Library of
Davidson College

THE RIGHT WING INDIVIDUALIST TRADITION IN AMERICA

The Right Wing Individualist Tradition in America

Advisory Editors:
Dr. Murray N. Rothbard,
Polytechnic Institute of Brooklyn
Jerome Tuccille,
New School for Social Research

EDWARD ATKINSON

The Biography of an American Liberal

1827–1905

BY
HAROLD FRANCIS WILLIAMSON

Arno Press & The New York Times
New York · 1972

923.3
At875w

Reprint Edition 1972 by Arno Press Inc.

Reprinted from a copy in The State Historical Society
of Wisconsin Library

LC# 79-172239
ISBN 0-405-00448-6

The Right Wing Individualist Tradition in America
ISBN for complete set: 0-405-00410-9
See last pages of this volume for titles.

Manufactured in the United States of America

EDWARD ATKINSON
The Biography of an American Liberal
1827–1905

EDWARD ATKINSON

*The Biography
of an American Liberal*

1827–1905

BY

HAROLD FRANCIS WILLIAMSON

*Instructor in Economics at Harvard University
Lecturer in Economics and Finance at
The Bentley School of Accounting and Finance*

INTRODUCTION BY

F. W. TAUSSIG

Boston
OLD CORNER BOOK STORE, Inc.
1934

COPYRIGHT, 1934, BY HAROLD FRANCIS WILLIAMSON

ALL RIGHTS RESERVED

The Riverside Press
CAMBRIDGE · MASSACHUSETTS
PRINTED IN THE U.S.A.

PREFACE

WHILE a biographical approach to history is apt to give a false perspective because of an almost unavoidable tendency to give undue importance to the work and influence of the subject, yet the study of an unusual or outstanding personality serves a most useful purpose in stating historical development in terms of the personal reactions of those who were a part of that development. It is therefore believed that this study of the life of a man who was keenly interested in the major economic, political, and social developments in the United States between 1860 and 1905 will add to the already acquired knowledge of the events which occurred between these dates.

It would be difficult to find a man, prominent during that period of American history, whose interests ranged over a wider field than those of Edward Atkinson of Boston. Cotton manufacturer, fire insurance executive, friend of the 'new' South, writer, tariff reformer, sound-money agitator, anti-imperialist, statistician, economist, dietician, inventor, speaker, are among the titles to which he could lay claim.

In each of these capacities Mr. Atkinson made interesting, and in many cases significant, contributions to the economic and political history of the United States. As treasurer and financial agent for several important cotton textile mills between 1850 and 1878, Mr. Atkinson became generally recognized as an authority upon the various phases of the cotton industry. He was an active member of the New England Cotton Manufacturers' Association, wrote extensively upon subjects having to do with the production, handling, and manufacture of cotton, and as an expert, exerted a considerable influence, especially during and immediately following the Civil War, over the governmental policy toward cotton growing and cotton manufacturing. Even after his withdrawal from cotton manufacturing in 1878, Mr. Atkinson never lost interest in cotton, and continued throughout his life to speak with authority on the subject.

In 1878, Mr. Atkinson became president of the Boston Manufacturers' Mutual Fire Insurance Company, a position which he held until his death in 1905. In addition to doing effective work in promoting the interests of this company, he became an ardent advocate of fire prevention. He was in no small degree responsible for the widespread adoption of the automatic sprinklers and the practice of fire-resisting or slow-burning building construction.

Tariff reform, sound money, and anti-imperialism constituted Mr. Atkinson's major political interests. As a proponent of lower tariff duties, he was out of sympathy with most of his New England contemporaries among business men and manufacturers, but an early acquaintance with the writings of Adam Smith and Frédéric Bastiat had convinced him of the soundness of a tariff for revenue only. It was his impatience with the failure of the Republicans to lower tariff duties after the Civil War that prompted him to become one of the leaders in the abortive Reform-Republican Movement in 1872.

As much as lower tariff duties interested Mr. Atkinson, the soundness of the monetary system seemed yet more important to him, and on the several occasions when he was forced by the stand of the two major parties to choose between high tariffs and sound money, or the alternative of low tariffs coupled with unsound money (be it in the form of greenbacks or silver), he had no hesitancy in choosing the former. His attitude on these two questions made it impossible for him to adhere consistently to the party policies of either the Republicans or the Democrats. As a consequence, while the Cleveland Democrats most closely approached his ideas in respect to tariff and money, on the whole he tended to be an independent in respect to his political affiliations.

Mr. Atkinson's anti-imperialistic and pacifistic tendencies showed themselves in his strong opposition to President Cleveland's belligerent stand on the Venezuelan affair in 1895, and in a vigorous attack upon the McKinley Administration for retaining the Philippine Islands after the Spanish-American War. He abhorred war because of its attendant destruction of life and property, and he objected to colonies because of their potentialities as a cause of conflict between nations.

Mr. Atkinson's political activities took two principal forms. He did effective work by personal contact in Washington, where he was a familiar visitor, and by writing numerous pamphlets, newspaper articles, and letters, upon the subjects he wished brought to the attention of the voters. In both rôles he exerted a considerable influence. His pamphlets were widely circulated, and there was scarcely a time after the Civil War when he did not have friends who were important either in Congress, or in the Administration, or both. Among the persons prominent in United States history whom Mr. Atkinson knew and with whom he corresponded were the following: David A. Wells, Hugh McGulloch, Charles Nordhoff, Horace White, Charles Sumner, U. S. Grant, James A. Garfield, J. M. Forbes, Henry Wilson, Professor A. L. Perry, William B. Allison, Henry L. Dawes, Francis A. Walker, William Morrison, Grover Cleveland, W. C. P. Breckinridge, J. G. Carlisle, William L. Wilson, Roger Q. Mills, J. R. McPherson, George F. Hoar, Z. B. Vance, Andrew Carnegie, and A. B. Farquhar.

His early interest in the South as a source of cotton was extended, after the war, to include an appreciation of the general economic possibilities of that region, which he publicized by articles and speeches. His work in this direction bore fruit in the form of the International Cotton Exposition held in Atlanta, Georgia, in 1881, considered to be one of the important events in the awakening of the 'new' South.

As an inventor, Mr. Atkinson's greatest contributions came from the enthusiasm he inspired in others to take up specific problems. He had tremendous faith in the ability of science to solve many of the problems of mankind, and was constantly on the alert to see what possibilities a new principle or idea offered. Specifically, important discoveries in the science of lubrication, building construction, illumination of rooms by ribbed glass, and an automatic fire door, are to be credited to him. Mr. Atkinson also made experiments in the art of preparing food and invented a cooking apparatus which he called the Aladdin Cooker, and which he hoped would revolutionize the existing methods of cooking in the interests of the poorer classes.

Mr. Atkinson enjoyed a widespread reputation as a statistician and economist. He wrote extensively upon subjects of current interest throughout his life, and while his contributions to economic and statistical theory were not outstanding, he did much to popularize these subjects and to draw attention to the issues of many controversies.

Mr. Atkinson was a voluminous writer. Over two hundred and fifty pamphlets, few of them brief, hundreds of letters to various newspapers and magazines, plus a few books testify to the prolific nature of his pen. The subjects about which he chose to write reflected his various interests. He had a pleasant, interesting style, and although addicted to an extensive use of statistics in many of his articles, possessed a faculty for making them understandable. Much of what was characteristic of Mr. Atkinson's writing applied to his abilities as a speaker. He both wrote and spoke with a positiveness and surety that carried conviction to his readers and listeners.

Physically, Mr. Atkinson made an impressive appearance. Tall, massively built, his natural dignity was accentuated by his moustache and full beard. He was genial and urbane in manner and delighted in social contacts. He made his home in Brookline the gathering place for interesting people from all countries.

In his philosophy Mr. Atkinson was essentially an optimist. He profoundly believed that this was the best possible of worlds, and that all that prevented greater human progress was the stupidity of man in not recognizing and removing bad laws, unnecessary legal restrictions, and other impediments to the operation of benevolent natural forces. For this reason, the spirit of the reformer was strong in him, and he worked vigorously throughout his life for the principles which he espoused. He possessed an

PREFACE

egotism born of a strong conviction of the correctness of his attitude toward certain political and economic questions. Aside from these questions, however, he was eager to grasp new suggestions, and possessed an imagination which could visualize to a remarkable degree the possibilities of new ideas, especially those of a scientific nature.

To him the world was an intensively interesting place, full of fascinating possibilities, and he felt that his own function, in part at least, was to call the attention of experts to the many things that should be done, with the notion that once having aroused their interest, he could hurry on to a consideration of something else. Not hindered by the inhibitions of a scholar, or scientist, he would often deliberately overstate the possibilities of a new idea in order to incite controversy, and on numerous occasions expressed the opinion that an article or speech was of little use unless it 'stirred things up a bit.' He would capitalize on his mistakes in the same spirit, feeling that if they had caused an examination or a re-examination of the subject under consideration, they had not been without value.

An outstanding feature of Mr. Atkinson's character was his frankness of expression and the utter lack of guile or duplicity in his relations with others. It was not in his nature to be otherwise, even though his outspoken manner sometimes injured the causes for which he worked. On the other hand, his very frankness and honesty gave him strength among those who appreciated such virtues, and even those who disagreed with him were forced to recognize his sincerity of purpose.

The material for this biography was drawn almost entirely from original sources. The first, and most important, was the copy-book record which Mr. Atkinson kept of almost all the letters he wrote between 1855 and 1905, amounting in all to over fifty thousand pages. A large number of letters written to Mr. Atkinson formed a second valuable source of information, although this collection is far from complete. Mr. Atkinson's printed pamphlets and other publications were helpful in giving a more elaborate and organized exposition of many of the subjects touched upon in his correspondence. The final source of original information came from interviews with those who knew Mr. Atkinson personally.

This work was originally presented as a doctoral thesis to the Department of Economics at Harvard University. Among the many persons who aided in its preparation, the writer wishes to acknowledge his indebtedness to the following who have aided in this work. He feels under special obligation to Professor Edwin F. Gay who first suggested this study, and who lent his valuable aid in getting the project under way; to Mr. Edward W. Atkinson for permission to use his father's papers; to him, and to Miss Caroline P. Atkinson and to Mr. William Atkinson for their time spent in reading and checking the manuscript; to Mr. J. H. Tuttle, librarian of the Massachusetts Historical Society, who allowed the writer the use of the facilities of the Society for almost two years, and who gave assistance at many specific points; to Mr. L. H. Kunhardt, Mr. Joseph P. Gray, and Mrs. A. C. Patterson, of the Boston Manufacturers' Mutual Fire Insurance Company, and Mr. E. V. French, of the Arkwright Mutual Fire Insurance Company, for their help on the chapter on Mr. Atkinson's work as a fire insurance executive; to Professor C. L. Norton, of the Massachusetts Institute of Technology, whose reminiscences of his work and friendship with Mr. Atkinson were most helpful; to Professor Arthur H. Cole, whose generous contributions of time spent in reading and correcting the entire manuscript, and whose numerous searching and helpful criticisms are deeply appreciated; and finally to my wife, who at every stage of the work gave both valuable suggestions and untiring labor in preparation of the manuscript.

HAROLD FRANCIS WILLIAMSON

CAMBRIDGE, 1934

CONTENTS

INTRODUCTION	xiii
I. EARLY LIFE AND CONTACTS, 1827–1865	1
II. EXPANDING INTERESTS: COTTON, RAILROADS, CIVIC AFFAIRS, 1865–1880	33
III. POLITICS: FREE TRADE, GREENBACKS, REFORM, 1865–1880	57
IV. BUSINESS EXECUTIVE: FIRE INSURANCE AND FIRE PREVENTION	99
V. MONEY, THE TARIFF, AGRICULTURE, THE NEW SOUTH, 1880–1892	134
VI. PROBLEMS OLD AND NEW: THE TARIFF, FREE SILVER, IMPERIALISM, SOCIAL REFORM, 1892–1905	178
VII. ECONOMIST AND PUBLICIST	242
APPENDIX A. GENEALOGICAL CHART	278
APPENDIX B. FREE LABOR COTTON COMPANY	279
BIBLIOGRAPHY	283
INDEX	299

INTRODUCTION
By F. W. Taussig

EDWARD ATKINSON belonged to the generation which, in the last quarter of the nineteenth century, maintained the unqualified liberal faith — the generation of which other conspicuous members in the United States were David A. Wells, Arthur L. Perry, and William G. Sumner. These men stood for the belief in competition and the devotion to liberty which characterized their English predecessors and contemporaries, and, not less, held to the optimism about America's future which remained unshaken among their own countrymen through the century. They were the reformers of their day. The path of reform seemed to them clear and straight. Liberty, the restriction of Government functions, abolition of favors and privileges, extirpation of monopolies — these were the conditions of prosperity and progress. Between nations, as between men, freedom was the ideal. If there must be duties on imports, let them be as low as possible and assessed primarily for revenue. Combinations alike of capitalists and laborers were condemned. Labor unions were as bad as monopolies of employers, and were inimical to the workmen themselves.

With all this went a common-sense and conservative attitude toward current questions not necessarily connected with the liberal creed. Government was to be more honest and efficient, the spoils system eradicated, the civil service reformed. The vanquished South was to be treated in a spirit of sympathy and helpfulness. 'Fiat money' was to be got out of the way, and the specie standard, abandoned during the Civil War, to be restored. When the agitation for silver coinage set in, it was treated as merely another form of the cheap-money heresy; and the fight against free silver brought with it hostility to every move toward any monetary system other than the free coinage and circulation of gold. The gold standard was a corner-stone of the creed.

Mr. Atkinson stood for all these things. The faith in liberty, in letting people attend to their own affairs without interference, in the ideal results which must come from unfettered competition, were expressed by him as by his fellows without qualification or reservation. The large and often loose phrases which they used were characteristic of the period. In Mr. Atkinson's case, this faith was combined with a practical strain. When handling the concrete problems of his day he saw the necessity for compromise and for the acceptance of the best that could be secured under the going conditions. And having the Yankee's eye for mechanical devices, he was keenly interested in practical matters of another sort. The main business interest of his later years (the manufacturers' mutual insurance organization) was based on better construction in the mills. Quite outside the range of his direct business problems was the interest in such contrivances as the farmer's silos and the workman's cookers. Great things were expected from these devices, and the optimism about the gain from their wide use by individuals was of a part with his general philosophy — the faith in individualism, self-help, freedom, spontaneous betterment.

This optimism has had its day. We cannot face the future with any such untroubled hopefulness as that of the nineteenth century. Yet not all the tenets and precepts of the age in which Mr. Atkinson lived are to be cast aside. He was a representative figure in a period the like of which cannot come again, but which left its permanent impress on the national character. From his varied experiences as recorded in this story of his life, we learn something, not only about the past, but about traditions and ideals that shaped the present and will not be completely set aside in the future.

EDWARD ATKINSON
The Biography of an American Liberal
1827–1905

EDWARD ATKINSON

CHAPTER I

EARLY LIFE AND CONTACTS

1827–1865

BORN in Brookline, Massachusetts, February 10, 1827, Edward Atkinson was the fourth of the six children of Amos and Anna Greenleaf Sawyer Atkinson. His father, Amos Atkinson II, was an old-time Boston merchant, partner in the well-known and long-lived firm of Atkinson and Rollins.

Ancestry on both sides of the family was predominantly English with a slight mixture of French. The first American ancestor of Amos Atkinson II was John Atkinson, a native of Bury St. Edmunds in Sussex, England, who settled in Newbury, Massachusetts, about 1663. His great-grandson, Amos Atkinson I, grandfather of Edward, served as a lieutenant in the Revolutionary War and fought at the Battle of Lexington. Other family names on the paternal side include Myrick, Cheney, Bailey, and Knowlton. Included among the ancestors of Anna Greenleaf Sawyer were such names as Moody, Pierrepont, Coffin, Stevens, Patch, Rogers, and Titcomb, to mention only a few. Both sides of the family had been residents of New England since about the middle of the seventeenth century.[1]

The first few years of Edward Atkinson's life were spent in Brookline, then a small village, where he lived the active, pleasant life of a young boy in the country. He began school in Brookline, but when he was nine, his father moved to Boston to secure better educational facilities for his children, and it was there, in various private schools, that the remainder of young Edward's formal education was obtained. He studied the subjects usually

[1] See the Genealogical Table, Appendix A.

taught in the primary and preparatory schools of the day, including mathematics, French, literature, Greek and Latin. He also learned to write a clear and distinctive hand, an accomplishment which was then held in great esteem.

He had planned to enroll at Harvard College in 1843, but the year before, when he was fifteen, the family met with financial reverses, and instead he entered the employ of the firm of Read and Chadwick, drygoods merchants who had a store in Liberty Square in Boston.

Mr. Atkinson said of his duties with Read and Chadwick, 'I had to get up before breakfast, go down and open the store, sweep the floors; in winter build the hardwood fires, get everything ready and then go back to breakfast, returning to pack and unpack cases.'[1]

His first advancement was to the position of shipping clerk which he filled in an able fashion. From this type of work he graduated into the accounting department of the firm, and although he had had no special training in the subject, he possessed a natural aptitude for the work, and within a few years had become an expert accountant.

This experience set the course of his early business career. A few years later his ability came to the notice of Mr. George O. Hovey, a member of the chief cotton goods commission firm in Boston, J. C. Howe and Company. As a result of this friendship, Mr. Atkinson was subsequently appointed treasurer for some of the cotton mills served by Mr. Hovey's firm.[2] One of his first responsible duties came when he was appointed as treasurer and financial agent for the Ogden Mills, a subsidiary of the Cohoes Mills, located at Cohoes, New York. This appointment, made in 1851 when he was but twenty-four years of age, is an indication of the confidence his employers had in his ability.

---

[1] *Edward Atkinson, 'His Egotistography,'* p. 42. This is an unpublished autobiographical manuscript in the *Atkinson Collection.*

[2] To those unacquainted with the business organization of the New England cotton mills, it should be explained that the treasurer ordinarily assumes responsibility for the management of the business. All the officials are in turn responsible either directly or indirectly to him and it is to him that the stockholders look for dividends.

EARLY LIFE AND CONTACTS

To this company were added others from time to time, until, by 1860, he was treasurer and agent for a number of manufacturing establishments, including six cotton mills operating approximately 70,000 spindles and 1500 looms.[1] The result was that more and more his business interests became centered upon cotton manufacturing, and, although his duties were primarily concerned with the financial rather than the manufacturing side of the business, he set out to become an authority on all phases of the cotton industry from its growth on the plantation to its final sale to the consumer as a manufactured article.

Mr. Atkinson could not have chosen a more opportune time to become established in the cotton manufacturing business. The decade beginning 1850 was for the United States in general a period of great commercial activity and of expansion, checked only by the panic of 1857. The effect of this growth on New England was to hasten the process of industrialization, as increased transportation facilities accentuated the advantages of territorial division of labor. Between 1850 and 1860 the cotton industry in particular enjoyed the greatest prosperity it had yet experienced.[2]

In addition to his business affairs, Mr. Atkinson took a keen interest in the political events of the time. There was much to stimulate such an interest in the decade before 1860, for these years saw the growing cleavage between the North and the South over the extension of slavery, which resulted in the final break after Lincoln was elected President.

Mr. Atkinson followed the events leading up to the Civil War with a keen interest. He was, by training and environment, an Abolitionist and a Free-Soiler.[3] His opinions upon the extension of slave territory were rather forcibly expressed in a letter to his

---

[1] In addition to the Ogden Mills, the companies for which he was treasurer at various times were, The Lewiston Bagging Company, The Cohoes Iron Foundry and Machine Shop, North Vassalborough Manufacturing Company, The Lewiston Water Power Company, The Continental Mills, The Franklin Mills, and Indian Orchard Mills.

[2] Copeland, M. T., *The Cotton Manufacturing Industry of the United States*, pp. 14–15.

[3] In 1851, for example, he joined the Committee of Vigilants of Boston, a group who gave aid to escaped slaves in their efforts to avoid recapture. Other members of the group included John A. Andrew, Richard Dana, Jr., Charles Hovey, George Minot, and Samuel Thayer.

friend Edward Philbrick, dated February 25, 1850: 'Do you know much about politics and the movements in Washington? I watch with a good deal of anxiety; it seems to me the prospect is rather dark, I say damn compromise, if compromise — damn union.' Then in the postscript: 'In speaking of infernal things, I deem it excusable to use infernal language.'[1]

He translated this feeling into more positive action in 1855 by helping to raise funds for the extension of the free territory in the West. A list headed, 'Subscription of the Citizens of Brookline in aid of the Free State Cause in Kansas,'[2] shows that he, as treasurer, helped collect over a thousand dollars for this cause. (Incidentally, most of this money was used to equip John Brown and his men with rifles and ammunition.)

There is an interesting connection between his anti-slavery feeling and a desire to develop an alternative source of supply of cotton shown in the following letter, dated April 20, 1859, and written to Thomas Clegg:

> I am a cotton manufacturer, at the same time an anti-slavery man. I wish to import sample bales of African cotton and if the cotton can be obtained and forwarded so that middling cotton shall not cost me *here* more than 14 cents per pound I want 4000 pounds. If I can get the 4000 pounds at or under 14 cents, I shall work it by itself through one of the mills under my charge, weave the cloth on a 64 and no. 30 yarn, and then, by exhibiting the cloth and the cotton to other manufacturers and to merchants, endeavor to interest them in the enterprise of procuring a larger quantity.
>
> The most I expect to accomplish in this matter is to demonstrate the fact that cotton of good quality grows in Africa and can be imported at a low price, at present in small quantities but with the prospect of large increase.

This movement was watched by others interested in cotton and the anti-slavery movement. Benjamin Coates, writing to Mr. Atkinson from Philadelphia on August 10, 1859, commented:

> The importance of this measure as an anti-slavery enterprise, I think it would be difficult to over-rate. If you can afford to sell cloth

---

[1] In the *Atkinson Collection*. Unless otherwise noted, all letters quoted are in the *Atkinson Collection*.
[2] *Ibid.*

from African cotton obtained from England at the same price as that made from American cotton, what must be the result when the production is increased sufficiently so as to be exported to the United States, so as to undersell our own slave-grown cotton? It will be a difficult matter in the course of a few years for slavery to compete with the cheap labor and cheap land of Africa. The great stimulus given to the culture of sugar in Liberia within the past two years has made a wonderful change there. They are now exporting sugar and molasses as well as cotton and coffee to Europe and America.

Lack of further evidence regarding this experiment, and the fact that such foreign cotton as was used during the war came mostly from India, would indicate that Liberia was not a satisfactory source of supply.[1]

Mr. Atkinson was restrained, after the Civil War began, from becoming a combatant because of the necessity of providing for his dependents. He had married Mary Caroline Heath in 1855 and at this time had two small children. In addition, he was the chief contributor to the support of his parents and his two unmarried sisters. He found much, however, to occupy his attention during the years between 1860 and 1865 in giving aid to the Union cause.

In the latter part of 1861, for example, he made an important attempt to strengthen the position of the North in the war by publishing a pamphlet entitled *Cheap Cotton by Free Labor*. This brochure, the first of a series of pamphlets and articles which did much to enhance his reputation and spread his fame as an authority on cotton, was designed to remove the fears of those users of cotton who felt that this staple could not be grown cheaply except under a system of slave labor.

His arguments in brief ran as follows: Because of the imminent possibility of European recognition of the Southern Confederacy, and the danger of war between the North and such countries that gave this recognition, every effort should be made to crush the rebellion as rapidly as possible. To accomplish this, there

---

[1] It is interesting to note that Mr. Atkinson imported what was probably the first Egyptian long-staple cotton brought into the United States. The shipment consisted of fifteen bales and the date of the invoice was January 27, 1864. The price paid was twenty-eight and one-half pence per pound, plus transportation charges.

should be an immediate emancipation of the slaves because slavery enabled the South to maintain a large army without being obliged to draw on its labor force. In addition, if the opportunity of 'owning a nigger' were denied to the poor whites, much of that group's enthusiasm for the sectional struggle would be lost.

There existed, however — so Atkinson said — a reluctance on the part of many persons, especially those interested in cotton, to grant emancipation because of the belief that a sufficient supply of cotton could be grown only with compulsory labor of colored workers. Mr. Atkinson denied the truth of this argument. He cited the results in the British West Indies to prove that the Negroes were effective workers under freedom.

But, he continued, should the emancipated slave prove to be inefficient in the cultivation of cotton, there was an alternative possibility which could be developed into a large source of supply. This was cotton grown by white labor. According to estimates made in 1850 and 1852, about eight hundred thousand slaves were used in growing cotton. In the same years approximately one hundred thousand white laborers were used for the same purpose. To these white (and free) laborers, found chiefly in Tennessee and Texas, Mr. Atkinson attributed about one-ninth of the cotton crop. This being the case, in the event of the failure of the Negroes to provide an adequate supply of cotton after emancipation, there was no reason why a sufficient crop could not be grown by white labor.

To offset a commonly held idea that the Southern climate was unhealthy for white men, Mr. Atkinson demonstrated, by the means of comparative temperature readings, that the South compared favorably with a large part of southern Europe. As further proof of his position, he called attention to the fact that in 1850 there were over one million white workers active throughout the Southern States.

With the elimination of the slavery system, Mr. Atkinson thought that the wasteful methods of cultivation which seemed to be characteristic in the growing of cotton would be eliminated. Further, the seeds of the cotton, thrown away under the existing system, would be utilized under a more enlightened type of agriculture.

Based on the foregoing, Mr. Atkinson's conclusions were that cotton could not only be grown, but grown cheaper with free labor (white, black, or both) than with slaves. He therefore proposed that free labor be put in competition with slave labor on a large scale by opening Texas to colonization by free labor and by purchasing and freeing the slaves there. The large number of German colonists in Texas would make this a good place to initiate the scheme, and the relatively small number of slaves would not make their purchase a heavy financial burden. The constitutional difficulties could be met, since 'let it not be forgotten that this most ungrateful State has utterly repudiated the Constitution.'[1]

To facilitate the plan, he urged the building of a railroad from St. Joseph, Missouri, to Mobile, Alabama, which should run through Lawrence, Kansas, and across the valleys of the Arkansas and Red Rivers. This would make it easy for settlers to enter the region and would also provide adequate transportation facilities to the Northern markets.

The ideas expressed in this pamphlet were favorably received by Northern newspapers and public men. For example, on December 3, 1861, *The National Republican*[2] commented editorially:

> *Cheap Cotton by Free Labor* — The above is the title of a pamphlet of fifty-two pages issued in Boston during the past summer by 'A Cotton Manufacturer,' Edward Atkinson. He treats the subject from the point of view of his business as a consumer of cotton, and the considerations which he presents are entitled to have and will have great weight in forming public opinion upon pending questions.[3]

---

[1] *Cheap Cotton by Free Labor*, p. 30.
[2] Published at Springfield, Massachusetts.
[3] The London *Spectator* commented upon the pamphlet: 'The strongest objection entertained by the English friends of the South to sudden emancipation is, we believe, a secret one. They fear that the slave once emancipated would not work, and that without his labor cheap American cotton would be an impossibility. We would recommend all such doubters to peruse a short and exceedingly plain-spoken pamphlet on the question, just issued by Mr. E. Atkinson, an American cotton-spinner. It will not take them an hour, and we are greatly mistaken as to the effect of argument on minds rendered keen by self-interest, if it does not disabuse them at once and for ever of that special form of delusion.' From an undated clipping in the *Atkinson Collection*.

From this grew a scheme to send a military expedition into Texas in late '61 and early '62 to make Texas a free territory. Dwight Foster, writing on October 21, 1861, spoke favorably of the project as follows:

> I quite agree with you as to the indispensable necessity of emancipation in Texas and all the northern tier of slave states, although I have doubted the present expediency of announcing in advance the intention to adopt such a measure by leading Republicans like Mr. Sumner.
>
> West Texas and its German settlers have been objects of hope and expectation with me for several years and I now believe that, should troops be sent through Mexico into that state, they would receive a good deal of support from the Germans and Governor Houston.

But the plan was doomed to failure. The difficulties were expressed by Senator Sumner who wrote to John Bright on August 5, 1862:

> The letters which I enclose from Mr. Atkinson, a most intelligent and excellent person, will let you see the chance of cotton from the South. Do not count on it. Make your calculations as if it were beyond reach. His plan of opening Texas reads well on paper; but thus far we have lost by dividing our forces. We must concentrate and crush. The armies of the South must be met and annihilated. If we start an expedition to Texas there will be another division. Climate, too, will be for the present against us.[1]

Mr. Atkinson's interest in the advancement of the Southern Negro found positive expression when, early in 1862, he became associated with the Educational Commission, which later became the New England Freedmen's Society. This organization arose as a result of the needs of the newly freed Negroes located in the Sea Islands just off the coast of South Carolina. These islands were seized by the Union forces early in the Civil War. E. L. Pierce was appointed as a special civilian commissioner in general charge of the Islands. The Government had made no provision for the care or close supervision of the Negroes who numbered about eight thousand. Pierce felt that the close proximity of army camps would be harmful to his charges and that without educational guidance they would be unable to assume properly

---

[1] Pierce, E. L., *Memoirs and Letters of Charles Sumner*, vol. IV, p. 82.

EARLY LIFE AND CONTACTS

the duties and privileges of freedom. He accordingly appealed to New England for aid in meeting this problem.[1]

There was an almost immediate response. On February 4, 1862, the Educational Commission was founded with the Reverend E. E. Hale as chairman, William Endicott as treasurer, and Edward Atkinson as secretary. Mr. Atkinson was also chairman of the finance committee. The purpose of the organization as set forth in the constitution was, briefly, to seek 'the industrial, social, intellectual, moral and religious improvement of persons released from slavery in the cause of the war for the Union.'

The Commission did effective work throughout the war and post-war period. According to the second annual report,[2] over $35,000 had been raised during the two preceding years. In the spring of 1864 the Commission and its affiliated societies in New England were employing thirty teachers among the freedmen. Later the Society joined the United States Commission for the relief of the National Freedmen, which combined the various societies performing activities of a similar nature. Finally the bulk of this work was taken over by the Federal Government under legislation which became effective March 3, 1865, and which set up the Freedmen's Bureau.

Meanwhile Mr. Atkinson continued in his efforts to promote the growing of cotton with free labor. In an article in the *Springfield Republican* on March 8, 1862, he told of the large profits from the growing of cotton which were possible in Georgia. He also wrote at the same time a magazine article entitled 'Is Cotton Our King?'[3] and published a map called *The Cotton Kingdom Defined*, both of which developed the ideas first presented in the pamphlet *Cheap Cotton by Free Labor*.

In 1863 he took steps to try out his theories of cotton production and to be of positive aid to the freedmen by organizing a

---

[1] The description of conditions in the Sea Islands and the request for aid is contained in a letter in the *Atkinson Collection* from E. L. Pierce to the Reverend J. M. Manning, January 19, 1862.
[2] April 21, 1864.
[3] *Continental Monthly*, vol. I, pp. 247–56.

company called the Free Labor Cotton Company.[1] The background for this movement lay in the occupation of the lower Mississippi Valley by Union forces. As the Northern armies moved south in the spring of 1863 to begin the siege of Vicksburg, many plantations were abandoned by their owners who fled before the approach of the Northern forces. This abandoned property, much of it with crops still standing in the fields, was taken over by the Government along with other property seized by General Grant in the prosecution of the war.

In order to gather the crops and, more important, to give employment to the many Negroes who had taken refuge with the Union forces and who were becoming an increasing burden upon the personnel of the army, these abandoned plantations were leased to private individuals on the condition that they employ the Negroes as laborers.

This plan was only moderately successful in the spring and summer of 1863, due to small crops and unsettled social and economic conditions brought on by frequent guerilla raids. Nevertheless, the Government prepared to continue this policy, and in the fall a Commission of Plantations was appointed to take over the administration of rebel property. A rather elaborate set of rules governing these leases was formulated by the Commission, providing among other things that only persons loyal to the Union cause would be given leases, that one able-bodied Negro should be hired for every eight acres of cultivated land, that these laborers should be paid at the rate of seven dollars per month in addition to food and clothing, and that schooling should be provided for the freedmen.[2]

The opportunity to raise cotton proved extremely attractive. One writer says of the movement: 'The commissioners were overwhelmed with applications for leaseholds, for the price of cotton was phenomenal ($250 per bale), the land fertile and labor cheap. From far and near the applications came, many from Northern

---

[1] For the names of the men connected with this company and the rules and regulations which were to govern its operation, see Appendix B.

[2] Contained in an article in the *New York Evening Post*, December 11, 1863. This article was reprinted by the *New England Loyal Publication Society*, no. 147, December 18, 1863.

men who knew little of the methods of cultivating the cotton plant. One lessee invested $13,000 in a crop and sold it for $135,000.'[1]

It is not surprising that under the circumstances, Mr. Atkinson and his associates were attracted by the possibilities of large profits in cotton-growing. In addition the experience of Edward Philbrick in the Sea Islands had been very encouraging. He had, in 1863, purchased plantations there at public auction for a group of Boston men and, using a share system with the Negroes, had made a profit of about $80,000 over and above interest, labor costs, and depreciation.[2]

Mr. Atkinson was optimistic about the possibilities of the company during December, 1863. He wrote to J. M. Forbes on December 11, saying that he was almost ready 'to spring a scheme' for a cotton company and had raised over $25,000, which he would turn over to Mr. Forbes, if the latter had a better plan.

A letter to Mr. Atkinson from Captain T. E. Ellsworth, written at Washington for General Wadsworth, dated December 19, 1863, said that the General endorsed the facts contained in an article printed in the *New York Evening Post* of December 11, 1863. This article had given a glowing picture of the possibilities of plantation leasing on the Mississippi. The General further indicated that there was plenty of land in the vicinity of Vicksburg which could be protected against guerilla raids.

In February of 1864 their plans did not look as promising as they had earlier. Discouraging news in the form of a letter written by H. Brown on the sixteenth to J. P. Williston and relayed to Mr. Atkinson told of the difficulties encountered in trying to establish a plantation. A lack of co-operation from the military leaders, plus the danger of raids from guerilla bands, had almost stopped their plans.

Nor was the outlook more encouraging in the spring, if one may judge from the account sent by Mr. Williston to Mr. Atkinson on May 27, 1864:

[1] Garner, James Wilford, *Reconstruction in Mississippi*, p. 251.
[2] *Second Annual Report of the New England Freedmen's Society*, April 21, 1864.

The investment in your company is not so near a failure as our Northampton Company is likely to be. I enclose extracts from letters written me by Mr. Brown, who accompanied Mr. Hunt. They located with a considerable company about 30 miles below Vicksburg on the west side. There is hardly a place on the river so defensible as the peninsula they occupied. Hunt and Brown had planned 400 to 500 acres before this last raid, and planted a considerable part. This Reverend Winchell was one who was in company with them. As the guerillas came in such force the concern will be abandoned unless Mr. Brown succeeds by offering 10 per cent of the crop to induce a large wood contractor to locate on the entrance to the peninsula with a large force for cutting wood for the governmental boats. He will locate if General Slocum consents. But even then it will be hazardous and very uncertain enterprise. Mr. Brown says that of 20 men whom he personally knew who have leased plantations, eight have been murdered.

I think the time is near at hand when we shall have to use India cotton again unless our aims meet with much better success. The enemy is much stronger and more determined than we had supposed.

In spite of these adverse reports of the difficulties encountered attempting to grow cotton along the lower Mississippi, Mr. Atkinson and his associates determined to carry out their original plan. The outcome of the project is contained in the following letter sent to the persons associated with the venture:

Boston, Apr. 28, 1865

Sir:

A meeting of the subscribers to the fund contributed for the purpose of cultivating Cotton upon the Mississippi River was held this day, and a final report was made by Captain A. H. Kelsey.

It will be remembered that seventy-five per cent of the capital subscribed was returned upon the report from Captain Kelsey that it was not expedient to undertake large operations and that one plantation only was leased. Upon this plantation operations were begun under the assurance of protection from the commander of what was known as the Marine Brigade, Mr. A. Warren Kelsey remaining upon the premises while Captain A. H. Kelsey came North to purchase supplies.

The promise of protection proved entirely delusive, no sufficient protection was given, guerillas attacked the premises, capturing Mr. A. Warren Kelsey, and carrying off our stock. Mr. Kelsey was released by the first band, but remained to protect our interests until he had been four times captured. Being then convinced that he must retire, he made arrangements with the head negro, who had formerly been 'negro driver' on the premises, to carry on the plantation on which 300 acres had been planted in Cotton. Supplies and money were from month to month sent to this man and the trust imposed upon him was faithfully performed.

Unfortunately for our pecuniary interest, the army worm attacked the crop and from 300 acres planted, only 18 bales of Cotton were made. These were delivered by the negro overseer upon the bank of the river, and have been sold. The proceeds would have allowed an additional division of about twelve and one-half per cent; but as Mr. A. Warren Kelsey had risked his life to protect our interest, and having realized no profit, he would not be entitled to any compensations, it was voted that the final dividend to the subscribers should be ten per cent, and that the remainder should be paid to him.

I now enclose a check for ten per cent upon your subscription, and request you to sign and return the enclosed receipt.

EDWARD ATKINSON, *Trustee*

It was natural that Mr. Atkinson's attention should be directed to Washington during this period. As a cotton manufacturer he was interested in the many governmental rules and regulations covering the cotton trade and manufacture. And as an authority on cotton, he was called on for expert advice by various governmental agencies.

In 1864 and 1865 Mr. Atkinson became more and more impressed with the necessity of opening up the cotton trade with the South. In part his eagerness to promote this trade was the high price of cotton which prevailed especially in 1864. An interesting sidelight upon his efforts in this direction is contained in the following extract from the *Diary of Gideon Welles*, Secretary of the Navy under President Lincoln. He described the Cabinet meeting of July 5, 1864, as follows:

Mr. Fessenden appeared at Cabinet meeting as a successor of Mr. Chase. Although the regular day of the meeting, all were specially notified and all promptly attended. The President appeared more constrained and formal than usual.... The subject of trade and especially trade in cotton with the Rebels was the subject of general interest which the President desired to lay before us. He appeared to have no fixed purpose in his own mind. Alluded to a Mr. Atkinson who had called on him — said that Mr. A. had impressed him with some very striking facts. The most prominent was, that although the Rebels sold less cotton they received about as much for it in consequence of high price as when they had more of the article. The President thought it might be well to take measures to secure the cotton, but was opposed to letting the rebels have gold.

Seward was voluble but not clear and pointed. Fessenden had seen Atkinson, had interview with him, thought him intelligent. On subject of trade with the Rebels was not posted. Stanton made extended, and in the main sensible and correct remarks, being wholly opposed to fighting and trading at the same time with the Rebels, ground which I have uniformly taken, but have not always been supported.[1]

By 1865 another reason prompted Mr. Atkinson's attempts to remove trade restrictions on cotton. He was anxious to draw the bulk of the cotton out of the South before the end of the war, because he was convinced that the future supply of cotton would be grown by free labor under the direction of industrious and energetic planters attracted from the North. But if the cotton stored in the South were to be dumped upon the market at the end of the war, the effect would be to lower the price to such a level that potential cotton-growers would be discouraged. It was his hope that immediately after the war there would be a series of crops selling at prices high enough to give the 'free labor' growers an opportunity to get well started. He said of this:

> You will see... that I believe there may be a temporary depression of cotton to a much lower point than present price, and the depression may be so great as to carry the price to a point lower than the probable cost of production in the first year of free labor. It is therefore of the utmost importance that the lowest price should be reached and a rising market established before the time when the arrangements for planting the new crop are begun.
>
> I want to see free trade at once, get the lowest point as early in the autumn as possible and establish a rise before January 1, 1866.
>
> If there are *not* from two to two and a half million bales of cotton in the South, all this calculation is of no value. The price of cotton will remain high enough to stimulate production.[2]

In this and other matters during 1865, Mr. Atkinson worked closely with his friend, John Murray Forbes, famous merchant and railroad executive, who had taken a house in Washington in December, 1864, for the purpose of being near his son, an officer

---

[1] *Diary of Gideon Welles*, vol. II, p. 66.
[2] Letter to J. M. Forbes, May 3, 1865.

EARLY LIFE AND CONTACTS

in the Union armies, and to be 'at the center of things' during that important period in American history.[1]

In the latter part of January and early February, Mr. Atkinson urged Mr. Forbes to lend his influence toward removing the restrictions on the purchase of cotton.[2] They also had some correspondence regarding a tax on cotton. Negotiations by letter did not seem satisfactory. Accordingly, Mr. Forbes wrote from Washington on February 19:

> Your letters are full of interest, but during the next week we have got to settle some of the biggest questions of the year, and much is often done in these last few days, so I wish you could be here to throw your experience and weight into the *right scale*. Now is the very focus of the year. I agree with you fully about the duty on cotton in the *long run* being high enough at five cents, but doubt about it *this year*, and I think you had better sacrifice a good deal to be here, for men's minds are so divided that you might turn the scale. I could do something if I were posted, but I am not and so I can only *suggest* where you could dictate. *Come by all means* if you can and come soon, for the Tax Bill will be up in Senate on Wednesday (possibly Tuesday) and you ought to have your say on it, or if too modest, you can help me speak.

Mr. Atkinson accepted the invitation to come to Washington and arrived there on February 22. The following letters written to his wife during his stay there give an excellent picture of the nature of his activities and the things in which he and his friends were interested:

> February 24, 1865
>
> Here I am domiciled with Mr. Forbes in the most pleasant and easy way. I reached Washington at 7 P.M. night before last, went to Willard's in the mud and rain, could not get a room and found no message or note from Mr. F. so I began to say to myself, what a fool I had been to come, but I left my valise and paddled off through such mud as you have no conception of, to Mr. Forbes' house, where I found him tied

---

[1] Hughes, Sarah Forbes, *John Murray Forbes, Letters and Recollections*, vol. II, pp. 125 ff.

[2] Section VIII of a law passed by Congress July 2, 1864, provided that agents of the Treasury could go beyond the lines of the army in certain districts and purchase cotton, paying two-thirds of the purchase price in currency and one-third in supplies, not contraband of war. The total purchase price should not be more than three-quarters of what the cotton would bring in New York. See the *Congressional Globe*, Thirty-Eighth Congress, Second Session, 1864–65, p. 1351.

by the toe with an attack of gout. He had sent a note to Willard's which they had neglected to give me asking me to come here. He sent down for my traps and now I feel as much at home as if I had known the family all my life. Mrs. F. is delightful, the other members at home are Miss Alice and a young son and daughter and Mrs. Russell's baby. Mrs. R. has just gone to New York to be treated for weak eyes.

Mr. Forbes immediately set me at work by sending me to the Senate with notes of introduction, and I was at once called before the Finance Com. who are at work on the tax bill, where I gave my evidence, and then went into the House of Rep. where I had pleasant talks with many of the members. Yesterday afternoon Mr. McCulloch who is probably to be Sec. of the Treasury and his wife, dined with us and we talked late into the evening. Mr. McC. wants me to remain a week and try to get correct ideas about the cotton question into the heads of the Senators, so I feel bound to stay over Sunday at any rate, and I shall find enough to do. Mr. Forbes is now writing an invitation to Senator Grimes and Mr. Fessenden to dine. If he could move about we should do more for I don't know the ropes.

Today the sun is out bright and clear and it won't be so hard to get about, the mud dries in a minute almost. I am going to see Mr. Fessenden and to see the President if I can get at him, then to the Senate and House again.

February 25, 1865

I am having a very satisfactory time even if I don't accomplish much. It is very pleasant to meet the future Secretaries and Senators, etc.

Today Mr. Fessenden and Senator Grimes are to dine with us. Yesterday I was at the capitol almost all day and was introduced to Senators Howe and Sherman by Mr. McCulloch who is to be Sec'y of the Treasury. Mr. McCulloch wants me to stay here as long as I can and talk with the M. C.'s on certain points on which he thinks I am right, and try to prevent some legislation which he doesn't like, and as he thinks I can do some good I am glad to work. I am very much pleased with him and I think he will make a very strong secretary, a vast improvement on Mr. Fessenden.

I meant to go about among the freedmen tomorrow but I find that Mrs. Forbes is a little afraid to have me do it for fear I may come in contact with some contagious disease and bring it to Mrs. Russell's baby, so I shall merely go to see our teachers and leave my visit to the schools until my last day here.[1]

---

[1] The schools referred to by Mr. Atkinson were the schools established by the New England Freedmen's Aid Society in Washington for the benefit of the liberated Negroes.

EARLY LIFE AND CONTACTS

February 26, 1865

I am still at work with my head full of facts and figures and doing work for which our manufacturers will have to thank me when they know the danger they will have escaped by my being here.

Yesterday was all spent at the capitol in the Senate and House and last evening I cooled my heels two hours in the President's ante-room by appointment but did not see him after all, he is very much pressed.

Two hundred and fifty deserters came in yesterday morning, they had deserted from Lee's army in one squad. Mrs. Forbes talked with some of them. I am going to the Marshal's office this morning to see some of them. Today I hope to find time to see Emma Ware and to go to one of our schools. Then to the weary work of watching legislation.

March 2, 1865

I wrote you last evening a hurried note. Congress has just passed a bill which will enable our factories to settle some long pending claims against the Government, and as I may by staying two or three days more, save Mr. Bates a journey to Washington, I thought I ought to write him that I would stay, and I shall depend on his telegram. If he doesn't want me to remain I shall leave tomorrow evening, reach New York on Saturday morning and get home Sunday morning, unless I should decide to remain in New York until Sunday evening to have a chat with C. W.

Yesterday we went in the carriage, Mrs. F., Miss Alice and myself to see our Boston school. I was really surprised to see how much the children had learned and I have taken one of the writing books to bring home. The school is kept in a church and they have no desks, when they write they have to kneel on the floor and put their books on the seats. You would think they were all saying their prayers.

Then I went to the capitol and saw the tariff amendment which I had caused to be made, safely passed by the House, it is in no danger in the Senate. The opposition in the House had no idea of the importance of the amendment or we should have had trouble. I have also got the leading men all right on the cotton tax and I expect to see that passed exactly as I want it. One funny thing happened. I made two memoranda for Mr. Sumner on which he was to argue on the cotton tax, one to be used in case the tariff was amended and the other in case it was not, and he made a mistake and used the wrong one. It doesn't matter much as it happened.[1]

I think I did not write you about my talk with rebel deserters.

---

[1] An examination of the provisions of the tariff amendment fails to show any change which might be considered so important. The principal difference was a provision for an increase in the duty on cotton from two cents to five cents per pound. Cf. *United States Statutes at Large*, 1866, p. 439.

Two hundred and fifty-six came in in one squad mostly South Carolina men, I had a long talk with some of them and was astonished at their intelligence; this war has taught them many things. They all said their politicians had deceived them, that they had learned that they were fighting for a class interest and against their own, that northern systems, schools, etc., were much better than theirs, and if the officers would only stand aside and let the men settle the matter they would throw down their arms, shake hands and be better friends than ever before. One said the Peace Commissioners who met Lincoln might have made peace to suit the men but they chose to try to save the leaders, and that this army would not fight to save Jeff Davis and his crew, for his part he hoped Jeff would be hung. This man was superior to the others, he said he had had a fair education and that he had 'written hundreds of letters for his comrades, for,' said he, 'you know half Lee's army cannot read and write.' He said that more men were deserting and running into West Virginia than came north. A Georgia man said it had only been pride that kept him from deserting long ago, but it was now so common that pride no longer kept a man back. All agreed on the ration being now three-fourths a pound of corn meal, and one-fourth pound bacon a day, and that this was very small.

Yesterday I went again to see some more but I was too early, there were 148 in the yard just being mustered into line to take the oath, and in a room overlooking the yard were 35 Confederate officers just brought in as prisoners. I exulted in seeing them watch the performance.

Mrs. Forbes went later to talk with them and one told her that 1000 deserted last week and that it was agreed in Lee's army to stop the war in this way. I should not wonder at this in the least.

All these men agree that desertion and discouragement are the order of the day and the common talk in Lee's army. I almost think there may be no more great battles. I shall try to see some more of them today.

Mr. Forbes wants me to try once more to see the President, but I don't believe I shall, it takes too much time.

March 4, 1865

When I last wrote you in detail I thought my tariff amendment was all made, when I went to the Senate I found Mr. Morrill had made a mistake, having only corrected the error in one place instead of two. I had to get it corrected in Senate, watch the enrolling clerks when they engrossed it, escort the bill over to the House again, see it safe through a conference committee, and last evening it was finally passed.

Now I am going to prove to you that I am a United States Senator. Day before yesterday old Mr. Blair dined with us, in the evening we explained to him our ideas that Government should no longer confiscate cotton, but should rather entice owners to bring in their cotton by giving them a voucher convertible at the end of the war into a United States bond for its value. He saw the force of the argument and at once advised me to see the President and get his influence upon it. I went to Mr. McCulloch, but we could not reach the President, so we went down to the Senate where Mr. McC. introduced me upon the floor, a very rare privilege — I was the only one not a Senator or Cabinet officer. One by one I explained the matter to about a dozen Senators and then at Mr. Cowan's desk drew up an amendment to a pending law, covering my point. This I gave to Mr. Wilson who moved it yesterday morning and it passed with only 3 opposed. Last evening I went to the House, converted this man and that, got the bill called up and at 1 o'clock A.M. I had the satisfaction of seeing it pass almost unanimously. I have no doubt the President signed it and it is now a law. And it changes radically the whole previous policy of the Government.

This was an amendment to a bill before Congress designed to stop any further commercial relation with the Southern States. This trade, principally in cotton, had been the subject of bitter discussion. The military authorities condemned it on the grounds that it gave substantial aid to the enemy. Other opponents pointed out the inconsistencies of maintaining any commercial relations with the Southern States while at war with them. On the other hand, the high price of cotton, the Northern commercial interests, and, in the early part of the war, a desire to furnish cotton to the British market for diplomatic reasons, combined to put pressure upon the Government to allow this trade.[1]

It was at the height of an acrimonious debate on the above bill that Senator Wilson introduced Mr. Atkinson's amendment. Quoting from the *Congressional Globe*:

> Mr. Wilson: I offer the following amendment as an additional section to the bill: And be it further enacted that all cotton seized by the military or naval authorities, or surrendered to said authorities, shall be delivered to the officers of the Treasury, and vouchers shall be given to the owner or claimant of such cotton, entitling such owner or claimant, personally, to payment for such cotton at the end of the war, less taxes and expenses, in bonds of the United States, bearing six per cent interest, redeemable in twenty years.[2]

---
[1] Cf. Rhodes, J. F., *History of the United States*, vol. V, pp. 274–313.
[2] Thirty-Eighth Congress, Second Session, p. 1352.

This was obviously a compromise measure and as such was passed by both houses as an amendment to the bill up for discussion. The plan possessed the advantages that it would stop any legal trade with the enemy and at the same time would allow the owners of cotton to convert their holdings at the then current prices.

The 'Cotton Purchase Bill' was fated not to become a law in spite of Mr. Atkinson's optimism concerning it, as it was vetoed by President Lincoln. Mr. Forbes expressed his disappointment in a letter to Mr. Atkinson on March 8:

> You can hardly imagine my disgust after you left at finding that old Abe had pocketed our Grand bill — I could have wrung his long neck! I suppose the cotton speculators around him were too many for him.
>
> It is sad to see the impression which this and other things give that whether *he* gets anything out of it or *not*, his course is influenced by those who do. The next best thing now is to try and get him to give an order that all cotton seized shall be certified to the owners, leaving Congress to decide thereafter upon what should be done with the proceeds. As this course would help the cotton speculators and increase the quantity of cotton by encouraging holders to bring it in instead of burning it, I should think he would do it if properly moved thereto. Cannot you get your Chamber of Commerce to make a petition to that effect, referring to the action of Congress and either send on a deputation to present it or send it to me promptly while I can get a Senator to back me up in presenting it? I write Low in the same sense.

Mr. Atkinson seemed less disappointed than Forbes. Writing on the same day he said:

> I am sorry to learn that the President did not sign our bill.... However, we have the eighth section unrepealed and I am satisfied that is the next best thing.[1]

The cotton situation failed to improve as Mr. Atkinson wished. On May 3, 1865, he again wrote to Forbes on the matter:

> I have given Mr. McCulloch the substance of the following letter but I want you to have the facts in your mind.
>
> Under existing regulations an owner of cotton on the Red River or

---

[1] This eighth section referred to allowed the trade to continue as it had since July 2, 1864. *Supra*, p. 10.

in the interior of Alabama and Mississippi had better leave it to rot than to try to get it to market.

The trade law requiring 25 per cent to Government still stands, and in addition a war tax of 4 cents, internal revenue 2 cents, fees and stealing indefinite. I know that it has cost 29 cents per pound to get cotton from Red River on board ship at New Orleans and when it got to New York it would not pay cost allowing nothing for value of cotton at the starting point. There is now a lot of 50 bales at Providence, R.I., on which the charges are so heavy that the consignees will not take it away.

What is needed is to have all the country east of the Mississippi declared to be within the lines of actual military occupation. This annuls the trade law requiring purchase on behalf of the United States.

Second, abatement of all taxes and charges except the legal revenue tax of 2 cents per pound.

Third, to abolish Mr. Mellens' complicated regulations for trade *within* the lines and have Mr. Risley make new and simple ones.

It was Mr. McCulloch's belief, however, that there were not over one million bales of cotton in the South which would come on to the market.[1] If this were true, he did not see the necessity of removing the trade restrictions, as the prices of this comparatively short supply would remain high enough to attract the cotton owners to sell it. In addition, the tax yielded a substantial revenue. Mr. Atkinson was skeptical of this estimate. His letter of May 8 to Mr. Forbes presents his views on the subject as follows:

> I must sum up the cotton question in answer to your letter, leaving you to present the case to Mr. McCulloch if you see fit.
>
> As to the estimate of the quantity of cotton in the South. I will not gainsay Mr. M.'s figures, *if measures have been taken by the Government to ascertain the facts.* If not, then I claim that the estimates of the men now here from the Atlantic States are not to be relied upon. Many of them have an interest in cotton and they want to keep up the price. They also represent a section of country which contains all the spindles of the South and therefore where consumption has been greatest, and their section has also supplied blockade runners. These Atlantic men give the low figures.
>
> Now as to the evidence from Southern men as a whole. T. W. Pierce, of the firm of Pierce and Bacon, whose Southern proclivities you well know, has just returned from New York where he has been

[1] Letter of Mr. Atkinson's to Mr. Forbes, May 6, 1865.

for several weeks. He says the average statement of Southern men for each week and for his whole stay was 1,600,000 bales of sound cotton. Now I believe that you should make an allowance of at least 25 per cent for the interest of the parties, but accept his average.

Total stock now	1,600,000

We have satisfactory evidence that a crop of at least 500,000 has been planted in Texas where hordes of negroes have been concentrated.

Lee surrendered long before the planting season had passed, cotton can be planted up to May 10 with fair chance of making a crop. If there is the small quantity in the Atlantic States, will not every man who had an acre prepared for corn, plant half of it in cotton? If such planting gives only 200,000 bales, the total supply to come to market prior to May 1, 1866 would be:

Average Southern estimate of stock	1,600,000
Texas crop	500,000
Cis-Mississippi crop	200,000
Total	2,300,000

You are well aware that B. F. Nourse keeps well informed. His figures are:

Stock east of Mississippi River	1,600,000
Stock west of Mississippi River	700,000
Planting in Texas and West La.	700,000
Planting east of Mississippi River	300,000
Total	3,300,000

Now, since there are judicious men who have heretofore been well informed, who believe in these figures, I think the policy of the Government should be to allow the actual facts to be developed at once by the removal of restrictions, purchasing agency, and all other Government charges except the internal revenue tax of 2 cents per pound.

The little ring of mills to which I belong propose to employ a cotton detective to go to Savannah and thence through Georgia, Alabama, and Mississippi in pursuit of accurate information, can you procure from Mr. McCulloch a proper pass with liberty to have our agent carry letters of introduction, we agreeing to give the Secretary all the information we may get?

Now as to the actual present. The heavy losses suffered by all who have attempted to move cotton during the past three months has checked the receipts on private account and very little cotton can be expected to move on the new plan of Government taking one-quarter in kind.

Speculators understand this and are not afraid to purchase the Government cotton. From this an advantage accrues to the Treasury, but on the other hand the price of middling having reached 60 cents, the starting up of spindles has been checked, the demand for goods is ceasing, and the industry of the country is embarrassed. I believe the Treasury will lose more from the loss of internal revenue on the manufacture of cotton than it can possibly gain from any system of purchase or trade or tax beyond the tax of 2 cents.

And, if we prove to be right, as we may prove to be in our large estimate, by-and-by the price must break clear down and next spring's planting will be seriously impeded.

I suppose our imports this autumn will not be excessive and that they may be balanced by necessary exports other than cotton or gold. If so, cotton will be a surplus export to be paid for in gold. I therefore wish to see it come out as freely as possible in order to bring back specie payment. If, on the other hand, our imports should be large, how much more need of the cotton, be the quantity large or small.

The effect of this letter upon McCulloch was described by Forbes:

I presented your cotton letter to Mr. McC. He thinks you prove too much. If cotton is going to keep up here to 50 cents he thinks three-fourths of that in the Rebel States will be price enough to bring it out freely.[1]

Mr. Atkinson remained unconvinced. Writing again to Mr. Forbes on May 18, he said:

I have yours of the 16th and note contents. Whether cotton keeps up or goes down does not affect my argument. I claim uncertainty and fluctuation as the consequence of Government interference in trade.

For instance, under pressure of the Government cotton, the price went down to 30 cents, a price at which we could make goods which looked very cheap compared to previous prices. At the same time the price of cotton (30 cents) was one low enough to warrant mills running without great risk of loss, even although the managers expected lower prices soon. Everyone began to start up, even the oldest fogies. Now had there been no onerous Government interference receipts would have continued, but the charges and taxes had been so heavy that private receipts almost ceased. Speculators saw this and the price was run up to 60 cents. Mills ceased to start and some began to stop and yet goods paid a better profit on the 60 cent cotton than on the 30 for a little while, but we don't dare carry the necessary stock at 60 when we believe it is three times too high.

Another effect, previous to the fall to 30, we were making arrangements to reduce wages 20 per cent, but when the mills began to start up freely, we found that help was very scarce....

[1] J. M. Forbes to Mr. Atkinson.

I bought heavily at 30 to 35 cents and am now running on that cotton. I now expect a decline on the first receipts under new regulating, because the owners must press forward some cotton. The price will fall, rivers will be low, owners first needs met, and then they will hold back again. Speculators take that opportunity and up goes the price once more.

I am arguing against my interest in advocating free trade in cotton. Personally, I like these fluctuations. I always go in on the declining market and have always succeeded in beating the average. In six months ending December 1, I beat the average $90,000 on one mill, then bought in England on credit and so got down from 1.90 to 30 without loss.

This matter was finally settled by a removal of trade restrictions with the South in June, 1865.[1] Mr. McCulloch wrote to Mr. Atkinson on the 22d:

The removal of all restrictions upon trade with the Southern States is to me personally a great relief. The only objection there can be to the Executive action is that it will keep out of the Treasury a large amount of money which at the present time is very much needed.

I am hopeful, however, that the Government will be compensated for this loss, by the increased deliveries of cotton, and by being freed from the odium which has attached to the trade operations in the South under Treasury Regulations.

It should not be conceived that Mr. Atkinson's advice and recommendations to Secretary McCulloch concerning cotton and other matters connected with the administration of the Treasury were unsolicited. On his return from Washington in early March, 1865, Mr. Atkinson received a note from Mr. McCulloch, written on the ninth, thanking him for his past assistance. The note continued: 'I shall be pleased at all times to hear from you in relation to the cotton trade and to all other subjects connected with the public revenues. You will doubtless hear from me frequently through our mutual friend Mr. Forbes.' The correspondence and cordial relations thus begun lasted throughout Mr. McCulloch's terms as Secretary of the Treasury.

When the problem arose concerning the disposal of the Sea

---

[1] The accompanying table shows the price fluctuations of which Mr. Atkinson complained. With the cessation of the war and the removal of trade restrictions a much steadier price ruled in the market.

Table Showing Fluctuations in the Price of Cotton in the United States

	1861			1862			1863			1864			1865			1866		
	High	Low	Av.	High	Low	Av.	High	Low	Av.	High	Low	Av.	High	Low	Av.	High	Low	Av.
Jan.				38	31	35	90	67½	74	84½	81	82½	1.26	83	1.04½	51½	48½	50
Feb.				32	20	26	92	85	90	84½	79	82	88	80	84	50	43	46
Mar.				29	23	27	89	60	75	81	70	76	84	43	65	45	39	42
Apr.	14	12½	13⅛	30	27¼	28½	74	60	67	84	75	79	58	31	36½	41	30	37
May	14¼	12¾	13⅞	31½	26	28	67	49	60	1.05	83	89	57	44	30½	42	32	36½
June	14⅝	13½	14	38	30½	31½	74	51	59	1.52	1.06	1.29	47	40	43	42	35	38½
July	16¼	14¼	15¼	50	36½	43	73	55	64	1.70	1.50	1.60	53	46	49	38	35	36
Aug.	20½	16	18¼	49½	45	47	69	63	67½	1.90	1.62	1.76	49	42	45½	38	32	34½
Sept.	22½	18¾	20⅝	58	48	55	83	65½	70	1.88	1.20	1.54	46½	42	44½	40	32	34¾
Oct.	22½	20½	21½	61½	54	59	92	81	86½	1.28	1.10	1.19	63	44½	58	45	37	40½
Nov.	29½	22¼	23⅞	70	58½	65	87	75	84	1.45	1.23	1.34	58	49	53	41	33	37
Dec.	40	27¾	33⅞	68½	66	67½	82	78	80	1.34	1.14	1.24	53	48	50½	37	33	34
	40	12½	19⅜	70	20	42½	92	49	73⅛	1.90	70	1.17	1.26	31	57	51½	30	38⅞

The above Table is taken from pages 90–91 of a pamphlet entitled, *Proceedings of a Convention Held in the City of New York, Wednesday, April 29, 1868, for the Purpose of Organizing the National Association of Cotton Manufacturers and Planters.*

Island cotton captured at Savannah, Secretary McCulloch turned to Mr. Atkinson for advice as to the best method. At first it was planned by the Treasury to send the cotton directly to England for sale. Mr. Atkinson pointed out a danger in this procedure, as there was a question as to the ownership of the cotton. Some of the cotton seized by the Union forces as Confederate property was claimed by Great Britain for her citizens. Through Mr. Forbes, Mr. Atkinson advised the Secretary to rebale any cotton shipped to England, as otherwise it might be replevined by the British Government pending a decision concerning its ownership.[1] Rather than risk any trouble with England, it was decided to sell the cotton at auction in the United States.

With the close of the war, the amount of cotton available in the South became of vital importance to the cotton manufacturers. Opinion varied greatly as to the correct figures. Mr. McCulloch wrote to Mr. Atkinson on this subject: 'I trust you are right in your estimates of the amount of cotton in the Southern States. Opinions of Southern men are so conflicting, that I have ceased to place reliance upon any of them. General Hamilton estimated the amount in Texas to be not less than 1,250,000 bales. Other persons, who ought to be about as well posted as himself, think that there are not in that State more than 300,000. Different citizens of Georgia estimate the amount in *that* State all the way up from a 150,000 bales to 625,000.'[2]

Finally, to end as far as possible the uncertainty connected with this subject, Mr. Atkinson persuaded a group of his associates in cotton manufacturing to join with him in sending a representative throughout the South to determine as accurately as possible the amount of cotton there. Captain Albert Warren Kelsey was chosen for this task, and left early in August, 1865, for a tour which lasted through December and thoroughly covered the cotton-growing region. His reports to Mr. Atkinson, in addition to information about cotton supplies, contained an

---

[1] Letter to J. M. Forbes, March 10, 1865.
[2] Letter dated June 16, 1865.

interesting account of the social and economic conditions in the South in the period immediately following the war. Captain Kelsey's final estimate gave a total supply for the season of 1865, including old and new cotton, of a little less than 2,000,000 bales.[1]

It was unfortunate that Mr. Atkinson did not either accept this figure as a conservative estimate or retain his original estimate of approximately 2,300,000 bales,[2] for the supply for the season of 1865 finally amounted to 2,269,316 bales.[3] But by October, 1865, he had revised his original figure to a much lower amount. He wrote to Maurice Williams in Liverpool on the fifth: 'I am fully confirmed in my last estimate of not over 1,250,000 bales old cotton on hand at the end of the war and a new crop which may not be over 250,000 and certainly not over 400,000. I have my year's stock in one mill over which I follow my own judgment, at about 46 cents at mill.'

Throughout the remainder of 1865 he continued in his belief of approximately 1,750,000 bales. The continued low price was attributed to the heavy accumulations at the ports as the fall rains made the rivers more navigable, and to the stringency in the money markets.

With what he figured to be a relatively short supply, he evolved a plan to make the British, who had been slow about ordering American cotton, pay a good stiff price for their supplies. He presented this plan by letter to Secretary McCulloch on October 27, 1865:

> I am, as you are aware, urgently desirous to see a contraction of the currency, an end put to speculation and even to the extravagant profits of my own branch of business. It is unwholesome.
>
> New England has taken six months' stock of cotton at an average of less than 50 cents per pound. England has taken no stock ahead. She must have our cotton, all that we can spare at any price up to thirty pence per pound.
>
> The present prices of cotton are high enough to draw cotton from the interior. There is a heavy stock at the ports. About November 6, we shall get news here of the advance in Liverpool caused by the rise

[1] Letter to Secretary McCulloch from Mr. Atkinson, January 3, 1866.
[2] *Supra*, p. 22.
[3] Brown, Harry Bates, *Cotton*, p. 484.

here from 50 to 62 cents for middling in New York. Such news will probably cause heavy shipments and relieve us from the present pressure of stock at ports. But another and probably greater temporary pressure of cotton at ports will soon follow. The Southern rivers are now beginning to rise. From November 10 to January 1, the means of transportation will be much easier and cheaper than they have been. If during the period from November 1 to January 1, the screws are put upon the money market here, it will be, to all intent and purposes, seconding the Bank of England in an effort to procure cheap cotton for English manufacturers, and cheap cotton means a large export of English goods to America next spring.

If your general policy will admit, money should remain comparatively easy until about January 15, by which time England will have been obliged to take her largest supply at a high price. After January 15, there will be a competition between England and America to secure the remainder of the cotton without much regard to the money market, unless we are in error in our present estimate of the supply.

My own information would lead me to believe, and in my opinion I am confirmed by one of the leading men in the house of A. T. Stewart and Company, that English manufacturers have taken contracts for all the goods they can make for three to four months to come and they only look to us for a sufficient supply of cotton. The amount at sea from East India and China is about 200,000 bales less than last year.

At this time, two things combined to convince Mr. Atkinson that England would not only have to buy from the United States but at fairly high prices. One was the supposed shortage of the East Indian and Chinese crops just suggested. The other arose from what he considered an erroneous way of determining how much cotton remained in the South for potential purchases.

The method which he criticized assumed that practically all cotton passed through the ports en route to market. Accordingly, the total of receipts at the ports plus the amount in transit, subtracted from the total estimated supply, gave a figure that was accepted as being the amount still to come from the South. It was his opinion that these calculations failed to account for a fairly large proportion of the supply at the ports and in transit, cotton which was already assigned to New England manufacturers, and that they omitted the direct rail shipments from the South to New England, which had been unusually heavy. Thus such an estimate would give an impression of a much larger supply than was actually the case.[1]

But the supply of Indian cotton proved to be larger than he had anticipated, and, as already noted, the American supply was about 500,000 bales greater than he estimated. The result was the comparatively weak market for the year beginning October, 1866.[2]

On the whole, Mr. Atkinson and his associates were pretty much mistaken in their estimates of the available cotton, in spite of having taken what seemed to be the best of precautions. He wrote to John Bright, April 13, 1866: 'In regard to cotton, I must admit in our low estimates we were deceived. We took the utmost pains and the Northern spinners as a body acted upon estimates of much less than 2,500,000 bales.' In his own business Mr. Atkinson came out slightly ahead for the year. 'A few of our New England mills on heavy goods will make a bad six months, but all those with which I am immediately connected will make up a good account, having gone in so early as to make a good average on their cotton.'[3]

Mr. Atkinson's estimates received a good deal of publicity and undoubtedly had considerable influence upon the market. Parts of his letter to Maurice Williams in Liverpool were quoted in the English papers. He had Captain Kelsey give a résumé of his findings in *The Nation*.[4] Mr. Atkinson himself entered into a controversy with an English brokerage firm concerning the supply of cotton, which was aired in both English and American papers.

About the only satisfaction he derived from the cotton situation as it developed in 1865 and early 1866 came from the fact that the Southerners received about $50,000,000 more for their crop than they would have if the estimates had been higher. He felt that these funds helped meet a great need of Southerners for capital and also made them conscious of the economic possibil-

---

[1] Cf. letter from Mr. Atkinson to Maurice Williams, November 10, 1865.
[2] See table, p. 25.
[3] Letter to Maurice Williams, May 21, 1866.
[4] Vol. II, pp. 79–81.

ities of the freed Negro. If Southern cotton-growers realized that they could make money hiring the former slaves, they would be anxious to treat them well and not to drive them from the region. He concluded the above letter to Mr. Bright, 'I cannot regret this (low estimate) as the high price is now giving the freedmen about the only protection from abuses which they now have since the sad defection of our President [Andrew Johnson].'

It should not be supposed that Mr. Atkinson's attention during the war period was confined exclusively to problems in connection with cotton. He was, for example, greatly interested in the methods of financing the war, and as might be expected, was a 'hard-money man,' and favored taxation and the sale of bonds instead of inflation as a method of raising governmental funds.

He was especially sharp in his criticism of the Government's policy, if one may judge from a letter of defense from Alexander H. Rice, member of the House from Massachusetts:

> I have just received your letter of yesterday, which I regard as disrespectful to myself and to other members of Congress. The estimate which a somewhat limited acquaintance has given me of your character leads me to believe, however, that this characteristic of your letter is attributable to the fervency with which your views are advocated rather than to any deliberate purpose of offence; and therefore I give it this notice. I must be permitted, however, to say in answer to your emphasized remark that 'those who control the elections... *will have men* who have the courage to tax them,' that if you apply that remark in any manner to me, they will also possibly find that while I am in this place, I shall discharge my duties according to my best understanding of them, and shall not be likely to be intimidated by such threats from any quarter. It is now too late for argument; but if you suppose Congress has any fear of imposing such taxation as is necessary to meet the wants of the Government, I think you are gravely mistaken. The Secretary of the Treasury sent in his annual estimate of the wants of the Government and nothing that he has asked for has been refused. It is the opinion of the Financial Committees of the two Houses of Congress that the measures which have been adopted will raise the amount required; and I presume it is time to say that they do not deem it right or expedient to add to the other and inevitable calamities of war the burdens of *needless* taxation.
>
> I have read your views at length in relation to free trade in cotton, and believe them worthy of much consideration; and the general proposition in favor of high taxes is sound; and Congress has acted upon

EARLY LIFE AND CONTACTS

it; but most men believe that a disturbed currency is to be attributed to other and unavoidable causes while we are in a state of war; such as the great absorption of the productive power of the country in waging the war; the conversion of nearly a million producers into consumers only; the sudden demand for vast expenditures for land and water defences, for ships, ordnance and clothing and other supplies; to the excessive importation of foreign luxuries in foreign ships; the destruction of our commerce by pirates fitted out under the protection of our commercial competition; and for the present, and in respect to the high price of gold, to the lack of that degree of the military success which everybody seems to have anticipated in this campaign.

There may be an honest difference of opinion about a financial policy. What Congress does is not the opinion of an individual, but the result of the study of men upon whom rests the responsibility of success or failure, and whose opportunities for a full view of what ought to be done and what can be done are supposed to be not inferior to those possessed by the general public. Its action is as near the recommendation of the fiscal officers of the Government as can be obtained in a deliberative assembly of equals in authority and privilege gathered from widely scattered constituents various in opinions and interests. I understand at this moment that the Ways and Means Committee have under consideration an additional tax bill; and if they deem it necessary, it will be promptly passed, I do not doubt. The session is in its last hours; and the opportunity which you invoke for Congressmen to meet the 'righteous indignation' of the people is at hand. The rapid and astonishing decline in gold today upon the announcement that one of these Congressmen had been appointed Secretary of the Treasury, the one chiefly responsible for the financial action of Congress, would seem to indicate that however intense that indignation may be in individual cases it is by no means universal.[1]

Mr. Atkinson hoped that the public confidence might be established in respect to both the immediate and ultimate value of the greenbacks. To this end, early in 1865, he dunned the Treasury for a public statement regarding the movements of gold during the preceding ten years, and for an estimate of the existing supply. It was his opinion that there was more gold in the United States in 1865 than there had been in 1861. If this were true and generally known, he believed it would do much to combat the idea that a scarcity of gold would prevent an early retirement of the greenbacks.

At the same time, he wanted a Secretary of the Treasury

[1] July 1, 1864.

appointed who really believed in the value of greenbacks, for, 'Given a Secretary of the Treasury who really believes a greenback to be as good or better than gold, the people will believe it, and their faith will make it true.'[1]

He was against any financial plan which would recognize that the difference between gold and paper was anything but temporary. It was his opinion also that the redundancy of the currency was not as great as was generally believed. 'Does not our present cash system absolutely require twice as much currency in circulation as the old credit system? It seems to me that it does. If so, our redundancy is not over 40 per cent, and the withdrawal of State circulation this year will be nearly as much as one year ought to bear. In addition to that, the simple knowledge that Mr. McCulloch will at the proper time retire greenbacks will be sufficient.'[2]

Mr. Atkinson advocated the use of the cotton held by the Treasury after the capture of Savannah, as a lever to enforce the Government's fiscal policy. On March 27, 1865, he wrote Mr. Forbes to the effect: 'I would risk the addition of a sufficient addition to the currency to pay up arrearages. I hold that the effect would be to start forces up again, but the moment they went too far, sell some cotton and make exchange plenty and you check the advance. Give stability by playing cotton against any too rapid rise, you then start trade, make people feel cheerful and hopeful in business again.'

His opinions regarding national financial policies were in the process of formulation during this period.[3] But on the whole, despite some slight concessions as to the usefulness of the greenbacks, he was in favor of their contraction and a resumption of gold payments as rapidly as possible. And in the subsequent controversy over the greenbacks he became a strong opponent of their continued use.

---

[1] Letter to J. M. Forbes, February 14, 1865.
[2] Letter to J. M. Forbes, March 17, 1865.
[3] 'I argue these matters [of governmental financial policies] with great diffidence. I am not used to these large matters except on cotton.' To Mr. Forbes, March 15, 1865.

CHAPTER II

EXPANDING INTERESTS: COTTON, RAILROADS, CIVIC AFFAIRS

1865–1880

FOR more than a decade following the close of the Civil War, Mr. Atkinson's chief business interests continued to be centered upon cotton manufacturing, although (as will be shown subsequently) by no means to the exclusion of other subjects. Unfortunately, in respect to his business career, only a few of his records have been preserved, and it is only by drawing upon scattered evidence that the course of these activities can be traced.

For the cotton manufacturers, the years immediately following the war and those of the depression in the 'seventies were not conducive to financial success. The fluctuations in prices in the immediate post-war period, and the succeeding industrial stagnation combined to make the situation a difficult one to meet.[1]

Mr. Atkinson found these years very trying in many respects. Being a young man in comparison with most of his associates, he felt hesitant, in case of disagreement, to push his own ideas of the financial policy which he thought should be followed by some corporations under his immediate control. As his most successful cotton mill was the Indian Orchard Mills, of which he owned a substantial share and over which he had complete control, some of the restrictions placed upon him during this period by owners or boards of directors of other mills for which he acted as treasurer, proved very irritating and onerous. Because of these circumstances, Mr. Atkinson was tempted several times, between 1865 and 1878, to withdraw from his duties as treasurer, and to devote his entire time to the operations of a mill of his own.[2]

---

[1] Cf. *Boston Board of Trade, Reports on Cotton*, 1865–80.

[2] For example, on September 18, 1866, he wrote to Amos Lawrence: 'I have concluded that it is great folly for me to run corporations for a salary any more, as I have ample means of my own to build a small mill, and I want to bring up my boys to be manufacturers.'

The following letter sent to one of his business associates sheds light upon Mr. Atkinson's business methods and also shows some of the difficulties he had to meet:

Boston, January 16, 1868

Friend Brodwell:

As you have not sent back your hasty and impulsive missive which was not unexpected when I received it, I will try to make a frank statement and to use such tact as I am possessed of in making it. I have no intention of dictating, or being impertinent and have not been.

The simple case is this. I am paid by the C. M. [Continental Mills] and the F. Co. [Franklin Company] to attend to the duty of a Treasurer. I am paid by Mr. Bates to assist him and to keep the details of the A. M. [Anderscoggin Mills] and B. M. Co. [Bates Manufacturing Company] right. The details of their accounts are in my opinion all wrong. Their money goes into the cash account of F. S. and Co. [Francis Skinner and Company] and we have no knowledge of how the account stands. I prepared a statement of the account of the Continental Mill, the Anderscoggin Mill and the Bates M. Co., wrote the letter containing the proposed votes, and submitted it to Mr. Bates.

He approved the letter but said instead of writing on the Bates and Anderscoggin take your memo of their account over and have a talk with Brodwell.

Now why am I anxious upon this point? simply because the times are dangerous, and the questions which have been asked of me of late and the rates at which your paper sells indicate such a state of feeling as might embarrass you in case of a panic. I say this plainly because I believe it is the most friendly act I can do.

But you must admit that with such a feeling in my mind it is my duty at any risk to myself (for I don't wish at present to give up my position) to see to it that in such contingency there should not be the least danger of embarrassment to the corporations for which I am either directly, or as Mr. Bates' assistant, responsible.

On this point, I have tried to resign rather than face the probability of a contest, and I can only blame myself for not having taken the positive ground I now take long ago. I have made up my mind that I must either do one of three things. 1st, have the accounts properly kept, 2d, be convinced that my views about the proper methods were wrong, or, 3d, resign my offices upon the ground, to be distinctly stated, that I could not have this matter arranged according to my views of what is right in the premises.

Now, as to the matter of directions for using up surplus yarn in the Anderscoggin Mills. Mr. Bates asked me to get the orders from you. I tried 4 or 5 days, every day, and reported to Mr. B. and I said to him what I said to you that there was no system or method about such matters of detail in your concern. I leave to Mr. B. to say whether he agreed with me or not. Is it not true?

I tell you honestly and as the best and most friendly service I can do you, but which I should not volunteer, were I not obliged to do it, by my views of my duty to the corporations, that in the general opinion of the Directors of our corporations who know anything about it, that their interests are suffering because your house is not well organized.

You cannot retort upon me, I have advised you over and over again that the Franklin and Continental should have all the time of one man. I have made mistakes, as all do, but I have done as well as I know how to do and have proved to be tolerably competent by moderate success. My small measure of success has been due to method and system more than anything else.

I disclaim any personal feeling in this matter except the personal feeling of being obliged to do a very disagreeable thing, and I tell you, as between man and man, you owe me an apology and I know you well enough to believe you will come to the same conclusion. You would be the first man to declare me unfit to be Treasurer if I had failed to do what I have done.

Yours truly,
E. A.

He continued to aid in the direction of the above mills until September, 1870, when he resigned his position as treasurer of the Continental Mills and the Franklin Company. This action is explained by a letter to Mr. C. J. Barker, dated September 30, 1873:

I have ample time and am ready to become Treasurer of any good mill that now offers and I should be glad to take the Barker Mill. I could probably get some additional stock taken if more capital is needed, by a good commission house. If there is a chance that such an arrangement would be satisfactory to your associates, I will come down in October and have a conference with you.

In general I will now say that I have always taken such care to act as Treasurer only for concerns that would be sure to pay debts in any event that my name as such Treasurer, now carries confidence with it.

When I became distrustful of F. S. and Co. long before the failure, although I dared not whisper my doubt, I resigned all the small Treasurerships I had held with them and retained only the Franklin and Continental.

For two years more I kept silent and sought to protect their property rather than make money. In that period I lost reputation as a money-making Treasurer but in the end I was fully justified; but it nearly killed me. Since then I have rested somewhat, and I now feel able to do better service than ever before. I have only the Indian Orchard Mills as Treasurer and they are on brown and dyed goods.

I believe an ex-Governor is one of your number, can't remember which but I think Perham. If so, one of my friends who is intimate with him would back me.

As a result of these negotiations, Mr. Atkinson took over the duties of agent for the Barker Mills. At the same time he assumed the office of treasurer of the Masconamet Mills. The latter company had suffered serious financial difficulties, but Mr. Atkinson felt that it was fundamentally sound and with some reorganization would prove profitable.

But he was wrong in his estimates, for the company was unable to survive the troublesome times, and in 1876 the mills were sold at public auction. In respect to his own part in the difficulties, he wrote to a friend: 'I did everything a man could do, but of course I am the scape-goat with some men.'[1]

In the same letter he again expressed the wish to build an ideal mill: '... somewhere between Boston and New York where taxes are low, coal cheap, houses plenty, etc., etc., say Bristol or New London if they meet the first condition. I want 50 acres of cheap land, ample room, and a two-story mill — then help operative families to build and own their houses as we do at Indian Orchard.'

But this plan remained only a plan, and a little over a year later he accepted the appointment as president and treasurer of the Boston Manufacturers' Mutual Fire Insurance Company, which appointment took him out of active participation in cotton manufacturing (of which more in a later chapter).[2]

The remedy to the difficulties which the cotton manufacturers faced during the years of the depression, in Mr. Atkinson's opinion, lay in the recapture of the foreign markets for cotton goods, which had been lost to the American manufacturer during the Civil War. He wrote: 'I have long been of the opinion that during the period of prosperity and large home consumption, we

[1] Letter to Henry Lewis, October 19, 1876.
[2] Cf. Chapter IV.

failed to foster our exports of cotton goods, and the result has come, a very small accumulation has caused an undue depression. In the present emergency everyone is interested in exports, even the most intense protectionists.'[1]

He converted his thoughts into action, and in 1876 was able to interest a number of cotton manufacturers in preparing samples to be sent for display purposes to various markets. Mr. Atkinson personally undertook to arrange the details in connection with their shipment and destination. In October of that year, some sixty cases, each containing two hundred samples of cotton fabrics, were sent to the principal cotton-consuming countries of the world.

Mr. Atkinson also worked to remove some of the obstacles which hindered the exportation of American cotton goods. One of these was the imitation of well-known American trade-marks by certain British manufacturers. Mr. Atkinson protested to Hamilton Fish, Secretary of State, and secured a petition signed by a long list of representative cotton manufacturers urging that steps be taken to eliminate this practice. It was discovered on investigation, however, that the British law on the subject had recently been changed so that redress against imitators could be secured in British courts by the American manufacturers.

These actions, sponsored by Mr. Atkinson, are of interest as indications of the methods followed by the manufacturers in building up their export trade after 1876.[2] In his correspondence, he makes no further reference to the subject, which may be accounted for by his withdrawal from the cotton manufacturing field the following year.

Meanwhile, Mr. Atkinson had not lost his early interest in the future supply of cotton and the general problems connected with its culture. He predicted in December, 1867, 'that the sys-

---

[1] Letter to George E. Woodward, December 31, 1875. M. T. Copeland, in his *The Cotton Manufacturing Industry of the United States*, p. 221, says that for twenty years after 1873 the American cotton manufacturers used the foreign market as a 'safety valve in keeping the home market fairly stable.'

[2] The average annual export between 1871 and 1875 amounted to $3,100,000. Between 1876 and 1880 it increased to $10,000,000. Cf. Copeland, *op. cit.*, p. 220.

tem of raising cotton is to change from large plantations to smaller farms, and that from this change there will come in time large crops from a small number of acres.'[1]

He was interested in encouraging immigration into the Southern States, but felt that it would come only as it was demonstrated that there was a profit to be made in cotton-growing. For a while he entertained the idea that cotton would be grown at a low cost in the South by Chinese labor. With the completion of the Union Pacific Railroad, he thought that the Chinese laborers engaged in its construction would make their way into the southwestern cotton area and 'solve the cheap cotton problem.'

In 1867, Mr. Atkinson secured the co-operation of the United States Department of Agriculture in introducing a new type of long-staple cotton, which was grown in Egypt, and which seemed adapted to certain sections of the South. He wrote an article setting forth the advantages of this variety for the publication of the department, and had samples sent to various of his friends in the South. A few years later, he personally imported a quantity of cotton seed from China, which was of a particular hardy type and distributed it to a number of interested persons.

Mr. Atkinson's reputation at this time as a cotton expert is shown by the following request made of Benjamin F. Nourse by a Mr. C. Kerckoff, of New York City, who was preparing a résumé of the cotton industries of various countries. The letter, forwarded to Mr. Atkinson, read in part, '[I hope] that you will kindly prevail upon Mr. Atkinson to furnish his important co-operation as far as the manufacture of American cotton is concerned, he being reported the best statistician on the continent, and the most competent authority on the matter.'[2]

Mr. Atkinson's interest in the economic rehabilitation of the South after the Civil War prompted many Southerners to seek his help when they were attempting to raise capital in New England. Although he felt that the South potentially would offer much as an investment field, Mr. Atkinson was personally unwill-

[1] Letter to Messrs. Epping Houserd and Company, December 4, 1867.
[2] July 8, 1871.

COTTON, RAILROADS, CIVIC AFFAIRS

ing to take an active part in any of the many propositions which came to his attention in the years immediately after the war, even though on several occasions he arranged necessary introductions for his Southern friends. In 1873, however, he was strongly tempted to aid in the promotion of a Southern railroad which seemed to possess attractive features. In that year, in company with Mr. Henry Saltonstall, he was invited to become a member of the board of directors of the Little Rock and Fort Smith Railroad, a small line which was being constructed in western Arkansas. A preliminary investigation of the financial arrangements of the company did not entirely please Mr. Atkinson.

He wrote to a friend:

> The proposition for a release of the State lien, as I understood it, was that one million common stock should be issued to the State of Arkansas and $360,000 State bonds or $180,000 cash deposited with a banking house whose name you know. To whom the deposit with the banking house was to go, I have not ascertained, nor do I think it is fully understood in State Street.
>
> I shall be glad of any information on the subject, but of one thing you may be assured, if I become a director in the Little Rock and Fort Smith Railroad, no payment, deposit or other expenditure will be made by my consent that is not to be entered on the books of the company as paid to certain persons thereon named for purposes thereon designated. From the date I enter on the duties, until I go out, every transaction must be open, clean and of record.[1]

Subsequent study of the proposition convinced Mr. Atkinson and Mr. Saltonstall that they did not wish to become associated with this railroad company. In a joint letter they expressed their reasons as follows:

Boston, February 28, 1873

Elisha Atkins, Esq.

Dear Sir,

Having reason to suppose that you have received a notice from the proper recording officer of the Little Rock and Fort Smith Railroad of Arkansas that we have been elected as directors in said railroad, for which position we have not yet qualified, we hereby decline to accept

---

[1] Letter to W. D. Crane, February 14, 1873.

such position and we intend to persist in such declination, because we find upon an inspection of what purports to be a copy of the records of said railroad that all the action intended to have been taken by the new board of directors has been forestalled by the making of contracts with Josiah Caldwell for the completion of the road, the disposition of bonds, for the construction of certain bridges and the payment of certain tolls and other matters.

We take this action at the earliest moment possible after the receipt of said records, and the reading of a part. The condition of our hereafter undertaking any duty or service in connection with said corporation will be the annulment of all said contracts and an alteration in the personnel of the board alleged to have been chosen at the last meeting.

It will be borne in mind that we made it a condition precedent to our acceptance of the office of director that we should have an opportunity to inspect all the records before we entered upon the duties.

EDWARD ATKINSON
HENRY SALTONSTALL

Mr. Atkinson's attention seems to have been drawn by the foregoing to the financial possibilities of railroad construction, for a year later he became deeply interested in another railroad project. This second interest in the railroad industry came in conjunction with a State-wide attempt to improve railroad transportation facilities in Massachusetts during the 'seventies. It was the hope of the commercial and industrial interests, particularly of Boston, not only to increase the direct exchange of goods with the West, but to build up the port of Boston as an important exporting center. Great emphasis was placed upon Boston's closer proximity to Europe than New York, Philadelphia, and other American exporting points, and it was generally felt that, given proper railway facilities, Boston could greatly increase its importance as a port.

In this connection, one of the important problems was the necessity of giving the railroads convenient access to ocean steamers in order that transshipment of goods might be facilitated as much as possible. Efforts were made to induce the railroads and other interested groups to construct their terminal facilities in such a way that ocean traffic would be stimulated. For example, the Boston Board of Trade passed a resolution

COTTON, RAILROADS, CIVIC AFFAIRS 41

November 19, which read: 'Resolved, That the Boston Board of Trade would at this time earnestly press upon the attention of the various railway companies whose lines connect this city with the west and the north, the urgent necessity which exists for the construction of new elevators and other terminal facilities at East Boston, Charlestown, and South Boston, for the accommodation of the rapidly increasing foreign commerce of the port, with the least possible loss of time.'[1]

In 1874, there were eight different railway lines terminating in Boston.[2] Of these, only three, the Hartford and Erie, the Boston and Maine, and the Eastern Railroad had constructed lines which gave convenient access to harbor facilities.

The general situation was complicated by the discussion concerning the disposition of the Hoosac Tunnel, which had been completed in 1873. This project, begun in 1854, had been built by State aid and Massachusetts had spent over ten million dollars in its construction. Opinion differed regarding its use. Some felt that the State should operate a railroad line using the tunnel, a scheme which would, presumably, retain the benefits of the tunnel to the people and give healthy competition to the privately owned lines. Others advocated that the tunnel should be used by private railroad companies under some form of ownership or lease. This latter point of view was expressed in a resolution of the Boston Board of Trade passed June 1, 1874:

> WHEREAS, This Board and the community, have long and patiently waited for a solution of the vital question of our day, viz: — The Hoosac Tunnel question, which rightly will give Boston advantages as an export city, equal to any port on the Atlantic coast; and whereas, it is feared the Legislature is about to adjourn and leave this important matter unsettled for another year; Resolved, That in the judgment of this Board, a further delay in this matter is not only uncalled for, but will be attended by great harm to the interests of this State and City.
>
> Resolved, That a public meeting be called in the name of this Board, in Faneuil Hall on Thursday next, at 3 1-2 o'clock, P.M., to indorse the

[1] *Annual Report of the Boston Board of Trade, for the Year Ending January 8, 1873*, p. 69.
[2] Cf. *Map of Boston and the Country Adjacent Showing Rural Parks*, as proposed by Ernest W. Bowditch, 1874; Massachusetts Historical Society.

following proposition; 'The interests of this State and this City demand a through and independent line of railway from Boston, by way of the Hoosac Tunnel to the West, and the Legislature should perfect and adopt a plan in answer to this demand, before the adjournment of the present session.'[1]

More adequate transportation to the West and better terminal facilities were closely associated in the current discussion during this time. For example, in 1876, the Secretary of the Boston Board of Trade reported:

> Closely connected with this question of additional avenues of railroad to the interior and the West, is the one of terminal facilities in our city, for with adequate means to bring increased products to our doors, we must have the requisite conveniences, so that the supplies may be cheaply and expeditiously distributed.
>
> At the present time the only efficient terminal facilities at tide water, are those possessed by the Boston and Albany Railroad at East Boston, and only by this road and at this place, can the cereals of the West be brought to and exported from our city. While wishing to say nothing whatever in disparagement of this single line of railroad, it must be clearly apparent to all that a great city like Boston cannot safely allow itself to be restricted to so limited an outlet. The plan for utilizing the South Boston Flats for terminal facilities is therefore one that vitally interests every business man of our city, and the early completion of the enterprise is of the first importance.
>
> In view of all these matters, it is absolutely necessary that connections be formed with the Hoosac Tunnel line, thus virtually giving to Boston a trunk road connecting with the principal cities of the West; and the great desideratum is that Boston shall have that close connection with and virtual control of these lines, that shall place it beyond possibility that she shall be discriminated against in the matter of charges in favor of New York. We do not complain of the prosperity of our sister city, on the contrary, we wish her success, but we must insist on equal rates.[2]

Mr. Atkinson's interest in this matter and the germination of his later plans are contained in the accompanying letter to J. A. Wenzie, dated May 9, 1873:

> I have very little knowledge in regard to railroad matters and have just begun to study the questions now at issue.

---

[1] *Annual Report of the Boston Board of Trade for the Year Ending January* 1, 1875, pp. 35–36.

[2] *Annual Report of the Boston Board of Trade for the Year Ending January* 1, 1876, pp. 13–14.

It has seemed to me that the tunnel controversy has turned mainly upon the terminal grounds now in the possession of the Lowell Railroad, and that the alleged necessity for the consolidation of the Lowell and the Fitchburg is based upon the supposed need of connecting the track of the Fitchburg with the terminal grounds of the Lowell. This is all very well — But, how much area do those grounds comprise? Are they very ample even for the business of the Lowell and Fitchburg as they now are with their share of the tunnel business added? I *guess* not. Now suppose the Massachusetts Central reaches the tunnel and is obliged to use the terminal facilities of the Lowell, what chance would it have?

If the State owned and operated the tunnel line, or leased it as proposed by the minority of the committee, no other road would have a ghost of a chance to do tunnel business. On the other hand, if the Consolidated Corporation owned the terminal grounds at this end, it would squeeze out of a competing line all that it possibly could. Hence, in any view of the matter the road that competes at the tunnel must be free at this end. This is imperative.

Now any arrangement made with the Lowell Railroad *as it now is* could not be allowed by the public interest to hamper and cripple a line that was not a competing line with the Lowell when the contract was made, but which may become a competing line with the new corporation in which the Lowell may be merged. Especially would it be true that no such crippling contract could stand, if thereby it was made impracticable to connect the interest of the State in the tunnel with the interest of the State in the flats at South Boston.

Let the Massachusetts Central only show this possibility. First, of a line to compete with the Consolidated Lowell and Fitchburg from this tunnel to the sea. Second, that the new line would unite the tunnel and the flats. Third, in order to compass these ends the Massachusetts Central may unite at Mount Bowdoin with the New York and New England (late Hartford and Erie) and thus help save the interest of the state in that line. And what results would follow? I think the whole absurd scheme of State ownership would fall because wholesome competition would be sure and the necessary legislation to secure such results could be had for the asking.

If I were a Massachusetts Central Railroad manager, I should first promote the plan of the majority of the Railroad Committee and then ask leave to put my road over to South Boston flats.

Further study of the situation convinced Mr. Atkinson that the development of the terminal facilities should be put into the control of an independent corporation which should undertake to construct the proper terminal facilities on the South Boston flats. In order to make these facilities available, the corporation should also construct a junction line which would link together the railroads terminating in Boston with this property. This would guarantee a comprehensive development of the property, and would insure to all interested parties equal accessibility to the terminal grounds.

There were several reasons why such a plan would appeal to Mr. Atkinson. In the first place, it fitted in with his strongly developed interest in public welfare. More personally, the development of this project would undoubtedly mean that he would assume an executive position with the new company, which was desirable in view of the unsettled state of his cotton business. Finally, the proposed line would pass over some property owned by Mr. Atkinson in West Roxbury.

To carry out his ideas, Mr. Atkinson, early in 1874, organized the Boston and Northwestern Railroad Association. The immediate purpose of this organization was to raise sufficient money to perform all the necessary preliminary steps and to form the nucleus of the corporation which should subsequently be organized to undertake actual construction. Some $170,000 was pledged to the Association upon which a ten per cent assessment was levied for the purpose of making surveys, securing options, and other necessary preliminaries.

The route which was chosen for the proposed junction line was as follows: Starting at the flats in South Boston, the road was to proceed by tunnel under South Boston, through West Roxbury, Brookline, Newton, across the Charles River at Riverside Station, finally to stop at Weston. The total distance was approximately fifteen miles. The proposed route had many advantages from a construction point of view. Fifty per cent of the line was level; there would be few grade crossings; and the nature of the terrain was such that the necessary excavations could easily be made. In addition, the road ran through regions which were not thickly settled, which insured a minimum difficulty in securing the rights of way.

The line would cut across and connect with the following railroads already built: The Shawmut and Old Colony, the New York and New England (Blackstone Division), the Boston and Providence, the New York and New England (Woonsocket Division), and the Boston and Albany. Connections could easily be made with the Fitchburg Road and eventually with the Massachusetts Central.

Before much progress could be made, the use of the South Boston or Commonwealth flats by the proposed railroad had to be secured. These flats, which were owned by the State, consisted in about three hundred acres of tide water, and other land on the northeastern or harbor side of South Boston. The State had spent considerable sums from time to time to improve this property, but to this time no use had been made of this area.

Experience with the Hoosac Tunnel and other railroad construction in Massachusetts had caused a strong reaction against any further State aid to railroad ventures either by direct subsidies or the issue of State bonds. From the point of view of the State the South Boston flats represented a considerable investment, and, although in its existing form the property was of little use, it was unlikely that the flats would be turned over to a private company without exacting a high price. On the other hand, Mr. Atkinson's company was unprepared to pay any large sum for the use of this property to the State. It was felt, and not without reason, that the railroad would be the chief contributor to the ultimate value of the flats, and Mr. Atkinson and his associates were unwilling to make any large payment for this property in addition to building the railroad.

In an attempt to solve this dilemma, Mr. Atkinson worked out the following plan: To safeguard the financial interests of the Commonwealth, the Governor would be empowered to appoint one or two of the executive officers of the Boston and Northwestern Railroad Company, who were to have the final decision in respect to the investment of funds. In this manner, the State could transfer the flats to a private company and yet avoid the evils of a direct subsidy. And, with the use of the property insured to his company, Mr. Atkinson anticipated no difficulty in raising sufficient funds to complete the proposed railroad project, including some rather extensive improvements on the flats themselves. The State should donate the use of a portion of the flats to the Boston and Northwestern Railroad Company, and in return would receive a substantial part of the stock issued by the Company.

In November, 1874, Mr. Atkinson presented a petition to the Massachusetts Legislature for permission to organize a company for the purpose of developing the terminal grounds at South Boston according to the plan suggested above, and for the construction of a junction railroad. The petition was referred to a joint Committee of the House and Senate, which was instructed to make a thorough investigation of the plan.

The substance of this Committee's report, made in 1875, was as follows.[1] It recommended that a comprehensive plan be adopted for the development of the terminal facilities at the flats. The disposal of the flats was to be put in the hands of a competent commission which should deal 'upon liberal terms' with those who wish to develop the flats upon some such comprehensive plan. The Committee felt that the most feasible route for the junction railroad was the one proposed by the Boston and Northwestern Railroad Company. In respect to the Boston and Northwestern Railroad Company, the Committee stated:

> Energetic and influential men, who fully appreciate the opportunity now offered to Boston by the proper use of the new railroad are active in its management.... They will make the whole property accessible to railroad business, and will add much to its value. It will be for the Legislature to determine how, and to what extent, not by payment of money, but by gift or sale of land (at present of little value), this railroad may be aided so that its construction, without unnecessary delay, may be assured.[2]

The final result of this and other committee reports [3] was the enactment of a law May 19, 1875, which authorized the Governor to appoint three persons who were 'to make contracts for the improvement, filling, sale, use or other disposition of the lands

[1] *House Legislative Documents*, 1875, no. 100.
[2] *Ibid.*, p. 42.
[3] *Ibid.*, nos. 365 and 388.

COTTON, RAILROADS, CIVIC AFFAIRS   47

at and near to South Boston... known as the Commonwealth Flats.'[1]

Section Five of the Act applied particularly to Mr. Atkinson's project:

> Said agents may, with the consent of the Governor and Council, make bargains for the sale of portions of the flats to any persons or corporations which shall undertake to construct a junction railroad to connect one or more existing railroads with the said lands, upon such terms and conditions as are hereinafter provided.

Mr. Atkinson's plans received considerable attention from those interested in the improvement of transportation facilities. For example, the secretary of the Boston Board of Trade commented:

> In connection with this question of trunk lines of railroad to the interior and the West, is one of terminal facilities in our city, and on this point, the scheme of Mr. Edward Atkinson for a line of railroad to connect the existing lines of roads with tide water at South Boston, and the erection at that place of elevators and warehouses, is an important one.
>
> This plan has been explained to our merchants by Mr. Atkinson, and a Committee of the Legislature has carefully considered the matter during the recess, and it is understood, will present a very thorough and exhaustive report on the subject in January.[2]

Although the Act passed in 1875 authorized the proper authorities to negotiate with the promoters of a junction line, progress in this direction was blocked by the general railroad law of Massachusetts which prohibited railroads from connecting with each other except under restricted circumstances. Branch lines in the vicinity of Boston and grade crossings were also prohibited. In addition to these difficulties, the railroads having actual or potential interest in the South Boston Terminal grounds or who wished to develop rival facilities began to move against the plan. The chief members of the opposition were the Fitchburg, the Boston and Albany, and the New York and New England railroads.[3]

---

[1] *Laws and Resolves of Massachusetts*, 1875, Chapter 239.
[2] *Annual Report of the Boston Board of Trade for the Year Ending January*, 1875, pp. 15–16.
[3] *House Legislative Documents*, 1879, no. 289, p. 10.

To solve the legal difficulties involved, Mr. Atkinson caused a bill to be introduced into the House in March, 1876, which would allow such inter-railway connections as would be necessary for a junction railroad.[1] But the opposition was too strong, and it failed even to get a third reading in the House.

As a result, save for the completion of necessary surveys and other similar work, nothing was accomplished in this matter between 1876 and 1878. Late in 1878, Mr. Atkinson again petitioned the Legislature on behalf of the Boston and Northwestern Railroad Association for an act of incorporation and for the passage of a law permitting the necessary inter-railroad connections. This petition was eventually referred in March, 1879, to a joint committee composed of the Land and Railroad Commissioners who were instructed to make a thorough investigation of the proposition and to report to the next legislative session, which would meet in 1880.[2] Obviously, this meant a postponement of any action for at least another year.

Such a delay was most unwelcome to the promoters of the Boston and Northwestern Railroad. On March 10, 1879, this Commission sent a letter to the Governor urging the necessity of immediate action upon the subject.[3]

In their opinion it was not only necessary to enact needed legislation in order to improve the property, but to prevent injury to it as well. The ability of Mr. Atkinson and his associates was praised and they were described as 'men who have the means to do the work, and every incentive to undertake it.'[4]

The letter continued:

> They do not ask the State to spend another dollar on the South Boston property; but they do ask that they may be permitted to build a junction railroad which shall connect one or more roads not now connecting with the South Boston property. Under the general laws, such a railroad cannot now be built.... This Commission appeared before the Committee on Railroads to aid in securing such a railroad (junction road).... Opposition to the special charter asked for was made by existing railroads; and it was urged that a company to build

[1] *House Legislative Documents*, 1876, no. 151. [2] *Ibid.*, 1879, no. 211.
[3] *Ibid.*, 1879, no. 289.   [4] *Ibid.*, p. 2.

COTTON, RAILROADS, CIVIC AFFAIRS

the road should be first organized, and that then, if special provisions were required, the organized corporation should petition for them.... This would defer action until another year, and would virtually defeat the objects of the petitioners.[1]

As the situation then existed, the flats could not be leased except to a company which was organized for the purpose of building a junction road. Yet, money would not be invested in a company which was prohibited by law from doing the thing which it was organized to do. To solve these difficulties, the Commission suggested a bill which would make the necessary changes in the general railroad law of Massachusetts to permit the construction of a junction line.

In spite of such a strong plea for immediate action, the bill failed to pass and the matter was referred to the special Committee.

After considering the matter, this Committee reported favorably on the necessary legislation which would provide for the construction of a junction road and branch railroad lines. Their bill was passed by the Legislature and became a law early in 1880.[2]

This action did not result in the carrying-out of the plans of the Boston and Northwestern Railroad Company for several reasons. In the first place, Mr. Atkinson's personal interest in the project had been lessened because he had, in 1878, assumed the presidency of the Boston Manufacturers' Mutual Fire Insurance Company, and in addition had disposed of property which would be benefited by the road. But probably the greatest obstacle lay in the attitude of the Committee which made the report on the law and which was authorized by the law to negotiate for the use of the flats.

While admitting the great need for proper terminal facilities, the Committee continued:

> But we do not believe that this land should be given to any party for such use, or for any use. We cannot regard railroads or shipping enterprises as subjects for charitable action on part of the State. The time has passed when the Commonwealth could be properly asked to

[1] *Op. cit.*, 1879, no. 289, p. 3.
[2] *Laws and Resolves of Massachusetts*, 1880, Chapter 252.

aid any commercial scheme by gifts or loans. We do not therefore recommend any grant of money or land, nor any sale or contract which from its terms would be equivalent to a grant... even if it could be shown that these flats would be more rapidly improved by the grant of a special charter to individuals with peculiar advantages and liberal grants, it would by no means follow that this course was desirable.[1]

Such a policy precluded any grant of the flats to the Boston and Northwestern Railroad Company, and meant that several million dollars of capital would have to be raised to build the railroad, to construct warehouses, and to purchase the flats. In view of the uncertain co-operation of the railroads, it is not surprising that no further action was taken.

Mr. Atkinson made several attempts to interest various railroad executives in taking over the plan. Altogether the Association spent about nine thousand dollars upon surveys and securing options. Although some interest was evoked, nothing came of his efforts.

Whether such a plan for combined terminal grounds would have increased Boston's importance as an exporting and importing center, is a matter of conjecture. Subsequent development of railroad terminal facilities has resulted in their location at various points on Boston Harbor. Such a system undoubtedly necessitates transshipments which would be avoided by union terminal grounds.

In respect to Mr. Atkinson, the whole plan is indicative of the scope of his activities. It shows his ability to plan along comprehensive lines and in terms of social welfare.

In 1842, Mr. Atkinson returned from Boston to Brookline, Massachusetts, where he made his home throughout the remainder of his life. He at once became actively interested in town and social affairs and was the moving spirit in many of the latter, planning dances, concerts, dramatic entertainments, sleighing and skating parties for his contemporaries.

[1] *Land and Railroad Commissioners' Report, Accompanying Legislative Document,* 252, 1880.

It was during these years that he met Mary Caroline Heath, who became his wife in 1855. Their marriage proved a most happy one, as she was ideally suited to his temperament. She had a calm, serene nature which served to balance her husband's more volatile enthusiasms, and he depended a great deal upon her judgment on all matters connected with his career.

Early in their married life they built a house on part of her grandfather's estate now known as Heath Hill.[1] Though it may have been a wrench for her parents to give up their only daughter, it was not long before Mr. Atkinson became an important and much-loved member of the family. All of them, including many of Mr. Atkinson's relatives who also lived on Heath Hill, became dependent upon his judgment and consulted him in matters of business as well as in the more intimate family problems.

By 1878 nine children had been born into the Atkinson family, two of whom, Caroline Heath and Lincoln, died in infancy. The remaining seven, Anna Greenleaf, Edward Williams, Charles Heath, William, Robert Whitman, Caroline Penniman, and Mary Heath, completed a family group which enjoyed the pleasures and associations possible only in a large family.

Mr. Atkinson took great pride and pleasure in his family. He was able to give each of the boys a college or university education and each of the girls had an equivalent in special training and travel. He was especially proud of the musical talent possessed by his wife and the various members of his family, and liked nothing better than to have them sing and play for his guests. He himself was not talented musically, but possessed a keen appreciation of good music. He would occasionally join in the family choral singing with what he called his 'three and only bass notes.'

[1] Heath Hill in Brookline overlooks the old Boston Reservoir and the city itself. It consists of about twelve acres, being what was left of a large farm originally owned by an English gentleman. The latter was loyal to the Crown in Revolutionary days and migrated either to Canada or back to England. Thereupon the property was confiscated by the Colonial Government and the farm was purchased by the original John Heath from the Colonial Government. It was worked as a farm for many years and later on was gradually either sold or divided among his descendants. At present there are six houses occupied by his descendants on Heath Hill which is the only part of the original farm that remains. The oldest house now existing thereon was built in 1791, the original older house having been torn down many years ago.

He made his home an open house for his many friends and acquaintances. His wife and daughters, whose responsibility it was to plan the meals and to care for visitors, became accustomed to receiving unexpected company.[1] But as he entertained easily and without undue ceremony, both his guests and his family enjoyed the informality of these occasions.

The many persons who enjoyed the hospitality of Heath Hill reflected the broad range of his acquaintances. Among the more noted or unusual visitors were Governor Andrew and his staff, Walter Hines Page, Booker T. Washington, Lord Herschell, Archibald Geikie, Professor Frank Emmons, a Buddhist priest from India called the Anagarika Dharmapala,[2] Bonami Price, Thomas Potter, Francis A. Walker, Professor and Mrs. Robert E. Richards, W. Z. Ripley, David A. Wells, Charles Nordhoff, Lord and Lady Farrer, Geoffrey Wedgwood, Sir Swire Smith, the Henry Yates Thompsons, Colonel Henry Lee, Colonel Theodore Lyman, Judge John Lowell, J. Elliot Cabot, Moses Williams, and others.

Mr. Atkinson found keen enjoyment in various Brookline and Boston clubs to which he belonged. Probably the most famous of these was the Thursday Evening Club, composed of a cosmopolitan group of business and professional men living in and around Boston. This group was able at its monthly meetings to present the leading authorities in various branches of knowledge who spoke about their special fields. Mr. Atkinson was a faithful attendant, and on one occasion had the pleasure of entertaining the entire group at a bountiful dinner cooked entirely in his Aladdin Cooker.

---

[1] His daughter Caroline related of the time when a half-hour before meal-time she saw her father coming up the drive with seven school teachers whom he had brought home to dinner.

[2] Anagarika Dharmapala came to the United States to study improved agricultural methods with the object of introducing them into India. He met Mr. Atkinson, who was also interested in this subject, and the two became such good friends that the priest spent two months at Heath Hill. Some years after Mr. Atkinson's death he again visited the United States and came to the house on Heath Hill with the particular object of paying deference to Mr. Atkinson's memory. He went through the ceremony of lighting a candle in front of Mr. Atkinson's picture and then bowed his head in silent prayer, after which he arose, and joined the members of the family who had gathered to see him.

A more intimate and more social group in which he found a great deal of pleasure was the Brookline Whist Club which met on Saturday evenings. This group was organized informally in 1873 for the purpose of playing whist and enjoying one another's company. In addition to Mr. Atkinson the original members were John C. Abbott, insurance underwriter; William I. Bowditch, conveyancer; Charles D. Head, stock broker; Thomas Parsons, philanthropist; Edward Philbrick, civil engineer; Henry V. Poor, railroad statistician; and Moses Williams, lawyer. Each member would entertain the group three times throughout the season, which began in early November and lasted to May, usually providing a light supper for his guests during the middle of the evening. Edward Stanwood, who became a member in 1881, wrote of these meetings: 'The host of the evening signifies to his fellow members that his house is theirs for the time being by leaving his door so that there is no need of a latch-key or of a maid to open the door. Absolute good-fellowship prevails. During the twenty-five years the writer of these chronicles has been a member of the club he has never heard an intentionally severe word spoken by one member to another, nor observed any incident which ruffled the universal harmony and good-will.'[1]

Attendance at meetings was compulsory in the sense that only the most imperative reasons kept members away. Mr. Atkinson, for one, lived up to this rule scrupulously and would plan his absences from home in such a manner as to be away as few Saturday evenings as possible. Stanwood says of Mr. Atkinson's association with the club, 'We remember him as a genial host, the charming companion in our hours of relaxation, the personal friend full of acts of kindness.'[2]

Mr. Atkinson also belonged to several other discussion groups including the Round Table at the Union Club, the Examiner Club, and the Economy Club. Numbered in this last group were such recognized leaders in their respective fields as Henry Lee, Moses Williams, William Minot, R. D. Smith, S. Wood, E. R. A.

[1] Stanwood, Edward, *Annals of the Brookline Whist Club*, p. 5.
[2] Stanwood, Edward, *op. cit.*, p. 21.

Seligman, A. L. Perry, C. F. Dunbar, Horace White, F. W. Taussig, A. T. Hadley, and J. Laurence Laughlin. At this organization's periodic meetings various members or invited speakers would address the group and lead in the discussion which followed.

Few persons enjoyed traveling more thoroughly than did Mr. Atkinson. In addition to numerous excursions south and west in the United States, he made no less than seven trips to Europe during his lifetime. He sought comfort rather than luxury on his trips, but refused to start out on journeys unless he could travel easily. He made it a point on his journeys to get acquainted with as many persons as possible and was ever eager to get new ideas and facts from all possible sources. He was a delightful traveling companion and some of the pleasantest memories cherished by his children have to do with the companionship they enjoyed while accompanying him on various trips.

Mr. Atkinson's sense of civic pride and responsibility prompted him to take an active part in the development of the town of Brookline. As was the case with his national interests, these activities ranged over a broad field. Probably the most important of these exists today as a permanent record of his foresight and energy. This had to do with the preservation of the reservoir located on Boylston Street. This body of water, which adds so much to the beauty of its surroundings, served as a reservoir for the city of Boston until the 'eighties, when other facilities were developed. Some years later a group of real-estate promoters conceived the idea of purchasing the site of the reservoir with the purpose in mind of filling it in and making it residential property.

With characteristic vigor, Mr. Atkinson moved to stop this project. He succeeded in getting the abutting property owners to subscribe $100,000 toward the purchase of the reservoir. To this the town of Brookline added another $100,000, and the property was purchased from the City of Boston, and was dedicated forever to park purposes. Anyone who drives over Boylston Street or views this body of water from any one of the numerous vantage-points surrounding it will agree that Mr.

Atkinson did well to preserve its beauty for the enjoyment of future generations.

Brookline, like so many of the New England towns, has always been governed through the medium of town meetings. It was in these meetings that Mr. Atkinson would find numerous opportunities of giving verbal support for the projects which he favored. An able and forceful speaker, he enjoyed these meetings and was thoroughly convinced that this was the ideal method of government. To his friends from foreign countries he held up the town meetings as the most nearly perfect of democratic institutions.

In the early 'seventies Mr. Atkinson bought the old town hall located on Walnut Street next to the First Parish Church for the purpose of establishing a school for his own children and those of his neighbors. And it was here, first under the guidance of Miss Clement and later Miss C. M. Rideoute, that all of his children and their playmates attended school. Later, the building was used for the gatherings of what was known as the Schoolhouse Club. This club held meetings every fortnight at which games were played and musical entertainment given. Mr. Atkinson enjoyed this sort of thing immensely, and he was never happier than when engaged in some social activity with his family or friends. When the school had fulfilled its purpose, the building was purchased by the First Parish Church and is now known as Pierce Hall and is still used for church gatherings.

A present-day Brookline institution which owes its foundation to Mr. Atkinson and his friends is the Brookline Savings Bank, founded in 1871. Feeling that Brookline needed facilities for the accumulation of savings, Mr. Atkinson and his friends, J. C. Abbott and Moses Williams, Jr., petitioned the Massachusetts State Legislature for a charter to establish a savings institution in Brookline. The charter was granted in February, 1871, and in April the first regular meeting of the Corporation was held.[1] At this meeting, Amos A. Lawrence was elected presi-

---

[1] The following distinguished list of persons were members of the Corporation: John C. Abbott, Edward Atkinson, George Baty Blake, Amos A. Lawrence, Alanson W. Beard,

dent with Edward Atkinson, Alanson W. Beard, and Charles U. Cotting as vice-presidents. When Mr. Lawrence found it impossible to serve in this capacity, Mr. Atkinson was elected to the presidency in May, 1871.

In this position Mr. Atkinson successfully guided the new venture through the troublesome years of the 'seventies and laid the foundations for the subsequent success which this institution has enjoyed to date. He was forced to withdraw from this office in May, 1877, because of ill health, and it was with profound regret that the trustees accepted his resignation.

In addition to the activities already mentioned, Mr. Atkinson found time to take an active part in some of the most important political questions of the day, to write numerous articles and to make several important speeches on various subjects. He also busied himself with several inventions and initiated some important scientific experiments.[1] It may be of more than passing interest also to record that he was one of the original founders of *The Nation*, and was a frequent contributor to its pages.

Charles U. Cotting, William A. Wellman, Charles D. Head, Alfred Kenrick, Jr., Thomas Parsons, William I. Bowditch, James Driscoll, Philip Duffy, Martin Kingman, John W. Candler, George F. Fabyan, Ignatius Sargent, Austin W. Benton, Charles H. Stearns, Horace James, Moses Williams.

[1] As these various subjects will be described in some detail in subsequent chapters (*vide*, Table of Contents), they are only mentioned at this point.

CHAPTER III

POLITICS: FREE TRADE, GREENBACKS, REFORM
1865–1880

THE appointment of Mr. David A. Wells in 1865 as the chairman of the Commission to revise the Government's hodgepodge taxation structure which had grown up during the war, prompted Mr. Atkinson to write to him suggesting one or two persons who might serve upon the Commission. This correspondence marked the beginning of a friendship between the two men which was firmly based upon mutual admiration and respect. Mr. Wells consulted Mr. Atkinson freely upon many of the problems which arose in connection with his work and relied considerably upon the latter's judgment upon various matters, particularly those relating to cotton and tariff.

One of the most important questions in connection with the revision of the revenue system was the fixing of the tax upon raw cotton. It was the procedure of the Revenue Commission of which Wells was chairman, to call into conference representatives of those industries which were affected by changes in the taxation system. Accordingly, representatives of the cotton industry met with the Committee to discuss the effect of a tax upon cotton and other provisions in connection with this measure.

In the opinion of most of these experts, whose testimony was the subject of a special report by the Revenue Commission,[1] a tax upon cotton would fall upon the consumer, and with one exception they favored such a tax as a source of revenue.[2] Mr.

---

[1] *House Executive Documents, Thirty-Ninth Congress,* First Session, 1865–66, *Appendix to Special Report,* no. 3.

[2] It may be of interest to note in this connection that of the seventeen men whose testimony appeared in this report, only one was a cotton-grower; the remaining sixteen were from New England. The only objection to the tax on cotton came from A. H. Kelsey, whose extensive tour of the South immediately after the war (*supra,* p. 26) convinced him that Southern rehabilitation would be furthered by the elimination of such a tax.

Atkinson's testimony before the Commission is of particular interest because of the extensive use of tables and other statistical evidence to back up his statements. His conclusions, which coincided in general with those of his associates, were that cotton could probably be taxed five cents per pound with no serious consequences either to the producer or consumer, although he preferred a lower rate. He felt that the consumer would bear the tax, but as the average annual per capita consumption of cotton was about twelve pounds, such a tax would not be excessively heavy even at five cents. The tax, he thought, should be collected at the mills because of the small number in comparison with the plantations. On cotton for export, the tax should be collected at the ports.

To protect the exporter of cotton goods who was forced to compete with cotton goods produced from Indian and other tax-free cotton, he strongly recommended a drawback equivalent to the amount of the tax. Also, as a part of the whole plan, an equivalent tariff duty should be levied upon cotton imports.

In their report to the Treasurer, the Commission recommended legislation identical to that outlined above, namely, a tax of five cents per pound to be levied upon the manufacturers, and upon exported cotton a drawback equivalent to the tax, and a tariff upon cotton goods of equal amount.[1] The bill as proposed by Mr. Wells met some objection. He wrote to Mr. Atkinson on April 7, 1866:

> They have decided that our cotton bill will not hold water constitutionally, and in connection with this I have drawn a new bill substantially on the plan of the existing one, which will probably pass. The drawback section will be fought by the Western men and I doubt if it can pass. What shall I do? Will it answer to limit the drawback to no. 20 yarns? Or shall I try and kill the bill if the drawback fails? And yet I feel as though we must have some revenue from cotton. The statements I hear are discouraging from manufacturing interests. It seems as though they must have relief or perish temporarily. The committee have made little progress since you were here. Take counsel in Boston and advise me. Can you stand the tax without the drawback?

[1] *Op. cit.*, *Special Report*, no. 3.

FREE TRADE, GREENBACKS, REFORM 59

In his answer to Mr. Wells, Mr. Atkinson gives an interesting picture of the situation as it then existed. Dated April 11, 1866, the letter read:

> I have your letter of the (?) I have received the drawback regulations and think they meet the case.
>
> As to the general subject. You are afraid that many manufactures will be killed by the burthen of taxation and you need the tax upon cotton to give relief. To this I answer:
>
> First, the high rates of exchange have caused the establishment of many manufactures and the great extension of others before the time in which they would have had a natural growth. They are like hothouse grapes, if you remove the glass they will be killed, yet if circumstances require the removal of the glass you would not endeavor to regulate the outward temperature so as to save the grapes.
>
> The representatives of such forced growth will appear before you and will be among the most urgent for relief. Those upon whom the tax has not proved a severe burthen do not appear before you. You therefore get a one-sided view.
>
> Second, in consequence of the forced diversion of labor into unnatural channels and the withdrawal of labor into army, labor advanced and has become too independent. The wages of a large portion of the labor of the country are now unnaturally high and the laborers do not do a full day's work. The prices of commodities and of all material and manufactures are therefore high, yet they may pay no profit, in many cases a loss.
>
> What must be the result? A period in which production must cease for want of profit — and yet prices of commodities remain high — and the wages of labor be reduced. This will give hard times, it will be dangerous. Yet if you attempt to avert it by legislation you are attempting to stop not the rise but the fall of the tide.
>
> Gold is today the cheapest of all commodities. In order to reduce other things to the level of gold, production must cease for a time in order that we may *accumulate a surplus of labor* and get full days' work, then on rates of wages established on a gold basis make or raise commodities and manufactures on the same gold basis. Hard on labor — but necessary and wholesome in the long run. You cannot prevent injury to some, destruction to others unless you attempt to legislate for the continuation of an abnormal state of things. Industry adjusted itself slowly to a state of war. It must adjust itself to a state of peace.
>
> Now as to cotton, the bill should not pass for the following reasons:
>
> First, as the old cotton keeps coming and the prospects of new crop improve, it becomes evident that the world will have a surplus of cotton much sooner than we thought last summer. When there is

a surplus the untaxed product regulates the price and the taxed product will pile up — *five cents is too high.*[1]

Second, the drawback is essential. During the war production of heavy goods stopped and the looms have never fully started again. They are now starting again on an export demand; stop that, and they will stop and only start again on a home demand. There is a surplus of coarse machinery and unless there is a foreign outlet, any attempts to establish cotton manufactures in the South or West will be swamped. The beginning of cotton spinning in the West must be on coarse work. What can the West do in competition with a surplus of coarse spindles standing at half or one-third the present cost, with New England skill and capital ready to run them on quarter of a cent per yard profit?

Third, you cannot collect the tax in the manner now proposed. In witness of this you have not and are not now effectively collecting it.

Fourth, you cannot mark the bale so that the bale itself will prove payment of the tax, and unless a receipt is claimed for each bale separately, you cannot furnish documents to prove the payment of the tax.

Fifth, a tax of five cents on cotton is six cents on a grain bag or three cents per bushel.

You will get some income from cotton if you kill the new bill and let the present law stand unchanged. This I hope you will do. The consumption of cotton north of the Potomac does not now, and has not since the war, exceeded 12,000 bales per week, or three-fourths the capacity of the mills. This proves the idleness of the coarse looms.

I have called a meeting of all the spinners who gave testimony before you by advice of Mr. Gory and Mr. Crowinshield to meet tomorrow morning and consult. Will write you on result.

Get drawback on all of no. 20 or lower numbers at any rate, but better leave the present law unchanged.

At the same time, Mr. Atkinson moved to preserve the drawback provision in the cotton bill. He addressed letters to various influential persons who might lend their aid to the measure. The following to Justin S. Morrill, Chairman of the House Ways and Means Committee, is a good example:

> We have been informed that there may be some opposition to the drawback section of the new law imposing a tax upon cotton, and have therefore caused the enclosed memorial to be prepared and signed by as many of the cotton spinners as can be found at one day's notice.
>
> If Western members oppose the drawback section, I should meet

[1] Mr. Atkinson's shift in opinion respecting a tax of five cents per pound can be accounted for by the difference between his estimate of the cotton supply made in 1865, and the actual supply which was known by this time. Cf. *ante*, p. 29.

them upon the following ground. It is desirable to establish the manufacture of cotton in the West and South, the beginning must be upon coarse fabrics. There is now in existence in New England a surplus of coarse spindles for any home demand. A large portion of the coarse looms have been stopped since the beginning of the war but are now starting up on the demand for export.

If the export demand should cease from the absence of the drawback, these looms would again be idle, but always ready on any increase of home demand.

How can the West and South establish manufactures in the face of the competition of this surplus of spindles unless they give a foreign outlet for goods of Eastern make?[1]

[1] April 13, 1866. This letter was accompanied by the following memorial:

'The undersigned, engaged in the manufacture of cotton cloth, believe that the aggregate of existing taxes on raw cotton, and on goods manufactured of cotton, makes as large a burden as can wisely be imposed, whether regard be had to the interest of the manufacturers, or consumers, or of the Government in its financial measures:

'That if any increase be made in the tax on raw cotton, a corresponding reduction should be made in the tax on the manufactured product:

'That it is essential to the manufacturing interest of the country and to the general interest of the Nation, that a drawback should be allowed on all manufactures of cotton exported, equivalent to the taxes assessed on the raw material of which such manufactures are made, and on such manufactures themselves.

'We have always had close competition in Foreign Markets, with other manufacturing countries, when raw cotton was free of tax; and unless such tax be remitted on goods exported, this outlet will be stopped, to the detriment of the country at large:

'1. By depriving it of one of the means of paying its foreign indebtedness.

'2. By compelling the disposal of all cotton manufactures at home.

'3. By reducing the wages of labor as a necessary consequence.

'4. By preventing the development of the manufacturing resources of the States not already engaged in this business.

'We are all of the opinion that it will be better for the country to have no additional tax on cotton, if an equivalent additional drawback on the manufactured product be not allowed, and in view of the embarrassments of the subject, in collecting the tax on the raw material, in the fluctuations in its value at the present time, and with the difficulties of adopting a policy which can be regarded as permanent, it seems to us that the general interest will be promoted by leaving the existing taxes on raw cotton as they now are.

'We believe that the immediate interest of manufacturers would be favored by taxing raw cotton more highly, and repealing the tax on manufactures of cotton, always assuming that a drawback be allowed; but for the present we all think that the interest of the Government, and of the country will be best served without a change.

'The tax on manufactures is easily and economically collected, and, if the duties on foreign imports be so regulated as to enable us to pay the tax, we believe the common good will be promoted. We shall be glad to see a reduction in all taxes whenever it can safely be made.

'We are very respectfully yours, (signed)

William Gray	George R. Richardson	D. N. Spooner
Saml. Batchelder	Walter Hastings	F. L. Richardson
W. Amory	Minot T. Hooper	Edwd. Atkinson
Geo. Atkinson	Charles Amory	Geo. L. Ward
Saml. R. Payson	E. R. Mudge Sawyer Co.	Gardner Brewer Co.
William Dwight	B. F. Nourse	Lyman Nichols
	John D. W. Joy'	

It was supposed by Mr. Atkinson and others at this time that the annual cotton supply for 1866 would be greatly curtailed because of the influence of the war upon planting in 1865. With short crop, a tax of five cents would not work a hardship upon the growers, for the price would be high. But an unexpected supply of old cotton held during the war, coupled with a favorable current planting, began to come upon the market and the prospects were for a low price.[1] This made it questionable if such a high tax were advisable. Mr. Atkinson expressed his doubt on this point in a letter to Charles Nordhoff dated April 16, 1866: 'I see that you have begun to doubt the expediency of a tax upon cotton. So have I in view of the large quantity of old cotton and the better prospect for new. Yet I am willing to stand at three cents, the mark which I gave in my testimony before the Revenue Commission. I enclose some ammunition, which you must use as the basis of editorials and not as a communication; if you use it at all.'

In the enclosure Mr. Atkinson expanded upon the inadvisability of a tax of five cents per pound. Such a tax upon American planters would have the effect of raising cotton prices to such an extent that production in India, Egypt, and other places would be greatly stimulated. At most, only a temporary tax of three cents with a drawback on exported goods should be resorted to.

The legislation on the cotton tax which was finally enacted included the provisions recommended by Mr. Atkinson. It called for a tax of three cents per pound with an equalizing drawback and tariff.[2] This measure, which was approved July 13, 1866, was changed the following March, when the tax was reduced to two and one-half cents per pound, with a corresponding decrease in the drawback and tariff provisions.[3] In his second annual report, Mr. Wells recommended that the tax be removed entirely.[4] The matter was finally closed by the removal of all

[1] For the reasons for Mr. Atkinson's estimate of a short crop, see *ante*, p. 21 ff.
[2] *U.S. Statutes at Large*, 1866, Thirty-Ninth Congress, First Session, Chapter 184.
[3] *Ibid.*, 1867, Thirty-Ninth Congress, Second Session, Chapter 169.
[4] *House Executive Documents*, 1867–68, Fortieth Congress, Second Session, no. 81, Appendix G. The reasons for his recommendations were, first, that the low price of cotton

internal taxes on cotton grown after 1867, and the removal of import duties on cotton and cotton goods after November 1, 1868.[1]

The question of the cotton tax, however, was soon dwarfed by the larger aspects of the growing tariff controversy. During the Civil War, internal taxes had been extended and expanded in all possible directions and import duties had kept apace, partly in order to equalize the internal taxes and in part to raise additional revenue. It was generally supposed that the revamping of the revenue system would include a downward revision of the tariff rates.[2] But as attempts were made to secure revision, strong opposition began to show itself and there developed the important tariff struggle which saw the defeat of the free-traders at the Reform Republican Convention at Cincinnati in 1872.

In this struggle both Mr. Wells and Mr. Atkinson played leading rôles. One commentator described Mr. Wells's part as follows: 'Undoubtedly the most potent influence over American thought with reference to the tariff during the years immediately succeeding the passage of the Wool and Woolens Act of 1867, was exerted by Mr. David A. Wells.... At the beginning of his service on the first revenue commission, he was a protectionist; when he completed his work as special commissioner, he had become — the adverb is used in no offensive sense — violently anti-protectionist, and had made himself the leader of those whose aim was free trade.'[3]

In this fight over tariffs and revenue reform, Mr. Atkinson took an important and enthusiastic part as an ally of Mr. Wells. He was truly on the firing-line and directed his energies over a wide field ranging from personal contacts and advice, to the releasing of 'broadsides' in the form of pamphlets and other

---

made the burden excessive; second, that the tax was stimulating production in India, and other places; and, finally, that the United States needed cotton to pay for our imports and the interest due to foreign holders of our bonds.

[1] *U.S. Statutes at Large*, 1868, Fortieth Congress, Second Session, Chapter 5.

[2] Cf. Taussig, F. W., *Tariff History of the United States*, p. 73, and Secretary McCulloch's Report, *House Executive Documents*, Fortieth Congress, Third Session, no. 2, p. 16.

[3] Stanwood, Edward, *American Tariff Controversies in the Nineteenth Century*, pp. 158–60.

printed material. It was Mr. Atkinson's purpose not only to show that national interests would best be served by a tariff for revenue only, but that the interests of special groups of manufacturers and laborers lay on the side of lower import duties.

Although he favored the principle of low tariffs for revenue only, Mr. Atkinson believed that any changes should be made gradually. He felt, in respect to proposed legislation on tariff in the latter part of 1865 and early 1866, that such legislation would be of a temporary nature and would pave the way for later revision. It was only as the protectionist forces began to show their strength that he became more and more an ardent exponent of free-trade principles, although he never relinquished the idea that revisions should be made gradually.

It was not inconsistent, therefore, for Mr. Atkinson, during 1866 particularly, to work for favorable tariff rates and conditions for the cotton industry.[1] The following letter sets forth his position on this matter in detail.

Boston, May 30, 1866

Hon. James G. Blaine
Dear Sir:

I write to you at the suggestion of our mutual friend Mr. George L. Ward, by whom I am informed that my position is sometimes brought up in a manner to make it difficult for our friends in Congress to make an argument even in favor of such measures as I most honestly advocate, as in the case of the proposed drawback upon cotton fabrics exported, which drawback I advocate, not as a matter of protection in the technical sense of that word, but simply as an offset for the tax on raw cotton, and for the purpose of putting us on an equality only with the foreign manufacturer who makes cotton goods similar to our heavy export cottons, from untaxed India cotton.

Upon the general question of protection, my position is this. If we had never framed a tariff except for the simple purpose of collecting revenues, I would never do so, but inasmuch as we have in the past had tariffs, framed for protection, and our industry has thereby been forced into channels which it would not have naturally followed, any change in policy must be very gradual.

Second, no change should be made toward a reduction of duties

---

[1] In addition to his personal interest, Mr. Atkinson was chairman of the Cotton Spinners' Committee of New England, organized to secure the best interests of the cotton manufacturers.

upon cotton manufacturers or any other article unless a general change is made; because in order to compete with England we must have access to her machine shops and buy cheap machinery. We cannot make cotton goods with machinery, in the manufacture of which the iron master and the machinist have been protected, unless the cotton fabric be also protected. Neither can we compete with England unless we have all our raw material free of duty as she has.

Third, all our internal taxes must be offset by corresponding duties before the duty begins to be effective even to the point of the incidental protection offered by a revenue tariff. For instance, our average consumption of cotton cloth in this country is coarse, about no. 24 yarn. A no. 24 fabric is one that can be made in England from untaxed India cotton at a disadvantage as compared with American, but such disadvantage would be far less than our proposed tax of five cents. Therefore our first element in the tariff should be a duty of not less than five cents per pound on cotton fabrics imported. There would be no technical protection in this.

Next, we are to pay five per cent tax upon our finished product besides all the taxes on the starch, oil, iron, etc., etc., which is used — now as our tax is levied upon gross market value and the duty is upon the net foreign cost, it follows that we require about double the amount of ad valorem duty, or ten per cent to offset our tax. There is therefore no technical protection in the first ten per cent of the duty on foreign fabrics.

Now, I believe all authorities agree, both the free trade and protection — that 25 per cent duty is not above the revenue point. Mr. Allison stated that the existing duties were equal to about 28 per cent on the foreign cotton fabrics. (I have not examined this myself but take it he is correct.) Now if the present duty is 28 per cent, and I am correct in claiming that we must deduct double the rate of internal tax, or at present 12 per cent, and under the new law ten per cent, it follows that the real duty is only 16 to 18 per cent, or not even up to the revenue point, to say nothing about the necessity of an offset for the tax upon cotton.

It therefore follows that if technical protection be defined as being a tariff duty above 25 per cent, and the whole tariff duty now levied is only 28 per cent, we have now no technical protection at all, and my claim that instead of a reduction in the present duty if any change is made there should be an additional duty levied on cotton fabrics by the pound as an offset to the increase of the tax on cotton from two to five cents, is perfectly consistent with my position that we do not need an increase as a matter of technical protection.

I write this, as I have said, at Mr. Ward's suggestion in order that you may use it in case my plan is called upon the other side.

I should not advocate any change in the tariff on cotton fabrics, for while the present rates of duty may be only 28 per cent upon present values, yet as they are largely specific, they will as cotton goods fall in price, represent a larger per cent. This statement applies to piece goods only. There are some articles, like cotton hosiery on which there is only an ad valorem duty now, but which absolutely need an additional specific duty; such cases will have been duly presented to the Committee of Ways and Means, and no doubt provided for.

I have assumed Mr. Allison's statement of 28 per cent to be correct. I have the impression, however, that the duties are now more than 28 per cent upon present values.

Yours very respectfully

EDWARD ATKINSON

In 1866, Mr. Wells reported two bills to Congress. One recommended a general revision of the internal revenue system and became a law in July, 1866, substantially as he presented it. The other bill related to tariff and called for a moderate revision of duties to adjust them to the revenue bill. Naturally Mr. Atkinson took a keen interest in these bills, especially as they related to cotton. During the time when the tariff measure was being framed, he was in constant communication with Mr. Wells, suggesting various changes and giving information concerning the various problems which arose in connection with the work.

The tariff bill was reported by the Ways and Means Committee to the House on June 25, 1866. As presented by Mr. Wells, and amended by the Committee, this bill was in no sense a free-trade measure, but was intended to equalize the tariff duties with the changes in the revenue system. After a spirited debate in the House of Representatives, the bill was passed and sent to the Senate on July 12, just a few days before adjournment. As a result, the consideration of the measure was postponed until the next session met in January, 1867.

Debate on the tariff measure provoked sharp criticism from the opponents of protection, much of which was directed at the New England manufacturers. Mr. Atkinson came to the defense in a characteristic fashion. To Charles Nordhoff, editor of the *New York Evening Post*, he wrote:

FREE TRADE, GREENBACKS, REFORM 67

You quote big dividends of cotton mills and say the cotton manufacturers ask more protection. YOU CANNOT PROVE IT, and I tell you that some of the managers of the very mills you quote are against the present movement in Washington. The only movement of the cotton spinners upon the tariff that I know about has been to look out for the blunders and to get a correction made in the tariff on some articles not enumerated before, and on which the burthen of taxes was so great as to discriminate against the home manufacturers, and we have got more than we asked.

I honestly believe that a majority of the New England manufacturers are opposed to tariff now being discussed, and you do New England *gross injustice* in putting the onus upon us.

This is a Western tariff carried by combination with Pennsylvania iron. We cannot move against it because the result would be a reduction of the duty on manufactures and this imposition of duties on wool, iron, etc., etc.

Remember this is a private letter, but I beg you not to hurt your own cause by damning your own friends.[1]

Mr. Atkinson felt a real anxiety lest New England manufacturers should be blamed for sponsoring protection, and the Republican Party be definitely committed to that policy. He wrote to Henry Wilson:

When the tariff bill opens in the Senate, I hope you will put it clearly on record that the bill now under discussion is not a New England measure. It is carried by a combination of the West and Pennsylvania. All that New England asks is an even tariff at the revenue point of 25 per cent, and this is what she has to look out for to see that if heavy duties are put upon wool, iron, dye stuffs, etc., etc., the tariff on manufacture shall be 25 per cent beyond these. The real fact is, the old idea of framing a tariff for protection and not for revenue simply, is growing weaker and weaker here. The strongest men in the trade are more afraid of the unskillful competition built up at home by high duties than they are of foreign competition, but we can't move now, the only result would be to get lower duties on manufactures, with high duties on coal, iron, wool, etc., etc.

What this country wants is cheap iron. Our cotton mills now cost to build $30. per spindle complete with looms, etc., etc., against $10 to $12 in England.

What I want to guard against now is to prevent the odium of the tariff being thrown on us. In any ordinary time such a tariff would kill the party that passed it. Please keep this private, as I don't want

[1] July 5, 1866.

a controversy with Edwards — Bigelow, etc., but if it comes I can call in on my side Gray — Dwight, O. H. Perry, and many more.[1]

It was in connection with the framing of the tariff bill then before the Senate that Mr. Wells began to recede from his original protectionist point of view. He wrote to Mr. Atkinson on July 17, 1866:

> As you know, the tariff bill is laid on the shelf until next winter, and on the whole I am not very sorry for it. I sent you a copy of the Senate bill with the House Amendments. The idea of a tariff commission will not be acceptable; but the general idea instead is that I should take the matter up and make a bill for next winter, on conditions which will allow of the adoption of rates of a permanent character. I will have all the force and help and money I want, and after the hot weather is over, and I have got a little rest, I think I can go into the matter with zeal and accomplish something. I mean to put myself early in connection with you and other Boston friends for consultation and advice. I have changed my ideas respecting tariffs and protection very much since I came to Washington, and am coming over to the ground which you occupy. I am utterly disgusted with the rapacity and selfishness which I have seen displayed by Pennsylvania people, and some from other sections on this subject. Congress will probably adjourn in a week, and soon after that I think of going to Mt. Desert and will stop a day or two in Boston.

In September, Mr. Atkinson expressed the fear that the possibility of increased tariff rates would cause abnormal imports into the country. He wrote to Mr. Wells:

> I am quite convinced that unless something is done to counteract the impression, large orders for foreign goods will be given this autumn in the expectation of a heavy advance in the tariff at the next session of Congress, and I therefore hope you will get an order issued by the Secretary as we proposed at the last Club dinner, and I have had the audacity to spend Sunday in writing the Secretary's order and your answer which are herein enclosed. I have written them out in this form as it is so much easier to write with a definite point in view.
> I am very sure that if some such positive statement of proposed action can be at once made public, any danger of excessive imports will be avoided, and at the same time the moderate men of all parties will so give utterance to their approval as to give direction to the action of Congress. We want neither ultra free trade nor Japanese protection, but we must have revenue. The free traders are satisfied

[1] July 7, 1866.

FREE TRADE, GREENBACKS, REFORM 69

to allow the incidental protection of a revenue tariff and the protectionists generally ask no more. If you think my documents of sufficient value, please read them to the Secretary with my regards, and ask his pardon for my presumption in writing a document as his representative.[1]

In October, Mr. Atkinson headed a group of New England men which spent an intensive two weeks in Pennsylvania making observations and interviewing various persons in the interests of moderation. The result was not reassuring to Mr. Atkinson. He wrote to Secretary McCulloch:

> I found many men in Pennsylvania entirely crazy on tariff and currency, but I think our Massachusetts party have had a good influence upon such men as have not entirely lost their judgment. We preached moderation and support to you and to Wells and I hope we have done some good. Wells will give you an account of our doings.[2]

In anticipation of the discussion in the Senate of the tariff bill scheduled to come up for consideration in January, Mr. Wells turned his attention to the drafting of new measures which would be more satisfactory to the free trade opponents of the bill then pending. It was hoped that these changes might be made in the Senate as amendments to the original bill.

Again Mr. Atkinson contributed much technical advice and in addition counseled Mr. Wells not to be led into difficulties by making changes to meet special interests. On this point he wrote:

> I beg of you to be careful. Settle your averages and let specialities take their chance. Avoid opposition by making few changes. Beware of such changes as a heavier duty on soda ash. I take this as a specimen case. By yielding to such a special claim, you would array paper, glass, soap and printers against you, and what is worse, they would be right![3]

By the middle of January, Mr. Wells felt discouraged about the possibilities of getting his suggestions adopted. He wrote to Mr. Atkinson on the fifteenth from Washington:

> Things do not look very satisfactory here. I am afraid the extremists and inflationists will have it pretty much their own way. The machinery people are here asking 80 per cent duties on machinery. The

[1] September 2, 1866.   [2] October 27, 1866.   [3] November 10, 1866.

committee have raised from 35 to 45. The bill will probably come up in the Senate on Thursday. With the best part of Congress my views find great favor, but special interests override all other considerations.... I am afraid Congress will set much higher than is anticipated. In regard to creating a Bureau of Revenue, it would do no good I think to agitate just now. For myself, I ask nothing. I get so despondent at times in view of the manner in which legislature is constructed, that I feel as though it was no use and I had better retire. The only way to accomplish results is to work on public opinion outside of Congress and let the influence be reflected back....

The more I know about this wool matter, the more iniquitous it seems. I wish you would set all the engines you can in motion to defeat it. You will get some reductions of internal revenue, but the feeling is, that a heavy reduction of internal taxation, and a large and almost prohibitory increase of the tariff — especially on wool and woolens — are incompatible, and so we will go over the old way, without system, or sense.

Discussion upon the tariff bill in the Senate proved Mr. Wells correct in his fears concerning higher rates. In the course of the debate, numerous amendments were proposed and adopted which called for higher duties than those made by the Revenue Commission.

Mr. Atkinson's immediate reaction to this procedure was expressed in the following extract of a letter to a friend: 'I have since written him [Wells] that if the exorbitant duties imposed upon wool and woolens, linens, silks, etc., are to prevail, the rate on all cottons should be put up ten per cent so that we may all tumble together within two or three years. I have no idea that the bill can pass at all as it now stands and think the work will all have to be done over again upon a moderate basis.'[1]

But when the Senate finally passed the amended bill and returned it to the House on the first of February, he assumed the position that the measure should be defeated. He wrote to Mr. Wells on February 6, 1867: 'I have your note with the Senate bill. I don't need to examine this abortion as I have followed it closely in the *Congressional Globe*. I think you have but one thing to do. *Defeat it if you can.* If you want to risk your office now for a strong position in the future, I think you have

[1] Letter to James Park, Jr., January 28, 1867.

FREE TRADE, GREENBACKS, REFORM

the chance. If not, the Secretary can take the chance without risk.'

Mr. Wells shared Mr. Atkinson's feeling that the bill should be defeated. On February 10, he wrote the latter urging him to come to Washington and stay until the Senate tariff bill was defeated in the House. Greenough, Walker, and Nordhoff had already come on to aid in the fight.

Mr. Atkinson accepted the invitation and remained in Washington until the bill was finally defeated in the House on February 28, 1867. He outlined his part in the defeat of the bill in a letter to J. W. Labouisse, March 4, 1867: 'I have just returned from two weeks' stay in Washington where I have been fighting the high-tariff men. I have for some time been satisfied that the idea of protection was unsound, and that the only thing to be considered in framing tariffs was to get revenue in the least injurious manner. The necessity for revenue will require a high tariff for some time to come and with that New England will be content, but Pennsylvania and Ohio are rapacious and prohibitive in their ideas.'

The picture of this period would not be complete without some mention of the Wool and Woolens Act of 1867, which secured for the woolen interests approximately the same protection which the defeated tariff bill had included. This measure, at first introduced into the House by Judge Bingham of Ohio, provided for higher rates upon wool and lower rates on some woolen manufactured goods than those proposed by the general tariff bill. Objection was made by the woolen manufacturers to these changes and a compromise was reached which restored the rates of the House bill.

The bill passed the House and was sent to the Senate July 28, 1866. Consideration was postponed until Congress met again in January, 1867. During the Senate debate on the tariff bill, nothing was done about the wool and woolens measure, but with the defeat of the former, the friends of the woolen interests in the Senate secured the passage of the Wool and Woolens Bill on March 2.

It seemed doubtful if President Johnson would sign the bill to make it a law. Opponents to special protection brought pressure to prevent him from signing the measure, and it was not until just before midnight on March 3, the time which marked the end of the session, that he affixed his signature.[1]

Although he had led the fight against the tariff bill, Mr. Wells lent his influence toward getting the President to sign the Wool and Woolens Bill. On March 5, Mr. Wells wrote to Mr. Atkinson from Washington:

> The papers will have informed you before now about the Wool Bill, and the difficulties which the Department finds in putting it into execution. It was doubtful for a considerable time whether the President would sign it. He was very reluctant to do so and kept it back till the last moment. I don't think he would have signed it had I not advised; but I found that there was an intense feeling among many of the Western members on the subject, and I was afraid that if it were not signed the whole subject of the tariff would have come up again this week, in which case we might get a worse bill, and an indefinite prolongation of the Session. The iron and other interests are a good deal dissatisfied, and say the *two best horses have been taken out* of the tariff team, which will make the road the harder to travel.

With the questions of revenue and tariff changes settled for the time being, Mr. Wells decided to make a trip to Europe for the double purpose of getting a much-needed rest and to make a study of European financial systems. He was very eager to have Mr. Atkinson accompany him, particularly as he wanted the latter to make an intensive study of the English cotton industry. But business conditions were such that Mr. Atkinson felt obliged to decline the invitation. Mr. Wells expressed his disappointment:

> Now, about the... momentous question of going abroad, I feel that I must go, but when I think of going without you, the whole project seems uninviting. My whole scheme is based upon your participation in it, as counsellor and friend. The Government will give me a special commission, and Seward told me yesterday that he would detail Dudley, our consul at Liverpool, to go with me to the manufacturing districts.... I think, notwithstanding your talk about business, it is

---

[1] Cf. Stanwood, Edward, *op. cit.*, pp. 154–58.

FREE TRADE, GREENBACKS, REFORM 73

the disinclination which every 'home man' feels to saying good-bye to his family and everyday life, which induces you to hesitate.[1]

But even this plea failed to convince Mr. Atkinson that he should leave his business at the time, and Mr. Wells was forced to sail without him.

During the remainder of 1867, Mr. Atkinson's interest in the tariff question was directed toward an attempt to mobilize public opinion in favor of more moderate tariff schedules. Probably his most important single contribution in this direction was the publication and wide distribution of his pamphlet entitled, *On the Collection of Revenue*.

Mr. Atkinson gives the genesis and purpose of this brochure in the preface:

> The following Essay was originally written for the purpose of testing the results of my own thought and experience by the formulas of the free-trade economists, and was afterwards read at a meeting of the Economic Section of the American Social Science Association, held in Boston in January. Some extracts then published, having caused considerable remark, as emanating from a New England cotton manufacturer, I have thought that the publication of the whole might do a service in bringing public sentiment to what I consider just views on a momentous question, and might perhaps cause an abatement of the prejudice existing in some quarters against New England manufacturers, in consequence of views in which they are erroneously supposed to be unanimous.
> There is nothing new in the Essay; but it is often useful to apply well-known principles to passing events and present circumstances in a form that will bring them to the observation of those who are too busy to read elaborate treatises.   E. A.
>
> Boston, April, 1867.

The essay is an interesting presentation in simple terms of the principles of *laissez-faire* economics, especially as applied to the subjects of taxation and free trade. The following is a brief presentation of his arguments:

The well-being of a nation is dependent upon the combination of labor, capital, and natural resources in such a way as to insure the greatest possible production. Every effort should be made to

[1] March 21, 1867.

eliminate those practices and elements in society which lower production. Such things as gambling, extravagant living, expenditure for war, and the like, are in this category. Also included is inconvertible paper money, which by its nature greatly stimulates price fluctuations and unduly increases the number of persons engaged in speculative fields.

Taxes should be levied in such a way as to impede production as little as possible. In this connection, a tax on capital as such is bad, for although such a tax is supposed to be beneficial to labor, the reverse is true. Bastiat is quoted to the effect that an increase in capital increases the absolute, but decreases the relative share of production going to the capitalists, whereas both the relative and absolute share of labor is increased by a larger supply of capital.[1]

Among the worst of the influences which prevent the efficient utilization of the factors of production are tariff laws which force labor and capital into unnatural channels.

> The greatest progress of a country will be secured by the application, on the part of the people, of the greatest number of hours of labor, consistent with health and education, to the production of raw materials for use by the process called manufacturing. We may be sure that God has indicated the direction in which such labor can be expended with the best results, by giving to different countries different conditions of soil and climate; and that to interfere with the natural distribution of labor in accordance with these great laws, as has been done by all so-called protective legislation, is to cramp civilization and prevent the spread of Christianity throughout the world.
>
> Commerce is the most effective agent of civilization, but protection, if carried to its legitimate result, would cause each nation to satisfy, as far as possible, all its desires within its own limits, and there could be no foreign commerce.
>
> To illustrate this point. The Kaffir of South Africa was formerly a savage warrior; he is now a peaceful shepherd in whom some of the desires of civilized life have been developed. How has this come about? By the desire of the civilized men of Europe and America for a kind of wool which the climate and soil of South Africa will produce. It happens that, upon the hills of South Africa, wool can be raised with

---

[1] Atkinson, Edward, *On the Collection of Revenue*, pp. 7–8. It is interesting to note that Mr. Atkinson favored an income tax as a source of revenue, as it taxed income and not the productive process.

FREE TRADE, GREENBACKS, REFORM 75

no labor except that of the shepherd to tend the sheep and the annual shearing, but the wool is absolutely useless in that climate. On the other hand, wheat, tobacco, butter, cheese, ironware and tools cannot be raised or made there at all. What has happened from these conditions? The first settlers tempted the Kaffirs to become shepherds by offering them good bread, butter, cheese, iron, and other luxuries hitherto unknown to them, but yet real necessities for the full development of the manhood in them. Europe and America took the wool and gave the wheat.

But now the United States say, or rather Ohio says, we can raise all this wool. True, but instead of expending only the labor of a Kaffir who can do nothing else, we must build great barns to protect our sheep in our cold winter, we must employ farmers to raise hay and roots to feed them; and we must expend two days' labor of a civilized man, where the half-civilized Kaffir need expend but one, yet we ought to be protected in our labor; we, the educated, civilized men of Ohio and Vermont and Massachusetts need to be protected against that poor, half-civilized creature, we are afraid of him. God has given him more sunshine and a better position than ours, and, if he advances, we shall be degraded.[1]

The arguments advanced by protectionists in favor of their principles are not sound nor logical. For example, the idea that a revenue tariff will give incidental protection is shown to be false, 'because just so far as a tariff stimulates the home production of the commodity upon which the duty is imposed, just so far it prevents the importation of that commodity, and therefore it so far fails to yield a revenue.'[2]

In respect to the 'infant industry' argument, experience has shown that the healthiest and most permanent growth has come to industries which have not been coddled nor aided by props.

> This claim for protection of infant manufactures never ceases. Under its operation they never seem to grow to manhood, but the larger they grow the more urgent the demand for artificial support. The most urgent and imperative demand for protection now comes from the iron-masters and the wool-growers.
>
> American iron was born into the world more than a hundred years ago, when Pennsylvania was a colony. Great Britain was the midwife who presided at the birth, and endeavored to strangle the infant in its cradle; but he, being tough and of a fibrous quality, lived and grew apace, until now he could stand alone, if he would only think

[1] *Op. cit.*, pp. 25–26.   [2] *Ibid.*, pp. 26–27.

so. But having been propped up with baby-jumpers and crutches, shoulder-braces, etc., he fears to stand lest he should fall, and demands now to be encompassed with a high wall over which no rude shove shall reach him.[1]

The common belief that foreign producers are always organized in a plot to destroy domestic industries, is met in an interesting fashion.

It is alleged that because we have begun the manufacture of Bessemer steel rails in this country, the price has been reduced by the English manufacturers from $150 to $110 a ton, or about in that proportion; but those who make this absurd allegation make no note of the enormous extension and improvement in this manufacture in England. If their allegation is true the trade in steel rails in England would be conducted in the following manner. Suppose the parties to be the English manufacturer, the Agent of the Pennsylvania Central Railroad, and the Agent of the Pacha of Egypt.

Penn. Agent — What is the price of steel rails?
Manufacturer — For what railroad?
Penn. Agent — For the Pennsylvania Central.
Manufacturer — The price is $110 per ton, delivered.
Agent of the Pacha — I want an equal quantity at same price.
Manufacturer — Our price for Egypt is $150.
Agent of Pacha — Have you two prices?
Manufacturer — Yes, sir; they are endeavoring to establish the manufacture of steel rails in Pennsylvania, and all the English manufacturers have combined to break them down; we charge $110 to Yankees and $150 to all others.
Agent of Pacha — But you make a profit at $110.
Manufacturer — Oh, yes, certainly; we don't make a practice of selling at less than cost.
Agent of Pacha — Good morning, sir; I will get my rails in Prussia, or wait until the Americans get started. If you make a profit at $110, and charge me $150, Pennsylvania will soon supply me at less than $150, even if you supply her own railroads at $110.

I believe that any business man must see that the alleged effect of the few small steel-rail establishments in this country is as nothing compared to the effect of the competition in England. We cannot cripple our whole railroad system, cause all our transportation to be more costly, and retard the development of our western country, by granting any higher bounties to a few rail-makers, than we now pay.

[1] *Op. cit.*, pp. 33–34.

Yet I do not ask Pennsylvania to cease at once to demand duties upon iron and steel, nor would I willingly submit at once to a great reduction in the duties upon cotton manufactures. Any such abrupt changes would destroy capital and reduce production.[1]

There is more than a suggestion of Bastiat's style in the following:

> There is a danger in the abundance of things. We are flooded with foreign commodities — flooded with comforts and luxuries. Protect us, in order that we may labor; it is a privilege to labor; we want to work harder, to get what we consume, than our natural condition requires. Create an artificial scarcity, so that we may enjoy our full right to labor. Is it right to labor for which we should so strive? Is labor the end? Is it not rather what labor will give us that we seek? And if we can get what we want with little labor, instead of much, do we regret it?[2]

To remedy the evils which have grown up under the protective system, there should be established a permanent Board of Revenue Commissioners. This Board, which would be non-political in its nature, would have the function of guiding production back into its natural channels, and, 'would prepare changes and give fair warning, thus giving each branch of industry time to prepare, and preventing disaster.'[3]

Tariffs should be reduced to a system of 'British Free Trade,' which would mean that a relatively few articles would be taxed, and for the purpose of raising as large a revenue as possible. Other taxes should be levied on licenses, incomes, stamps, banks, and other similar sources of revenue.

In this pamphlet, Mr. Atkinson also answers the question as to why a New England cotton manufacturer of cotton goods should have such unorthodox views on the subject of tariff.

> As some surprise has been expressed that these views should emanate from a manufacturer of cotton goods, I will add, that I believe a gradual and judicious reduction in the duties upon foreign commodities, in the manner proposed — of course preceded by an entire abolition of the internal taxes upon manufactures — will result in a more permanent and uniform condition of prosperity in the manufacture of textile fabrics, as well as of all other commodities, than we have ever

[1] *Op. cit.*, pp. 35–36. [2] *Ibid.*, p. 32. [3] *Ibid.*, p. 41.

yet enjoyed. If we can come slowly but surely to what is called British Free Trade, we shall share in the increase of wealth which that system has brought to Great Britain, only the benefit to us would be greater, as our natural advantages and variety of resources are greater.[1]

The essay, *On the Collection of Revenue*, was received enthusiastically by the group which was working toward lower tariff duties. Mr. Wells said of it: 'Taken all in all, I think it one of the most powerful, convincing articles I have ever read, and think it will make a sensation.... So the fight is beginning. Yours is the first real hostile gun.'[2]

Mr. Nordhoff was equally enthused. He wrote: 'I have just read your pamphlet which came this forenoon. It is splendid, and I congratulate you heartily. Our Free Trade League meets on Thursday. I shall propose to them to take nearly your whole edition. They can distribute it to newspapers and Congressmen.'[3]

His friend, Professor A. L. Perry of Williams College, whose position and writings in favor of free trade were well known, wrote to Mr. Atkinson: 'I have read your pamphlet carefully, and with great satisfaction. You have the art of putting things. I hope it will be widely circulated and read.'[4] Many others also wrote to Mr. Atkinson praising this publication.

The pamphlet was widely distributed. A particular effort was made to place it in the hands of Congressmen, editors, and political leaders who might be favorably impressed. Mr. Wells marked a list of the Thirty-Ninth Congress who should receive copies. Secretary McCulloch gave out several to friends. Mr. Atkinson sent one hundred copies to a friend in England to give to prominent Britishers.[5]

Mr. Atkinson was in danger, by his free-trade propaganda, of antagonizing many of his friends and business associates. He had already provoked criticism on the part of the woolen interests who objected to his share in the fight against the tariff bill in the early part of 1867. Accordingly, in response to Nordhoff's

[1] *Op. cit.*, p. 51.   [2] April 9, 1867.   [3] April 23, 1867.   [4] April 30, 1867.
[5] Cf. letter to Maurice Williams, April 29, 1867. It may be of interest to note the following names which were on Mr. Atkinson's list: Walter Bagehot, John Bright, Platt Brothers, Baring Brothers, Lawrence Oliphant, and W. S. Jevons.

FREE TRADE, GREENBACKS, REFORM

suggestion that the American Free Trade League should distribute his pamphlet, Mr. Atkinson wrote:

> I have yours of the 23d and am much gratified by the contents. I will write you frankly about this matter and I want you to keep what I say to yourself. I think I have written a good pamphlet not for originality but for the plain and practical application of principles to circumstances. In publishing, I have run a good deal of risk because I have made a break among the corporation men who are a powerful body. Among them I have many sympathizers, but not a majority, and of course the man who makes the first division may have to be sacrificed. If any such result should happen, I should not consider myself a victim, or call myself wronged in any way.
>
> But, as I take the risk, I mean to pay the bills, and not to receive any money from anyone. Neither do I want to be in any manner identified with your League, and simply because the League is unjustly identified by the public with New York importers.
>
> I will send a copy of the pamphlet myself to every member of Congress, and I will send you personally 500 copies, which you can give to the League if you wish to do so. I give them to you. I play a lone hand and don't mean to be euchred.
>
> Now I am not above vanity and consequent vexation of spirit. The pamphlets will cost me about 20 cents each, and if the members of the League choose to present me with a well-chosen book of engravings or something of the kind with the notes of presentation from Mr. Bryant, it would be the sort of thing I should like to leave to my children. If you don't think this suggestion is out of the way, you may act upon it....
>
> N.B. The pamphlet is not copyrighted. I want comments or criticisms of the press or others so I may print another edition next winter.[1]

But Mr. Atkinson did grant permission to the League to reprint the pamphlet for distribution which did not associate him officially with the organization.

An interesting adverse criticism came from the American economist, H. C. Carey, whom Mr. Wells quoted as saying that Mr. Atkinson's pamphlet was 'all twaddle!!'[2]

When Carey wrote a pamphlet favoring protection soon after this, Mr. Atkinson wrote to him:

> I have received a copy of your pamphlet containing your letters to Senator Wilson. May I ask whether it is published and for sale, as I wish to procure two or three copies for some of my friends. I

---

[1] April 24, 1867.   [2] Letter to Edward Atkinson, May 2, 1867.

will frankly admit that I am rejoiced at its publication as it will relieve our New England men from any supposed or implied obligation to vote for protective measures next winter, as many of them did at the last session against their own convictions. We have had to bear the odium of what I call the Pennsylvania policy, but hereafter our defense will be easy, and we can join the north-west and the *new* South in promoting a simple revenue system and a speedy return to specie payments.[1]

Mr. Atkinson was much encouraged by general reaction to his article and what seemed to be the popular sentiment on the tariff question. On June 20, 1869, he wrote to Senator J. W. Grimes:

> I am much gratified by your approval of my pamphlet, which I sent you as well as to all the Members of Congress. I have printed 1500 copies of it (of which I have sent out about 1200) and by Wells' advice have had it stereotyped, hoping that when the question comes up, there may be a call for another edition. I have been unable to provoke the Protectionist papers into an attack. They either dare not or care not to notice me, and therefore, I have not made as much of a mark as I hoped. I learn from Allison that White of the Chicago Tribune means to reprint.
>
> I think I represent fully one-half of our manufacturers, especially the younger men; but the older ones, while in reality desiring only very moderate duties, in fact, are fearful of yielding what they call the principle of protection. Our Boston papers are timid and wait rather than lead.
>
> Among the mass of the people I am sure that the old protective theories are dying out. If you could by any means cause my pamphlet to be the basis of a discussion in the west, I am quite confident you would force our papers to come out, and you would find a decided change in their tone. I can send you 50 or 100 copies for this purpose, and hope you will not impute to me any desire for personal notoriety in making the offer. I think Sumner will come out for Free Trade next winter, but he does not lead the business community.
>
> I never read Mr. Webster's speeches, but shall do it. In fact, I have read very little upon the subject. And, in fact, my brother who is the scholar of the family, penned my work severely so that I might not seem to claim originality for old ideas.

In a letter to Secretary McCulloch, he expressed the same opinion and urged the latter to take the lead in an attempt to force Congress into line:

[1] November 11, 1867.

FREE TRADE, GREENBACKS, REFORM

The publication of this pamphlet has led me to a much greater insight into the state of public opinion upon the revenue question. Let the reconstruction matters be once settled, and the fight between Protection and Free Trade will be upon us, and Free-Trade views will win. The substantial points made in my pamphlet will in my opinion be backed up by the majority of New England manufacturers. I am much surprised at the general approval I have received. Congress will not be permitted to trifle with the matter again, and you will have a glorious opportunity when you make your next report. If you take strong ground for a pure revenue system against the claims of all special interests, you will have hearty support and will have the unwilling acquiescence of Congress. The people are getting enlightened very fast by the present condition of affairs.

I am rejoiced that Morrill has gone into the Senate and hope we may have a good Chairman of Ways and Means *not* from New England.[1]

And to Mr. Wells, who was in Europe, Mr. Atkinson wrote:

You say that old castles, etc., no longer entice you, but don't forget that we have a big fight to go through next winter and unless you give yourself some rest you won't be in condition to use the ammunition you are now collecting.... I am pretty well satisfied that Pennsylvania is floored for the next heat on the tariff, and that you will find men's minds prepared to digest all your work and apply it reasonably.... Remember what I say. Force yourself to take some time for play before you come home.[2]

By the next winter, however, Mr. Atkinson's political interests were dominated by the problem of specie redemption almost to the exclusion of the tariff. This shift of interest is not surprising, for, aside from the problem of Southern reconstruction, there was no political question which attracted more attention and excited more heated controversy in the decade and a half following the war than the subject of the resumption of specie payments. When Secretary of the Treasury McCulloch assumed office in March, 1865, one of the major tasks which confronted him was the disposal of the United States notes which had proved to be such a disturbing element in the monetary system.

It was generally supposed that the reorganization of governmental finances on a peace-time basis would include the early redemption of the demand notes of the United States Govern-

[1] May 28, 1867.   [2] July 23, 1867.

ment (greenbacks) as well as other evidences of Federal indebtedness.[1] Under this assumption, Secretary McCulloch, soon after taking office, proceeded to retire greenbacks out of surplus revenue, and his policy was not only sanctioned by Congress, but he was given the further power by that body to issue bonds if necessary to carry out the process of redemption. But opposition began to develop before redemption had been carried very far, and in the following April, Congress passed an act limiting the amount of contraction to a total of $10,000,000 during the succeeding six months, and to a maximum of $4,000,000 in any one month thereafter. Thus began what one writer has called 'a decade of debate and delay,'[2] which ended only with the passage of the Resumption Act in January, 1875.

Mr. Atkinson took a keen interest in this struggle to secure specie resumption. He entered the controversy with the enthusiasm and energy which characterized his earlier attention to the question of tariff reform. As will be shown in this and succeeding chapters, he felt that of the political questions which were considered in the forty years ending in 1905, sound money ranked above all the others in importance. At times, for example, when the issue seemed to be between sound money and protection on one side, and low tariffs accompanied by free silver or expansion of greenbacks on the other, he had no hesitancy in relegating the tariff to a secondary position. His most active work for tariff reform came, therefore, at times when there was no question in respect to the soundness of the monetary system.

As was indicated at an earlier point,[3] Mr. Atkinson was in favor of the earliest possible resumption of specie payments, but he had felt no special concern in regard to the matter during 1865 and 1866, chiefly because he had faith in Secretary McCulloch's intention and ability to resume specie payments at an early date.

But as the opposition to contraction grew stronger after

---

[1] Cf. Barrett, Don C., *The Greenbacks and Resumption of Specie Payments, 1862–1879*, p. 131; Noyes, Alexander D., *Forty Years of American Finance*, pp. 7–9.
[2] Barrett, Don C., *op. cit.*, p. 159.   [3] *Ante*, pp. 31–32.

1866, his anxiety over the question increased proportionately. Especially was he concerned lest Secretary McCulloch's loyalty to President Johnson should, in view of the increasing sentiment for impeachment, cause the removal or the resignation of the Secretary and the appointment of a successor to the Treasury post who did not hold sound views on money. Accordingly, Mr. Atkinson counseled Secretary McCulloch to put himself in a position which would not be threatened by the removal of President Johnson. 'Separate yourself from A. J., and let it be known that while you do not approve the action of Congress, you submit to its decisions and desire to work in harmony.... Give the Republicans who hold sound views on financial questions a chance to support you as the Secretary of the United States Treasury, and not as a member of the present Cabinet, and you can almost dictate the future policy.'[1]

His failure to convert Secretary McCulloch to this point of view made Mr. Atkinson apprehensive during the subsequent impeachment proceedings, and he worked vigorously both before and after the trial to enlist support for Secretary McCulloch and the sound-money policy. One of the most interesting letters in this connection was to Henry Ward Beecher, dated October 10, 1867. He said, in part: 'The great moral question of today is the currency question. Capitalists, speculators, and middlemen are *stealing* the share of annual product which under natural law belongs to labor, by the use of false money.... Have you studied the matter? It needs your attention.'

Mr. Atkinson was successful in getting Horace White, editor of the *Chicago Tribune*, to modify his opposition to Secretary McCulloch's policy. Several letters from Mr. Atkinson backing Secretary McCulloch and advocating specie resumption were printed in the *Tribune* by Mr. White during September and October, 1867.

He also tried to get Senator Sumner to come out firmly for sound money. He appealed to the latter's consuming desire at the time, when he pointed out the possible danger of Democratic

[1] August 7, 1867.

success in elections on a platform embodying specie payments and free trade. Such a success would 'sacrifice the cause of equal rights' for the Southern Negroes, for which Senator Sumner was working so fervently. Mr. Atkinson was unable to get Mr. Sumner to take a strong position against greenbacks, although the Senator was much interested in Mr. Atkinson's views on the subject and consulted freely with him upon the subsequent development of the question.[1]

In addition to the foregoing instances, Mr. Atkinson kept in communication with various other of his friends and acquaintances who were in a position to influence the course of monetary reform. He overlooked no possible arguments to substantiate his principles. To Senator Grimes, for example, he pointed out the danger of universal suffrage, free trade, and *expansion of currency*, with Benjamin F. Butler as a Presidential candidate.[2]

Letters to William B. Allison, David A. Wells, and others carried strong opposition to any attempt to limit the process of currency contraction and specie resumption.[3] The plan which

---

[1] Mr. Sumner's point of view is well expressed in the following:

Private   Senate Chamber, 17th Feb. '68

Dear Mr. Atkinson:

I always value all your suggestions and consider them carefully. But let me ask you if you are not hasty, if not sharp, in your criticism of me for not sooner embarking in the Finance discussion.

There is in the Senate as elsewhere, a division of labor. Mr. Sherman is Chairman of the Finance Committee with six associates whose special duty is to consider questions of Finance. Of course, any Senator is at liberty to do the same; but all generally look to the members of the Committee to take the lead.

It so happens that I am Chairman of the Committee of Foreign Relations. This is my speciality. All the business of that Committee passes through my hand. This has been during the present session very heavy. Already this session I have reported and carried through *six* different treaties, and there are *three* others still pending, these latter of great importance, occupying much of my thought. All this is in secret session.

I begin my work at 8 o'clock and rarely leave off before midnight, and I am engaged constantly on my public duties. Thus far in public affairs I believe that I have not failed to be heard at the proper moment.

Ever sincerely yours

CHARLES SUMNER

[2] Letter dated September 10, 1867.

[3] To William B. Allison, he said: 'As to paper money, I am opposed to expansion utterly, totally and morally. It would be folly, fraud, treachery, dishonor, theft, stupidity and everything else that is weak, miserable and cowardly combined. I mean every word I say and I am as sure of it as that two and two make four.' December 13, 1867.

FREE TRADE, GREENBACKS, REFORM 85

he, personally, favored for specie resumption included the legalization of gold contracts and the conversion of greenbacks into bonds. Opposition to the gold contracts bill he attributed to 'Carey and his crew because it would make foreign trade safer.'[1]

Mr. Atkinson tried in the Congressional elections of 1868 to remove what he considered one of the greatest menaces to gold resumption, tariff revision, and other reforms advocated by himself. This was an unsuccessful attempt to defeat General Benjamin F. Butler, then Congressman from Massachusetts.[2] Richard H. Dana, Jr., was General Butler's opponent in this campaign, but he and his associates were no match for the General, who was an expert politician. Mr. Atkinson's part in the campaign consisted in raising funds and in giving publicity to certain phases of General Butler's war record, which were not above criticism. Mr. Atkinson was greatly disappointed at the result of the election, but 'we have made our protest, kept him at home and shall ultimately beat him unless he changes entirely from motives of policy.'[3]

The results of the Presidential election, however, were distinctly encouraging to the opponents of inflation, for the proposals of President Johnson in December, 1868, to repudiate the public debt had forced the Republicans into a strong declaration for its preservation. This position was strengthened when President Grant, in his inaugural address, strongly advocated payment of all debts in gold.[4]

Before turning to a consideration of Mr. Atkinson's subsequent part in the development of this and other subjects, some further mention should be made of his attitude upon the important topics of reconstruction and impeachment. On the subject of reconstruction, Mr. Atkinson tended to reflect the views of those who

---

[1] A letter to William B. Allison, June 25, 1868.
[2] No one could have been found who so typified the antithesis of Mr. Atkinson's principles as did General Butler. The latter believed in the payment of government bonds in greenbacks ('the same money for the bondholders as for the people'). He was against contraction and specie resumption, and favored a high protective tariff.
[3] Letter to Lester S. Taylor, November 7, 1868.
[4] Cf. Barrett, Don C., *op. cit.*, pp. 171-72.

wished to see the Negroes given full political and economic rights in the South. He was strongly opposed to the readmission to Congress of Southern Representatives until such rights had been conferred on the former slaves. He did think, however, that given a good price for cotton, the Southern delegations might safely be readmitted in the winter of 1866, 'when these Representatives would be safe men. They would represent a constituency with pockets full of national currency, the proceeds of the crop, and in whose minds the promise of the future would far outweigh the value of any claims for the past.'[1]

Mr. Atkinson did not favor impeachment, largely because he distrusted some of the elements working for the removal of the President, and also because, as already noted, he feared that such action might remove Mr. McCulloch as Secretary of the Treasury; and especially was he opposed to the attempts, after impeachment, to 'ride out' of the party the Republican Senators who had voted against the conviction of the President. To one of their number, Senator Fessenden, he wrote: 'while expressing my regret that while impeachment was entered upon it could not have been carried through, [I wish] to express to you my hearty respect for the independence you have manifested in rendering your verdict.'[2]

This support threatened the cordial relations which existed between Mr. Atkinson and Senator Sumner when the former acted as a sponsor for a dinner given in Boston in honor of Senator Fessenden and some of his 'renegade' colleagues. It was with some difficulty that Mr. Atkinson convinced Mr. Sumner, who was exceedingly bitter on the subject, that there was no personal criticism implied against him by this action.[3]

In January, 1869, Mr. Atkinson gave the following three prin-

---

[1] Letter to Secretary McCulloch, January 8, 1866.   [2] May 5, 1868.

[3] His reasons for sustaining Senator Fessenden are succinctly stated in the following extract from a letter written to Senator Sumner, June 22, 1868: 'I have little confidence in the stability or permanent success of a party which submits to the leadership in the House of B. F. Butler, and attempts to cast out Fessenden. If Butler is allowed to take upon the Republicans the odium of the present corruption by defeating the efforts of honest men to reform the revenue system, thus knowingly or otherwise making himself the advocate of the whiskey ring, all men who have any self-respect will leave the party which he thus betrays as soon as the exigencies of reconstruction will allow them to do so.'

ciples as his program for the promotion of reconstruction and the building of a true union between the North and the South.

1. Complete reconstruction on basis of impartial suffrage.
2. Re-establishment of specie standard as speedily as possible.
3. As near an approach to free trade as the necessity of revenue will allow.[1]

In view of the pronouncements of Congress and President Grant in favor of specie redemption, he chose the last of these as his immediate objective, and during the period between 1869 and 1872 concentrated upon the task of influencing public opinion in such a way that there would be a popular demand for revenue and tariff reforms.

To this end, he wrote a series of articles and pamphlets advocating the above principles, and in his private correspondence continued to emphasize the importance of the general subject of revenue reform to his friends and acquaintances. A few years before, he had undertaken the task of editing a publication modeled along the lines of the 'Broadsides' issued by the New England Loyal Publication Society, which had done such important service in molding opinion in the North on the slavery question prior to and during the Civil War. Mr. Atkinson's plan called for the publication of 'Broadsides' containing short articles upon economic questions which were to be sent to various newspapers which might care to reprint them. The scheme was quickly launched, and, in October, 1869, he reported that two thousand copies were being sent out weekly throughout the country.

Meanwhile, neither tariff reform nor specie resumption was making much progress under Grant's first administration. Congress assumed the policy of letting the country grow up to the expanded currency, much to the disgust of the supporters of sound money, while the combined Tariff and Revenue Act of 1870 was not acceptable to the tariff reformers.

In December, 1871, in order to facilitate action on these important matters, Mr. Atkinson promoted the establishment of an information bureau at Washington, called the Taxpayers' Union.

[1] From a letter to a Mr. Haskell, January 11, 1869.

The Union was put in the charge of William Grosvenor of St. Louis, well-known tariff reformer, who was charged with the duty of securing the proper direction of tax and monetary legislation. Particularly was he instructed to furnish data and lend aid to members of Congress and others who wished to further the objects of the organization.[1] The Union was financed jointly by a group of New England men favorable to revenue reform, for whom Mr. Atkinson acted as treasurer, and the National Reform League of New York.

The Taxpayers' Union under Mr. Grosvenor's leadership was the center of the attempts during the first few months of 1872 to push tariff reform through Congress. It served as the clearing-house for all matters relating to revenue reform. Although the Union was pledged to the general principle of reduction of tariffs to a revenue basis, its supporters were far from united in their ideas as to how such a reduction should be achieved. Mr. Atkinson, for example, wanted immediate free raw materials, especially iron and wool, followed by lowered duties upon manufactured goods in the future, a plan which he worked out in detail later.[2] This suggestion did not appeal to the Western free-traders who desired lower duties on manufactured goods as well as on raw materials, and were not inclined to favor New England in such a fashion. The situation was complicated by other supporters of the Union who had certain pet measures they wished to have supported. These diverse interests, of course, made Mr. Grosvenor's position a most difficult one. In spite of them, however, he was able to accomplish effective work in concentrating the growing feeling of dissatisfaction with Grant and his Administration, although such management did not result in the passage of legislation.

It was natural that most of those associated with the Taxpay-

[1] The Executive Committee included W. M. Grosvenor, of St. Louis, Missouri; David A. Wells, of Norwich, Connecticut; Mahlon Sands, of New York City; Edward Atkinson, of Boston; Horace White, of Chicago; and Jacob Cox, of Cincinnati. The object of the Union as it appeared on its letter head was 'Not to interfere with any existing organization, but to afford means for combining the efforts and information of all who desire reduction of tariff to a revenue basis.'

[2] *Post*, p. 136.

ers' Union should see in the Liberal Republican Movement of 1872 [1] an opportunity to register a protest against existing political conditions and to secure a positive remedy for the evils in the tariff legislation. Mr. Grosvenor, especially, urged his associates to bend every effort toward making the Cincinnati convention of the Liberal Republicans a success. He was particularly anxious that New England should have a strong representation, and looked to Mr. Atkinson to secure leading men to serve as delegates.

Mr. Atkinson was not specially enthusiastic about joining the Reform Republicans, even though he consented to secure delegations from New England. For one thing, he had not entirely lost faith in the effectiveness of the Taxpayers' Union, and similar organizations to achieve the needed reform — a fact which made him reluctant to split the party. In addition, Horace Greeley's endorsement of the Missouri platform was discouraging. On March 30, 1872, Mr. Atkinson wrote to Grosvenor on this point: 'I cannot get the names I want for Cincinnati. The Greeley movement hurts it, and if it is to be a mere bolt, I shall not attend.'

But Grosvenor was able to convince Mr. Atkinson that if there were strong delegations of low-tariff advocates present, they would be able to control the convention in such a way that it would not be a mere party bolt. He wrote to Mr. Atkinson: 'I do not think you and Wells can afford to leave the Cincinnati convention to be controlled by those who oppose us without effort or protest on your part.' [2]

Mr. Atkinson continued, however, to experience difficulty in getting the men he hoped would back the movement. Especially

---

[1] This movement began with the gubernatorial elections in Missouri, in the fall of 1870. In that election the Republicans split over the question of removing from office those officials who had been aligned with the Confederate cause during the war, a policy favored by Grant; and the dissenting wing, under the leadership of Senator Carl Shurz, elected their candidate Gratz Brown, as Governor. In January, 1872, this same group met in State convention and issued a call for a national convention to be held in Cincinnati the following May, for the purpose of securing a Presidential candidate and a platform pledged to reform the abuses attributed to the Republican Administration under Grant. Cf. Rhodes, J. F., *History of United States*, vol. VI, pp. 412-13.

[2] April 5, 1872.

was he disappointed at being unable to get the active support of Senator Sumner, who was considered as a possible Presidential candidate for the convention. He wrote to Mr. Sumner: 'I am getting a few names, not just what I want, but good ones and shall print our call early next week. But we want a leader. I long for your letter. Would not the rights of the colored people be more fully secured by the support of Democrats on the Missouri platform than by anything else that can happen? So it seems to me. The apathy of many, and Forbes' advice [not to take part] disheartens me, but I shall act on my convictions and be one of the forlorn hope, if, so it shall be. Endicott agrees.'[1]

The convention which met in Cincinnati on May 1, 1872, was made up of three general classes; those advocating civil service reform, those who wanted a liberal Southern policy, and finally the section which hoped for 'a genuine reform of the tariff.' It was in this last category, of course, that Mr. Atkinson was included. With him were the outstanding free-traders of the day, including David A. Wells, Horace White, William Cullen Bryant, Mahlon Sands, and others.

It was apparent, even before the convention was assembled, that there would be substantial agreement upon all principles except the tariff. Consequently, the tariff reformers were prepared to make a fight to keep this principle before the convention, but they met defeat at the outset when the Committee on Resolutions decided, in respect to the tariff, to 'remit the discussion to the people in their Congressional districts, and to the decision of Congress thereon, wholly free from executive interference or dictation.'[2]

This action made it incumbent upon Mr. Atkinson and his associates to secure the nomination of a Presidential candidate who would be favorable to their principles. He and Mr. Wells personally desired Senator Trumbull, or J. D. Cox, but were prepared to sustain Charles Francis Adams, if neither of the other two could be nominated.

[1] April 11, 1872.
[2] Rhodes, J. F., *op. cit.*, vol. VI, p. 420.

But none of the low-tariff men were prepared to accept the nomination of Horace Greeley, which came on the seventh ballot of the convention, for it would have been difficult to find a more bitter opponent of tariff reform than Horace Greeley. As editor of the *New York Tribune*, he had consistently favored high protective duties, and had opposed any attempts at revenue reform that involved tariff reduction. His nomination at Cincinnati came as a result of the plea that he was the man who 'was most likely to defeat Grant.' Greeley's sympathy toward the South, which led to his subsequent nomination by the Democrats, made him acceptable to one part of the convention, but he had not been friendly toward civil service, and was the antithesis of what the tariff reformers had expected.[1] Thus it was, that what started out as a movement based upon genuine principles of reform, ended in what amounted practically to a party bolt, just as Mr. Atkinson had feared.

Mr. Atkinson returned from the convention greatly disheartened at the result. He expressed his own feeling and that of others when he wrote: 'Everyone here seems most bitterly disappointed. Had we nominated Adams, we should have swept the State. One of the most active and prominent Grant leaders said to me yesterday, "I would rather have cut off my fingers than not to have voted for Adams."'[2]

For a time he hoped that another convention might be held which would nominate Adams upon a genuine reform platform, but his attempts with Wells and others in this direction resulted in a failure. Between Grant and Greeley, Mr. Atkinson much preferred the President as the lesser of two evils, and consequently he voted the regular Republican ticket in the November election.

There was a distinct change in Mr. Atkinson's attitude toward tariff reform after 1872. His statement, made a few days after the convention, 'I have just returned from Cincinnati where I lost my scalp,'[3] testifies as to his immediate reaction, and he

---

[1] Cf. Rhodes, J. F., *op. cit.*, vol. VI, pp. 411 ff., and Stanwood, Edward, *op. cit.*, pp. 184–86.

[2] Letter to E. W. Kittridge, May 5, 1872.   [3] Letter to Harvey Kent, May 5, 1872.

made the resolve, 'to return to my proper function of writing and not to meddle much with the executive department for which I am unfitted.'[1] This resolution was strengthened by the fact that his work for free trade had made enemies among many of those with whom he had business relations, his activities being, in one case, a contributing factor in forcing his resignation from a mill treasuryship.[2]

For these reasons, he withdrew his active support from the free-trade movement as such. He did not relinquish his convictions in respect to the benefits of free trade, nor did he doubt the ultimate success of the movement in the United States,[3] but events at Cincinnati had convinced him that a better method of securing tariff reform lay in the adoption of a compromise position which would secure united action from those whom he termed the 'judicious' men on both sides. The following extracts from a letter written to David A. Wells in 1875, shed further light upon his changed point of view:

> I am more and more satisfied that if we avoid controversy as between protection and free trade, we shall secure good sound legislation by consent of both sides.... We must take men and facts as they are and remember that England took from 1824 to 1846 before the corn laws were repealed, and it took 20 years more to perfect the work.
>
> We must have a large tariff revenue. Try to frame it and you come to but one result. We must restore tea and coffee duties, make wool and other primary forms commonly called raw materials free, and then put 20 to 25 per cent on goods; *you can't get your revenue any other way*. Now if free traders in theory will admit this, necessity in fact, the antagonism between them and the manufacturers will cease....
>
> As I grow older I become less eager for immediate action, and more confident in the steady growth of ideas. Protection has now no in-

---

[1] Letter to Mr. Grosvenor, May 11, 1872. The Taxpayers' Union, incidentally, expired with the Cincinnati convention.

[2] Concerning this difficulty, he wrote: 'I have felt it to be my duty both as a public service and for the special interest of cotton mills to take a good deal of public work on me, especially on free trade. That fact has made me enemies, and has hurt me personally; if it is raised against me, I desire to say, not for the purpose of getting office, but that the facts may be known, that I have retired from public action until I can afford to retire from business.' Letter to C. F. Barker, September 30, 1873.

[3] On the contrary, as will be noted later, more than once was he afraid that a disastrous sweeping tariff reform would be achieved.

FREE TRADE, GREENBACKS, REFORM 93

tellectual force behind it; it is only a vested interest. It must die but it will take time. People will not submit to special legislation and any effort of the Iron and Steel Association or the Wool Association will only hurt themselves if we let them alone.[1]

As will be shown in subsequent chapters, Mr. Atkinson's later part in the tariff struggle consisted largely in an attempt to guide sentiment and legislation into a middle course which would, through a gradual, not sudden change, finally achieve the benefits of a tariff for revenue only. This policy resulted in many of the difficulties which one would expect from an attempt to ride two independently minded horses at the same time, even though the ultimate goal of both might be identical.

In the year and a half immediately following the Cincinnati convention, Mr. Atkinson turned his attention chiefly to matters other than politics, but he could not remain indifferent to the danger of currency inflation which appeared in the latter half of 1873.

In October of that year, Secretary of the Treasury Richardson had, with the consent of President Grant, paid out some $26,000,000 in greenbacks previously retired by Secretary McCulloch. This action seemed necessary because the panic of 1873 had so depleted the Treasury that there were no funds to meet the ordinary expenses of the Government. After Congress met in December, it was apparent that there was a strong sentiment not only to legalize the issue of greenbacks made by Secretary Richardson, but under the pressure of hard times, to enter into a definite policy of inflation. A flood of proposals were made to expand the issue of greenbacks in the interests of cheap money.[2]

On February 2, 1874, Mr. Atkinson wrote to Representative Henry L. Dawes of Massachusetts:

> I regret to see that there is any possibility that the re-issue of the cancelled notes may be legalized. The mischief of the unwarranted inflation is already apparent in every direction. If you legalize this issue of bad money you will give a precedent for a Secretary of the Treasury to collect a forced loan without authority of law at any time.

[1] November 11, 1875.   [2] Barrett, Don, *op. cit.*, pp. 177–78.

It seems to me there never was a time when courageous resistance to false measures was more needed. Pardon me if I speak warmly. I am one of those who cannot forbear denouncing a fraud when I see it, and I consider the continued use of bad money without any real attempt to make it good, a most infamous fraud. When the masses realize the cheat, as they surely will, there will be no forgiveness for any man, however true he may have been, if he has failed to resist the clamor of knaves and fools, like Butler and Kelly. 'Prosperity' Boutwell should read the history of 'Prosperity' Robinson, afterward Lord Goderick, and see where he landed.

The following month, Mr. Atkinson made a trip to New York for the purpose of speaking against monetary expansion at a large meeting at the Cooper Institute. While in New York, he and other sound-money advocates decided to set up an organization to counteract the efforts of the inflationists. The following, written March 28, 1874, gives the nature of this movement: 'I have telegraphed you to appoint a permanent committee, also to start Holton in Milwaukee. We must have a permanent league for hard money to control the nominations for Congress next fall, and go for good money irrespective of party. Headquarters in the West — New York is at white heat — We only wait so as not to prejudice the case by too much eastern action.' [1]

Mr. Atkinson had an almost immediate opportunity to utilize this organization. On April 14, Congress passed what was known as the 'Inflation Bill.' This provided that the total amount of greenbacks outstanding should be increased from $382,000,000 to $400,000,000 and that an additional issue of paper money, amounting to $46,000,000, should be permitted in the form of more National bank notes. Immediately after the bill went to the President for consideration, Mr. Atkinson wired to the Western men who were opposed to inflation, 'to rain in letters and telegrams of protest' against the measure. It was thought by Mr. Atkinson that these protests, coming from what was supposed to be the center of the agitation for cheap money, would make a decided impression upon the President. Several years later, in a personal conversation, Grant, unaware of Mr. Atkinson's part

[1] Letter to A. M. Wright.

FREE TRADE, GREENBACKS, REFORM

in the affair, told him that it was these letters and telegrams signed by influential Western men, whom he knew to be sound in their views, that made him decide to veto the bill — as he did on April 22.[1]

Although Grant's veto marked the turning-point in the inflation movement of this period, the advocates of paper money were not immediately silenced, and much remained to be done before resumption of specie could finally be accomplished. The Resumption Act itself, passed in January, 1875, was not clear in its terms as to how the greenbacks were to be redeemed.[2]

Mr. Atkinson had his own plan whereby the value of the greenbacks could be restored to par and actual specie resumption achieved. After a careful reading of the legal-tender acts passed in 1862 and 1863, he concentrated on the phrase in the Act of March 3, 1863, which read that the United States notes once returned to the Treasury, 'may be reissued from time to time as the exigencies of the public service may require.'[3]

Upon this basis, Mr. Atkinson argued that a forced loan during peace-time, such as was effected by the greenbacks, did not come under 'the exigencies of public service,' and that their reissue was illegal. For this reason, all greenbacks paid into the Treasury should be deemed *functus officio*, and not permitted to go out into circulation again. Further, because the Secretary of Treasury had never lost his power to receive these notes (the legislation limiting contraction, in Mr. Atkinson's opinion, applied only to positive action in respect to deflation), and because it was an executive function to determine the duration of 'the exigency of public service,' Mr. Atkinson suggested that the President should make a positive statement to the effect that public welfare did not require the reissue of a forced loan, and should further instruct the Secretary of Treasury to retire the United States notes as they were received.

[1] In an article written for *The Journal of Political Economy*, vol. I, pp. 117–19, Mr. Atkinson gives the details of this conversation with former President Grant.
[2] Barrett, Don, *op. cit.*, pp. 187 ff.
[3] *U.S. Statutes at Large*, Thirty-Seventh Congress, Third Session, Chapter LXXIII, Section 3.

He first advanced this plan early in 1875 in the hope that specie resumption might be speedily resumed under its operation. But as he was unable to secure any strong support for the measure, he let it drop for the time. Two years later, however, while on a visit to Washington, he was able to put his ideas directly before President Grant.

Encouraged by the interest which the President showed in his proposals, Mr. Atkinson, on his return from Washington, wrote an open letter, dated January 29, 1877, to the President giving his arguments in full. At the same time he addressed a private communication to him which read in part:

> Since my return from Washington, I have made a more complete examination of the acts passed subsequently to the legal-tender acts and I can find nothing to conflict with what I hold to be the essence of the Acts of 1862 and 1863. I hope the law officers of the Government may confirm my views.
>
> I am the more solicitous in this matter because I know that very prominent Democrats take my view, that a note paid in for taxes is dead, and I desire earnestly that it shall be buried under Republican administration. I hope nothing may be left for a possible Democratic administration to do that it may be claimed that a Republican administration might have done.
>
> I have caused my argument to be printed and I send herewith twenty copies. I retain a number of copies, but shall not allow them to be issued unless I learn that you have permitted the suggestions to be made public. In such event, I should be glad to have your authority to distribute some of them among my friends whose support of the measure might be of great value, and I shall be much gratified to have your permission to distribute them....
>
> I have been much honored and gratified by the attention you have given to my suggestions, and a letter from you would be a valuable bequest to my descendants.

The President made the following cordial reply:

> Executive Mansion, Washington
> February 7, 1877
>
> Dear Sir:
>
> After our conversation on the subject of specie resumption on the occasion of your recent visit to this city, I made inquiries of the Secretary of the Treasury as to his views upon the subject of his power under all existing acts of Congress to do what I believed would prac-

FREE TRADE, GREENBACKS, REFORM

tically bring legal tender notes to par; or near par, with gold. I found that there was a positive prohibition to any diminution of the issue of legal tenders except as provided for in the Act authorizing an unlimited increase of National bank circulation. Under these circumstances, I believed some legislation to be necessary authorizing the retirement of a portion of these notes, to accomplish a result so essential to the public good as I believe specie resumption to be. I have accordingly embodied my views on this subject in a short message to Congress, which will be delivered tomorrow.

I am much obliged to you for your kind note of the 30th inst. and hope that you, and all who desire to see sound currency take the place of our present fluctuating medium of exchange will give the subject such attention as will be likely to lead Congress to feel the necessity of action on their part. I feel anxious only as to the result, not as to the means by which it is accomplished. Any member of Congress who will devise a measure that will cure the present currency evil — be he Democrat or Republican — will receive my hearty co-operation.

With my best regards
Your obedient servant
U. S. GRANT

Edward Atkinson, esq.

In his message on February 3, 1877, President Grant recommended a funding arrangement whereby the greenbacks would be acceptable for four per cent Government bonds.[1] But his term of office ended in less than a month and it remained for Secretary Sherman to accomplish specie resumption under the next Administration.

Mr. Atkinson was deeply disappointed at the failure to get action on his plan. He confided to a friend, 'I think the President was inclined to act on my proposition that a note returned to the Treasury for taxes is *functus officio*, but Secretary Morrill was not equal to it.'[2] And to another he said, 'I wish I could have remained [in Washington] and induced Grant to act.'[3]

During the remainder of the period under consideration, Mr. Atkinson's interest in the subject waned, and other matters,

[1] Richardson, James D., *A Compilation of the Messages and Papers of the Presidents, 1789–1897*, vol. VII, pp. 425–27.
[2] Letter to J. S. Abbott, February 7, 1877.
[3] Letter to Hubley Ashton, February 17, 1877.

largely outside the political field, occupied most of his attention. In the Presidential election of 1876, he favored Hayes, although Blaine's characterization of the Congress of 1874–76 as 'the Confederate Congress,' almost turned him to the Democrats. He looked upon the controversy over the election as being unfortunate, but in April, 1877, expressed the opinion that 'we are enjoying a calm after a great political storm, and I cannot but think we are gathering up our strength for an era of great prosperity.'[1]

[1] Letter to Gustav Herrmann, April 11, 1877.

CHAPTER IV
BUSINESS EXECUTIVE: FIRE INSURANCE AND FIRE PREVENTION

ALTHOUGH what might be termed his avocations — that is, his activities as an economist, free-trader, anti-imperialist and publicist — brought Mr. Atkinson to the attention of a greater number of persons, it is probable that his most important and lasting contributions came from his vocational career after 1878, and the public relations thereof. In that year Mr. Atkinson withdrew from active participation in cotton manufacturing and assumed the duties of president-treasurer of the Boston Manufacturers' Mutual Fire Insurance Company, an office he was to hold until his death in 1905.

No one can study the history of fire insurance and fire prevention during the past century without being impressed by the importance of these subjects, which have largely been neglected by economists. Only those who remember or those who have made a study of former fire losses can appreciate the tremendous progress which has been made in the elimination of fire hazards and the consequent saving of life and property. This statement applies particularly to factories, hotels, warehouses, and similar types of construction. Architecture, chemistry, physics, and other sciences have contributed jointly to make these improvements possible, but it is to the fire insurance executives and their engineers that the chief credit goes for adapting scientific principles to their specific needs and in securing a widespread use of safety measures.

In respect to organization, fire insurance companies are divided into two general classes; stock companies and mutual companies. Briefly, the difference between the two types is as follows: Stock companies insure various types of risks, charging a premium rate, in each case fixed at a point high enough to cover probable losses, plus the expenses of operation. The paid-in capital of the company represents a reserve which may be drawn upon in case of unusual losses, and any profits from the operation of the business are paid to the stockholders as profits or used to build up a surplus.

The mutual plan differs from the above on one or two important points. Under this plan, persons interested in insurance associate themselves in a company for the purpose of carrying their own insurance risks. Premiums are also charged upon a basis of probable risks, but any surplus revenue above operating expenses and an amount necessary to maintain a reserve is returned to the members as 'dividends.' In case of unusual losses, members are subject to a *pro rata* assessment, sufficient to make up any deficit.

Although by far the greatest amount of the fire insurance business of the United States is done by stock companies, the mutual companies have played an important part in fire insurance history. Of particular significance among the latter group have been a small number of fire insurance companies, located chiefly in Massachusetts and Rhode Island, known as the Associated Factory Mutual Fire Insurance Companies of New England.[1] These companies have not only been outstanding examples of the practicability of the mutual type of organization, but in addition have led the way in the advancement of the technique of fire prevention. The Boston Manufacturers' Mutual Fire Insurance Company, with which Mr. Atkinson became associated as President and Treasurer, has been a leading member of this Association.

The first factory mutual fire insurance company in the United States was started by Zachariah Allen in 1835. Mr. Allen was the owner of a woolen mill at Allendale, Rhode Island, and a pioneer in the study of fire prevention. When he found that, although he had reduced the fire hazards in his mill, he was unable to secure lower rates of insurance in any of the stock companies of the time, he set about to interest a group of his friends in a mutual company. The result was the organization of the

---

[1] There were at one time several smaller companies in Philadelphia and two in Chicago also associated with the main group.

FIRE INSURANCE AND PREVENTION

Manufacturers' Mutual Fire Insurance Company of Providence, Rhode Island, a company which has had a successful history, and is today an important member of the factory mutual group.

The success of this company led other groups of manufacturers to follow its example with the result that between 1848 and 1900 approximately twenty-five companies were organized on the mutual plan. These companies and their dates of organization are shown in the accompanying table.

ASSOCIATED FACTORY MUTUAL FIRE INSURANCE COMPANIES

ORGANIZED [1]	NAME OF COMPANY
1835	Manufacturers' Mutual Fire Insurance Company
1848	Rhode Island Mutual Fire Insurance Company
1850	Boston Manufacturers' Mutual Fire Insurance Company
1854	Firemen's Mutual Insurance Company
1855	State Mutual Fire Insurance Company
1855	Worcester Manufacturers' Mutual Insurance Company
1860	Arkwright Mutual Fire Insurance Company
1868	Blackstone Mutual Fire Insurance Company
1870	Fall River Manufacturers' Mutual Insurance Company
1871	Mechanics Mutual Fire Insurance Company
1873	What Cheer Mutual Fire Insurance Company
1874	Merchants' Mutual Fire Insurance Company
1874	Enterprise Mutual Fire Insurance Company
1875	Cotton and Woolen Manufacturers' Mutual Insurance Company
1875	Hope Mutual Fire Insurance Company
1877	American Mutual Fire Insurance Company
1880	Philadelphia Manufacturers' Mutual Fire Insurance Company
1884	Rubber Manufacturers' Mutual Insurance Company
1884	Mercantile Mutual Fire Insurance Company
1884	Keystone Mutual Fire Insurance Company
1886	Paper Mill Mutual Insurance Company
1887	Protection Mutual Fire Insurance Company
1890	Industrial Mutual Insurance Company
1893	Manton Mutual Fire Insurance Company
1895	Mill Owners' Mutual Fire Insurance Company

Developed first among the textile industries of New England, the factory mutuals have expanded their business until in 1931 they included approximately eight thousand large industrial plants throughout the United States and Canada,[2] and carried

---

[1] *Manufacturers' Mutual Fire Insurance Company, Annual Report for the Year Ending December 31, 1931*, p. 33. It should be mentioned that between these dates there were several other companies started which subsequently failed or were absorbed.

[2] Pamphlet, *The Inspection Department of the Associated Factory Mutual Fire Insurance Companies*, p. 1.

insurance for their members amounting to over nine and one-half billion dollars.[1]

Mention has been made of the leadership assumed by the factory mutual fire insurance companies. One writer has described their influence and the pressure which they brought to bear upon the stock companies in the following words:

> It was during this period [before 1890] that the Factory Insurance Association was organized by some of the stock companies in order to meet the competition of the 'factory mutuals.'... For many years they [the factory mutuals] had been especially active in New England, where, by advanced methods of fire protection, they had cut the cost of insurance among their members to a remarkably low figure. It had become difficult for the stock companies to compete with them for the better types of factory risks. By 1883, the mutuals carried $350,000,000 of business in Massachusetts and Rhode Island alone. Soon after this, the Phenix (of Brooklyn), the Queen and the New Hampshire Fire, all stock companies, followed in the footsteps of the mutuals and co-operated in improving their factory risks, particularly by means of installing sprinklers, with a corresponding rate reduction.[2]

The author continues:

> Better methods of construction were devised, and fire fighting devices were installed, but the chief contribution of the 'mutuals' was the introduction of the automatic sprinkler, the most effective weapon in the whole arsenal of fire protection.[3]

The success of the factory mutuals in providing satisfactory insurance for their members, and in leading the way in adopting fire-prevention methods, has been due to several reasons. In the

---

[1] *Annual Statement of What Cheer and Hope Mutual Fire Insurance Companies*, January 1, 1932, p. 18. Among their risks are included some of the most important industrial organizations in both countries. The following is a list of a few of the most prominent companies which were members of the Factory Mutuals in 1931:

Aluminum Company of America	Eastman Kodak Company
American Can Company	Ford Motor Company
American Tobacco Company	B. F. Goodrich Company
Amoskeag Manufacturing Company	International Harvester Company
Bibb Manufacturing Company	R. J. Reynolds Tobacco Company
Canadian Cottons, Limited	Standard Brands, Incorporated
Dominion Textile Company, Limited	Studebaker Corporation

Annual Report, Firemen's Mutual Fire Insurance Company, Mercantile Mutual Fire Insurance Company, and Narragansett Mutual Fire Insurance Company, 1931, pp. 23, 24.

[2] Brearley, Harry Chase, *Fifty Years of a Civilizing Force*, p. 73.

[3] *Ibid.*, p. 166.

first place, they have avoided two difficulties, which, according to one authority, have beset most fire insurance companies organized as mutuals. Too often mutual fire insurance companies have failed to keep their risks confined within a geographical area that would lend itself to adequate supervision, or they have assumed types of risks so varied that fire-prevention technique was difficult to develop.[1] By confining their risks to one general type, and by expanding their territory only as they were able to supervise the extended area, the factory mutuals have avoided these obstacles.

A second factor in the growth of the factory mutuals was the early recognition of the principle that the primary function of the fire insurance company was to prevent losses and not merely to distribute them after fires had occurred. In carrying out this idea, every effort has been made to make the members feel that they are partners in a joint enterprise, the success of which depended largely upon their co-operation with the officers of the company in adequately safeguarding their property against fire hazards. Mr. Atkinson put this principle into stronger words: 'The only persons who can prevent loss by fire are the owners or occupants of the insured premises. Upon them rests the responsibility for heavy loss, if any occurs, in nearly every fire. All that the Insurance Company can do is to pay indemnity for loss, which, if large, in nine cases out of ten is due to the lack of apparatus for preventing loss, or to lack of care and order in the conduct of the work.'[2]

Therefore the history of the companies has been largely that of the development of the technique of fire prevention, and the education of members to the point where they realized that self-interest demanded the adoption of all possible safeguards. Except for the perfection of the automatic sprinkler, which stands out as the greatest single invention for the control of fire, there has been little of the spectacular in this history. Rather it has con-

[1] Cf. Oviatt, F. C., 'Historical Study of Fire Insurance in the United States,' *Annals of the American Academy of Political and Social Science*, vol. XXVI, no. 2, pp. 345 ff.
[2] Atkinson, Edward, *The Prevention of Loss by Fire*, p. 11.

sisted in discovering the numerous small factors which combined made for the danger of fire, and in eliminating them through education, persuasion, and in some cases through pressure on the members.

The period between the beginning of Zachariah Allen's venture and 1878 demonstrated the effectiveness of the plan of self-insurance. The officers and members of the companies had found that an intelligent study of fire hazards and the adoption of preventive measures resulted in fewer losses and lower insurance costs.[1] But as these problems were being met, changing conditions were introducing others. Factory buildings were being built larger, machinery was being speeded up with a consequent increase in friction, and other changes were being made, all of which called for new energy from those interested in fire prevention.

After 1878, there was a period of twenty-five or thirty years which formed a fairly definite chapter in the development of the factory mutuals. It was in 1880 that the first serious effort was made to push the use of the automatic sprinkler among the members. The end of the chapter came between 1900 and 1910 when practically all risks were protected by this device. The effectiveness of this and other methods of fire control is well demonstrated by the steadily lowered net cost of insurance to members.[1]

In any analysis of the success of the factory, or New England mutuals as they are sometimes called, credit must be given to the officers of the various companies who filled their positions with great energy and ability and who visualized the purpose of fire insurance in terms of fire prevention.

Mr. Atkinson's name ranks among the most forceful and able of these officials, and he was responsible in no small degree for many of the improvements made in this field between 1880 and 1905. This statement in no way detracts from the contributions and accomplishments of his associates. As is so often the case where many minds are directed toward the same general pro-

[1] Note table on page 105.

blems, it is difficult to give credit for particular ideas to those who deserve it. Often the same solution will occur to two or more persons at the same time, or a suggestion from one source, added to others gathered elsewhere, will emerge as a completed idea from an individual who has synthesized them.

NET PREMIUM COST OF $100 INSURANCE PER YEAR [1]

DECADE ENDING	BOSTON MANUFACTURERS' MUTUAL FIRE INSURANCE COMPANY	ARKWRIGHT MUTUAL FIRE INSURANCE COMPANY
1870	27.9 cents [2]	31.8 cents [2]
1880	25.3 cents	29.4 cents
1890	22.7 cents	21.8 cents
1900	14.3 cents	14.3 cents
1910	6.7 cents	6.5 cents

DECADE ENDING	MANUFACTURERS' MUTUAL FIRE INSURANCE COMPANY
1845	84.0 cents
1855	39.0 cents
1865	30.8 cents
1875	35.5 cents
1885	22.9 cents
1895	16.2 cents
1905	11.2 cents
1915	6.6 cents

Mr. Atkinson's greatest service to the prevention of fire came from his capacity to see value in the ideas of others, and in his ability to interest others in the major problems in the field, and in his success in popularizing the various practices which in his judgment should be followed. In his own words, his rôle was described as follows: 'Having no truly scientific mastery of any of the applied sciences, it has been my function to select men who might each in his own branch of science work out the problems as they have been presented.' [3]

[1] The data for this table were taken from the following sources: *Annual Report of the Manufacturers' Mutual Fire Insurance Company and Associated Companies*, 1931; *Annual Report of the Boston Manufacturers' Mutual Fire Insurance Company*, 1931; and, French, Edward V., *Arkwright Mutual Fire Insurance Company*, p. 121.

[2] The net premium costs for all the factory mutuals will not vary appreciably from these figures.

[3] Atkinson, Edward, *op. cit.*, p. 51.

The remainder of this chapter will deal with Mr. Atkinson's work and association with the Boston Manufacturers' Mutual Fire Insurance Company, and his efforts to secure a general adoption of the principles of fire prevention developed in connection with the work of the factory mutual companies. Incidentally, it should be noted that, while in the following discussion chief emphasis will be placed upon the Boston Manufacturers' Mutual Fire Insurance Company, the history of this company so closely parallels that of the other factory mutuals that its development may be said to give a representative picture of the group. In addition, the fact that improvements and suggestions in this field, unlike advances achieved by competing commercial firms, were made common property and used for mutual benefit, makes for a common chronology.

The Boston Manufacturers' Mutual Fire Insurance Company was started in 1850, the third of the group of factory mutuals. It was the first company to be organized in Massachusetts, and has consistently carried the largest amount of risks of any of the group. Mr. Atkinson's first official connection with the company came in 1865 when he was elected a member of the board of directors. His active work, of course, did not come until he assumed the duties of president and treasurer in 1878.

The business methods of the company at the time are well described by Mr. Atkinson: 'Before 1878 no customary or regular meetings of the directors had been held. Inspections had been made in a desultory manner by the presidents or secretaries of the several companies about once a year, usually a few weeks before the expiration of the policy. Modern safeguards had not been thoroughly investigated. Automatic sprinklers were known, but had secured little or no attention. There were no experience tables, no classification of risks, and no real comprehension of the relative hazard on different classes.'[1]

This condition of affairs was changed soon after Mr. Atkinton's election as president. In the first meeting over which he

---

[1] Atkinson, Edward, *op. cit.*, p. 14.

FIRE INSURANCE AND PREVENTION

presided it was voted that thereafter the directors of the company should meet regularly once each month.[1]

At the same meeting, the first step was made toward securing a more efficient and orderly system of fire inspections, when funds were appropriated for the services of extra draughtsmen who were to make complete plans of the premises of all the risks insured by the company. In this way the fire hazards of each risk could be studied more efficiently and suggestions made for their elimination. Arrangements were also made to keep complete and permanent records of the important phases of the business.

Also in 1878, the Boston Manufacturers' Mutual Fire Insurance Company organized an inspection department with Mr. William B. Whiting, secretary of the company, in charge. This department began a system of regular quarterly inspection of all the risks upon the books of the company. These early inspections were not complicated, the principal idea being to maintain general order and cleanliness in the mills in order that small fires could be controlled and extinguished with water pails or small hose lines. Pumps and hose lines were tested and special attention given to waste boxes, spittoons, and other spots where fires might originate.

As the risks of the Boston Manufacturers' Mutual Fire Insurance Company were in practically all cases shared to some extent by the other factory mutuals, the advantage of sharing the inspection information soon became obvious, and arrangements were made whereby the Boston Manufacturers' Mutual Fire Insurance Company supervised the work and prorated the expenses among the other companies upon a basis of the amount of the risks held by them. This arrangement remained in effect until 1887 when the Associated Mutuals set up a Bureau of Inspection to take care of this work.

Another of Mr. Atkinson's first tasks was to eliminate the poor risks from the books of the company. Between 1878 and

[1] *Minutes of Board of Directors of the Boston Manufacturers' Mutual Fire Insurance Company,* January 31, 1878.

1880, the board of directors, at his suggestion, canceled a considerable number of policies representing manufacturing establishments which were deemed as being particularly subject to fire hazard. During the same period, however, new business was added with the result that there was a net gain for these two years.[1]

Mr. Atkinson's next step was to make an analysis of the causes of fires as shown by the past experiences of the insurance companies. A study of former fires showed that broken lanterns and spontaneous combustion accounted for about fifty per cent of the fires, while friction was responsible for another twenty per cent.[2] He finished his report in March, 1878, and immediately set about to remedy the situation. He had circulars printed and distributed to all who might be interested, and addressed the National Association of Cotton Manufacturers upon the subject, pointing out to the members of that group the necessity of eliminating as far as possible these chief causes of fire.[3] He strongly recommended the use of improved types of lanterns which were less likely to be broken by careless handling.

The case of the lanterns well illustrates the point that fire prevention consists in the elimination of small factors. It also shows the trouble sometimes encountered with what seems to be a simple problem. Mr. Atkinson tells of the difficulties. An examination was made of all lanterns used in mills.

> Not a single safe lantern could be found in use. All were badly made, liable to melt at the joints, and insufficiently guarded. On searching for good lanterns none could be found except expensive brass lanterns made for the railway service. Warnings were given, due precautions taken and, in connection with the firm now called the F. O. Dewey Company, safe lanterns at moderate cost were invented, but it took five years to perfect this apparantly simple device. Many improvements have been made, and there are now two or three types of safe and suitable lanterns for mill use, burning either animal oil, mixed oils or mineral oils. Since that study of the lantern question, there has not been a loss of any considerable amount in any of the

---

[1] Atkinson, Edward, *op. cit.*, p. 15.
[2] Cf. *Proceedings of the National Association of Cotton Manufacturers*, no. 24, pp. 57–60.
[3] *Ibid.*, no. 24, pp. 14–17.

works insured by this company which could be reasonably attributed to fault in the lantern. Careful attention to lanterns would doubtless save many fires and losses in city risks, but what owner or occupant ever gives his personal attention to this insignificant cause of very heavy losses?[1]

Many of the fires, attributed both to spontaneous combustion and to friction, were caused by the poor or uncertain quality of lubricants. In response to the demand for increased production, machinery had been speeded up without a corresponding improvement in the quality of the oils used in their lubrication. The result was that the oils became gummy on the working joints, increasing the friction, or under the increased friction of faster moving parts, the more volatile types gave off gases which were extremely susceptible to ignition or explosion.

In addition, there was great variation in the costs of lubrication to manufacturers. In a selected group of fifty-five print mills it was found that oil prices varied from twenty-nine cents to a dollar and five cents per gallon. In terms of lubrication per thousand pounds of cloth, the costs varied from sixty-eight cents to two dollars and fifty-eight cents.[2]

Mr. Atkinson saw the importance of greater and more precise knowledge concerning the nature of various types of lubricants, both for the prevention of fire and as an aid toward securing lower operating costs for manufacturers. He persuaded the several mutual companies and some of the stock companies to contribute jointly for the purpose of making a scientific investigation of lubricating oils, and secured the services of Professor John Ordway, of the Massachusetts Institute of Technology, to undertake and supervise the experiment.

The chief purposes of the experiment were to determine the rate of evaporation, the viscosity, flashing points, and other qualities which would determine the usefulness of the lubricants.

This series of experiments presented considerable difficulties of a technical nature. Special apparatus, for example, had to be

---

[1] Atkinson, Edward, *op. cit.*, pp. 27–28.
[2] *Ibid.*, p. 31.

designed which would give identical condition for the various tests.[1] These obstacles were overcome one by one and the results finally achieved were of practical value to the manufacturers and the insurance companies.

The chief items which interested the manufacturers were the flashing points and rates of evaporation of the various oils. It was found, for example, that the rates of evaporation of the various oils submitted for the experiment by various users varied from 1½ per cent to 25 per cent for a ten-hour period at a temperature of 140° Fahrenheit. As this temperature was not uncommon for bearings, the expense and danger involved in the use of the more volatile oils can readily be seen.

The flashing point or temperature at which the oils burst into flames, showed a variability ranging from 180° to as high as 540°.[2] In the interests of fire prevention, the oils with a low flashing point were to be avoided, as their use in bearings gave rise to the danger of ignition from friction. Only one mineral oil of those tested was found which was well distilled and safe for lubrication. Mr. Atkinson accordingly served notice on the makers of the other oils that unless their product was improved, warnings would be sent to members of the insurance companies not to buy or use these inferior oils under any circumstances. Quoting Mr. Atkinson directly:

> This led to a threat of a suit at law for interfering with their business, which I immediately urged them to enter in Court, as I desired to publish the facts; but I advised them to settle the patent rights and to change their methods of distillation, which advice was taken. A year later, wishing to secure some of the volatile oil for experimental purposes, none could be found in the market. The price and cost of lubricating oil were very greatly reduced, all oils being brought to a uniform standard; very great benefit in money and increased safety have since ensued. From the conclusion of that investigation to the present time, serious losses from hot bearings have been very rare; in fact, there is not one of any moment on our record that I can recall. Several members reported to me that their savings in the cost of

---

[1] *Proceedings of the National Association of Cotton Manufacturers*, vol. 26, speech by Professor Ordway, p. 17 ff.

[2] *Ibid.*, vol. 25, pp. 61–71.

FIRE INSURANCE AND PREVENTION

lubricants in the next two years, resulting from this study, had been more than the cost of their insurance in the same period.[1]

Another subject which came in for the early attention of the inspection department was the nature and efficiency of the fire hose. Too often hose was hung up more to impress the underwriters or insurance inspectors, than to be used as an aid for the extinguishing of fire. Numerous qualities and grades of fire hose were used, some of which would not carry enough pressure to throw a stream more than a few feet.

In connection with the inspection department, complete tests were made of both fire hose and nozzles, and a standard was set up which was required of all members. Any manufacturer who made hose of this grade was entitled to label it as *underwriters' hose*, making it easy to identify by purchasers.[2]

To Mr. William B. Whiting goes the principal credit for the elimination of another small but important fire hazard. As was the case in numerous similar situations, Mr. Atkinson was responsible in seeing that the idea received wide attention. This subject had to do with the proper place of the steam-heating pipes in factories. It had been customary to fasten them to the walls near the floor where they were apt to collect combustible material and possibly to char the wood with which they might come in contact. It was urged by Mr. Whiting and Mr. Atkinson that the pipes be suspended from the ceilings which would eliminate fire risks and increase the efficiency of the heating units. This suggestion did not meet with immediate favor. Mr. Atkinson writes: 'No improvement which has been presented by the undersigned ever encountered so much distrust, almost ridicule, as this; but by coaxing the incredulous to try it in some small room, the result soon justified the recommendation, and the pipes were moved throughout the works. The most satisfactory case was in a high basement with a stone floor, in which no one could work except in wooden shoes such as are worn in England in stone-floored weaving-buildings to keep the feet warm. When

[1] Atkinson, Edward, *op. cit.*, p. 32.
[2] *Ibid.*, p. 38.

the pipes were put overhead, the stone floor was soon warmed, and the room was put to use.'[1]

After these immediate difficulties had been remedied, attention was next turned toward the subject of mill construction and its relation to fire control.

Some of the early mills had been constructed in such a way that once a fire started, it was liable to spread rapidly. This was due primarily to the type of roofs, and the construction of the flooring. The earliest roofs were steep and contained a good deal of combustible material. The fire hazard was often increased by loft floors that formed attics. These were inaccessible in case of fire and often harbored rats' nests made of combustible materials. The fact that rats and mice often carried matches and oily rags and the like to their nests gave an added danger.

The floors were usually made with a joisted type of construction. As a result, in case of fire, it was difficult to reach all the parts of the ceiling (formed by the floor of the room above) with a hose stream or sprinklers because of the partitions formed by the joists. In such a construction the floor boards were usually of two layers of one-inch stuff which would soon burn through.

Mr. Atkinson and his associates advocated a type of factory construction which had long since been used in the better-constructed factories which became known as 'mill construction,' or 'slow-burning construction.' The main emphasis was placed upon improving the floor and roof construction. Instead of the steep roof, a comparatively flat roof with a pitch of from one-half to three-quarters of an inch per foot was recommended. This did away with objectionable features of the older type as it eliminated attics and much combustible construction.

Floor construction was improved by the use of heavy cross timbers about twelve inches by sixteen inches instead of joists, spaced eight to ten feet apart. The floor consisted in a bottom layer of thick planks and a top layer of either a hard wood floor usually placed at right angles to the planks, or of a layer of soft-wood flooring laid diagonally to the lower planks and covered

---

[1] Atkinson, Edward, *op. cit.*, p. 42.

FIRE INSURANCE AND PREVENTION

by the hard-wood flooring. Such construction gave the minimum amount of exposed space and resisted fire very effectively. In addition, the ceilings were easy to flush with hose lines.

Columns supporting the roof were of the same heavy type of construction. Experiments showed that timbers of from twelve to sixteen inches gave the best results. It was found that steel supports, unless protected by thick coverings or insulating materials, would buckle and warp under conditions which would only char the wooden pillars.

In an article in *The American Architect* for April, 1893, Mr. Atkinson summarized Mill Construction as follows:

What Mill Construction Is

1. Mill construction consists in so disposing the timber and plank in heavy solid masses as to expose the least number of corners or ignitable projections to fire, to the end also that when fire occurs, it may be most readily reached by water from sprinklers or hose.

2. It consists in separating every floor from every other floor by incombustible stops — by automatic hatch-ways, by encasing stairways and belts either in brick or other incombustible partitions — so that a fire shall be retarded in passing from floor to floor to the utmost that is consistent with the use of wood or any material in construction that is not absolutely fire-proof.

3. It consists in guarding the ceilings over all specially hazardous stock or processes with fire-retardent material such as plastering laid on wire-lath or expanded metal or upon wooden dovetailed-lath, following the lines of the ceiling and of the timbers without any interspaces between the plastering and the wood; or else in protecting ceilings over hazardous places with Asbestos Air Cell Board, Sheet Metal, Sackett Wall Board or other fire-retardent.

4. It consists not only in so constructing the mill, workshop or warehouse that fire shall pass as slowly as possible from one part of the building to another, but also in providing all suitable safeguards against fire.[1]

This type of construction was recommended to all members who contemplated the construction of new factory buildings. The members were aided by plans for an ideal mill which were drawn up and distributed by the mutual companies. In addition,

[1] Cf. *Report No. 5, Insurance Engineering Experiment Station*, 'Slow-Burning or Mill Construction.'

arrangements were made for officials of the companies to look over proposed plans for specific construction for the purpose of eliminating possible fire dangers due to construction. As experience warranted it, these plans were added to and changed, but on the whole the principles just outlined have remained the principal features of construction.

With the perfection and lowered cost of reinforced concrete construction in recent years, much of this phase of fire prevention has been solved. Yet a large number of existing textile mills have heavy plank and timber floors and roofs, and many of the most recent mills have followed this type of construction.

The automatic sprinkler has already been referred to as the greatest single improvement ever made in the development of fire control. Its place in the history of fire prevention is well described by C. J. H. Woodbury, one-time vice-president of the Boston Manufacturers' Mutual Fire Insurance Company, who wrote in 1892: 'The normal hazard of manufacturing establishments has greatly increased in the last ten years; buildings have been made larger, crowding into one structure a greater number of possible dangers; the speed of machinery has been increased; the chemical changes due to more rapid dyeing and drying processes have increased the fires from spontaneous ignition of textile fibers; and the inevitable tendency of all these destructive conditions was leading to the most serious results to owner and underwriter, when the automatic sprinkler system, as an invention in due time, met these dangers in such potency as to reverse the conditions of greater hazard and diminish the fire risk.'[1]

Inventors had been working on the idea of an automatic sprinkler for at least a hundred and fifty years before it came into commercial use. The first patent for a self-operating sprinkler was granted in England to Ambrose Godfrey in November, 1723. His device consisted in a cask of fire-extinguishing fluid which contained a pewter chamber of gunpowder connected to a series of fuses. His apparatus was tried out and in several authenticated

---

[1] Woodbury, C. J. H., *Modern Development and Early History of Automatic Sprinkler*, p. 15, circular of the Boston Manufacturers' Mutual Fire Insurance Company.

FIRE INSURANCE AND PREVENTION

cases operated successfully, although it never became popular.[1]

Another patent was taken out by John Carey in 1806 for, 'An apparatus for the extinguishment of fires in gentlemen's apartments and warehouses.'[2] It consisted in a rose-sprinkler connected by pipes to a tank of water. The valve in the sprinkler was controlled by a combustible string which would release the water when ignited. This type was impractical because of the tendency of the string to contract and expand.

Some few years later, Major A. Stewart Harrison, of England, developed an apparatus which consisted in, 'a large rose-head containing numerous perforations counter-sunk on the outside. Water was shut out at the neck of the sprinkler by a cup-shaped rubber piston-valve resting on a disk at the top of a rod, which was in turn supported by a conical plug held in place at the bottom of the sprinkler by fusible solder.'[3]

As Harrison could not interest anyone in helping him produce his invention, he was unable to do anything with it, even though it had all the essential features of the sprinklers which later became widely used.

The predecessor of the automatic sprinkler in the United States was the perforated-pipe sprinkler, a device introduced about 1852, probably from Great Britain.[4] The most successful of the perforated-pipe sprinklers consisted of lines of wrought-iron pipe with small holes drilled at short intervals resembling a long lawn sprinkler. The holes were drilled in such a way that the small streams were directed toward the ceiling. The sprinklers of each floor or section of floors were controlled by separate valves located at convenient places. In case of a fire in a mill, the valve for that section was turned on and the place deluged with water.

The merits of the system over the former methods of fire control are obvious, and by 1880 perforated-pipe sprinklers were quite generally used in the sections of the mills particularly susceptible to fire hazards, such as picking-rooms and other

[1] Woodbury, C. J. H., *op. cit.*, p. 2.   [2] *Ibid.*, p. 2.   [3] *Ibid.*, p. 3.
[4] French, Edward V., *Arkwright Mutual Fire Insurance Company*, pp. 16–17.

departments liable to rapid spread of fire or difficult of access.[1]

Although a great advancement in the progress toward the successful control of fire, the perforated sprinklers were not entirely satisfactory. Probably the greatest trouble was that they had to be turned on in case of fire, and while in some of the mills the pipe sprinklers were well planned and effectively used, there were numerous instances of their failure to operate properly. There was, for example, some difficulty with the valves which would sometimes be open when the pumps were started up for inspection, thus flooding a section of the mills. Sometimes in the excitement of a fire, valve stems would be broken by being turned in the wrong direction, making the apparatus useless. And there was one instance related of a whole mill being wet down by a person who mistook moonlight on the window for a fire. Mr. Woodbury writing on this subject said, 'These accidents have by no means been confined to irresponsible persons, as an instance has been known where the agent of a mill wet down a large carding room while in the act of illustrating to the president of an insurance company how easily the valves of his fire apparatus worked.'[2]

The first automatic sprinklers which were produced for commercial use were the invention of Henry S. Parmelee, of New Haven, Connecticut.[3] His sprinkler, patented August 11, 1874, was in the shape of a small turbine with a brass cap soldered to the lower part of the rim. It was simple in design and efficient in its action, and although it was superseded by other types, many of the early Parmelee sprinklers operated successfully after several years' installation. The manufacture and distribution of these sprinklers was handled by the Frederick Grinnell Company, which has since become the most prominent company associated with the automatic sprinklers.

Colonel T. J. Borden was among the first to use the automatic sprinklers to any considerable extent. In 1875 he installed some

[1] French, E. V., *op. cit.*, p. 18.
[2] Woodbury, C. J. H., *Joint Report for Year 1888, Associated Factory Mutual Insurance Companies*, p. 10.
[3] *Ibid., Modern Development and Early History of Automatic Sprinklers*, p. 4.

twenty-five hundred Parmelee sprinklers in his mills at Fall River.[1] Their use spread slowly, however, due partly to the usual apathy of persons toward new inventions and partly to several specific objections made by mill-owners and managers. Among other things, they felt that installation costs would be excessive; that the sprinklers would fail to operate after being in position any great length of time; that they would not be able to control any except small fires that had made little headway; and finally, that there was considerable danger of damage from sprinkler leakage.

The producers of the Parmelee sprinklers pushed their product vigorously, making numerous experiments and calling attention to its successful operation in early fires. Mr. Grinnell, at Mr. Atkinson's suggestion,[2] gave the first talk on automatic sprinklers before the National Association of Cotton Manufacturers in April, 1878, including in his speech a report on tests of the Parmelee sprinkler.[3]

Mr. Atkinson was by this time thoroughly convinced of the effectiveness of the automatic sprinklers and desired to promote their use. He worked under a handicap at first, however, because for several years the Parmelee sprinkler had a monopoly in the field, and he felt hesitant, in his official capacity, to push its use vigorously because of possible criticism. But by 1880, he and his associates felt that the efficiency of the Parmelee automatics more than offset any such possible criticism, and in that year they issued a special bulletin which read, in part, 'The officers of this company cannot hesitate to recommend the adoption of the automatic system of sprinklers in almost all cases where sprinklers are needed.'[4]

Within a few years there were several sprinklers invented and

---

[1] French, E. V., *op. cit.*, p. 42.
[2] *Boston Manufacturers' Mutual Fire Insurance Company, Special Report*, no. 3, December, 1880, p. 9.
[3] *Minutes of the Board of Directors of the Boston Manufacturers' Mutual Fire Insurance Company*, November 26, 1885.
[4] *Boston Manufacturers' Mutual Fire Insurance Company, Special Report*, no. 3, December, 1880, p. 9.

placed on the market so that prospective users had a number from which to choose. In 1885, Mr. Woodbury made the first of a series of comparative tests of the various automatics then on the market, and was able to show which operated most successfully.[1]

The work of these early automatic sprinklers was watched with keen interest. As examples began to accumulate showing their efficiency in the checking and extinguishing of fires which, without them, would have meant serious losses, the task of spreading their use became somewhat easier. The following table of fire losses, classified according to equipment, shows the favorable results of the use of automatics.

	With Automatic Sprinklers	Without Automatic Sprinklers
Total fires	206	759
Total loss	$87,600	$5,707,000
Loss per fire	1,080	7,500 [2]

Meanwhile, Mr. Atkinson was pushing the use of the automatic sprinklers with a great deal of vigor. He arranged for practical demonstrations of the sprinklers for the benefit of the members, and had numerous reports on their operation printed and circulated among prospective users.

The board of directors of the Boston Manufacturers' Mutual Fire Insurance Company co-operated with him in bringing pressure to bear upon members to install automatics. It was voted on December 1, 1881, to increase the rates on risks not adequately protected by sprinkling or other apparatus, with the exception of those under agreement to get such protection. A year later it was voted: 'That on and after January 1, 1883, the executive officers of this company be instructed to increase rates on such risks as have not adopted adequate sprinkling as in their judgment may be equitable.'[3]

[1] *Minutes of the Board of Directors of the Boston Manufacturers' Mutual Fire Insurance Company*, November 26, 1885.
[2] French, Edward V., *op. cit.*, p. 46.
[3] *Minutes of the Board of Directors of the Boston Manufacturers' Mutual Fire Insurance Company*, December 1, 1882.

FIRE INSURANCE AND PREVENTION

In spite of these efforts, the adoption of the automatic sprinklers by the mutual risks was slow. Six years later the minutes of the board of directors again read that, 'in the opinion of the directors every effort should be made, even an advance in rates, to hasten the substitution of the automatics for perforated pipes.'[1] As a matter of fact, it was not until between 1900 and 1910 that automatic sprinkler protection among the mutual risks approximated one hundred per cent.[2]

Gradually the principal objections to the automatic sprinklers were overcome. It was demonstrated that they could be depended upon to operate, even after being installed several years, and that they could control or check fires that were of serious proportions. Members found that the costs of installation could be met to a considerable degree out of lower insurance costs.

One of the main objections made by the users to the automatic sprinklers was that they had no protection against water damage caused by the accidental opening of one of the sprinklers. In 1886, Mr. Atkinson discussed with his board of directors the possibility of insuring their risks against such danger.[3] It was found, however, that the laws of Massachusetts prohibited the mutual fire insurance companies from issuing water damage insurance policies. For a few years the plants which wished to carry such insurance took out policies with outside stock companies.

In 1895, Mr. Atkinson made a determined effort to secure a change in the State law to permit the mutual companies to issue water damage policies.[4] His efforts were successful, and in 1896 the Boston Manufacturers' Mutual Fire Insurance Company wrote its first policies against leakage damage.[5] For six years these policies were written separately from the fire insurance policies. By that time the mutual companies had had sufficient experience with the automatic sprinkler to have faith in its reliability. As a result, after 1902, full coverage from loss due to

[1] *Minutes of the Board of Directors, op. cit.*, December 26, 1888.
[2] French, Edward V., *op. cit.*, p. 121.
[3] *Minutes of the Board of Directors, op. cit.*, March 3, 1886.
[4] *Ibid.*, November 6, 1895.
[5] *Ibid.*, July 8, 1896.

leakage or breakage of sprinkler equipment was included in all fire insurance policies with no extra premium deposit.[1]

Another development in which Mr. Atkinson had a part was the adoption of the blanket type of insurance policy for the factory mutuals. During the early years, it was customary to specify each insurable item with the amount of insurance carried by each. The chief complaint against such policies is that there may be excessive insurance on one part of the plant and insufficient coverage on another.[2]

On January 29, 1880, Mr. Atkinson introduced the subject of a blanket type of insurance policy at the meeting of the board of directors of the Boston Manufacturers' Mutual Fire Insurance Company.[3] At that meeting it was voted to send this plan to the other mutual companies for consideration. At the meeting of the board in June, Mr. Atkinson presented a specific form of blanket policy which was approved, and the directors recommended that this be presented to the other companies for approval or alteration.[4] This was done and the president was able to report in September: 'that the project for a blanket form of policy was substantially adopted by all the mutuals.'[5]

The policy which was finally adopted was simple in form. Under it, all buildings, machinery and stock were covered in one item, and in case of fire the total damage was estimated and paid by the insurance companies. This form of insurance was in keeping with the spirit of the mutual companies which was to keep relations between the members and the officials of the companies as free from technicalities as possible. Mr. Atkinson expressed himself on this point:

> It may be remarked, that since the main or sole purpose of this and other factory mutual companies is to find out the exact measure of indemnity due to each member and to pay it, the technical form of

[1] French, Edward V., *op. cit.*, p. 115.
[2] *Ibid.*, p. 113.
[3] *Minutes of the Board of Directors of the Boston Manufacturers' Mutual Fire Insurance Company*, January 29, 1880.
[4] *Ibid.*, June 29, 1880.
[5] *Ibid.*, September 2, 1880.

the policy or contract is of little moment. In ninety-nine cases out of a hundred each member would be as safe under a record made on his own and on the books of the insurance company without the execution of any policy of insurance as he is with it. The writer can recall but one instance of a reference to the technical phrases of the contract having been required in making the settlement of a loss. There have been a few instances of reference to the substance of the contract rather than to the form in order to find out under what head the building injured had been listed. Now and then a loss has occurred in an outside building which the owners assumed to be included in the policy of which the underwriters had no knowledge. In such cases we have been reluctantly obliged to decline paying the loss.[1]

It is not to be expected that Mr. Atkinson would confine his efforts toward eliminating fire hazards within the confines of the factory mutuals. He possessed far too much public spirit and zeal not to try to secure a widespread adoption of fire prevention and control principles throughout the general community.

One fact which was of deep concern to Mr. Atkinson was that the principles of slow-burning construction and the other methods of eliminating fire hazards, used so successfully by the members of the factory mutuals, were not generally adopted by architects and engineers in the planning and construction of buildings of all kinds.[2] He saw no reason, for example, why beauty of design and maximum safety from the danger of fire should not be combined in the same structure. Yet it seemed to him that had architects deliberately set out to design buildings which would ignite and burn with a maximum of efficiency, they could not have improved upon many of the structures already in existence. He wrote:

> We burn nearly two hotels every day in the United States. We destroy one hospital, asylum, or almshouse, by fire every two weeks,

[1] Atkinson, Edward, *op. cit.*, pp. 56–57.

[2] In a letter, dated March 1, 1902, sent to the clients of the Boston Manufacturers' Mutual Fire Insurance Company, Mr. Atkinson wrote in part, 'The only drawback to the interest and satisfaction which I have enjoyed in the development of our own system of preventing loss, and in the evolution of an applied science almost without our being really conscious of it, has been in witnessing the bad faults in construction and occupancy outside our own field — in witnessing the constant and continued practice of combustible architecture, almost always at a much higher cost for the buildings than would have been incurred if safe methods had been adopted; lastly, the toleration of dangers in occupancy almost criminal in the carelessness implied.'

customarily with the loss of one or more lives. Some of our Massachusetts public buildings are among the most costly and dangerous examples of this art of combustible architecture. In them hundreds of incapable persons are now exposed to danger. Aside from public buildings, I know of large buildings in some of which fires are certain to occur, and in which a greater or less loss of life is equally sure to follow, if these fires occur in the daytime. I have been myself threatened with suits for damages for pointing out some of these dangers to the proper authorities. I know very well that in many cases these dangers are not due to any unwillingness of the owners to avoid them by proper measures. They are mainly due to the incapacity of those to whom the owners have delegated the work of planning and constructing the buildings.[1]

To aid in changing this situation, Mr. Atkinson proposed that a Department of Insurance Engineering be established at Massachusetts Institute of Technology, which would have the double function of teaching the knowledge already acquired, and, more important, would develop through tests and experiments advanced principles to be followed in the practice of fire prevention and improved building construction.[2]

The Institute, however, was in no position financially to undertake this work without a sufficient endowment. Accordingly, Mr. Atkinson set out, in the early part of 1902, to raise funds for this purpose. He appealed to members of the factory mutual companies, to stock companies, and others who, he thought, might be interested in the project. But as the accumulation of funds from these sources was slow, it was decided to begin upon a limited number of experiments in order to demonstrate what could be done with such a plan. The result was the organization in the latter part of 1902 of the Insurance Engineering Experiment Station, under the general supervision of the Boston Manufacturers' Mutual Fire Insurance Company, with

[1] Letter written by Mr. Atkinson to the *Boston Herald*, dated March 8, 1888.
[2] Attention should be drawn to the fact that the Associated Factory Mutuals Fire Insurance Companies had in 1890 established laboratories in connection with their inspection department. The work done in these laboratories, however, was confined to testing devices of immediate concern to their clients. Mr. Atkinson proposed that the department of insurance engineering which he sought to establish should carry out its work on a broader scale, not limited by the immediate exigencies or interests of the clients of the insurance companies.

FIRE INSURANCE AND PREVENTION

Mr. Atkinson as director, and Professor Charles L. Norton, of the Massachusetts Institute of Technology, in charge of experiments.[1]

The work done by this organization covered an interesting group of subjects, most of which had a significance far beyond the immediate concern of the fire insurance companies.[2]

This was true, for example, of experiments upon 'fireproof' wood, as a result of which experiments, it was demonstrated that the claims for these materials were largely specious, and an end was put to a small industry which had been profiting by the credulity of uninformed buyers.

Also included among the reports of the Experiment Station was one on *The Diffusion of Light*. This report supplemented and brought down to date the results of experiments made a few years previous to the inception of the Experiment Station. In 1883, Mr. Atkinson had visited some English cotton mills which were using rough plate glass in their windows and skylights. He was interested to learn that this type of glass improved the lighting within the mills. Upon his return, Mr. Atkinson caused experiments to be made upon the amount and effectiveness of light transmitted by various kinds of window-panes. The result of these tests was that a type of glass known as 'factory-ribbed' was developed and used extensively throughout the textile mills of the time. The work, thus begun at Mr. Atkinson's suggestion, inaugurated in the United States the use of indirect illumination. This system has since become important in factories, schoolrooms, libraries, etc.

Experiments were also made by Professor Norton upon the corrosion of steel, a subject which was assuming considerable im-

---

[1] The Station had no official connection with Massachusetts Institute of Technology, although much of the work was done there.

[2] The following is a list of the reports issued by the Insurance Engineering Station between 1902 and 1904; No. 1, Fireproof Wood — So-Called. No. 2, Sound-proof Partitions. No. 3, Wired Glass — Diffusion of Light. No. 4, Corrosion of Steel. No. 5, Slow-burning or Mill Construction. No. 6, Mud Fuel, Coke, Gas. No. 7, Fire-resistant Roofs for Foundries and Machine Shops. No. 8, Diffusion of Light. No. 9, Second Laboratory Report on Corrosion of Steel. No. 10, Test of Columbian Fireproof Construction. No. 11, Fire and Heat Resistance of Luxfer Prism Glass Electro-glazed. No. 12, Bog Fuel, Coke, Gas and Secondary Products of Gas.

portance because of the increasing use of reinforced concrete building construction.[1]

Although the Experiment Station demonstrated what could be accomplished by such an organization, and the results were of real value to those who sponsored it, Mr. Atkinson was unable to interest enough persons to make the project self-sustaining, and the work was abandoned after 1903. The incident is indicative, however, of the keen interest which he took in the problems connected with improved building construction and fire-prevention.

Mr. Atkinson used various other methods in his attempts to awaken the consciousness of the public to the importance of adopting safeguards against fire. He would call attention to specific fire hazards, sometimes communicating directly with the owners or the proper officials, and sometimes by the use of the public press. He took a particular interest in the construction and safeguarding of public buildings such as hospitals, churches and the like. One interesting practice which he followed in this connection was to write to the officers of any colleges or universities which had suffered a fire loss, recommending to them the principles of slow burning construction and adoption of fire prevention methods in any reconstruction. A letter typical of this practice was written to the President of the Case Scientific School in Cleveland, Ohio, and read as follows:

> I observe with regret that you have met with a heavy loss. It is probably due to the fact that your building may have been a complete example of combustible architecture. I trust you will not think me officious in sending you a treatise upon construction in order that you

---

[1] One of the most interesting series of tests made by the Experiment Station had no connection with building construction or the prevention of fire. These were the experiments made to show the possibility of securing a cheap supply of fuel from the marshes and swamps of New England in a form which Mr. Atkinson called bog or mud fuel. The occasion for this study was a coal strike in 1902 which raised the price of coal sufficient to make an alternate supply of fuel of interest. It was found by experiment that a satisfactory type of fuel could be had by drying and compressing the ordinary black mud underlying the ordinary fresh water meadows. Although Mr. Atkinson vigorously pushed the idea of the immediate practicability of utilizing this fuel, he was unable to interest anyone in taking up the idea commercially in view of the cheapness of coal and alternative fuels. Should the price of fuel rise sharply at some future time, however, this supply may be of real importance.

FIRE INSURANCE AND PREVENTION 125

may avoid the dangers to which almost all such buildings are exposed from their very faulty construction.

I am myself a director in the Massachusetts Institute of Technology, and our last large building was constructed wholly in accordance with the principles laid down in the address which I now send you. It is considered a model of economy and fitness for its purpose.

There are some lessons which we have learned in the construction of this building which would be useful to you in the construction of your own. I might suggest a visit and a consideration of these plans. There are several architects who are thoroughly familiar with them, notably, Messr. Peabody and Stearns, and also Messrs. Shepley, Coolidge, and Rutan, successors to H. H. Richardson.

I have no personal interest in the matter other than that of an anti-combustion missionary. All our methods are well known to the managers of the Brush Electric Light Company of your city.[1]

Among the specific buildings which were criticized by Mr. Atkinson as being especially susceptible to danger from fire were Faneuil Hall in Boston and Memorial Hall in Cambridge. In a letter addressed to the editor of the *Boston Post* and dated February 14, 1890, he explained the hazards of Faneuil as follows:

I next visited Faneuil Hall, to which the so-called fire-escape corresponding to those now on many of our four-story school-houses has been attached. This fire-escape consists of a series of small platforms one above another, attached to one window on each story of the school-houses. On Faneuil Hall there are four on each side of the building, and two at one end. There is a hole in the bottom of this platform through which one person can pass at a time, provided a vertical ladder is ready for use. This vertical ladder, about one foot wide, folds into an iron case shaped like a U, from which it must be unfolded before it can be used. When examined two or three years ago, many of these ladders were found rusted in. They are liable to be frozen at any time; and those which are attached to the school-houses *are locked in with a padlock at the bottom!*

The 'Cradle of our Liberty,' Faneuil Hall, is occupied in the basement and on the first floor for dangerous purposes — the sale of greasy provisions; a single spit-box filled with sawdust into which a little grease may fall at any time, may set the historic building on fire any night, by spontaneous combustion. A few greasy rags in a drawer

[1] October 28, 1886. As a result of such a recommendation sent to Amherst, he received the following reply from Julius Seelye: 'Accept my thanks for yours of the 17th inst., with the interesting documents which you have had the goodness to forward me. I appreciate the wisdom of your utterance, and trust that our farther buildings of this college at least will not be wasted efforts.' April 18, 1882.

opened but a crack, may do the work of the incendiary. Neither of these floors is protected with automatic sprinklers, as they ought to be without delay. All persons are familiar with the outlet from the main Hall and from the galleries of this building. A large audience might escape by the stairways if there were no panic. But *if* fire-escapes are needed, these worthless attachments which I have described are not entitled to the name.

His efforts in respect to making this building safer evidently had some results, for in 1891 he wrote: 'after many years' work, with such support as I could give [Faneuil Hall], has at length been made partially safe.'[1]

In a letter to President Eliot of Harvard University, dated July 10, 1889, Mr. Atkinson wrote the following in regard to Memorial Hall:

> You once consulted me about protecting Memorial Hall from the danger of fire. You are now subject to another danger which affects the building in two different ways. The processes of cooking are hazardous not only on the property itself, but from the greasy materials which may gather in by-places, liable to spontaneous combustion. I should recommend you to have the whole cooking department protected with automatic sprinklers.

On occasion his zeal in calling attention to fire hazards got Mr. Atkinson into difficulties. One particular instance arose over a building erected by Jordan Marsh Company in Boston. This structure, a storage or annex building, was built at the corner of Bedford and Kingston Streets. Mr. Atkinson noticed what he considered unsafe construction methods being utilized in its construction, and accordingly wrote to Mayor Green of Boston outlining his criticisms:

> This note is not a pleasant one to write, and must be considered confidential unless it becomes necessary to cite me as a witness in a case which may make trouble if my fears are correct.
> Jordan, Marsh and Company are putting up a very large building on the corner of Kingston and Bedford Streets. I intend to caution the members of my family not to pass by that building lest it should fall and crush them. The girders over the second-story window, 18 feet between the posts, at least 21 feet on centres, are composed of *cast-iron*,

---

[1] Atkinson, Edward, *Prevention of Loss by Fire*, pp. 66-67.

FIRE INSURANCE AND PREVENTION

a treacherous material at best — the material which caused the terrible accident on the Gay Bridge; — a material which is being given up by all contractors and engineers who are fit to be trusted, where any great transverse strain comes upon it.

Upon these girders granite is being piled three or four stories high; and the construction of the floors is such that the ends of floor timbers of at least 24 feet span will rest upon the same support. I have a tolerably true eye — and I think the girder on the corner is already sprung, but it may be my imagination.

The building may stand so long as it is not exposed to heat; but the heat which will be generated by a small proportion of the probable contents of the second floor will make these cast-iron girders utterly unsafe.

I have no doubt the building is consistent with the Acts; the plans must have passed the supervision of the inspector of buildings.

It is not pleasant to interfere with the work of people with whom I am in such pleasant relations as I am with the owners. I can see no way except to present this case to you, trusting to your good judgment in the matter.

It would be better for me to be condemned as officious and meddlesome, than to have a bad accident when it is too late to apply the remedy.[1]

Later he elaborated upon his original criticisms as follows:

First, in case a small fire should occur on the second floor, the heat will attack the cast iron girders, which being unprotected will give way before a very moderate fire. When one yields, the thrust of the floor joist will throw the wall across the street.

Second, the bearing of the wooden girders which sustained the floor joist upon the post is insufficient — the material on which the girder rests is cast iron which is treacherous.

Third, the want of any stay or brace in any part of the building, taken in connection with the danger of the fracture of the cast iron girder over the windows, renders a very complete destruction possible from the giving way of a single post or the fracture of a single girder.[2]

The building was found to be within the terms of the building laws and nothing could be done to prevent its construction. Meanwhile, the architect, Mr. Samuel Thayer, threatened to bring suit for damages to his personal reputation against Mr. Atkinson. After some correspondence during which Mr. Atkin-

[1] April 27, 1882.
[2] Letter to Mayor Green, May 8, 1882.

son flatly refused to make any apology for his action, the matter was dropped.[1]

Some years later, Mr. Atkinson's judgment in respect to this construction was vindicated, for it was in this building that a disastrous fire originated on November 28, 1889, which swept through a considerable portion of the business district of Boston. A current newspaper account of the fire read:

> The largest fire which Boston has seen since the great disaster of 1872, broke out at 8.20 A.M. yesterday in the splendid block on the corner of Kingston and Bedford Streets, owned by F. L. Ames and occupied by Brown, Durrell and Company, and several minor concerns. For five hours the flames raged fiercely, and it was 1 o'clock before confidence was felt that it would spread no further. Twenty buildings, the majority of them large granite and freestone structures of modern build, were destroyed.
>
> The scenes about the fire were replete with excitement and activity. The police department was prompt in roping off the streets and keeping back the crowd, leaving ample room for the firemen. On every corner engines puffed and rumbled and emitted torrents of black smoke, while hose lines by the score lay in a twisted, tangled web up and down the streets for blocks on all sides of the fire. The territory bounded by Kingston, Bedford and Chauncy streets was the principal theatre of destruction, and here the conflagration levelled everything. Within an hour after the first alarm sounded, the whole structure of Brown, Durrell and Company's building collapsed with a tremendous crash. The flames were darting from doors and windows, and the interior of the block was a glowing furnace. The dry goods and other combustible materials, with which the floors were packed, burned to a white heat, granite crumbled and iron girders melted away like ice. The streams from the engines were dissipated in vapor before they touched the fire. Suddenly the cry arose 'The walls are falling! Back, back!' The crowd surged back for their very lives, startled by the shout. Firemen dropped their nozzles and ran to save their apparatus. Great gaps opened in the walls and the bricks from the cornices dropped into the street with ominous clatter....
>
> The lofty walls of the blazing building were tottering and the men were compelled to flee. There was a confused and deafening roar and a dense cloud of smoke and dust mounted heavenward. When it cleared away the luxurious palace of trade had vanished, only a fantastic heap of bricks, shattered stone, twisted iron beams and broken columns marking the site.[2]

[1] Cf. Letter from Mr. Atkinson to Samuel Thayer, July 29, 1882.
[2] *Boston Daily Advertiser*, November 29, 1889.

FIRE INSURANCE AND PREVENTION

The action of the fire upon the walls of the structure (at this time known as the Ames Building), and their subsequent collapse, show that Mr. Atkinson's predictions were well founded.

About 1884, Mr. Atkinson helped initiate a drive to secure adequate fire escapes for the public schools of Boston. Unfortunately, the result was the adoption by the city authorities of a ladder arrangement considered by fire authorities as wholly inadequate.[1]

Accordingly, in 1888, he again began a campaign to get a more adequate type of fire escape installed on the schools, proposing outside stairways similar to those used upon the most modern factory buildings of the time.[2] But his efforts were not successful. In spite of repeated attempts made over a period of almost two decades, he was unable to secure the desired improvements. In 1900 he described his difficulties:

> For many years I sought a remedy by appealing, year after year, to each new mayor, new school committee or other board which might be assumed to take cognizance of this subject. There were at one time nine public and private boards, committees or authorities taking supervision of this and other subjects connected with the schools. Each rejected all responsibility for existing conditions and put the charge of the remedy upon the other, the mayor turning it over to one body, the school committee to another, the inspector of buildings to another, but all disclaiming any power or responsibility in the matter. These conditions have remained the same for about twenty years. I sent one of my young men an hour ago to some of these schoolhouses, and there he found this so-called fire escape in position, in one the padlock rusted and the janitor condemning it as utterly worthless, himself unable to unlock the ladder.[3]

After some years' experience with fire commissions, building restriction, and public apathy, Mr. Atkinson decided that more drastic methods should be adopted to secure a more general use of fire-resistant construction and fire-prevention technique. To insure the adoption of these principles, he proposed to hold the owners and lessees of buildings liable for any damages from fire

---
[1] This device is described *ante*, p. 125.
[2] Cf. letter to *Boston Herald*, May 16, 1888.
[3] Atkinson, Edward, *Prevention of Loss by Fire*, p. 66.

that could be traced to negligence either in construction or failure to adopt proper safeguards against such a danger:

> I have pondered over this subject in many anxious and some sleepless hours. I can find but one remedy, and that is to hold the owners and lessees of every building liable for damages for every loss of life or injury to persons which happens in the property owned or occupied by them. Four-fifths of all the fires, in my judgment and that of my coadjutors, some of whom have had longer experience than myself in providing for the safety of factories, are due to stupidity, negligence, carelessness, or crime; less to actual crime than is commonly believed.
>
> Four-fifths of the losses by fire are, in our judgment, some one person's fault, and that person must be held responsible if the loss is to be saved. Those who are thus held liable can then combine to insure themselves from such avoidable losses by means of prevention. The agency may be a simple, inexpensive Landlords' Liability Insurance Company. I know that this can be done. There is no theory in the matter. Every man connected with the prevention of loss by fire in factories knows how it can be done.
>
> These remedies will not be applied until the owner or occupant of every building, in which loss of life or injury to person happens, is held in money damages for permitting avoidable dangers to exist. These faults may not be remedied until the owner, occupant, architect, and builder, by whom these costly and homicidal buildings are constructed or occupied, shall be held to trial by public opinion in open court, with a published inquest of the Fire Marshal as to the original cause of the injury to the building or the loss of life. The original cause lies back of the mere accident in which the particular fire originates, in the negligence of those who should be responsible to prepare for such accidents and have not done so....
>
> Mere building acts do not suffice; they can be, and are evaded. The only building act which will serve the purpose is to make the owner of the building understand that this loss of life by fire or injury to person is, in nine cases out of ten, due to causes *for which he himself and he only is responsible.* When this becomes a part of the common knowledge of the public, as well as of the owners, the hazard to life, if not to property, may be removed at a small cost by very simple precautions.[1]

Another public danger which Mr. Atkinson sought to avert was the spread of fires in the crowded business and warehouse districts of large cities. Once started, such fires easily assumed large proportions, and the history of practically every large city

---

[1] Letter to the editor of the *Boston Sunday Herald*, March 8, 1888.

FIRE INSURANCE AND PREVENTION

contains its 'great fires' which have caused serious loss of life and tremendous property damage. One of the greatest difficulties in the way of checking such conflagrations once they have started, comes from an inadequate water supply or pressure resulting from an abnormal drain upon available sources.

It was this problem that Mr. Atkinson proposed to overcome by providing buildings in such crowded districts with water supplies independent of the city water mains. The sources of these independent supplies were to be wells or connections with harbors, if the latter were available. A steam pump or pumps would provide pressure to boost this water to the roofs where it would be distributed through a series of hydrants arranged in such a way that each building could be protected from all four sides. With the pressure available, each building could be protected and considerable aid given to adjacent structures in checking the spread of fire.

Experience in large factory cities had proved the practicability of Mr. Atkinson's plan. On numerous occasions, fires had started in these cities which would have been very serious but for the aid which each mill could extend to the others in the form of fire apparatus and from roof hydrants.[1]

In co-operation with Mr. William B. Whiting, Mr. Atkinson wrote a report on the subject of roof hydrants in 1882, which was issued to members of the Boston Manufacturers' Mutual Fire Insurance Company, and others, in the form of a circular. Later he reported the following in regard to the adoption of the principles involved:

> The subject of roof hydrants of large capacity to be supplied by powerful stationary steam pumps, drawing water where possible from a separate source than the city pipes, was held to be of prime importance. Shortly after we were consulted by the owners of one of the largest warehouses in New York. A system of roof hydrants, supplied by a powerful steam pump, was there established under the direction of Mr. Whiting. Within a short time a destructive fire, which caused a loss of about four million dollars ($4,000,000), threatened this establishment. There was little doubt that the roof hydrants, throw-

[1] Cf. Atkinson, Edward, *op. cit.*, p. 21.

ing streams across a narrow, intervening street and over one of the buildings in the block on fire which was but little injured, prevented the advance of a fire under a high wind and probably saved a very extensive conflagration. In the recent very destructive fire in Philadelphia, we find another instance, and I may quote from a circular and letter issued by Henry W. Brown and Company, insurance agents, under date of January 10, as follows:

> 'It seems reasonable opinion that this threatening conflagration was limited to the area destroyed, and prevented from becoming a widespread disaster involving many millions of dollars chiefly through the instrumentality of a "Roof Fire Service," consisting of a powerful fire pump in a safe vault under the sidewalk, supplying a system of six large hydrants located upon the roof of the store of Messrs. Lit Brothers, by whom it was established upon the advice and suggestion of our firm, just in time to render its signal and powerful aid.'

In a private note to myself, Mr. Brown says of this report: 'I think it will interest you, especially as I owe the idea entirely to you. It is the first time I have ever seen it applied, and there is no doubt that it saved this city a vast conflagration. The attack upon the heart of the fire from the vantage point was irresistible.'

In one other very destructive conflagration, three private pumps working through private standpipes and hydrants from different levels unquestionably stopped the spread of a very threatening conflagration which had already burned over several acres of most valuable property. All these systems had been established mainly at the instance of this company, although in premises which we could not insure.[1]

It was Mr. Atkinson's opinion that the principles of mutual insurance could and should be much more widely adopted. He felt that churches, theaters, college buildings and the like might well be insured by companies organized along the lines of the factory mutuals. For example, he wrote to the President of the University of Tennessee, Dr. C. W. Dabney:

> I have yours of the 18th and wish I could help you. I have often wished that I were young enough to get up a mutual company for the protection of college buildings and schoolhouses. The factory mutual companies would not be permitted by their charters or by their policy to take them in. The destruction of buildings like that in Pennsylvania the other day, with libraries and contents that cannot be replaced, is dreadful; a useless sacrifice to the ignorant practice of com-

---

[1] Atkinson, Edward, *op. cit.*, pp. 22–23.

bustible architecture. Why don't you, being a comparatively idle man! nothing much to do! take up the subject and combine colleges for mutual prevention of loss by fire?[1]

In some respects it is difficult to measure with any degree of accuracy the contributions which Mr. Atkinson made to the fields of fire insurance and fire prevention. Especially is this true of his influence outside the sphere of the factory mutuals. General changes in such a field are the result of too many influences to gauge accurately the part played by one individual. There can be little doubt, however, that his influence was considerable in securing a more widespread adoption of safer building construction and better fire protection.

His leadership within the factory mutual organization can be appraised with much more certainty. Enough evidence has been given to show that he was quick to recognize the possibilities of new ideas and had an important part in many of the major developments adopted by the Associated Factory Mutuals during the period between 1880 and the time of his death in 1905.

Under his presidency, the Boston Manufacturers' Mutual Fire Insurance Company increased its business (insurance written and in force) from $43,166,718 in 1878 to $228,007,966 in 1905, while at the same time lowering the net premium cost of insurance per one hundred dollars from approximately 25 cents to a little less than 7 cents.[2]

---

[1] January 22, 1898. Cf. also a letter on Church Insurance to the editor of the *Daily Commercial Bulletin*, November 8, 1889.

[2] *Annual Report of Boston Manufacturers' Mutual Fire Insurance Company*, 1931, pp. 10–12.

CHAPTER V

MONEY, THE TARIFF, AGRICULTURE, THE NEW SOUTH
1880–1892

HAD Mr. Atkinson been able to follow his natural inclinations and desires after 1880, he would probably have devoted his entire time to writing, speaking, and working on questions of general public interest. But, as president of a large fire insurance company, his activities in this public nature were limited by the pressure of his duties and the nature of his private office. In spite of these limitations, he showed an interest in an amazing variety of subjects, and took an active part in some of the most important political and economic questions of the day.

Politically, Mr. Atkinson's interests were largely confined to a few of the major questions of the time, especially to those subjects which had to do with the tariff and monetary controversies. In his political affiliations, he remained an Independent, and cast his influence on the side of the principles and men in which he had faith. The election of James A. Garfield as President in 1880 was a source of great satisfaction to Mr. Atkinson. The two men had been associated in earlier tariff discussions and had kept up a friendly correspondence for a number of years. Mr. Atkinson wrote to the President-elect on December 2: 'I feel the most sincere personal as well as public interest in your success. You have the opportunity to place yourself where Lincoln or Andrew would stand if they were in your place.'

The assassination of the President was a severe shock to Mr. Atkinson, who felt keenly the loss of his friend from whom he had expected so much.

During President Arthur's term of office there was considerable agitation on the part of certain tariff reformers to make an attempt to secure lower import duties. David A. Wells and Charles Nordhoff and others were eager to make a fight on this issue, and they wanted Mr. Atkinson's active support in the

Boston Dec 2. 1880

Dear Garfield

Since my Atlanta speech I have been urged by some of the most prominent republicans here and elsewhere, to write you at length on the true method of breaking the solid south into fragments—

These men belong as I do to the independent and anti-stalwart wing, who wait your message to find out their own future place.

I know how you must be bored and harassed and I shall not assume to be an adviser, unless after you have read the speech, you shall give me leave

I feel the most sincere personal as well as public interest in your success You have the opportunity to place yourself where Lincoln or Andrew would stand if they were either one in your place

Your friend Edw Atkinson

struggle. This Mr. Atkinson refused to give for several reasons. In the first place, he felt that tariff reform was inevitable. No longer was there any question as to whether tariff reform was needed, the questions of importance were, when and how should reform take place.[1] Necessary tariff changes, he thought, would come from the industrial interests themselves, and he looked upon the appointment of the Tariff Commission of 1882 as an important indication of this movement. In addition, Mr. Atkinson had always opposed any sudden change in tariff legislation, and he feared that agitation for reform at this time would result in revisions which would work an injury to industrial interests.[2]

Again, his position as president of the Boston Manufacturers' Mutual Fire Insurance Company made his public participation in tariff controversies undesirable. Many of the members of his company were opposed to tariff reduction, and they felt that his statements, while president, carried the implied sanction and approval of his business associates. This limitation was at times irksome to Mr. Atkinson, although it fitted in with his belief that his greatest service would consist in quietly influencing leaders on both sides of the tariff controversy in such a way as to secure a 'judicious' and orderly adjustment in the movement which he thought inevitable.

A final reason for his refusal to enter the tariff struggle, especially in the early 'eighties, was the conviction that other questions were of more immediate importance. On this point he wrote to David A. Wells, December 31, 1883: '*Surplus* and *Silver* are our two great causes of danger and the tariff is *secondary*. The reduction in the rates of tariff should have begun long since — to make any reductions *now* which will decrease the actual customs revenues in any sufficient measure to affect the surplus would be very dangerous for the time being.'

---

[1] 'As a question of principle, it [tariff] no longer interests me — the intellectual fight is over. As a question of methods of reductions, I am not under obligations to make a personal sacrifice of time or health.' Letter to David A. Wells, January, 1883.

[2] The large surplus revenue of the time offered a strong argument for the reduction of internal taxes and revenue duties, and if the tariff issue were brought into prominence, the proponents of free trade, he thought, might succeed too well.

Mr. Atkinson's advice to let the situation rest between 1881 and 1883, pending settlement of the more important questions of the day, brought upon him the condemnation of many of his former associates in the tariff reform movement, and he was viewed by some as having deserted the cause.

In line with his determination to give the proper direction to the inevitable tariff reform movement, Mr. Atkinson quietly worked out a plan during the latter part of 1882, based on the general policy followed by Sir Robert Peel in effecting the tariff reform in England. This, he hoped, would appeal to the 'reasonable men' on both sides of the free-trade question. He wrote to William Morrison:

> What I am endeavoring to do is this — to suggest to you and others on the free trade side a plan of action consistent throughout, and directed toward a free trade policy as rapidly as circumstances ought to permit you or anyone else to go in that direction.
>
> As you will observe from the tables, the theory of this policy is to enlarge the free list immediately on all crude articles, articles of food, fuel, and timber; to add to the free list a large number of miscellaneous articles on which the duties do not pay the cost of collection; to treat chemicals, ores, raw flax, and other so-called raw materials by successive reductions of twenty per cent (20%) each until they are also made free five years hence; and to treat what are commonly called manufactures by successive reductions until the rates are brought down to an average not less than twenty-five per cent (25%), ranging from fifteen per cent on commmon or coarse articles, up to forty per cent on fine articles and on articles of fashion and fancy.[1]

Whereas both Morrison and Wells were inclined to favor this general policy, any sanguine hopes Mr. Atkinson may have had concerning the other side were destroyed when he presented his ideas to some of his associates. As much as they might prefer lower duties on raw materials and other products going into their manufacturing process (such as machinery), they did not think such a plan could pass in Congress for the reason that the representatives from many of the regions which were most urgent in their requests for reductions on manufactures, would block cor-

[1] December 28, 1882.

responding reductions on raw materials originating in those same regions.

As a result of this objection, Mr. Atkinson withdrew his plan for the time being. It was, however, the basis of most of his subsequent recommendations and activities upon the subject, and as such deserves special note at this point.

Forced into temporary inactivity in respect to the tariff, Mr. Atkinson found his political and economic interests aroused by the question of railroad regulation, which was attracting a good deal of attention at the time. The intensive railroad competition, particularly in the 'seventies, had shown a very unsatisfactory condition in respect to railroad rates and regulations, and proposals were being made for national legislation on the question.

Mr. Atkinson was much opposed to such legislation, legislation which he termed as 'meddlesome.' His objections were fundamentally those of a person who believed in the adequacy of competition as a means of securing the proper conduct of business. His main point in arguing on the subject was to show that railroad rates had been reduced tremendously since the Civil War, evidence which controverted, he thought, the claims of unreasonable or excessive rates. The claim of discriminatory rates he lightly dismissed by calling upon his own experiences in shipping cotton, in which he had had no difficulty in getting satisfactory rate adjustments.

These ideas found expression in an article entitled, 'The Railroad and the Farmer,' printed in *The Journal of the American Agricultural Association* on April 1, 1881. The article was most acceptable to those opposed to railroad regulation, and it was widely distributed in pamphlet form by various railroad executives.[1] In the subsequent discussion on the subject, Mr. Atkinson maintained a position in opposition to regulation. In December, 1886, and early January, 1887, he provided ammunition for the opponents, in and out of Congress, of the Interstate Commerce Act. The passage of the Act called forth the following: 'As

---

[1] Mr. Atkinson estimated that about 32,000 copies of this article were thus distributed. Letter to Theodore F. Lees, October 7, 1884.

the bill was to pass, it is lucky that it is so ambiguous as to be inoperative. Alas! Alas! with what foolishness we are said to be governed.'[1]

Mr. Atkinson took no active part in the subsequent political events of President Arthur's term. He did, however, grow more and more dissatisfied with the general policies of the Republicans, and the Presidential election of 1884 found him ranked with the 'Mugwumps.' He looked upon the election of Cleveland as an important step toward the rejuvenation of the Democratic party. To William Fowler he wrote: 'You are right in assuming that I was greatly opposed to the Democratic Party, so long as it sustained slavery, but a transmutation is in progress. The Republican Party has become corrupt and has become the chief support of an exorbitant tariff and of an intolerant system of protection, while the new South, permeated by new industries and new interests, is becoming truly Democratic, and therefore entitled to full consideration.... Philosophically speaking, I am a radical Democrat, and I therefore welcome the reconstruction of the Democratic Party on right principles.'[2]

The subsequent developments during President Cleveland's first term ended Mr. Atkinson's comparative inactivity in respect to national politics, and from that time until his death, over twenty years later, there was scarcely a time when he was not actively participating in the agitation relative to some major piece of legislation, or was not working to influence public opinion on some question of general interest.

It is not unexpected that the revival of the silver question between 1884 and 1887 should have been the event which brought Mr. Atkinson back into actual politics. As already noted, he looked upon this question as one of the most important of the day, and whereas he had encountered much opposition among his associates on the tariff, any support he might give to sound money would secure practically unanimous approval from this same group.

[1] Letter to H. V. Poor, January 15, 1887.
[2] December 15, 1884.

MONEY, THE TARIFF, AGRICULTURE 139

The condition which was causing the immediate concern of those who had worked for gold-specie resumption and who favored its maintenance, arose out of the operations of the Bland-Allison Act. It was thought by the framers of this act that silver dollars would be popular for hand-to-hand circulation. But the heavy dollars were not popular, and began to make their way into the Treasury in increasing amounts, with the consequent loss to the Treasury of other kinds of money. Hugh McCulloch, who served as Secretary of the Treasury during the last few months of President Arthur's Administration, expressed the fear in December, 1884, that gold payments might be endangered.[1]

In a letter to the Secretary of the Treasury, dated February 16, 1885, Mr. Atkinson suggested a remedy for the situation:

> I venture to protest against any further purchase or coinage of silver dollars on the part of the Secretary of the Treasury, until the obscurities and uncertainties of the Act to authorize the coinage of silver dollars shall have been corrected, amended, or removed by further legislation. Vide Chapter 20, 1878.
>
> This Act instructs the Secretary of the Treasury 'To purchase, from time to time, silver bullion at the market price thereof, not less than two million dollars' worth per month, nor more than four million dollars' worth per month, and cause the same to be coined monthly, as fast as so purchased, into such dollars.'
>
> The obscurities of the Act, which may render it inoperative and therefore unsafe for the Secretary of the Treasury to put into force without further legislation, are as follows:
>
> First, you are charged to purchase two million dollars' worth of bullion at its market price, but the Act does not define the standard by which you are to be guided, and there are two kinds of lawful dollars now in use in this country. One kind of dollar is made of gold. Another kind is made of silver. The quantity of bullion purchasable in the gold kind is much greater than the quantity purchasable in the silver kind. If the gold kind is used, the Secretary may exceed the purchase contemplated by law.
>
> Second, after such purchase of two million dollars' worth of silver bullion has been made, the Secretary is ordered to cause it to be coined into '*such*' dollars. The word 'such' is so used in this context that it may refer to the description of the silver dollar which is recited at the

[1] Noyes, A. D., *Forty Years of American Finance*, p. 103.

beginning of the Act, or it may refer to such dollars as have been made use of in making the purchase of bullion. The latter is apparently the true construction, and in such case, if gold dollars have been used in making such purchase, *such* dollars cannot be made of silver; or if gold dollars' *worth* has been expended, then the silver dollar coined from the bullion must be greatly increased in weight in order that it may be '*such*' a dollar as is contemplated in the Act.

In the construction of the Act, it must be assumed that Congress intended to authorize two kinds of dollars of equal value, as any other construction would impute a fraudulent debasement of the coinage, to the legislative department.

I, therefore, beg to present the matter for your consideration. Not being of the legal profession, I am not aware of the steps necessary for a citizen to take, in order to procure a legal adjudication upon an obscure or doubtful statute. May I ask if a Secretary of the Treasury can be enjoined from taking action by any proceedings in court, and thereby be caused to suspend action until alleged faults may either be overruled or cured by legislation?

A personal note accompanying the official letter is illuminating:

> Robert J. Walker once said to me that the first quality needed in a Secretary of the Treasury was 'to find law for what was necessary to be done.' By the same rule, why should not a Secretary find a *flaw* in a law for what is necessary to be done? If you suspend coinage before March 4, the present Congress cannot get at you, and it would be very unsuitable for your successor to begin coinage again until the legal point had been adjusted.[1]

Secretary McCulloch did not concur in Mr. Atkinson's interpretation of the law. He answered on this point: 'I regret that it is not in my power to suspend the coinage of silver, but there is no flaw in the statute, and it must be obeyed. Congress alone can undo what it most unwisely did.'[2]

Unable to get action upon the alleged obscurities in the Bland-Allison Act, Mr. Atkinson let the question drop for the time. In July, 1885, he felt that the matter was on the road to settlement. 'Under the vigorous leadership of the present most excellent and admirable Administration, I have great confidence that we shall repeal the Act for silver coinage, and reach a sound and suitable

---

[1] February 16, 1885.   [2] February 18, 1885.

MONEY, THE TARIFF, AGRICULTURE

fiscal system in the ensuing session of Congress, on the basis of the gold standard.'[1]

A little later, however, Mr. Atkinson became interested in another suggestion for the solution of the silver question. This plan was to issue silver certificates (not to be confused with those which were issued), which would represent specific amounts of silver held in the Treasury. But as these certificates were not to be made legal tender, their value would fluctuate as the value of silver changed, and could not therefore endanger the security of the gold standard. This plan received support from some of his friends but did not achieve any wide popularity.[2]

The declaration of President Cleveland early in 1886 that he would not push the repeal of the Silver Purchase Act in Congress was a great disappointment to Mr. Atkinson. He looked upon it as 'a very hard blow to the opponents of silver coinage.... If he [the President] had held his tongue, the suspension of the silver coinage would have been very certain. Now it is very uncertain.'[3]

Mr. Atkinson immediately set about to mobilize the antisilver forces in an attempt to secure action both by the President and Congress. Letters to Charles Nordhoff, David A. Wells, W. C. P. Breckinridge, and others reveal the plan to circulate petitions, secure letters, etc., in opposition to the silver interests. One of the most interesting of these is a letter to Henry George suggesting that the latter should submerge his single-tax feelings for the time and work against silver. The emergency passed, however, as a result of the combined effects of the issue of silver certificates in small denominations, the withdrawal from circulation by the Treasury of small legal-tender notes, and the reduction of national bank notes through the purchase of governmental bonds, which put an end to the immediate difficulties

---

[1] Letter to Henry Carey Baird, July 29, 1885.

[2] It may be of interest, even though there is no evidence to show any direct influence of Mr. Atkinson's, that this plan was practically identical with the one suggested by Secretary of the Treasury Windom to President Harrison in 1890.

[3] Letter to Moorfield Storey, January 8, 1886.

arising from silver coinage, and suspended agitation for the time over this question.¹

In April, 1887, Mr. Atkinson was greatly honored by being appointed by the President as a special monetary commissioner for the purpose of making a study in Europe of the possibilities of international bimetallism. Mr. Atkinson spent about four months in Europe working on this commission and conferred with the principal authorities in the field.

His report, which appeared as a special Senate Document,² may be summarized as follows: First, there was no prospect of any change of the European monetary systems which would necessitate any change or modification of the financial policy of the United States. Second, there was no indication of any change of policy among the principal European states which would make them seriously consider any treaty for international bimetallism. Third, bimetallism was not seriously considered except by small groups in any of these countries. And finally, no action on international bimetallism would be taken without the concurrence of Great Britain, and in England, public opinion was not concerned with the question.

Mr. Atkinson found it commonly believed by many Europeans that the United States could flood the world with silver at a low cost and that remonetization of silver would bring about a tremendous expansion of silver production. He did not believe this to be true, and on his return from Europe, obtained letters (incorporated in his report) from mining experts and geologists confirming his opinion.

Included in the appendix, however, was probably the most important part of Mr. Atkinson's report. (The part which he predicted would be 'the tail that wagged the dog.') This was the translation of A. D. Soetbeer's *Materielen*. This report, which was translated from the German by Professor F. W. Taussig, made available in English Dr. Soetbeer's authoritative data on the world's production of gold and silver since the fifteenth century.

¹ Cf. Noyes, A. D., *Forty Years of American Finance*, pp. 105 ff.
² Fiftieth Congress, *Senate Executive Document*, no. 34, 1887.

MONEY, THE TARIFF, AGRICULTURE

Although not a part of his report, Mr. Atkinson also came to the conclusion that the future trend of the price of silver would be upward. He thought that as commerce and industry increased in the more backward parts of the world, these regions would need larger supplies of circulating media. Because of its limited supply, gold would be too expensive for the countries in these areas, and they would be forced to seek a cheaper substitute in the form of silver. In particular, he looked upon India, Africa, and South America as forming this potential market.

It was this conclusion that made it possible for Mr. Atkinson to be unconcerned, after 1887, over the coinage of silver under either the Bland-Allison Act or the Sherman Silver Purchase Act. Such an increase in the price of silver as he anticipated would make the United States' silver dollars more valuable as bullion than they were as dollars — a situation which would cause them to disappear from circulation as rapidly as they were coined.[1]

It is not to be expected that Mr. Atkinson would be content for long to play the part of a spectator in any controversies that involved the tariff. Accordingly, in spite of the opposition which he had encountered a few years before from his associates, he again took up the subject (in so far as the limitations of his office would allow) as it developed during President Cleveland's first term.

In general, Mr. Atkinson's efforts were largely directed toward an attempt to secure tariff reforms patterned after the general plan which he had suggested in 1882.[2] He had the greatest admiration for Sir Robert Peel's methods and accomplishments, and he hoped to find an American counterpart.[3] Mr. Atkinson appealed from time to time to various Congressional and political leaders to assume the rôle of the American Sir Robert Peel, and

[1] He attributed the subsequent low price of silver largely to the uncertain status of silver coinage in the United States. In his mind the possibility that the United States might at any time stop the purchase and coinage of silver and take steps to get rid of the large stock of accumulated bullion, served unduly to depress the market for this metal.

[2] Cf. *ante*, p. 136.

[3] For example, he wrote to Charles Nordhoff, May 26, 1885, 'Who is the Peel of our time? Have we an Administration capable of framing and carrying a great measure?'

was greatly disappointed when they failed to measure up to those specifications.

During the latter part of 1885, Mr. Atkinson worked to have his ideas of a broad plan for tariff reform embodied in an administrative measure which he hoped would secure the backing of the Democratic Party. His ideas were well received by some members of the Administration, and he was urged by Secretary of the Treasury Manning to confer with party leaders on the subject.[1] Mr. Atkinson went to Washington and conferred with various persons there, including Representative Samuel J. Randall, a Democrat from Pennsylvania, who was working on a tariff measure. This alignment is significant because Randall was the leader of the protectionists in the Democratic Party. It was through him that Mr. Atkinson believed an acceptable compromise measure could be evolved. To a free-trade friend he wrote:

> I have your letter of November 4. I think that nothing can stand in the way of a reasonable and judicious settlement of the tariff question, unless it be the folly of the Democratic Party in failing to arrange and sustain an administration measure. I use the word '*administration*' as distinct from a party measure, for reasons which may hereafter appear, but to which I will make no further reference.
>
> I have had two long and instructive interviews with Mr. Randall. He is an honest, earnest, and able man. He has done good service in forbidding wasteful appropriations. He had impeded partial tariff measures, pending a full discussion and determination of the whole question. All reasonable and judicious tariff reformers should be grateful to him for having impeded even the consideration of such a *bastard* measure as that proposed by Mr. Morrison, which under the name of 'horizontal reduction' was anything but horizontal. It would have brought contempt and ridicule upon the whole party, if it had been passed as it might have been had it not been stopped where it was.
>
> Mr. Randall is fully aware of the necessity of tariff reform. He is

---

[1] The following letter from Charles Nordhoff to Mr. Atkinson is of interest at this point: 'I read your letter about Randall last evening to Secretary Manning. He is much struck with it. He is convinced that the Administration ought to prepare a tariff measure, and recommend it to Congress. But he said, "I am very busy. I don't think myself able to make a bill even if I had time; I *do* wish Mr. Atkinson could come here, talk over the matter with me and with Randall more in detail, and see if they two could knock out a bill which the Administration could recommend as its own, and in which all reasonable men could agree."'

MONEY, THE TARIFF, AGRICULTURE 145

informing himself judiciously upon the subject. He is not the attorney of Pennsylvania, but he is a broad-minded man. If he is to be subjected to prejudice and relegated to a subordinate place, the opportunity for a wise tariff reform may be lost; and it will then continue to be said of the Democratic Party of the future, as it has been said of the past, that when it has the opportunity, it has not the intelligence and capacity to grasp it.[1]

Meanwhile, Mr. Morrison, Chairman of the House Ways and Means Committee, was at work preparing a new tariff measure for Congress. His earlier bill calling for a general horizontal reduction in tariff duties had not achieved any great popularity even with his own party, and he set about to frame the new bill along more acceptable lines. His first attempts at compromise drew Mr. Atkinson's scorn in no uncertain terms, because the latter thought the measure would do more harm than good, especially to the manufacturing interests.[2]

Using the early attempts of Morrison and the efforts of others to frame tariff bills as object lessons, Mr. Atkinson urged those among his protectionist friends, notably Henry Saltonstall and

[1] Letter to the Honorable C. W. Woolley, November 10, 1885.
[2] In a letter to Mr. Wells, dated February 24, 1886, he said in part:

'You say, "Why not help Colonel Morrison instead of criticizing?" I have helped Colonel Morrison to the extent of my ability, by going to Washington and causing all the imports to be sorted into five classes according to their respective kind and use, under McCulloch; next by consent of Mr. Fairchild, I have caused all the imports to be sorted for the last five years; then the imports of 1885 — with the respective revenue from each article sorted; systematized columns arranged in great books for the consideration of the matter. And these books have been used — I know they have. And with these books, I left behind me a simple and consistent method which I *know* would have been sustained by moderate protectionists here as well as by free traders, if it had been followed.

'What has happened? This bill is not more consistent than the so-called horizontal reduction of last year. The horizontal reduction stopped at the worst possible and most dangerous point — on the necessary materials used here, left them not below 1861, etc., etc. What a farce to import an old act into a new bill! This bill... will affect the woolen industry very disastrously.... It reduced the duties on goods without reducing the duties on wool. There are no words I dare use to describe such a measure.

'The free list is good as far as it goes; but it is ridiculously inadequate in any sound principle of reform. But if the reform is to be guided and controlled by deference to the wool growers, and fishermen, then I have nothing more to say. The man who defers in that way is incapable of making a true bill.... I have the kindest personal feeling toward Colonel Morrison, but I can do nothing more in the matter.... Cleveland may have erred in waiving Executive influence — but the way the Democrats are throwing away their chance on the tariff; on silver, etc., makes one sick. It is a name and not a party, no cohesion, no policy and no sense.... Kick the Democrats and quit — Let us have a small minority with the sense and pluck of the civil service men.'

Jonathan Chace, who favored moderate tariff reform, to lend their influence toward giving the proper direction to the fight for tariff reform. 'That fight is bound to come,' he wrote to Mr. Chace, 'and in my judgment is bound to succeed. I fear it will come in a destructive way unless you and all other leaders of the New England protectionists accept the position and guide the changes.'[1]

Through the influence of Mr. Wells and others, the bill which Mr. Morrison finally presented to Congress in April, 1886, met with Mr. Atkinson's approval and he urged his friends to support it as the first step toward a judicious tariff reform.[2] To offset the interests opposed to tariff revision, he proposed that a convention of manufacturers and representatives of laborers be called in Washington which would give support to this measure.[3]

Mr. Morrison's bill, however, was defeated in the House, largely through the efforts of Mr. Randall, who had failed to take the lead in tariff reform which Mr. Atkinson had hoped for. In fact, Mr. Atkinson's opinion of Mr. Randall had undergone considerable revision. To Charles Nordhoff, he wrote: 'You remember that I had two or three interviews with Randall last autumn. I was astonished at the profound ignorance of the man, of the simplest elements of the tariff question, and I supposed that he would get his inspiration from the Treasury if he did anything. Whatever he does on his own hook will be absolutely worthless. His only merit is that he has not stolen anything in the twenty-three years in Congress. I never was more disappointed in a man in my life, but I thought I had stirred up his vanity and conceit and tried to make him believe he could perform the part

---

[1] March 9, 1886.

[2] The bill as reported had a large free list including copper, lead and iron ore, coal and salt. Duties on other way materials, including wool, was lower and there were moderate decreases in the rates on manufactured goods.

[3] It may be of interest to note in this connection Mr. Atkinson's opinion on the position of the wool manufacturers: 'From what I hear of the opinion of prominent members of the Wool and Woolen Association, they want the bill, and they wish they could support it; but they are tied by their alliance of 1867 with the wool-growers. I told them at that time, when I went to Washington with Edward Harris, that they were tying a rope around their own necks with which they might be strangled at some future time.' Letter to Charles D. Owen, April 23, 1886.

MONEY, THE TARIFF, AGRICULTURE

of Sir Robert Peel. So he could if he would let somebody else do the work for him.'[1]

During the remainder of 1886, Mr. Atkinson pushed his idea of getting some united support for tariff reform along the lines he proposed, but the inability or unwillingness of Congress, coupled with the lack of co-operation, served completely to discourage him. On December 22, he wrote to David A. Wells: 'I have been to Washington, Nordhoff and I agree exactly. I am out and you had better step out and watch the condemned fools fight it out on false issues and ignorance of facts. W. C. P. Breckinridge is the only reasonable man that I met. Morrison and Beck are hopeless.'

In spite of his determination to 'let the condemned fools fight it out among themselves,' less than a year later Mr. Atkinson was again tempted to participate in the tariff fight. In October, 1887, he was asked to aid Representative Leopold Morse in the preparation of a revenue bill which would reduce revenues eighty million dollars, without any reduction of sugar tariff.

Because this method of revenue reform did not fit in with his views on the subject, Mr. Atkinson refused to help on such a bill. He was willing, however, to frame a bill along the lines which he had previously suggested, provided the New England manufacturing interests would co-operate in pushing his measure. But a brief of his proposed reforms, which was presented to the Home Market and the Arkwright Clubs, was not approved, and Mr. Atkinson felt restrained from writing the bill. He again warned his manufacturing friends that they were making a mistake by not guiding the tariff reform movement, instead of standing against it. But one of their members stated the point of view of the majority of the manufacturers when he wrote to Mr. Atkinson, 'I believe none of us is prepared to guide such a measure as you propose, and if we must be drowned out, have no inclination to let in the water.'[2]

President Cleveland's famous message to Congress in December, 1887, which definitely made the tariff the issue of the next

[1] June 22, 1887.
[2] Letter from George Dexter, November 16, 1887.

election, won the immediate approval of Mr. Atkinson. 'I think the President has chosen wisely. I believe the country is tired of parties which represent no specific policy and that it will support a brave, bold man, who has proved himself so independent in many directions, as Mr. Cleveland has proved himself.'[1]

To the President he wrote directly, 'Whatever may be the result of the pending tariff discussion, I beg to thank you for the service you have rendered in forcing the country to take up a living question in place of a dead one.'[2]

But the action and speeches on the tariff in and out of Congress during the campaign convinced Mr. Atkinson that some of his worst fears were about to be realized, as both parties seemed to take extreme positions on the question. To his friend, Jonathan Chace, who had refused to become a party to tariff reform, Mr. Atkinson wrote: 'The intolerants and doctrinaries must have their way; in the meantime the ground swell is rising and in the next Congress I think New England can hope for very little influence in stemming the tide of change. She will be relegated to the position of Mrs. Partington with her broom. While I shall stand up on the end of the dock looking down upon you with your little brooms attempting to stop the tide, and just before you disappear under the wave, I shall shout to you, "Didn't I tell you so?"'[3]

It may be of interest to note at this point one argument which was used by the free-traders, especially during this period, which made Mr. Atkinson impatient. This was the argument that the tariffs brought exorbitant profits to the protected industries. In a letter to R. R. Bawkes, he expressed himself on this point: 'I [have] become more and more disgusted with the ordinary methods which have been adopted under the lead of Professor Sumner and Professor Perry and which have been taken up by Philpot and others. The exaggerations and misrepresentations which they make in respect to the alleged effect of the tariff in this

[1] Letter to Carl Schurz, December 8, 1887.
[2] February 14, 1888.
[3] March 2, 1888.

country upon prices and profits, tend to sustain the present system, rather than to remove it, by making men greedy to share bounties which have practically ceased to exist.'[1]

As much as he would have liked to give active support to Mr. Cleveland, Mr. Atkinson was prevented because of his position from taking any prominent part in the campaign of 1888. His attitude on the result of the election was well expressed when he asked Charles Nordhoff to tell the President, 'that I congratulate him on securing a four years' interval of rest between his two terms.'[2]

The result of the election of 1888 set aside any immediate fears which Mr. Atkinson may have had concerning a 'free-trade ground swell' which would sweep away existing tariff legislation to the detriment of establishing industries. On the contrary, he felt that the Republicans might be tempted to push revenue legislation to the opposite extreme. To combat this possibility, Mr. Atkinson renewed his efforts to secure the adoption of a moderate attitude toward the question of tariff reform. One method which he followed was to lend encouragement to a group of clubs in Massachusetts known as Question Clubs. These clubs, some seventy-five in number, were organized for the purpose of securing tariff reform, and their procedure was to send a list of questions on specific subjects to Senators and Representatives. Replies or the failure to reply were given publicity in the newspapers friendly to the movement.[3] Mr. Atkinson aided these clubs by making out various lists of questions calculated to embarrass the protectionists, and by conferring with the officers

[1] October 16, 1885. An extract from a letter to an English friend is also of interest: 'One of the chief obstructions to the progress of free trade in this country is the notion that Great Britain desires us to adopt it. If you are enough of a free-trader to run the risk of the temporary harm which would come to Great Britain from its adoption, no written article would promote the change in this country more than an English article objecting to the adoption of free trade by us for the reason that it would harm Great Britain. The Carey school have inoculated the people of this country so completely with the idea that Great Britain desires free trade in order to break us down, that this is one of the chief obstructions to building ourselves up. I wish you could write such an article.' Letter to Moreton Frewen, December 21, 1885.

[2] November 17, 1888.

[3] For an account of this movement, see Mendum, Samuel W., 'The Question Clubs and the Tariff,' *North American Review*, vol. 150, no. 3, pp. 301–09.

of the clubs in respect to their policies and actions. He urged his friends to organize similar clubs throughout the country with the ultimate purpose of having a national organization through which public opinion could be quickly mobilized on questions of the day. But aside from a few clubs which were started in Pennsylvania, this effort was not successful.

Mr. Atkinson continued in his efforts to get his New England protectionist friends to adopt a more moderate point of view on tariff reform. To General W. F. Draper he wrote in November, 1899: 'The signs of the times are very ominous, and if you and your associates hold out to the bitter end you may be swamped, and you have no influence in directing the inevitable changes. I think the great mistake was made in allowing the opportunity to go by to modify and direct the form of the Mills Bill, which could have easily been done with the cordial assistance of Mills and the two Breckinridges.'[1]

Mr. Atkinson proposed that he and the General should get together for an occasional quiet meeting to agree upon a 'business-like' treatment of the subject. He and General Draper did meet on several occasions, but there is no indication that the latter changed his views in any marked degree as a result.

As Congress, late in 1889, began work upon the legislation that finally resulted in the Tariff Act of 1890, Mr. Atkinson centered his attention upon this measure, and while the bill was in the hands of committees and before Congress, worked vigorously to eliminate what were to him objectionable features. His participation, as before, was largely unofficial and *sub rosa*, and took the form of advice and suggestions to members of Congress and influential persons outside, supplemented by personal conferences both in Boston and in Washington.

At Mr. Atkinson's suggestion, Representative Roger Q. Mills visited Boston, and, with Mr. Atkinson as guide, inspected various manufacturing establishments, including the Pacific Mills at Lawrence. During this visit, Mr. Atkinson was host at a private dinner for Mr. Mills, at which a selected group of New England

[1] November 8, 1889.

MONEY, THE TARIFF, AGRICULTURE

men was present for the purpose of discussing the proposed tariff.

His correspondence between December, 1889, and October, 1890, with the chief opponents of the McKinley Bill, including Representatives J. G. Carlisle, William L. Wilson, C. R. Breckinridge, W. C. P. Breckinridge, Roger Q. Mills, and Senators J. R. McPherson and Z. B. Vance, shows that Mr. Atkinson kept in close touch with the progress of the Tariff Act through Congress, and contributed a substantial share of the ammunition used against the measure.

There was little in the McKinley Bill which pleased Mr. Atkinson. The maintenance of the rates on iron and iron ore, and the higher duties on wool, were directly contrary to Mr. Atkinson's plan for low tariff rates upon raw and partially manufactured products.[1] But it was the proposal to raise the rates on tin-plate in order to start an industry in the United States which was at the time non-existent that exemplified to Mr. Atkinson the very worst features of protectionism. Even if it were true, as the advocates of this measure maintained, that the foreign price of tin-plate would rise directly proportioned to the remission of duties, Mr. Atkinson was doubtful if the tin industry was one which we wanted to foster in the United States. 'It is a nasty, unwholesome work, which foreign paupers had better be left to do for us where they are, so long as they are willing to do it; we don't want them here.'[2]

Furthermore, according to Mr. Atkinson, a rise in the foreign price of tin-plate would put the United States upon more nearly equal competitive basis with the foreign producers of products utilizing tin-plate. Mr. Atkinson tried especially to convince Senator Dawes of Massachusetts of the inadvisability of voting for the tin-plate duties. But the latter refused to become a convert to Mr. Atkinson's point of view. He wrote to Mr. Atkinson, 'The idea that the consumer of tinned plate in this country will be better off if he lets the foreign producer fix the price

---

[1] *Ante*, p. 136.
[2] To Senator H. L. Dawes, February 11, 1890.

for him than he will be if the price is fixed at home, is an idea to which I have not as yet been able to accede.'[1]

Mr. Atkinson was also perturbed at the growing influence in the Republican Party of William McKinley. 'It seems to me that the old party which I esteemed so much in former days has committed political suicide by making McKinley its leader.'[2]

In another letter he wrote: 'I think Mr. McKinley himself is honest, but incapable of reasoning.... The whole Administration, including Congress on the Republican side, is below any reasonable standard of intelligence; absolute intellectual mediocrity or worse; worse where insincerity and dishonesty take the place of intellectual mediocrity.'[3]

At the time the Tariff Act was before the House, Mr. Atkinson gave Representative Mills some interesting advice: 'Your fight has begun. I do not suppose you can defeat the McKinley Bill, and if you cannot defeat it I should vote, if I were in your place, for every additional duty, and put every article possible *out* of the free list upon the dutiable list. Load it down.'[4] It is clear that Mr. Atkinson hoped that the bill would be so 'loaded down' that it could be easily 'sunk' at a later date.

The high rates proposed under the McKinley Bill were causing some concern and dissension in the ranks of the New England manufacturers. Mr. Atkinson saw in this situation another opportunity to push an insurrection among the protectionists. His center of attack was the Home Market Club. He proposed to several of the members that they hold a series of private conferences; 'to consult together what action can be taken to prevent this destructive measure [McKinley Bill] from becoming a law.'[5]

But a series of conferences were again unproductive of results and he was forced to admit in June, 1890, 'that the proposed rebellion, or Republican break here has fallen flat.'[6]

---

[1] To Mr. Atkinson from Senator Dawes, February 8, 1890.
[2] Letter to Senator Dawes, February 5, 1890.
[3] Letter to F. W. Cheney, April 1, 1890.
[4] May 7, 1890.
[5] Letter to F. W. Breed, May 22, 1890.
[6] Letter to J. G. Carlisle, June 9, 1890.

MONEY, THE TARIFF, AGRICULTURE 153

But he was not discouraged. In a letter to Horace White, dated June 20, 1890, he spoke of 'the crowd of timid manufacturers whom I am slowly and surely leading over to the right side, while many of them are not aware how fast they are going.'

Incidentally, Mr. Wells looked upon these efforts of Mr. Atkinson to safeguard the interests of the New England manufacturers and to direct them in the 'right' direction on tariff as being a thankless task. He wrote, 'What have you ever gained, but kicks, for all your attempts to save Boston protectionists from their folly?'[1]

During the time when the McKinley Bill was before the Senate, Mr. Atkinson was particularly active. He wrote a steady stream of letters, principally to Senators J. R. McPherson and J. G. Carlisle (appointed to the Senate in May, 1890), making suggestions and giving data for speeches. In September, when it looked as if the bill would be pushed through with all its objectionable (to Mr. Atkinson) features, he strongly recommended that the measure be held up in the Senate until after the Congressional election in November. He thought that if the Tariff Act were still pending at that time, such a strong protest vote would be registered that it would be necessary to make a thorough revision of the measure before it could become a law.

This maneuver, however, failed and the bill became a law in October, 1890.[2] In so far as the subsequent elections in November may be considered as registering a 'protest vote,' Mr. Atkinson's prophecy seemed to be well founded, for the Democrats swept the Congressional elections that year.[3]

To Mr. Atkinson the sweeping victory of the Democrats in the Congressional election of 1890 possessed inherent dangers; 'I would have much preferred that the Democratic Party had attained a small majority of twenty or thirty in the House. There

[1] From Mr. Wells, September 19, 1890.

[2] To Senator McPherson, Mr. Atkinson wrote, in part, on September 29, 1890: 'Perhaps this culmination was inevitable — you fought a good fight, of which the end is not yet.'

[3] In the Fifty-First Congress, which voted for the McKinley Bill, the Republicans had a majority of seven in the House. In the Fifty-Second Congress there were 236 Democratic and 88 Republican Representatives. Tarbell, Ida M., *The Tariff in Our Times*, p. 210.

is a great danger now of an ignorant rush to change existing conditions. I have laid all my lines with a view of becoming a force for the control and direction of financial legislation through the conservative men in the Democratic Party, who all have confidence in me. I think the time has come when independent men in both parties may be called upon to combine their influence and give direction to necessary reform.'[1]

To offset the danger of precipitate action on tariff, he urged the appointment by the Democrats of a committee, 'to the number of perhaps ten from different sections of the country, *who may consult the advocates of Tariff reform and the manufacturers whose industry is to be affected by the same,* and who may review the whole subject preparing a careful digest of expenditures and receipts for the last ten years, and preparing the way for a full and complete measure of internal and external taxation.'[2] This appointment was to be made in December, 1890, to prepare the way for tariff reform in the Fifty-Second Congress.

His friends among the Democratic leaders, however, did not share his fear of sudden action on the tariff, and thought that the next Congress would deal in a 'cautious and conservative manner' with the subject, and that no committee was needed to make a further study of the situation.[3]

The McKinley Bill had scarcely been passed when the silver question, which had lain practically dormant since the discussion over the Bland-Allison Act, again challenged public attention. The passage of the Sherman Silver Purchase Act in July, 1890, was made possible through the co-operation of certain anti-silver members of Congress, who feared a less satisfactory bill might be passed if they did not agree to the compromise. But the silver interests were far from satisfied, and in December, 1890, began a determined effort to secure free silver.[4]

[1] To Benjamin Butterworth, November 8, 1890.
[2] To Representative William L. Wilson, November 19, 1890.
[3] Cf. letter from William L. Wilson, December 2, 1890.
[4] Cf. Dewey, D. R., *National Problems,* pp. 220 ff. (*The American Nation,* vol. 24, A.B. Hart, editor.)

MONEY, THE TARIFF, AGRICULTURE

Mr. Atkinson had not felt any concern about silver since the early part of President Arthur's term and, as a result of his investigation as silver commissioner, had come to the conclusion that the growing demand for silver in South American and African countries would solve the problems arising from coinage under the Bland Act.[1] The passage of the Sherman Act did not cause him any anxiety for the same reason.

But Mr. Atkinson looked upon any attempts to bring about free coinage of silver under a bimetallic standard, unless in cooperation with European countries, as being most ill-advised. Such action, he felt, would lead to great uncertainty in respect to our money and credit system, and would probably bring about economic disaster. He therefore set out in December to offset what seemed to him to be an unwise movement.

In a letter to *Bradstreet's*, published June 21, 1890, he discussed the relative importance of the quantity of credit and the quantity of money upon the price level. Admitting a partial indebtedness to Macleod for the basis of his argument, Mr. Atkinson opined that credit, being a multiple (not a fixed ratio, however) of the quantity of money, is a much more important factor in the regulation of the price level.

With the quality of money firmly established, he thought that the quantity of credit would adjust itself to the commercial and industrial needs of the country. But should the quality of money be subject to question as it would be under the uncertainties of free silver coinage, confidence, upon which credit is issued, would be impaired with the result that credit would be greatly contracted. For this reason, he predicted that the remonetization of silver would cause an immediate fall in prices instead of the rise expected by the advocates of free silver.[2]

In an address before the Boston Boot and Shoe Club, December 17, 1890, he expanded these ideas and suggested that a new type of bank note be authorized in order to give flexibility to the

[1] *Ante*, p. 143.
[2] He did not consider the possibility of enough silver coinage to offset the decrease in credit, nor does he discuss the velocity of either money or credit.

monetary system. He would authorize banks in each of the several districts to organize a clearing-house. After depositing commercial paper as security with the clearing-house, the banks would be allowed to issue demand notes, backed by the security, and guaranteed by the clearing-house. Thus a flexible element would be added to the monetary system, for the volume of these notes would vary directly with an increase in the business activities of the community.[1]

Mr. Atkinson's avowed purpose in publishing this series of letters was to influence the 'responsible leaders of the Democratic Party. It is through their conversion between now and December, 1891, that we shall be saved from free coinage of silver.'[2]

To an objection of Horace White that his plan called for an additional type of currency which would be added to an already complicated monetary system, Mr. Atkinson replied, 'If we do not provide another safe kind of currency, there will be provided for us other very unsafe kinds, and who knows how many sorts?'[3]

Mr. Atkinson was zealous in getting his ideas brought to the attention of influential leaders in both parties, and he supplemented his letters in *Bradstreet's* with articles in other publications. But, although the plan created considerable discussion and some favorable comments among the anti-silver interests, he could secure no united, influential support for his project.

Mr. Atkinson placed the responsibility for the free silver agitation on the Republicans. On January 9, 1891, he summarized the situation for Mr. Cleveland:

> I think the demand for free coinage of silver both in the West and the East is a noisy, superficial, and ignorant call for that which will do great injury....
> The free coinage of silver in the United States at the present standard of sixteen to one is condemned alike by every intelligent student of the currency within my knowledge, whether bi-metallist or mono-metallist. I think it will promote a disaster or a panic such as we have

---

[1] The reader will note a certain similarity between this plan and the present method of issuing Federal Reserve Notes under the Federal Reserve System.
[2] To A. C. Stevens, December 4, 1890.
[3] December 24, 1890.

never seen, if it should pass. I think that the conditions are as follows:

For the purpose of passing a Force Bill the Republicans have admitted into the Senate the Senators from the so-called 'rotten borough States'; the new States, which all combined have hardly enough population for two Representatives, but which are represented in the Senate, ten or twelve Senators, who hold the balance of power. They have sold out the Republicans on the Force Bill for the purpose of gaining a benefit to the silver mines. The Republicans have now waived their right of objection to taking a vote, and have waived further debate, in order that, having been sold themselves, they may give the Democrats in the Senate the opportunity to *sell out their own party!* deprive it of the support of Independent votes, and risk, if not throw away, every chance of carrying any Eastern State. The Democrats have the field on the platform which originated with your reform and reduction of the tariff. That might have been kept the sole issue. It should be if it can be. If the Democratic Party now commits itself to the free coinage of silver, the stigma and responsibility will be removed from the Republican Party; it will be taken over by the Democratic Party, and they will lose the East without getting the West. I think the solid sense of the West is now against free coinage as it was against the greenback.[1]

He put the position of the Independents, who were at the time ranked with the Democrats, as follows: 'If they [the Democrats] are going wrong on the money question, I, and plenty more of my kind, will join any other set of men, whatever party they belong to, and help them to break the Democrats and crush them into powder; as they ought to be crushed if they behave like fools.'[2]

In early January, 1891, when the Senate seemed about to pass a free-silver measure, Mr. Atkinson suggested to Republican Senators Sherman, Aldrich, and Dawes that they form a coalition with certain Democratic Senators in order to defeat the proposition. To Senator Dawes, he wrote: 'The time has come when each and every man, and all men who desire to sustain the public interest without respect to party, may combine, split both parties on this issue and accept the result in the next election, whatever they may be. Have you and others a sufficient sense of the responsibility and duty which now falls upon you to join in

[1] To the Honorable Grover Cleveland.
[2] Letter to Edmund Hudson, January 3, 1891.

making this association with Democratic Senators? That is the test by which you are about to be judged.'[1]

Although Senator Dawes was impressed by the grave seriousness of the situation, he declined to co-operate on the grounds that an 'attempt to improve the currency by joining the Democrats has in it all the wisdom of the man who burns down his house to kill the rats in it.'[2] Nor was Mr. Atkinson more successful with Senator Sherman or Senator Aldrich.[3]

In letters and articles, Mr. Atkinson pointed out the possible dangers which would come to the South under free coinage of silver. Chief among these, according to him, was the probable cessation of the movement of capital into that region due to uncertainty in respect to the monetary standard. He saw a second danger in the probable fluctuation of prices of such export articles as cotton and timber, etc., which occur under a silver standard, and, finally, whereas the 'prudent men as well as speculators and gamblers' will look out for themselves, the small farmer and 'the laborer, whose wages are the last to rise, in view of the new conditions, will suffer most.'[4]

On January 14, the Senate passed a free-coinage bill. This act galvanized the opponents of silver into action. In Boston, for example, a large public meeting was held in Faneuil Hall, on January 21, to protest against free silver. At this meeting Mr. Atkinson spoke and was elected as a member of a committee which was instructed to go to Washington to work against the acceptance of the Senate measure by the House.

He worked with his committee in characteristic fashion. He sent a series of telegrams to various anti-silver men throughout the West, urging written and personal testimony from them against the Senate bill. The response, which showed that there was considerable sentiment in that section against free silver,

[1] January 7, 1891.
[2] Letter to Mr. Atkinson, January 5, 1891.
[3] Senator Aldrich declined to be drawn into the fight because he expected soon to retire from politics. There is no reason given for Senator Sherman, or any record of an answer.
[4] From a letter to *The Manufacturers' Record*, January 12, 1891.

was, in Mr. Atkinson's mind, an important factor in the final defeat of the free-silver measure.

He thought, however, that the real danger point was passed at a conference which he had with the Chairman of the Committee on Coinage of the House. He described this conference: 'The Chairman made the appointment, and having a legal mind, he very judiciously invited also one of the principle advocates of free coinage. He [the Chairman] was on the fence, doubtful about his duty, very conscientious. He kept myself and my opponent for a long evening. I felt perfectly sure that I had made my case, and presently so it appeared. There were three other men in the same boat with the Chairman, honestly doubtful. I carried them with him and in the test vote joining the four positive anti-silver men, decided the question by a vote of eight to five.'[1]

Whatever may have been Mr. Atkinson's influence, the Coinage Committee of the House reported the Senate bill adversely, and further action on silver was temporarily postponed.

Ex-President Cleveland's public statement that unlimited, independent free coinage of silver was 'a dangerous reckless experiment,'[2] was reassuring to Mr. Atkinson. It prompted him to comment to David A. Wells: 'Had he [Cleveland] not spoken on the silver question, he might have been nominated, but would have been defeated. Having spoken, he will be nominated and will be elected.'[3]

During the period between February, 1891, and the Presidential election in November a year later, Mr. Atkinson kept up his vigorous attacks on the silver interests, making speeches, writing articles, suggesting various plans to put business contracts on a gold basis, and assisting his allies in the fight.[4]

---

[1] Letter to Charles Nordhoff, August 24, 1891.
[2] Cleveland, *Writings and Speeches* (Parker edition), p. 374.
[3] February 13, 1891.
[4] One of the numerous plans which he advocated was contained in a proposed bill which he urged Mr. Cleveland to support. The plan included the following points: First, all contracts made after the Act should be payable in gold dollars unless otherwise specified. Second, all outstanding contracts should be payable in dollars which were legal tender at the time of their execution. Third, the coinage of silver bullion under the then existing standard should be stopped, and the volume of dollars already coined not contracted, but

In October, 1891, Mr. Atkinson thought the free silver was safely passed.[1] But his confidence was short-lived. The organization of the new Congress in December soon showed that the silver question was far from being a dead issue. Not only were several attempts to repeal the Sherman Purchase Act successfully opposed by the silver interests, but it seemed for a while that they might secure the passage in the Senate during March, 1892, of the Bland Act, which provided for free coinage of silver.[2]

As might be expected, these developments were very disturbing to Mr. Atkinson. He had tried unsuccessfully to persuade the new Speaker of the House, Charles J. Crisp, to appoint W. L. Wilson as head of the Coinage Committee. He wrote to Speaker Crisp: 'If William L. Wilson were placed at the head of the Coinage Committee, confidence would be given to the whole business community, and credit would be re-established. If Bland is put there, the very reverse will occur.'[3]

At the same time, he urged Representative Harter of Ohio, with whom he had co-operated closely on tariff reform, to support John Sherman for the Senate on an anti-silver platform, with the understanding that Mr. Sherman in return would take an active part in later tariff reform. He concluded his appeal by

---

kept in circulation and convertible into gold. Finally, he proposed the free coinage of silver into dollars which were 'to be made use of in all contracts or agreements in which silver dollars were specified,' but not otherwise. If possible such dollars should be coined at a ratio which would make the bullion content high enough that they would disappear from circulation, 'yet the coinage would be perfectly free.' Obviously such a plan would not appeal to the silver interests who would achieve a hollow victory in the 'free' coinage of silver dollars which would not possess legal-tender qualities, and which, if coined, would probably have less value as dollars than they would as bullion. In presenting this plan, Mr. Atkinson stated: 'I think there is something in this conception, even for practical purposes; but at any rate, its discussion brings out most conspicuously the separate and distinct purpose of the representatives of the silver miners as compared to those who, owning no silver mines, yet think there ought to be a greater abundance of money made of silver.' Letter to Grover Cleveland, February 19, 1891. This idea, although not important in itself, is an indication of the policy which Mr. Atkinson followed, of not missing any opportunity which might be utilized against the silver interests.

[1] He wrote to Mr. Wells on October 1: 'I think we can see the end of our work; it is within sight on the election of '92. It is manifest that each party will try to make capital of the other on the silver question, by the positive method in which each may declare their purpose to maintain silver at a par with gold.'

[2] Dewey, D. R., *op. cit.*, p. 233.

[3] December 22, 1891.

saying: 'The leaders of both the existing organizations are corrupt and unfit to be trusted. It is time to throw off their malignant control by an organization that will sweep them out of existence if it is managed rightly.'[1]

While the Bland Bill was under discussion in Congress, he expanded this idea of a new organization. He proposed, some time before the regular party conventions, to call a meeting of the Independents who favored sound money, tariff reform and civil service reform. This convention would not select a Presidential candidate, but would stand ready to oppose the party which failed to subscribe to their principles. Such a move, he thought, would insure the selection of Cleveland on a platform of sound money as the Democratic candidate, and would keep the Republicans in line on the tariff question. But as the excitement engendered by the Bland Bill began to subside, and it seemed more certain that Cleveland would be nominated, Mr. Atkinson no longer felt that the need was urgent for a third party.[2]

Mr. Atkinson took little part in the Presidential campaign of 1892. As there was little doubt that with Cleveland as a candidate the Democrats would sweep the country on the tariff issue, he took this occasion to leave, early in July, for a three months' vacation trip to Europe, which, he thought, among its other benefits, would keep him out of the campaign.

The substantial victory of the Democrats in the election again made Mr. Atkinson apprehensive lest the 'free-trade groundswell' had at last arrived, with its inherent dangers to the manufacturing interests which had been built up under the influence of the McKinley tariff. His efforts to secure, under the new Administration, the 'moderate and judicious' reform of the tariff

---

[1] December 24, 1891.

[2] So intensely did Mr. Atkinson work on the silver fight that he was compelled to take a short vacation in early April, 1892. The measure of his interest and the nature of his work on the silver question is well shown by an answer he gave at this time to a request that he deliver a lecture: 'I must beg off from any new lecture or address this spring. The silver question has interested me intensely, and you can have little idea of the amount of work that I have been called upon to do by members of Congress, editors, and others, so that I have been burning my candle at both ends for a while. Please excuse me this time.' To Colonel Charles W. Lippitt, March 31, 1892.

along the lines he had so long advocated, will, however, form a part of the subsequent chapter.

Mr. Atkinson by no means confined his political interests between 1890 and 1892 to the subjects of monetary and tariff reform. For example, one topic which greatly intrigued him was the proposal, made by himself, that the United States should buy the territory included in the Maritime Provinces (New Brunswick, Nova Scotia, and Prince Edward Island) from Canada in order to eliminate the recurrent friction over the knotty question of fishing rights. It was at this time (1887) that the relations between England and the United States were particularly strained over this question, and it seemed for a short period that war might result. Proponents of friendly relations between the two countries were trying to seek a more pacific method of settlement.

Mr. Atkinson made his suggestion while he was in England in the summer of 1887 studying the possibilities of international bimetallism.[1] The occasion was a meeting of the British Society for the Advancement of Science at which Mr. Atkinson was present as a guest of honor. In answer to a query as to what solution he would offer to the fisheries problem, Mr. Atkinson made the somewhat startling reply indicated above. He did not expect that his statement would be taken as anything but 'another scream of the American eagle,' but the serious attention which was given to his answer by the group present, made him think that some use might be made of the idea.

Accordingly, he took immediate steps to see that his plan received publicity and sent letters outlining his proposals to several American and Canadian newspapers. The response showed a keen interest in the matter, although the annexation features were not accepted as being wholly advisable or practical. The editor of the *Albert Maple Leaf*, a newspaper published at Albert, New Brunswick, wrote to Mr. Atkinson on this point: 'I do not altogether believe in annexation *only as alternative*. What I would like to see is full reciprocity between the countries, or commercial union. To take up your proposition too strongly at

---

[1] *Ante*, p. 142.

MONEY, THE TARIFF, AGRICULTURE

this moment would be likely to seriously impede the progress now being made by Mr. Wilman and others — in this country — in the way of commercial union.'[1]

Mr. Atkinson personally soon abandoned any hope that actual annexation was possible, but kept the agitation going as long as possible with the goal of close economic union in mind. He expressed himself privately on this point: 'If such a solution [annexation] of this question is impractical, nevertheless its consideration in this cannot fail to bring this fact into conspicuous notice; that the larger part of the benefits named may be secured by treaty, without annexation either by purchase or otherwise.'[2]

With this point in mind, Mr. Atkinson lent his support to the various proposals to settle the fisheries problem by a removal of trade restrictions between Canada and the United States, especially those upon the importation of Canadian fish into the United States. He looked upon the violent objections of the New England Congressmen to this plan as being wholly inconsiderate of the interests of the consumers of fish products. But letters to Senator Jonathan Chace and Senator Dawes and to others were ineffective, and his interest in the matter waned as the trouble with Canada on this point gradually subsided due to changed conditions in the fishing industry.[3]

It should not be supposed that all of Mr. Atkinson's interests outside of his business were confined to political questions. Cotton, scientific experiments, agriculture and a large number of other subjects attracted his attention, and were the objects of more or less extended treatment.

One of the most interesting of these had its beginning at the same meeting of the British Society for Advancement of Science just referred to in connection with Mr. Atkinson's proposal to buy the Maritime Provinces. In the course of a speech before that body on the subject of silver, Mr. Atkinson alluded to the fact that the lowered cost of railroad transportation, and of

---

[1] November 16, 1887.
[2] To F. B. Thurber, November 19, 1887.
[3] Dewey, D. R., *op. cit.*, p. 117.

growing wheat in the United States, would make it unprofitable for the British to attempt to grow wheat in England on any extensive scale. To use Mr. Atkinson's words: 'Our farmers [can] make as good a profit with wheat at 34 shillings per quarter in Mark Lane, as they did a few years since when the quotation was 50 shillings.'[1]

This statement was looked upon by English critics and newspapers as another example of 'American spread-eagleism.' The London correspondent of *Bradstreet's*, Mr. William E. Bear, wrote a series of articles in that publication characterizing Mr. Atkinson's remarks as amusing. Other critics were of the opinion that the low price of wheat was throwing most of the Western farmers into bankruptcy. This was a challenge which Mr. Atkinson accepted eagerly, and upon his return from Europe, he began an investigation to verify his estimate of wheat costs, and to discover the status of farm mortgages in the wheat-growing area.

After getting costs of growing wheat from various regions, he began to feel that his early estimates were too conservative. Information from several large mortgage companies doing business in the wheat-growing districts also seemed to confirm his opinion that the wheat farmers as a whole were not suffering from the lower price of wheat, and that it might be accepted as being permanently at a lower level.

Mr. Atkinson prepared a report based on his data, and sent it to the London *Times* in February, 1888. He hoped that it would be a '*coup-de-grâce*' to his opponents on the question. The *Times*, however, refused to publish Mr. Atkinson's articles, much to his disappointment and annoyance, especially as that paper had been one of his severest critics.

Accordingly, Mr. Atkinson had to content himself by addressing a series of letters on the subject to *Bradstreet's*.[2] These letters, four in number, took up the most important of the several

---

[1] Letter to *Bradstreet's*, May 14, 1889. The difference per bushel represented by these figures would be as between 85 cents and $1.25.

[2] Volume XVI, March 3, May 5, September 22, 1888.

objections made to Mr. Atkinson's original statements by his British critics. The first point which he sought to sustain was that the cost of transporting grain had been substantially and permanently lowered during the previous decade and a half. He computed that the cost of shipping one bushel of wheat from Chicago to Liverpool had been reduced a total of 37 cents between 1870–72 and 1887, of which 26 cents was saved on railroad freight charges alone.

He next pointed out that the costs of production had been greatly reduced by the extensive use of improved machinery both in cultivation and harvesting and in handling the crop at terminals. He received some particularly striking figures from the so-called 'bonanza' wheat farmers of the Northwest and California. Estimates from the most successful of these gave the cost of growing wheat at approximately 40 cents per bushel.

He summarized these results in the following table.[1]

SAVING, PER QUARTER, ON THE COST OF RAISING, HANDLING, AND SHIPPING WHEAT FROM CHICAGO TO EASTERN PORTS

Reduction of railway charge	7 shillings
Reduction on planting and reaping	2 shillings
Reduction on handling and elevating	1 shilling
Reduction in milling, etc.	2 shillings
Minimum reduction on cost of wheat without ocean charges	12 shillings

In terms of cost per bushel this would represent a reduction of approximately 36 cents. Ocean freights had been lowered about 8 cents, bringing the total savings on the cost of a bushel of wheat delivered in Liverpool, in 1887, to 44 cents under the cost in 1872. From these data, Mr. Atkinson concluded that his original statement that the farmers could make as good a profit at 85 cents per bushel delivered in London as they could at the former price of $1.25, had been substantiated.

In respect to the charge that the low price of wheat was forcing many wheat farmers into bankruptcy, Mr. Atkinson's conclusions were of a more general nature. A study of information

[1] *Bradstreet's*, March 3, 1888.

received from large farm mortgage companies and other sources, convinced him that the mortgage burden was not excessive, and on the whole the Western farmers were in a sound and prosperous condition.

Admitting that his conclusions regarding mortgages might be subject to criticism, it is safe to say that Mr. Atkinson's general thesis was correct, namely, that the costs of producing and transporting wheat had been greatly reduced in the period under consideration, and that it would no longer pay the British to grow wheat domestically on any large scale. To the extent that Mr. Atkinson called attention during the 'seventies and 'eighties to this significant trend toward lowered production and transportation costs, not only of wheat but of other staple agricultural crops as well, he may be said to have rendered a real service as a contemporary economic historian.

Another of Mr. Atkinson's most significant contributions of a non-political nature had to do with the economic development of the 'new South.' As has been noted in an earlier chapter, he was generally recognized during the war and post-war period as an authority on cotton, both in respect to its manufacture and its influence upon the South. His withdrawal from the manufacturing field did not diminish his early enthusiasm for the subject; on the contrary, it continued to be a topic of absorbing interest to him throughout his life.

Before proceeding directly to a discussion of the part he played in Southern development after 1880, it will be necessary to give a résumé of his activities in connection with the New England Cotton Manufacturers' Association.

Mr. Atkinson became a member of this organization when he was still treasurer of several cotton mills. He retained his membership after becoming president of the Boston Manufacturers' Mutual Fire Insurance Company because of his interest in the aims of the Association, and because it offered an excellent opportunity for him to spread the doctrine of fire prevention.

Between 1876 and 1883, the members of this Association were especially concerned with the poor quality and bad condition of the cotton they were getting from the South. It was poorly ginned and all too often the bales included dirt and other foreign matter for which the mills paid the regular cotton price.[1]

Various suggestions were made to improve this condition, including plans to ship seed cotton north for ginning, the establishment of central ginneries in the North or South, the identification of the shippers by tags on the bales, etc. One plan which received the sanction of the membership was to carry out a campaign of education among the planters in order to demonstrate that it was to their own best interests to improve the quality and handling of the cotton.

Mr. Atkinson was an enthusiastic supporter of this plan, and in 1880 he worked to put it into execution. In a letter to the *New York Herald*, dated August 10, he outlined the complaints of the cotton manufacturers, and in addition expressed the opinion that the South was not aware of the opportunities which were available to improve the quality of the cotton both in its culture and its preparation for the manufacturers. To overcome this situation, he proposed 'a great exposition exclusively devoted to cotton,' which should be held at some point convenient to planters and manufacturers alike.

His letter attracted immediate attention and was extensively reprinted with favorable comments.[2] Interest centered chiefly in his suggestion to hold an exposition devoted to cotton, and several groups interested in Southern economic development began to sponsor the idea. Meanwhile, Mr. Atkinson followed up his original communication with letters addressed to other papers and to friends throughout the South, expanding the ideas already noted.

Encouraged by the interest shown, he made a trip in October through the cotton States, in part to extend his knowledge of the region and in part to promote the educational work already begun.

---

[1] Cf. *Proceedings of the New England Cotton Manufacturing Association*, volumes 22–31 especially.

[2] For example, the leading article of *The Textile Record* in its initial issue in September, 1880, was a reprint of Mr. Atkinson's letter accompanied by favorable comments taken from the *Philadelphia Public Ledger*.

The highlight of his trip was an amazingly frank and daring speech which he made at Atlanta, Georgia, on August 20, 1880. Speaking in the State Senate Chamber before an audience made up chiefly of business men of Atlanta and State officials, he called attention to their ignorance of the resources of the South, to the lack of advanced methods in agriculture, and to the opportunities which existed for development, ending with an eloquent plea for an economic and political union with the North that should transcend sectionalism and party prejudices. In the course of his speech, he strongly recommended that the plans (then in a tentative form) to hold the Cotton Exposition in Atlanta be carried out, and gave some specific suggestions in respect to the nature of the exhibits, the construction of the buildings and similar subjects.

This speech stimulated action on the plans for the Exposition. A number of prominent Atlanta citizens, aided by a small group drawn from other centers, formed a committee to carry out the project. The date of opening was set tentatively for October 1, 1881.

Once started, the project moved forward rapidly to completion. Enthusiastic support came from both the North and the South and sufficient funds were soon raised to make certain its financial support.[1]

Mr. Atkinson accepted a place on the executive committee of the Exposition, and during the time when the plans were taking final form, kept in constant communication with the various persons connected with its management. In addition to giving advice upon the proper construction of the Exposition buildings and suggesting names of individuals who would assist in making the event a success, Mr. Atkinson made a number of other contributions which were very important. At his suggestion the scope of the Exposition was broadened to include exhibits of all Southern products instead of being restricted to cotton. He was active in

---

[1] General Sherman started the Northern subscriptions with $2000. Cf. *Charleston News and Courier*, March 8, May 3, 1881, quoted by Mitchell, Broadus, *The Rise of Cotton Mills in the South*, p. 123.

getting exhibits of machinery connected with the cotton-seed oil industry, and also secured the installation of silos and ensilage equipment at the Exposition. Finally, he prevailed upon the committee to secure what proved to be one of the most interesting of all the exhibits. This was a demonstration of the methods of hand weaving and spinning still being used at that time in the remoter mountainous regions of the South. In contrast with the most modern machine methods of spinning and weaving also displayed at the Exposition, this exhibit showed the striking advances made in cotton manufacturing.[1]

The International Cotton Exhibition was opened with appropriate ceremonies, October 5, 1881. Mr. Atkinson attended a few weeks later as a member of the official delegation from the New England Cotton Manufacturers' Association, and both he and his fellow members were received as honored guests. Mr. Atkinson personally received full credit and praise for first suggesting the affair, and for his later share in making it a success.[2]

It is no exaggeration to say that the International Cotton Exposition was one of the most important events in Southern economic history. Southern post-war industrial development had already begun to show itself,[3] and the Exposition came at the proper time to give a sharp impetus to this movement. One authority has said of it: 'The new statesmen of the South, industrially and not politically minded, found voice. Hints and hopes became certainties. "When the Atlanta Exposition closed... it began to be realized that the South was awakened to a new life. ... Intelligence was to take the place of ignorance in methods of cultivation; machinery was to take the place of exporting raw material and bringing back the manufactured article.... Capital

---

[1] To Mr. Atkinson probably should go credit for first introducing the soy bean into the South. He personally ordered several bags of the beans from China which were distributed during the course of the Exposition.

[2] As an expression of appreciation of Mr. Atkinson's interest in the South, he was elected in September, 1881, as an honorary member of The Society of Ex-Confederate Soldiers.

[3] Mitchell, Broadus, *op. cit.*, p. 123.

began to see the rich rewards waiting to be won, and prepared to occupy the vantage-ground.'" [1]

Another writer, a few years later, commented: 'One of the most important events in the history of Atlanta, and perhaps the most far-reaching in its beneficial results to the entire South, was the International Cotton Exhibition of 1881.... Novel and valuable agriculture processes, side by side with weighty economic theories, were demonstrated and, through the agency of the press spread broadcast. Its potent effect for good has been felt throughout the South, and from it has sprung the most important factors in the wonderful material development of the last decade.' [2]

Atlanta was amply rewarded for holding the Exposition. Not only were the promoters able to repay the original subscriptions, but the city experienced a rapid industrial growth, for immediately following the event, 'two cotton mills began operations, one in the Exposition Building itself; plow works were greatly enlarged; a cotton-seed cleaner company increased output; bridge builders extended their business; a cotton compress was erected; a company to manufacture a cotton planter commenced building; a cotton-seed oil mill was erected and other enterprises went forward.' [3]

With the important exception of the growth of cotton manufacturing, Mr. Atkinson anticipated most of the economic progress which was made after 1881. In an article written prior to the Exposition, he outlined several specific developments which he expected to follow from the Exposition. In addition to the improvement in the preparation of cotton, he expected that there would be an improvement in the types of tools and implements used by the Southern agriculturists, that more advanced

---

[1] Mitchell, Broadus, *op. cit.*, p. 124. Mr. Mitchell quotes from the *Baltimore Journal of Commerce and Manufacturers' Record*, July 15, 1882.

[2] Reed, Wallace P., *History of Atlanta, Georgia*, pp. 472, 475.

[3] Mitchell, Broadus, *op. cit.*, pp. 124–25. Also he quotes the *Baltimore Journal of Commerce and Manufacturers' Record*, September 20, 1882: 'In six months after the exhibition closed, $2,000,000 had been invested in manufacturing enterprises in that city of only 40,000 inhabitants, all of which was directly traceable to the exhibition.'

methods would be utilized in the treatment of all crops, especially tobacco, rice and sugar; that ensilage would be extensively used as food for cattle and other domestic animals; and that cotton seed would become an important source of oil, cattle food, and other products.[1] He also anticipated to a considerable degree the subsequent advances in the Southern mining and metallurgy industries.

On the other hand, one of his favorite plans, which was to raise sheep and cotton on the same farm, utilizing cotton-seed meal to feed the sheep and the sheep to fertilize the land, failed to take hold, although the use of cotton-seed meal and hulls for cattle food has since become of great importance in the Southern States. He was also wrong in a prediction made at this same time that the tide of immigration would turn toward the South after the Exposition.

In other words, Mr. Atkinson visualized the future growth of the South along lines which would be supplementary and not antagonistic to the economic interests of the North. He put this feeling into the following words: 'The greatest need of the present time is, that the citizens of the two sections that have been so widely separated until recent times should visit each other, learn the respective methods and opportunities of each State, and become convinced that in their mutual interdependence is the foundation of their true union.'[2]

The intense interest shown by Southerners at this time in the possibilities of cotton mills disturbed this carefully arranged picture of the future. It was because he sincerely believed in the superiority of New England in the field of cotton manufacturing that Mr. Atkinson felt obliged, although somewhat reluctantly, to advise against any extensive cotton manufacturing in favor of other more profitable investments of capital. In the preface

---

[1] Although the cotton-seed oil industry was established in the South before 1880, its significant development did not come until after that date. Cf. Tomkins, D. A., *Cotton and Cotton Oil*, p. 210.

[2] Pamphlet, *Address of Edward Atkinson of Boston Massachusetts Given in Atlanta, Georgia in October, 1880, for the Promotion of an International Cotton Exhibition*, p. 8.

of the pamphlet edition of his Atlanta speech, he wrote on this point: 'The Southern friends of the writer may not be averse to accepting an opinion that the South has a vast field of work in the manufacture and mechanical arts that promise a much greater profit than the manufacture of cotton fabrics can offer for many years to come.'[1] And he offered what almost amounted to a challenge when he continued: 'Let the Southern States visit the North and examine its methods of industry, and it will soon become apparent to them in which direction their attention should be turned.'[2]

In another article he amplified this point of view: 'Cotton spinning requires for its permanent success a large capital, a very few operatives, ample banking facilities, a thoroughly organized system of distribution, a machine shop on one side and a paper mill to work up waste on the other; but more than all, it requires habit and training for it or other like occupations in the mass of the community, and a cool or cold climate in which long hours of persistent but not arduous indoor labor can be sustained.'[3]

---

[1] Atkinson, Edward, *op. cit.*, p. 5.
[2] *Ibid.*, p. 8.
[3] Pamphlet, *Cotton*, articles from *New York Herald*, 1877, pp. 36–37. His position is given in some detail in the following letter addressed to F. C. Morehead, of Atlanta, one of the officials of the Exposition, dated May 6, 1881:

'This letter is for your personal consideration, not to be printed.

'The only point on which my views have been subjected to criticism by my Southern friends has been the discouragement that I have thrown upon investments in Southern cotton mills.

'I was almost forced into this discussion without intending to be. You will yourself fully credit me when I say that there is not the slightest sense of jealousy or fear of competition on the part of Northern manufacturers as to Southern cotton spinning. It will be almost impossible for you to increase your capacity to spin and weave as rapidly as the Southern States will consume cotton fabrics.

'I have never taken the ground that the climatic conditions were not favorable in many parts of the Southern States. They are especially favorable in some sections; for instance, in the Piedmont district of the Carolinas and Georgia, where the streams are exceedingly uniform, and the climate is better than ours.

'But we know by costly experience the difficulties of establishing this branch of industry. It is my private conviction that Massachusetts would have been better off today if there had never been a single cotton mill established within her limits. Very few exist that have not been sold out once, or else have had their capital cut down very heavily.

'The main point, however, is that it is a branch of industry that tends to concentration where all the facilities are to be had, and where the habit of the people becomes directed toward the kind of work.

'It is also true today, that no mill ought to be established and operated by a corporation of less than about 30,000 spindles. A mill can be fairly balanced on 15,000 or 16,000 or

THE NEW SOUTH 173

These expressions are typical of Mr. Atkinson's speeches and articles on the subject given both prior to and during the Exposition.

This discouraging advice tendered by Mr. Atkinson did not inhibit the Southerners in their determination to manufacture cotton. On the contrary, as Broadus Mitchell points out in his book, *The Rise of Cotton Mills in the South*, it was Mr. Atkinson's advice against Southern cotton manufacturing which was one of the important factors which stimulated its further development. Mitchell says:

> The question whether the South should manufacture cotton or be content with cultivation of the raw materials was made vivid by the opposition to Southern mills on the part of Edward Atkinson of Boston. It may almost be said that he conducted a propaganda to show that the South should devote itself to raising, ginning, and pre-

30,000 to 32,000 spindles or yarns ranging from 14s to 30s; but on any less number, the machine is not well proportioned, and cannot be, and the relative cost will therefore be higher. I speak of corporation mills, because the best skill is needed in the managers, and you cannot afford to pay for the best skill on a small mill. Smaller mills may be built and operated by individuals only who have been trained to the work; and if they are thoroughly trained, a small mill may be operated as skillfully as a large one; not otherwise.

'I do not like to see your people incur almost certain ultimate failure where they have as yet so little capital that ought to be risked in such business as this, when a little capital may be made so profitable and go so far in the preparation of the cotton for the spinner.

'You have an advantage in the proximity of the mill to the cotton field. But I will tell you privately that so far as Southern mills are now concerned, you are at a disadvantage far greater than this advantage amounts to.

'I have carefully examined all the census statements, being myself the agent for compiling the facts, as you know; and after making all allowance for the difference in work, and the different kind of mills operated in the two sections, I reach this conclusion — that the average number of hands to one thousand spindles ought to be about the same in New England and in the Southern States. In point of fact, you employ in your Southern mills, two hands where we employ one.

'I do not propose to publish this officially, or to give it the sanction of my name. It is stated to you confidentially.

'But it follows that even though your wages are much less, your cost is higher; and so far, in all the cost-sheets that I have ever seen, the excess of the cost of labor more than equals the advantage in the price of cotton.

'Further, your advantage in the price of cotton will be gradually diminished as time goes on; because in the consolidation of the railway service of the North and South, such as took effect ten or twenty years ago between East and West, there will be the same ratable reduction for moving merchandise. What this will be you will appreciate when I tell you that it costs less than one-third to move a ton of wheat from the wheat-fields of the West to Boston, compared to what it cost from 1866 to 1869 inclusive. The rates on cotton from South to North are now double what they will be three or four years hence.

'I name these matters in order that you may see what a vast interest you have in improving the handling and packing of cotton; and think you should give all your attention and all your money to that department before you risk it in uncertain enterprises in cotton spinning and weaving.'

paring the staple to be spun and woven elsewhere. A talented organizer of business, a not unkindly egotist, officious without being patronizing, gifted in social imagination, and one of the first New Englanders to concern himself actively in a public way with Southern economic affairs after Reconstruction, Atkinson sought, sometimes with semi-private purpose, to mirror the South to itself. The image he furnished, by its very distortion, assisted Southerners to a clearer view of their task. At that peculiar juncture in the South, he was listened to attentively, and negatively and positively exerted a striking influence.[1]

Or, in other words, because of his prominence as a cotton expert,[2] Mr. Atkinson's objections to Southern cotton manufacturing precipitated a spirited discussion of the possibilities of that industry, with the result that interest in the subject was greatly stimulated, and both Southerners and Northerners were made aware of the opportunities which existed in this field.

Positively, Mr. Atkinson's influence came from the Exposition itself, which gave a great stimulus to the manufacture of cotton. Mitchell, who dates the inception of cotton manufacturing in the South on any significant scale about the year 1880, says of the Exposition, 'It accomplished two things; first, it drew together the South's apostles of a new industrial order into confirmatory exchange of views and plans, and afforded concrete, tangible encouragement to already forming aspirations; second, it opened the eyes of the North to the field of investment that lay in the South, breaking down inter-sectional economic and political barriers of prejudice.'[3]

Edward Stanwood, in 1900, expressed the opinion in respect to Southern cotton manufactures that, 'The Cotton Exposition in Atlanta, in 1881, gave the industry an impetus which it has

---

[1] Page 117. *Note* — Although Mr. Atkinson originally suggested the Exposition as a method of getting improved cotton for the manufacturers, it is doubtful whether he felt any semi-private interest in advising against the construction of Southern cotton mills, even though there were included in the membership of the Boston Manufacturers' Mutual Fire Insurance Company, of which he was then president, a large number of cotton mills. At no place in his correspondence does he express any fear of Southern competition in this field, but is consistent with his expressions that there were other more attractive investment possibilities in the South.

[2] His opinions carried added weight because he had been commissioned to write the report on cotton and cotton manufacture for the Tenth Census.

[3] Mitchell, Broadus, *op. cit.*, pp. 9, 122. Cf. Copeland, M. T., *op. cit.*, p. 34.

never since lost. The possibilities of the region were shown when the Governor of Georgia appeared at the fair dressed in a suit of clothes made of cottonade manufactured on the grounds from cotton which had been picked from the stalk on the morning of the same day, in sight of the visitors to the fair.'[1]

Mr. Atkinson never entirely gave up the idea that the greatest opportunities for investment in the South lay outside cotton mills. He thought that the improvement in the preparation of the cotton,[2] the utilization of the by-products of the plant, improvements in agriculture, and the promotion of numerous small industries (which he maintained were the backbone of New England prosperity) were much more to be desired for the South than the rapid development which had taken place in the cotton manufacturing after 1880.[3]

He predicted that in a few years, as the native whites passed through the cotton mills into more highly paid occupations, Southern factories would be suffering from a lack of labor, for, unlike the New England mills, which had an unending stream of immigrants to draw upon, the Southern mills had no reserve or potential supply of workers to fall back upon.

As a result of the part he took in the Atlanta Exposition, Mr. Atkinson acquired a reputation as an authority upon the general subject of expositions. There was scarcely an exhibition or fair of any importance following 1881 upon which he was not asked to advise, or in which he was not invited to participate. He evolved the principle, which he expanded at every oppor-

---

[1] *Twelfth Census of United States*, 1900, vol. 12, p. 28.

[2] So convinced was Mr. Atkinson of the importance of improved ginning that in 1882 he organized the Cotton Improvement Company for the purpose of erecting a model ginnery at Hogansville, Georgia. The company was put under the direction of a young Southerner who lacked sufficient experience to make it a success, with the result that the company failed a few years later.

[3] On December 8, 1905, just a few days before his death, Mr. Atkinson wrote to the *Baltimore Manufacturers' Record* censuring the part played by that publication in promoting what seemed to him a one-sided Southern development. He said, in part: 'While you have poured capital, both Northern and Southern, into great factories and iron works, have you not neglected the very foundation of your prosperity, that is, agriculture? Have you yet surmounted the evils of the old system? What part of your cotton land has been subject to deep and thorough tillage, to renovation; to intelligent and intensive cultivation?'

tunity, that an exposition should be more than a large exhibition of products for advertising purposes. It was his feeling that such affairs should show the evolution of art and industry throughout history. In this point of view he anticipated to a remarkable degree the plan followed by subsequent events of this kind.

In June, 1889, Mr. Atkinson received further recognition of his aid to the South, when he was awarded an honorary LL.D. degree from the University of South Carolina. In addition to the personal satisfaction from such an honor, Mr. Atkinson felt that it was a sign of the progress which had been made in healing the wounds of the Civil War, when he, a former Abolitionist who had his first Southern contact in helping to equip John Brown's raiders with Sharp's rifles, should receive a degree from a leading Southern university.

Lack of space prevents extended treatment of any of the numerous other subjects to which Mr. Atkinson gave his attention, but perhaps the mention of one or two more may give an appreciation of the variety of his interests.

He was, for example, in charge of the Shaw Monument Fund, and was responsible for the successful completion of the monument honoring Colonel Robert G. Shaw, officer in the Union Army, and famous leader of Negro troops in that struggle. This monument was done by the well-known artist, Augustus Saint-Gaudens, and at present stands on Boston Common.

Mr. Atkinson was also prominent in the affairs of the Massachusetts Institute of Technology, and helped in the management of the school for almost twenty-five years. It was his purpose to secure for the students of the Institute a thorough background of a theoretical nature, coupled with actual experience in applying those principles. He was successful in securing funds and property for the Institute, and was an active member of various important committees. A difference of opinion with President Francis A. Walker over the nature of the curricula caused Mr. Atkinson to sever his connection with the Institute in 1892.

Mr. Atkinson was a member of the following clubs and societies: American Economic Association, American Statistical Association, British Economic Association, International Statistical Society, American Academy of Fine Arts, Twentieth Century Club, Thursday Evening Club, Reform Club of Boston, and Reform Club of New York.

Further academic recognition had come to him in the form of an honorary Ph.D. degree from Dartmouth College and an honorary membership in the Harvard University Chapter of Phi Beta Kappa.

CHAPTER VI

PROBLEMS OLD AND NEW: THE TARIFF, FREE SILVER, IMPERIALISM, SOCIAL REFORM

1892–1905

AT NO time, with the possible exception of President Garfield's inauguration into the Presidency, had conditions looked more promising for the fulfillment of Mr. Atkinson's hopes in respect to tariff and currency reform than they did in March, 1893. With Grover Cleveland in the White House there seemed little danger of the enactment of unsound monetary legislation; and in Congress, the Democrats, pledged by campaign promises to lower tariff duties, had large majorities in both the House and the Senate. Not that Mr. Atkinson did not have occasional misgivings, for the silver interests were strong, and, as has already been noted, there was a possibility, so he imagined, that tariff reform might be too sudden or sweeping. But on the whole, he looked upon the inception of the new Administration as an opportunity to put into effect his long-delayed plans for reform.

In a letter to Charles Nordhoff (vacationing in Coronado, California), he analyzed the situation as it existed in November, 1892:

> I have received your letters, and am always, of course, most glad to get them, but I could not find time until now even to sit down and dictate. I have been excessively busy, of which you have seen some signs. The revolution has come, and is more complete than I thought it would be. When I found that I could fill our great town hall of Brookline with a solid mass of Democratic voters, *not* of the type customarily interested in my kind of speaking, and hold them unwinking for over an hour, I made up my mind that the subject at length had hold of the mass of the people.
>
> Now comes the question how to direct it. I think that Cleveland will disappoint you both in his choice of a Cabinet and in his course. I do not expect to be called to the Cabinet, nor do I think that Wells ought to be. It would kill him, and he has neither the strength nor the

executive power for such a place. We are now in a better position as advisers than either of us could be in offices.

The leading men who will control the policy in the House and Senate will be Carlisle and McPherson in the Senate, and Wilson, Harter, and C. R. Breckinridge in the House. From all I can learn the new men found out how they blundered in the first session of the present Congress, and they will be prepared to follow the chosen leaders.

Moreover, I feel very little doubt that it will become necessary for the better class of Republicans to join with the intelligent Democrats in meeting the absurd demands that may emanate in the West and from other sources. I have reason to feel very sure that the break of Dr. McCune and the Southern Farmers' Alliance men from the Memphis Convention, was done with a purpose. The Southerners are quicker and more intelligent than the Western men. They have found out their blunder about the money question, and will soon support a sound national measure. Brawley, who voted against free silver and for honest money, and who expected to be defeated in the late election, was re-elected triumphantly from Charleston.

There will be no deficiency, so that the way to true tariff reform will be perfectly plain. I am framing all the tables that will be necessary to make the case as plain as daylight, and I have even secured the co-operation of Foster, the Secretary of the Treasury, and the annual statements of accounts from 1879 to the present day will be submitted in a separate computation, sorted and listed in my way, so that the exact income, the sources and proportions, and the exact expenditure, each will be very plain.

Raum will also submit a very different form of pension statement from the one formerly presented, which will show that even as a money question, the pensions will not stand in the way of an adequate reform of the tariff.

I have felt younger, stronger, and better since I came home from Europe than I have for many years, because I found out the true method of lightening my weight without starving myself while I was in London, and I feel more capable of work and a greater mastery of the work than in many years before. I wish you could be in Washington to assist us.

Immediately following the elections in 1892, Mr. Atkinson moved to have his views of tariff reform laid before the new leaders of Congress. He again outlined his plan for reductions of the duties on raw materials, to be followed by periodic adjustments of the rates on manufactured goods,[1] and on November 16, 1892,

[1] *Ante*, p. 136.

sent copies to President Cleveland, Senator John G. Carlisle, and Congressman W. L. Wilson, for consideration.

In his letter of transmittal to Senator Carlisle and to Mr. Wilson he said, 'If you will adopt substantially the plan which I have outlined in the enclosure, have it printed, and put it in circulation in the first half of the month of December, you will allay the fears, especially of the textile people, and you will secure an amount of co-operation on the lines I have laid, of which you little dream.'

To allay the fears of the manufacturers that the new Administration intended to initiate radical changes inimical to the industrial interests, Mr. Atkinson proposed that the Democratic leaders begin their work on tariff reform by immediately framing a series of questions to be answered by various manufacturers, which questions by their very nature would carry an assurance to those answering them, that reform would proceed slowly.[1]

From letters written to Mr. Atkinson during 1893, and early 1894, it is evident that numerous New England manufacturers agreed with him that the free-trade 'revolution had come,' and he was looked upon by many as one of the few barriers between them and a ruinous flood of imports about to be precipitated by the Democrats.[2]

---

[1] He put this point into the following words: 'I wish you especially to give thought to this method [of questions]: put yourself in the place of a timid manufacturer of woolens who is desirous to see tariff reform started and who wants free wool, but who is dismayed by the fear of what may occur in the interval. He receives these questions and then, when they become public, what will be the necessary inference? It will be this. He will say to himself, "Why, if this is the method on which these men who control Congress mean to act, we are perfectly safe. There will be nothing rash. There will be no great revolution. Everything will be done decently and in order. Let us help them all we can."

'On the other hand, the buyer of the goods having become informed of this method will immediately say to himself, "Why, if that is the way Congressmen intend to proceed, they have got some sense. There is no great danger of great revolution, and we can buy our goods with perfect assurance that there will be no great trap sprung upon us while we are making them up and getting them ready for sale." I think you will see this more quickly than almost any other member, because you know how business reasons, and you can explain this, if you concur with me, to others.' To M. D. Harter, December 6, 1892.

[2] The treasurer of a mill working on fine yarns wrote to Mr. Atkinson explaining the indecision of his board of directors in respect to a proposed expansion of their plant and equipment. He continued:

'While they [the directors] are convinced of the wisdom of making such changes, and that it ought to be done, yet I found them, in common with other business men, very reluctant indeed to expend any money for new machinery or improvements, feeling that

THE TARIFF

But with the exception of one textile manufacturer who wrote, 'Your tariff treatises are sound, conservative, and should be generally accepted by our manufacturers, but they are so permeated with the idea of high protection of each one's own special interest that they appear blind to changed condition of things,'[1] there is little evidence that the mill-owners as a whole would give enthusiastic support to Mr. Atkinson's plans for tariff reform.

with the uncertainty which hangs over us, through the incoming of the present Administration, they fear, of course, great changes will prevail, that duties will be lowered on manufactured goods both in cotton and woolen mills, as the Democratic Party say that protection is a fraud, and that free trade should predominate, and that it is a false principle to protect our American industries.

'Of course, I am not endeavoring in this communication to you to argue this question at all, that is not the point in view, for I told my directors that, so far as the present duties under which we are now operating are concerned, they were not sufficient to protect us from our competitors on the other side of the water. In other words, it is simply impossible for us to make yarns above no. 60's, and sell them in competition with the English manufacturers with our present duties so low. They have had the market practically, during the past two or three years on all the fine numbers in yarns above 60's.

'So I have told one and another, that I do not believe, when this is fully understood, that there would be any further lowering of the tariff upon the cotton yarn schedules.

'The writer knows that you have great influence in the present Administration, and that you have been called upon to give your views as to the formation and the framing of the new tariff bill, and further, you are the most thoroughly conversant with cotton manufacturing, and knowing as well as you do the conditions under which we work here in this country that it would seem to us you could not personally favor any reduction in the cotton yarn schedule. We need every bit of protection that we now have, especially for yarns in valuations from 25 cents to 60 cents per pound in English currency. So far as the yarns are concerned, in the higher values as above stated, we have been unable to make them in competition. I hope, therefore, that you will see that no reductions are made against our American manufacturers on yarns valued from 25 cents to 60 cents per pound in English money.

'You, of course, know the value of our plant here, and how much money it has cost to erect it, and also other similar establishments throughout New England. It would seem a pity to do anything that will endanger the interest of these stockholders that have put their money into them. It is not our wish to reduce our labor which we employ, but of course that would be the only and last resort which we should have to defend ourselves if the reduction of duties should follow, and I fancy we should make very little headway in reducing American labor in our cotton mills, and I hope we shall not be obliged to do it until we can reduce very materially the cost of our construction as it now stands upon the books.

'It would seem to me that we ought to apply to you, from the simple fact that you have been so long identified with the cotton manufacturing interests of New England. We look upon you as one of us, and we do not believe that you would for a moment do anything to injure the interest of those with whom you have been associated in business for so long a time....

'You will excuse me for writing you so plainly upon this matter, but, feeling as I do, and as our directors have done, I thought it would not be amiss for me to advise you in regard to same.' Letter dated May 6, 1893, from a cotton manufacturer.

[1] Letter from D. J. Johnston, August 14, 1893, treasurer of the Harmony Mills, Cohoes, New York.

It would be more accurate to state that they were willing to compromise upon free raw materials to be followed by subsequent reductions of manufactured goods, in lieu of a general scaling-down of all duties.[1]

Even Henry Saltonstall, treasurer of the Pacific Mills, designated by Mr. Atkinson as one of the 'reasonable' manufacturers who would, if given the opportunity, lend support to a liberal tariff reform measure, was not optimistic over the possible results from lowered duties on manufactured goods. He wrote:

> The great thing, of course, is to make a harmonious tariff. I mean one in which the duties upon certain materials or stages of manufacture shall agree or be in harmony with those upon other materials or other stages of manufacture. This is not the case at present. The duties on woolen yarn, for instance, are fixed by our friend Mr. Whitman at higher rates than many of the goods in which they enter.
>
> The subject is altogether too vast a one for a person who has not studied it as you have to put his finger into it. So far as the wants of manufacturers of my class of goods are concerned, I have already written you all I can say. At 25 per cent and free wool, I honestly believe we must stop manufacturing, and at an ad valorem duty of 40 per cent (which would not be practically 40 per cent), I doubt very much whether we should not be so swamped by foreign goods that we should have no home market. I believe it would take an actual duty of 50 per cent to properly protect a dress-goods maker, and in saying this you must remember that I am not a McKinley man, but in sympathy with the honest and conservative men of the present Administration.
>
> I would like to make two points: One, that the duties on yarn should not be as high as those on goods, because it is only a partially manufactured product, with less than one-half the labor as on goods, and does not need so much protection. Second, that the duty on

---

[1] While admitting its expediency, this compromise attitude was deplored by the official spokesman of the Home Market Club, Albert Clark, who wrote to Mr. Atkinson, September 29, 1893: 'While it is doubtless true that some protectionists who are manufacturers, and even some members of the Home Market Club, may connive at protection on the basis of free raw material, I am not advised that many are willing to make such terms, and personally I cannot see either the justice or expediency of it, from the protectionist standpoint. With a view to free trade, I can understand it, for, of course, the men who are deprived of protection will aim to get even at the next election. I believe that we ought to have either a protective bill of the general character of the McKinley tariff, or else a free-trade tariff like that of Great Britain. But as we are not likely to get either from a political Congress like the present, I do not question your wisdom in managing so far as you can to save as much protection as possible for our New England manufacturers, and I hope you will meet with a large measure of success.'

machinery and mill supplies, and drugs and dyes, should be lowered in proportion to the duties on goods.[1]

The last paragraph of the quotation just made suggests a further difficulty which Mr. Atkinson had to meet in trying to enlist united support. Each producer was reluctant to see duties on his own product or products lowered. General William F. Draper, for example, was fearful lest the duties on cotton machinery be reduced disproportionately to other rates, while a Pennsylvania representative of the coal and iron industries asked, 'Why, if the country is to get down from the protective stilts in part only, that certain interests should dismount entirely? Iron ore and coal employ the same kind of labor in mining and transporting as many other productions in the course of manufacturing and marketing, and if one is to be protected in any degree by taxes why not the so-called raw material?'[2]

Mr. Atkinson wisely sought to avoid these difficulties by confining his recommendations to broad principles of reform, and refusing as far as possible to name specific duties. 'My purpose,' he explained to one inquirer, 'is to establish the basis of facts, to procure and submit exact data to those who will frame a tariff bill, unbiased by personal interests and governed by just statements of the conditions as they now are... to regulate *the form*, so that there shall be no room for litigation, evasion and error, and to secure such adjustments of each part of the tariff bill to the other as will give justice to all.... It is not probable that I shall be called upon for specific rates. You will see at once that if I were to name rates on yarns I might run counter to the interests of the weaver. If I were to name rates to the weaver without consideration of yarns, then injustice might be done the other way.'[3] Believing as he did that 'the true protection to the industries of this country will ultimately consist in free trade, qualified only by the necessity of a moderate customs revenue,'

[1] Boston, April 7, 1893.
[2] Letter to Mr. Atkinson from H. R. Collins, of Pittsburgh, Pennsylvania, September 15, 1893.
[3] Letter dated May 10, 1893.

Mr. Atkinson could, of course, conscientiously advocate lower duties in spite of the objections of the manufacturers, particularly if he were able to secure moderate adjustments extending over a period of years.

With his friends who had definite tendencies toward free trade, Mr. Atkinson was more successful in securing co-operation. Mr. Wells wrote: 'I propose to stick by you. No crude stuff will go into our draft that we may submit, if a little tact is observed. All I want is that we improve our opportunity which may never come to us again. All the glory I want is to have something effectual done.'[1]

Mr. Atkinson also received assurances from various Democratic members of Congress that no revolutionary changes were contemplated.[2]

Meanwhile, there was the task of putting Mr. Atkinson's general plan into more specific terms in order that it might be used as a basis by the Ways and Means Committee in framing the new tariff bill. With the consent and approval of Secretary of the Treasury, Carlisle, Mr. Atkinson secured the co-operation of the Bureau of Statistics in the preparation of tables which showed, for the period between 1872 and 1892, the income and expenditures of the United States Government carefully classified as to specific sources and as to their definite disbursements. Mr. Atkinson worked closely with the Bureau on this work and gave many helpful suggestions concerning the form and nature of the tables.[3] With this material available, it would be possible for the Committee to determine which import duties yielded the most revenue, and the task of reducing the tariff to a revenue basis would be greatly facilitated.

[1] January 19, 1893.
[2] Senator J. R. McPherson wrote on the point, 'Unquestionably you will have much to do with outlining the policy of the Treasury in respect to the new tariff bill to be formulated, which, as everyone must see, must be fitted to present conditions rather than to theories.' February 22, 1893.
[3] These tables included for the several specified groups of articles affected by import duties the following information: tariff rate of duty, average ad valorem duty, average value per unit of quantity, quantity imported, value of the imports, duty thereon, and finally, duties collected in order of magnitude from each of the classes of goods considered. Cf. 'Mr. Atkinson's Plan for Tariff Reform,' *Tariff Reform*, vol. VI, no. 3, p. 4.

In the latter part of April, 1893, in company with Mr. Wells, Mr. Atkinson spent two or three weeks in Washington perfecting his plans and laying the groundwork for subsequent action. He returned to Boston much pleased with what he had accomplished. 'I think,' he wrote to Henry Saltonstall, 'I have planted some very important base lines in Washington.'

Under the heading, 'Mr. Atkinson's Tariff Plan,' his proposals appeared in some detail in the magazine, *Tariff Reform*, published by the Tariff Reform Committee of the Reform Club of New York.[1] In this article Mr. Atkinson called attention to the necessity for revising the McKinley Act, pointing out that many of its former strongest advocates were agreed that its passage had been a mistake. He outlined the two methods of tariff reform then being considered. One, sponsored by the Reform Club of New York, provided for a general horizontal scaling-down of the duties. The other plan, which he advocated and which, in current discussion bore his name, called for an immediate increase in the free list, an increase in the duties on luxuries and articles of voluntary use. Duties on raw materials and partially manufactured goods were to be substantially lowered or entirely removed as a means of promoting domestic industry. It was also suggested that the mixed system of duties, which had proved difficult to administer and was subject to fraud and evasion, be eliminated and specific rates substituted. He recommended that the measure be put into effect slowly in view of the uncertainties of the monetary situation, and in order to give manufacturers an opportunity to adjust themselves to new raw material costs.

Mr. Atkinson utilized the data he had caused to be prepared by the Bureau of Statistics to show that the normal costs of the National Government were met by the internal taxes and customs revenues from spirits, tobacco, beer, and wines. The extraordinary expenses, made necessary by the pensions arising from the Civil War and the sugar bounty, he proposed to meet by maintaining the duties, for the time being, on manufactured articles. Then, as the pension burden was subsequently lessened

[1] Vol. VI, no. 3, July 1, 1893.

(he estimated 1894 as the peak year), the rates on manufactured goods should be lowered correspondingly.

While admitting that this plan is not without definite merits as a rational approach to the solution of the tariff problem, it must be noted that the enactment of such a program into law would by its very nature encounter serious obstacles. Or, in other words, it lacked the qualities which would enlist the enthusiastic partisan support necessary for such important legislation.

As had already been shown, the manufacturers were willing for the most part to accept it instead of more sweeping changes, but if given their choice, would have left the protective system unchanged. On the other hand, Mr. Atkinson's plan by its very conservatism failed to appeal to the impatient tariff reformers who wanted more drastic and swift reductions of import duties. Accompanying Mr. Atkinson's article was a critical review by Mr. Ellery Anderson, a representative of the New York Reform League. In this review the objections of what may be termed the orthodox free traders were forcibly outlined. After admitting the value of Mr. Atkinson's plan for the raising of revenue, Mr. Anderson asked, '*But is this all there is of this great question?* The essential point of the great contest of 1892 was that it was unjust to compel the mass of our consumers to pay increased prices to American manufacturers and producers, in order to enable those in these particular industries to make them profitable.'

He then pointed out that the tariff was a tax, and continued: 'It was against the injustice of this compulsory exaction of tributes, small in detail but enormous in the aggregate, levied at all times and from everyone, that the people rebelled. They declared by their vote in 1892 that they did not choose to be taxed in order that special industries might flourish.'

His concluding remark was that the tariff reformers '... cannot accept a plan which, for the present, simply enlarges the free list as a redemption of the promises given to relieve our people from the burdens of unjust taxation.'

In spite of the lack of support from the free-traders, Mr. Atkinson had the satisfaction of having his ideas for tariff reform

THE TARIFF

adopted by the Treasury Department as the foundation for the Administration measure being prepared by it for the House Committee on Ways and Means.

There was reason to expect his plan would receive further support as a result of the appointment in August of William L. Wilson as Chairman of the House Ways and Means Committee, for Mr. Wilson by his training and temperament was inclined to favor such a reform as Mr. Atkinson recommended.[1] Subsequent developments proved this to be the case, for the bill which was reported by the Committee to the House (the so-called Wilson Bill) followed the outlines of the 'Atkinson Plan' in its essential features.

Mr. Atkinson kept in close touch with the Committee during the time when the tariff measure was being considered. He sought to offset the influence of the protectionists who were appearing before the Committee, by preparing sets of questions, the answers to which, he thought, would show the fallacies of the opponents to tariff reform. These questions he forwarded to Mr. Wilson. He also sent a carefully prepared list of names containing men on both sides of the tariff question who might well appear before the Committee as experts in their respective fields.

In September there was considerable talk in Washington about 'the Atkinson tables' and 'the Atkinson bill.' Mr. Atkinson was pleased at this indication of the influence of his work with the Treasury Department and the Committee. He wrote to Horace White in October, 'I have reason to believe that my logical formula for the adjustment of the tariff has almost absolutely controlled the action of the Committee of Ways and Means.'[2]

In the latter part of October, he went on to Washington at the request of the Ways and Means Committee. He later reported his work there to Mr. F. W. Cheney:

[1] Stanwood, Edward, *op. cit.*, vol. II, pp. 318–19, comments on Mr. Wilson: 'Mr. Wilson was a scholarly, well-informed, and sincere statesman and commanded universal respect. ... His mind was essentially logical, and he derived his economical views from the writings of economists rather than from personal observation of and acquaintance with the actual working of tariff laws.'   [2] October 27, 1893.

I have spent a week in Washington, each day with the Sub-Committee who were engaged in framing the tariff schedules, but I requested them at the outset not to give me any specific information in regard to rates, as it might embarrass them and would certainly embarrass me. My services in preparing the form and general scope of the new tariff were thus very welcome and were such as I could render without compromising myself in any way. You will know very soon what their exact decision is, but I think from what I inferred, not what they told me, that the bill will run very much on the lines of my plan in the Reform Club pamphlet.[1]

As already noted, Mr. Atkinson's high expectations were not unrealized. The principal features of the Wilson Bill as it was reported to the House were that it provided for such important free raw materials as wool, coal, iron ore, lumber, binding twine, and fish, and provided for moderate reductions in the rates upon practically all manufactured goods. Several of the individual rates, chiefly those on certain grades of woolens and worsteds, were not entirely satisfactory to him, but he thought that these defects would be remedied before the bill was finally enacted.

One feature of the bill, however, as it passed the House greatly disturbed Mr. Atkinson. This was the provision for an income tax. He thought such a tax had much to recommend it, but felt that its application was susceptible to fraud and abuse. Furthermore, according to his estimate of the revenue which might be expected under the new tariff, there would be no need for this added tax which was highly inexpedient from a political point of view. To C. R. Breckinridge he wrote concerning the income tax: 'I regard the measure itself as an economic blunder and political suicide for the Democratic Party. It will kill the party in New York absolutely, and without New York, what chance is there for controlling the country?'[2]

The proposed income tax gave Mr. Atkinson grounds for counseling his manufacturing friends to support the Wilson Bill as it originally stood, pointing out a desire on the part of many of the Western and Southern Representatives in Congress to declare

---

[1] November 18, 1893.
[2] February 7, 1894.

for out-and-out free trade, with the possibility of adjustments of the income tax to make up for any deficiency in revenue.

Notwithstanding these difficulties, Mr. Atkinson on the whole had every reason to feel that the Wilson Bill, as it was presented to the Senate, embodied the essential features of his original plan, and was to an important degree the result of his personal influence. Certainly the measure as it then stood involved a radical departure from the protective tariff policy which had been in vogue since the Civil War.[1]

Soon after the House Bill came up for discussion in the Senate, it became apparent that the measure would be subjected to sharp attacks and possible drastic changes. As was to be expected, Mr. Atkinson was disturbed by these possibilities. In answer to an invitation of Senator McPherson to come to Washington to aid directly in the fight, Mr. Atkinson answered:

> I do not believe it would be of any use for me to come to Washington, and I hardly dare to because my strength is not fully restored and I do not want to get into the anxiety and worry and turmoil of the conference. I did what I could to make the Wilson Bill, as you say, 'a good bridge,' but if it is to be broken down and a radical, revolutionary policy presented, I am out, I become a Mugwump again — the only comfortable political position that a man can hold.[2]

It will be noted that his fear at this stage was again that a radical, revolutionary policy might be presented rather than that the rates might be raised.[3] Subsequent action by the Senate proved that Mr. Atkinson's fears of radical measures were once more groundless. There proved to be unexpected protectionist strength even among the Democratic Senators, many of whom had special interests which they were pledged to aid by protective duties. Senator McPherson expressed the situation

---

[1] Cf. Taussig, F. W., *Tariff History of the United States*, p. 291.

[2] February 20, 1894.

[3] The bill was at this time being thoroughly revised downward by Senators Vest and Mills, who had undertaken its preparation for the consideration by the Senate. Cf. Stanwood, Edward, *op. cit.*, vol. II, p. 328. This fact prompted Mr. Atkinson to say to Senator McPherson: 'Perhaps it is just as well that this rank, aggressive, revolutionary spirit should show itself. It is what I have feared for many years and what I foretold in a letter to Secretary McCulloch in 1885 which now reads like a prophecy.' February 20, 1894.

graphically when he wrote to Mr. Atkinson on March 11, 'Only think of our desperate position as a party — in face of our pledges — We find sugar, coal, ore men first, then Democratic afterwards — but so it is.'

By the middle of 1894, Mr. Atkinson was more anxious to secure some positive, immediate action upon the tariff in order that business recovery might be encouraged than he was to retain the Wilson Bill in its original form. The protests of many of the textile manufacturers had, furthermore, convinced him that the rates on these products had been too sharply reduced. He was willing to compromise on the Senate amendments and so advised his friends in Congress.[1]

The tariff bill which finally became a law without the signature of President Cleveland in August, 1894, bore little resemblance to the original Wilson Bill. Free wool was the only important survivor of the extensive free list and other duties had been extensively adjusted, not on any broad principle of tariff reform, but to meet the special interests of certain groups. Many of the Democrats, including the President, were greatly disappointed at this result, for it was clearly no fulfillment of the promises made during the Presidential campaign.

Mr. Atkinson did not share in this disappointment. On the contrary, he seemed well pleased with the relatively small progress which had been accomplished. 'The reform of the tariff

[1] As early as February 21, 1894, he had written to Senator Mills:
'I fully comprehend the necessity for compromise, and provided I could carry the free wool and some other additions to the free list, coupled with a *well adjusted reduction of duties*, I should let iron ore and coal go back, because coal will presently be covered by a new treaty with Canada, and the supremacy in iron and steel, whether we have free ore or not, *has come to this side of the Atlantic to stay*. The duties on iron and steel with a few exceptions of some special kinds, will hereafter be substantially inoperative....

'I approve fully of a compromise on sugar for revenue purposes, and would not let the prejudice against the sugar trust prevent a slight discrimination between the raw and the refined. There is every reason for that discrimination in the foreign bounty system. Moreover, the tide has turned. McKinleyism is intellectually dead, and if you make a fair beginning *without revolutionary change*, and in such form on the textiles that the work will be given from here not to play politics, the matter will go on to its conclusion as it did in England as fast as it ought to. Within ten or fifteen years we shall be the greatest free-trade country in the world, simply for the protection of our own interests. All depends upon how the thing starts, and on that Gladstone spoke some wise words when he said, "that the road to Free Trade was like the road to virtue; the first step the most difficult; the last one the most profitable."'

has begun along true lines and it will go fast enough on its own merits,' he wrote in October, 1894.[1] He continued: 'I take no further interest in that question. The logic of the case will control events. There is great danger of disturbance on the silver and *fiat* money question hereafter, and on that I may still take an active part.'

At least two reasons were probably responsible for this lack of concern by Mr. Atkinson over the fate of his original tariff reform plan. In the first place, as has been noted, his policy was to guide the progress of tariff reform along conservative lines, and given his choice, he would have much preferred to see changes made in his scheme, looking to greater protection rather than toward immediate free trade, provided a good start was made toward an ultimate enactment of a tariff for revenue only. Of equal importance as a cause of his loss of interest in tariff reform was the possibility of the coinage of free silver. His earlier fears regarding this possibility were thoroughly aroused by the frequent demonstrations of strength on the part of the silver interests. To him the maintenance of sound money, as has also been noted, was much more important than tariff reform.

It is to Mr. Atkinson's part in the free-silver question which occupied such an important place in the economic and political discussions of the period that attention will now be turned.

Mr. Atkinson's activities in connection with the tariff fade into relative obscurity when compared with his interest and part in the free-silver fight which assumed such prominence after 1892. His participation in this latter question continued along the same general lines followed by him during the two previous Presidential Administrations, except that it was marked by much greater intensity.

Back of the strenuous efforts of the bimetallists to secure free coinage of silver after 1892 lay a complex pattern of economic, political, and financial events so interwoven that the individual threads are difficult to separate. The general situation was com-

[1] Letter to Alexander Hogg, October 2, 1894.

plicated in one important respect by the presence of a strong silver sentiment in Congress, and while movements in the direction of free coinage were checked by the uncompromising attitude of the President against any weakening of the gold standard, this condition made it impossible to secure, during Cleveland's second term, any thorough-going legislation which would remove the doubts concerning the monetary standard.

The condition of the Government's finances was in a most unsatisfactory state throughout the greater part of the period between 1890 and 1896. This situation arose from a number of causes, each of which had serious repercussions. In 1890, the failure of Baring Brothers in England shook the confidence of the British investors in foreign securities, and the resultant sale of American securities set up an unusual flow of gold exports from the United States. This movement of gold was aggravated by the operations of the Silver Purchase Act of 1890. Under this Act over $100,000,000 had been added to the circulating media of the United States by 1891. During the harvest season of 1890, the extra currency was absorbed without disturbing the money markets, but after crops had been moved, surplus funds began to move from the West into the Eastern financial centers. A substantial portion of these funds, in turn, found their way into foreign markets in the form of short-time loans for purchases of goods or as investments, thus renewing the flow of gold abroad. These exports of gold put a severe strain upon the United States Treasury, for much of the gold for export purposes was obtained by the presentation of legal-tender notes to the Treasury for redemption.

Pressure was temporarily lessened in 1891 by the coincidence of a large American wheat crop with the failure of that staple in the chief European producing areas. The consequent heavy exports of wheat reversed the gold movements during the last third of 1891, but after January, 1892, continued sale of American securities again set up a drain of gold from the Treasury, and before long the reserve supply of gold in the Treasury had almost reached the minimum of $100,000,000, a figure which had been generally accepted as an adequate reserve for the legal-tender notes. Secretary of the Treasury Foster, serving the last few months of Harrison's Administration, managed to postpone any decisive action until after March, 1893, with the result that when Carlisle took over the duties of the Treasuryship there was barely a $100,000,000 gold reserve left for the redemption of the legal-tender notes and only about $25,000,000 in general funds out of which to pay the operating expenses of the Government.

Secretary Carlisle set about to build up the depleted Treasury, but he was beset by numerous obstacles, chief of which came from Congress, which refused to pass any legislation that would strengthen the gold standard. He was further handicapped by the doubt which existed as to whether he possessed the legal authority to issue bonds for the purpose of strengthening his position.

The panic of 1893 added to the difficulties of the Administration, for in the depression which followed, the income of the Government from taxes and other sources was greatly diminished.[1] The President, who believed that the silver purchases were in a large measure responsible for the panic, called a special session of Congress in August, 1893, for the purpose of repealing this feature of the Act of 1890. The bill calling for repeal passed the House within a short time, but the strong silver interests in the Senate delayed its passage there for over two months, and it was only by pacifying certain Senators by judicious appointments and by splitting the Democratic Party that the repeal measure was finally ratified in the Senate, October 30, 1893.

Meanwhile, Secretary Carlisle tried without success various ways of securing the gold necessary to build up his reserves. The result was that by January, 1894, the condition of the Treasury was so bad (chiefly due to diminished income during the depression) that Secretary Carlisle was forced to issue bonds in the face of much opposition from a large part of Congress, many members of which thought that the cure for the current financial and

---

[1] The McKinley Tariff, which was still in operation, had, by its high rates, considerably reduced the income from import duties.

economic difficulties lay in the free coinage of silver. Two such bond sales were made in 1893, one in January and the other in November.

These bond sales by the Treasury were not successful in their purpose, which was to increase the gold reserves of the Government, because, while the bonds had to be paid for in gold, much of the gold used for this purpose was obtained by the presentation of legal tenders to the Treasury for gold redemption.[1]

Profiting by his experiences in 1894, the Secretary made arrangements in 1895 with the famous Belmont-Morgan Syndicate for the sale of bonds under conditions which would not cause a withdrawal of gold from the Treasury. This arrangement, although soundly denounced by the opposition, was successful in relieving the Treasury, and, followed by subsequent sales of bonds under similar conditions, successfully bridged the gap until 1896, when business recovery and the settlement of the silver question again put the Treasury in a strong position.

During the period under consideration the silver interests did not relax in their efforts to achieve free coinage. Their opposition to the repeal of the silver purchases has already been noted. The depression, with its customary liquidation, added to the burdens of the debtors, and gave added weight to the argument that silver should be coined as a method of relieving this class and promoting business recovery. This argument was especially popular when business failed to improve immediately after the cessation of the silver purchases. Various attempts were made in Congress to pass legislation providing for the coinage of silver, or its purchase under different plans, none of which was successful.

As the Presidential election of 1896 approached, it became evident that silver was to be the issue over which the election would be waged and, although McKinley attempted during the

[1] Congress' only contribution to aid the difficult situation of the Treasury was the passage of a bill in March, 1894, which provided for 'the coinage of the seigniorage,' a measure which was promptly vetoed by the President. The 'seigniorage' was the amount of silver theoretically acquired by buying silver at the market price and issuing of overvalued silver dollars.

early part of the campaign to emphasize the tariff, it was upon a platform calling for sound money that the Republicans succeeded in defeating Bryan.[1]

Mr. Atkinson watched with keen interest the vicissitudes of the Government's financial status and the developments of the silver fight. He was, of course, deeply concerned with the possibility of an abandonment of the gold standard and he overlooked no opportunity to make suggestions, both to friends in Congress and to members of the Administration, which he thought might aid in strengthening the position of the Treasury, and in avoiding any concession to the silver interests.

In May, 1893, while he was in Washington, Mr. Atkinson was asked by Attorney-General Olney to give an opinion upon one of the plans then being considered by the Administration to raise funds. This plan called for the sale by the Treasury of the silver bullion which had accumulated under the operations of the Silver Purchase Act of 1890, and for which Treasury notes had been issued in payment.

Mr. Atkinson lost no time after his return from Washington in carefully examining the legislation on the subject, and in seeking the counsel of his able legal adviser, Moses Williams, prominent Boston lawyer. The advice of the latter, that in his opinion the original intention of the Law of 1890 did not contemplate such a sale of the bullion, did not deter Mr. Atkinson in his belief that the bullion might well be sold as a method of relieving the pressure upon the Treasury. He explained to Williams: 'It is true that the law must be strained if the Treasury should sell silver bullion, and it may be admitted that such a sale was not contemplated by those who voted for the Act, even though it may have been contemplated by those who framed it. On the other hand, the sale of bonds is urged by yourself and others. Is it not equally true that the law must be strained to warrant a sale of bonds? None of the Acts in which that authority is found

---

[1] The foregoing résumé of the events between 1890 and 1896 was drawn from a number of sources, including Noyes, A. D., *Forty Years of American Finance*; Dewey, D. R., *Financial History of the United States*; Dewey, D. R., *National Problems*; and Taussig, F. W., *The Silver Situation in the United States*.

by indirection contemplated the sale of bonds for any present purpose. Now if the law may be strained for one subject, why not for the other; the more patent and thorough the remedy for existing wrongs, the more it should be strained if at all.' [1]

Mr. Atkinson developed this point of view in a brief which he sent to Mr. Olney. He also directed a letter to President Cleveland, stating that an emergency existed which should be met by the sale of the silver bullion in order to aid the Treasury in meeting the demands made upon it.

It was decided, however, by Mr. Olney and the Treasury Department, that the proposal for sale of the bullion was not legal, much to the disappointment of Mr. Atkinson, who had hoped for this comparatively simple method of easing the pressure on the Treasury. He did not immediately give up the idea, however, and during the subsequent action in Congress which led to the repeal of the silver purchase provisions of the Sherman Act, urged Secretary Carlisle and the President to use the possibility of the sale of bullion as a club to bring the recalcitrant members into line.[2]

The supply of silver held by the Treasury as a result of the silver purchases continued to bother Mr. Atkinson, with the result that he sought other methods of eliminating it as a factor in the Government's financial structure. One plan which he evolved provided for the sale by the Government of $100,000,000 worth of fifty-year annuities, backed by the silver bullion in the Treasury. To meet the payments on the annuities, two per cent of the bullion should be sold each year. This procedure, he felt, would raise needed funds and at the same time would liquidate the Government's supply of silver without seriously disturbing the silver market. This plan was subjected to many of the same

---

[1] May 9, 1893.

[2] Incidentally, Mr. Atkinson credited Senator Sherman with having the possible sale of silver bullion in mind at the time the Purchase Bill was passed. He wrote to the latter complimenting him upon his foresight and asked him to confirm this position. But Mr. Sherman declined to commit himself, and in his answer to Mr. Atkinson dated July 15, 1893, he said, 'As this subject is so soon to be brought before the attention of Congress, I do not care to express an opinion upon it, as it might embarrass the President and the Secretary, and cause needless discussion of the question.'

objections as was the outright sale of the silver bullion, and the result was that it received no substantial support.

Blocked in these moves, Mr. Atkinson proposed a third scheme to rid the Treasury of its supply of silver. He again sought loopholes in the law which had provided for the issue of the Treasury notes of 1890, and arrived at the conclusion that the Secretary of the Treasury possessed the power to eliminate the supply of silver if he adhered to a chain of reasoning which looked upon the Sherman notes when first issued as a forced demand loan; backed by a quantity of silver bullion, the original market price of which was equal to the value of the notes outstanding. If these notes were considered as evidences of a loan, once they had been paid into the Treasury for taxes, etc., their reissue could be construed only as an indication of another forced loan to the Government. According to Mr. Atkinson, however, the Secretary had no power to raise funds by borrowing, except by the authorization of Congress. It followed, therefore, that all the Sherman notes which had been paid into the Treasury should be considered as cancelled, or *functus officio*. Furthermore, to the extent that these notes were paid in, the supply of bullion would become redundant, and the surplus would be available for sale if Congress so desired.[1]

[1] The following brief which Mr. Atkinson sent to Secretary Carlisle on April 20, 1895, contains his arguments in more detail: 'The Sherman Act was an act for borrowing money by the issue of United States notes due on demand. These notes are evidence of debt. The purpose of borrowing was to buy silver bullion, a part of which has been coined. The purchase has been concluded. The original amount of the borrowing has been fixed by that conclusion. Under other provisions these notes have been made lawful money. As such they may be reissued in liquidation of demands on the Government. Their function as lawful money is separate and distinct from their original purpose, to wit, borrowing. The Treasury forced a loan to the Government by issuing them. The Act provides that the amount of such notes outstanding shall be no more and no less than the amount of silver bullion in the Treasury at its cost and the dollars coined therefrom. Whether they shall be and remain outstanding does not rest with the Secretary of the Treasury. He may use these notes as lawful money and under certain conditions of the Treasury, by so doing they may all remain outstanding, that is, they may remain unpaid and in circulation among the people or through the Treasury to and from the Treasury to the people who use them. It, however, rests with individuals to demand payment in coin. Under the mandatory provisions of the Sherman Act and in order to maintain parity, these notes are, have been and must be paid in gold coin. That payment ends that part of the loan. It is not within the lawful power of the Secretary of the Treasury to borrow again under that Act by reissuing a paid note. By analogy the Secretary of the Treasury might re-issue interest-bearing bonds which have been paid in anticipation of their maturity. In point of fact, a

Mr. Atkinson brought this plan to the attention of the Secretary of the Treasury and other members of the Administration at various times throughout 1895 and 1896. To hasten the redemption process, he suggested to the Secretary that bonds might be offered, payable only in Sherman notes, which would put the notes at a premium, and would insure their rapid withdrawal from circulation. This plan was attractive in its purpose to members of the Administration, but serious doubt was expressed as to whether it could be put into operation.[1] Secretary Carlisle, for example, did not feel that he possessed the power to retire the notes as Mr. Atkinson suggested. To offset this feeling, Mr. Atkinson seriously considered the advisability of securing a writ of mandamus to restrain the Secretary from reissuing the Sherman notes. He later decided that the Sherman Silver Purchase Act gave so much power to the Secretary that a court decision was unnecessary. But as Mr. Carlisle did not share this opinion, the matter did not develop further.

Incidentally, while it may be admitted that Mr. Atkinson's position in respect to the Sherman notes (he also applied the same reasoning to greenbacks) might possibly have been sustained by

---

certain part of this demand loan has been paid, we will say thirty million dollars ($30,000,000). Those notes now rest in the Treasury. Being paid notes, they cannot be considered as cash in the Treasury. It is not lawful for the Secretary to use them again as cash. The Sherman Act also provides for this contingency. These notes were to be sustained by silver at its cost so long as they remained outstanding or unpaid. The amount of the silver at its cost is to be no more and no less than the amount outstanding. The amount of the silver bullion now in the Treasury counted as cash is more than the amount of the unpaid loan. The Secretary has no power to sell this bullion, but the law is mandatory upon him to take out from the cash assets of the Treasury as much of the silver at its cost as would represent the amount of the loan secured upon such silver which has been paid. This can be done by a cross-entry and by opening a new account instead of the regular cash account of the Treasury. The accountant's entry would take the following form: *Silver bullion debtor to cash for ? ounces of silver at its cost transferred to a bullion fund of silver awaiting the instructions of Congress for its disposal, such bullion being representative of the amount of the loan originally negotiated for its purchase, which has been paid.* Respectfully submitted, Edward Atkinson.'

[1] Assistant Secretary of the Treasury, C. N. Jordan, wrote from New York, March 15, 1895: 'Much as I should like to agree with you [in this interpretation of the law] I am afraid that I can't. I suppose your idea is this: that having once redeemed a legal-tender note, the reissue of it constitutes a new loan, which is forbidden by law. But the Act of May 31, 1878, repeals all acts and parts of acts inconsistent therewith, and is mandatory in said Act. Send me the quotations which warrant your conclusion. If I can use them as you do, I will try to press them upon the attention of the Secretary.'

a court interpretation of the law, the political difficulties involved were more important. The question at issue was more than a legal technicality; it involved a fundamental struggle between the conservative East and the liberal West, between the creditors on the one hand and the debtors, aided and abetted by the silver interests, on the other.[1] In view of these facts, the Administration was probably wise in not further complicating an already complex political situation by introducing this new controversial point.

As another method of improving the financial structure of the United States, Mr. Atkinson sought to change the banking system in such a way as to give greater elasticity to the currency and to provide a satisfactory substitute for any circulating media which might be withdrawn by the retirement of the greenbacks or Treasury notes. As the first step toward improving the system, he favored the repeal of the tax on bank notes, 'in order that it may be in the power of every State and of every section to learn the lesson of sound banking in its own way.'[2]

To meet the requirements for an elastic currency, and to bridge the gap until the tax on banks was removed, he again recommended the use of clearing-house certificates as a satisfactory medium, a plan which he had advanced several years before.[3] Later this idea was modified to provide for the circulation of certificates of deposit. Mr. Atkinson felt that these certificates, issued by the banks as evidences of customers' deposits, would adequately fill the need for bills of small denomination, should the silver (and the Treasury notes) be withdrawn under his or similar plans, and would provide an elastic currency based in general upon the 'banking theory' to which he subscribed.

---

[1] Or, as one free-silver orator put the issue in 1892: 'Two great forces are forming in battle line: the same under different form and guise that have long been in deadly antagonism, represented in master and slave, lord and vassal, king and peasant, despot and serf, landlord and tenant, lender and borrower, organized avarice and the necessities of the divided and helpless poor. I appeal to the people of this great Commonwealth to array themselves on the side of humanity and justice.' Quoted in Barnes, James A., *John G. Carlisle, Financial Statesman*, pp. 254, 255.

[2] From a letter to the Editor of the *Manufacturers' Record*, July 7, 1894.

[3] *Ante*, pp. 155–56.

Mr. Atkinson worked hard to get this idea adopted. He secured a decision from Attorney-General Olney that such certificates would not be subject to the tax on bank notes. He wrote letters to Secretary Carlisle and others and had several articles published on the subject. He persuaded the Third National Bank of Boston, of which he was a director, to issue some $50,000 worth of these certificates, some of which he used on a trip to Washington. In spite of his efforts, he was again unsuccessful in getting any widespread interest in this idea. Mr. Atkinson attributed his lack of success to the uncertainty which existed as to the legal status of the certificates, in spite of the opinion of the Attorney-General.

While Mr. Atkinson was making the foregoing attempts to remedy the evils of the existing financial situation, he was overlooking no opportunities to discredit the free-silver movement. In this rôle he was at his best, and with speeches, letters, and articles made a sustained attack against the silver and cheap-money interests, concentrating his efforts, especially during the Presidential campaign, in the South and the West.

One of the chief arguments of the advocates of free-silver coinage was that there had been a disastrous fall in the price level since the Civil War, due to the appreciation of gold and the depreciation in the price of silver. This causal relationship Mr. Atkinson denied: 'Whenever that assertion is made, I ask my contestant to name the article or articles, and I affirm that there is not a single commodity which has been subject to a considerable fall in price since 1873 or 1865, of which that change or decline in price cannot be traced to specific applications of science or invention, subject to identification, either to the production or distribution of that specific article without any reference whatever to the change in the ratio of gold to silver or silver to gold.' [1]

There was also considerable agitation during these years for an international treaty relating to bimetallism. Mr. Atkinson

---

[1] Letter to the editor of the *Journal of Commerce*, September 25, 1896. In an article, 'The Battle of Standards, and the Fall of Prices,' which appeared in the *Forum*, April, 1895, Mr. Atkinson treated this question in some detail, calling attention to the various improvements which had been made in the production of various groups of commodities.

was strongly opposed to this possibility. To Senator Donelson Caffrey, of Louisiana, he wrote:

> The proposal for an international treaty of legal tender seems to be preposterous. We are the creditor nation of Europe on our annual trade to a very large amount of money. We produce the food that Great Britain must have, and the cotton that she must buy. She converts these into articles that are exported by her to the silver standard nations. Now, under an international treaty of legal tender, we should give the choice to Great Britain to pay for our cotton and for our corn in gold or silver at her option, while we should deprive ourselves of the right to refuse the silver. What a jolly good thing it would be for Great Britain to have such an option. But what idiots we should be to give it to her. It would be carrying on our corn and cotton trade, as I have said elsewhere, on the basis of Heads you win, Tails we lose.[1]

In Mr. Atkinson's opinion the legal-tender quality of the greenbacks, the Treasury notes, and the silver dollars, was highly undesirable. In his mind the true test of good money was the test of fire, i.e., the bullion value of a coin should be equal to its value in money. The fact that these forms of money had to be accepted in payment of debts made it possible for the Government to collect forced loans from its citizens. He placed a great deal of emphasis upon the point that each time the Treasury paid out greenbacks, silver certificates (or dollars), or Treasury notes, it was collecting a new forced loan. In a short article entitled 'Forced Loans,' which he sent to the *Journal of Commerce and Commercial Bulletin* in May, 1895, he outlined his position:

> The writer lately made the attempt to put the monthly statement of the national debt in a true form. The monthly statement which is issued by the Secretary of the Treasury is not in a true form. He cannot make it so because existing laws compel him to count as cash a

---

[1] Letter dated April 20, 1894. It is difficult to see how Mr. Atkinson could logically sustain this position. If, as the proponents of international bimetallism prophesied, the world market for both metals would give a steady market ratio equal to the mint ratios of the countries which were party to the agreement, then there would be no advantage in paying or receiving payment in terms of one or the other metal. If, on the other hand, the result were to be that one metal drove the other out of circulation, the fact that the United States was an 'annual creditor' would mean that the contracts for wheat and cotton would be made from year to year upon a basis of any change which might have occurred in the price level. It would be the holders of long-term bonds who ran the risk of losing by such a treaty.

part of the demand notes which have been paid in coin or redeemed by being paid into the Treasury for taxes. These notes are not cash. They are paid notes. Any private corporation, merchant, or firm who should make up his accounts in such a way would be regarded as a dishonest and disreputable person, unfit to be trusted. His credit would be gone if he submitted a statement to any bank or trust company from which he desired a loan, in which he counted his own paid notes as cash assets. The principle of law and the common practice are the same. A paid note is a dead note; in legal form it is 'functus officio.' The only true entry that can be made when such a note had been redeemed and paid is to charge it off to notes payable and thereby reduce outstanding liabilities. If such a note is put out again it works a new act of borrowing. It is evidence that another loan has been made by the promisor. A re-issue of such a note is not a continuation of a former loan; it is another, separate, distinct new loan. It matters not whether the same piece of paper is used or not. Bank notes which have once been in circulation and which have been paid by the bank are used over again. But no bank officer or director would ever pretend that, although the same piece of paper is used over again after having been redeemed, it is not a new transaction; a new, separate, and distinct obligation from any previous issue of such note....

The writer has been rebuked for telling the truth and for printing a true statement of the national debt. Even some of the advocates of a sound and safe monetary system seem to think that there is something discreditable to the Government in calling the greenbacks or legal-tender notes issued during the war 'a debt,' and in pointing out the fact that they only circulate at some periods by force, compelling the people of the country to loan money to the Government without interest when they do not wish to.

Under the decision of the Supreme Court both the people and the Secretary of the Treasury are compelled to treat the legal-tender notes of the United States as 'lawful money.' Neither that decision nor the practice of the people in receiving them can make these notes anything but 'fiat money.' The demand of the most crazy Populist or Greenbacker is justified if it is in the power of the Government to make its promises of dollars of the same monetary power as the dollars promised. That is the effect of the decision sustaining fiat money. Neither that decision nor any other can make fiat money true money.

If money is not true money, it is bad money. Legal-tender notes are bad money. They circulated originally only by force of law without regard to equality or justice except so far as the necessity of the war justified a departure from the ordinary rules of equality and justice. The forced loan collected for the purchase of silver bullion cannot be justified on any ground whatever. Both the Bland and Sherman Acts were a perversion of the power of public legislation to the purpose of private gain, at the instigation of the owners of silver mines and their representatives in Congress, themselves voting to put money in their own pockets at the cost of the people from whom they collected by way of these forced loans.

It is time to stop mincing matters and being mealy-mouthed. There is nothing sacred about the war greenback. It did its work. That work is done. It is not doing the work of war now. It is doing the work of fraud under the law in forcing a loan without interest from the people of this country to the Government, when the Government has or may have an ample revenue and does not need to collect a forced loan for any purpose whatever. Therefore it follows that any statement of the national account in which these paid or redeemed notes are counted as cash in the Treasury is not a true statement.

He also thought that this legal-tender quality of the 'fiat' money of the United States hid the essence of the difficulties with the coinage of silver. He claimed, for example, to be perfectly willing to have bimetallism in the United States if the legal-tender features could be modified.[1] In an open letter addressed to William J. Bryan in September, 1896, he advanced the following:

Our suggestion is a very simple one. May not the mints of the United States be opened to the free coinage of standard gold and standard silver dollars subject to provisions of legal tender by their specific name? Contracts in silver dollars to be enforced in silver dollars — contracts in gold dollars to be enforced in gold dollars — contracts in dollars without specification to be enforced in that dollar which at the date of the maturity of the contract is the best; that is to say, the dollar which would then buy the most goods either in this or any other country.

We submit that in this way a true and just bimetallic system may be established by which both gold and silver may be jointly used as money metals, subject to the free choice of all citizens, without im-

---

[1] In this connection, Mr. Atkinson advanced the theory that the conception of legal tender was born of fraud and deceit. In a letter to Henry Dunning McLeod he commented: 'I long since conceived that the origin of a conception of legal tender must have been in fraud of the public. Substantially all coins having originally been made of just weight corresponding to the name, there could have been no need of a decree or a statute to enforce their acceptance by a creditor; hence the very conception of a decree or statute of legal tender could only have originated when the coin was debased. In Ihne's *History of the Roman Empire* I have struck the first record which has ever been brought to my attention, to wit, in the Second Punic War the distress of Italy was so great under Hannibal's raid as to induce the Senate to reduce the weight of the Roman "as" with the customary disaster.' April 12, 1894.

pairing personal liberty or freedom of contract — but more than all in such a way that those who are not conversant with monetary science and who may not be aware of the danger of cheap or depreciated money may not be defrauded.[1]

One of Mr. Atkinson's major attacks upon the free coinage of silver centered upon the assumption by the United States Government of the functions of a bank of issue. He pointed out that this assumption had occurred under the laws which provided for the legal-tender notes, the silver certificates, and the Treasury notes. He correctly attributed much of the Government's financial difficulties during these years to the fact that the Treasury was faced with the necessity of redeeming its demand notes in gold. This, of course, could not have occurred if the Government had been restricted only to the coinage of such gold bullion as was presented to it for that purpose or the issuance of gold certificates. It was Mr. Atkinson's objective point, in his proposals for banking currency and reform, to take the Treasury out of the banking business in so far as the issue of currency was concerned, and to have that function exercised only by private banks.

Mr. Atkinson made extensive use of the foregoing material in the fight for the maintenance of the gold standard. His acquaintance with members of the Administration guaranteed a hearing for his ideas where their influence might be most effective. He occasionally wrote directly to the President, but for the most part communicated with Mr. Cleveland through the latter's close advisers.[2] Mr. Atkinson was highly gratified from time to time to see evidences of his influence in the President's speeches or actions. To Nordhoff on December 26, 1894, he wrote, 'I have been writ-

---

[1] It is not likely that this scheme was advanced for any purpose other than to embarrass Mr. Bryan by bringing out the differences in the value of the two metals, because the obvious confusion of having two monetary standards in existence at the same time would not make such a suggestion practical.

[2] A. B. Farquhar, of Pennsylvania, close friend of the President, for example, wrote to Mr. Atkinson concerning one of the latter's suggestions in respect to the currency question: 'I received your valuable monograph at the Shoreham Saturday afternoon and took it at once to the President, where it received the most careful attention, and a conference was arranged for Sunday noon.' Letter to Mr. Atkinson dated February 8, 1895. Mr. Atkinson also had personal interviews with the President during this period of currency problems.

ing very plainly during the past few weeks both to the President and to the Secretary, and I can see evidences of some of my phrases in Cleveland's message.'[1]

Mr. Atkinson kept in touch with Secretary Carlisle, sometimes by direct correspondence or interviews, but principally through the offices of the Assistant Secretaries of the Treasury, Charles Hamlin and C. N. Jordan. He became, at times, highly impatient at the refusal of Carlisle to act vigorously to preserve the gold standard. Such impatience is not difficult to understand, for the Secretary was cautious and conservative by nature, and his legal training prompted him to seek an interpretation of the laws under which he was called upon to administer his duties which would express the spirit of the legislation as it was originally passed, and he furthermore preferred, whenever possible, to lay questions before Congress instead of acting with vague or questionable authority.[2] On the other hand, Mr. Atkinson, as had been noticed,[3] was a believer in the principle that the end justified the means, and more than once sought to interpret the letter of the law in such a way as to effect the desired results. In addition, he would have much preferred to see the whole matter removed from Congress and placed in the hands of the Administration.

Mr. Atkinson's impatience with Carlisle reached its high point during the uncertain period just before the final arrangements were made with the Belmont-Morgan Syndicate. The Secretary was reluctant to make arrangements with the Syndicate because the terms seemed disadvantageous to the Government. This was due partly because the Treasurer had no authority to make the bonds payable in gold. He delayed for a few days after February 3, 1895, at which time preliminary arrangements had been made with Morgan and Belmont, hoping that Congress would

---

[1] Confirmation of his statement came from the Secretary of Agriculture, J. Sterling Morton, who wrote to Mr. Atkinson on January 29, 1895, 'The President's message of yesterday came as nearly saying what you desired to have said as though he had taken a photograph of your mental processes on the 11th day of January.'

[2] Cf. Noyes, A. D., *op. cit.*, p. 207.

[3] *Ante*, pp. 195–96.

pass the Springer Bill authorizing him to sell gold bonds. Congress rejected the Springer Bill on February 7, which made it impossible for the Government to do anything but agree with the Syndicate's terms.[1] It was this indecision on the part of Carlisle which prompted Mr. Atkinson to write two short letters to his friend A. B. Farquhar. One letter, marked *confidential*, read: 'The chief barrier to a return of confidence in the community is distrust of Secretary Carlisle. I regret that it is so but such is the fact. If Fairchild were recalled to the post it would be worth several per cent of the price of bonds. The President ought to be advised of these facts.' The other letter, marked *personal*, continued: 'I have stood Carlisle until I can no longer. He is not master of the situation. His fiddling with the coinage of the seigniorage and his want of clear grasp of all the conditions has destroyed the confidence of the men whose support is now most needed. Can anything be done?'[2]

To these letters Mr. Farquhar made answer, in part, on February 8: 'Your letters referring to Mr. Carlisle were read with sad interest. I am afraid you are correct. Carlisle is my friend, as I believe he is yours, but there are times when public duty must transcend the claims of personal friendship, and I have been debating in my mind whether I should see Mr. Cleveland in regard to the matter. I cordially approve of the selection of Mr. Fairchild. Carlisle, I am distressed to say, has not been a success. He is an able man, would have been valuable in the Senate, but does not size up to the Treasury.'

Both Mr. Atkinson and Mr. Farquhar were appeased by the successful completion of the arrangements with the Syndicate, which insured the continuance of gold redemption by the Treasury, although they inclined to give full credit to the President for this achievement.[3]

---

[1] Cf. Barnes, James A., *John G. Carlisle, Financial Statesman*, pp. 363 ff.

[2] Both letters were dated February 6, 1895.

[3] Mr. Atkinson wrote concerning the Syndicate arrangement: '... it seems to me that the President's action corresponds very closely to Grant's veto of the Inflation Bill. That veto killed the greenback movement. The present action of the President will kill the free-silver movement.' Letter to A. B. Farquhar, February 21, 1895.

While Mr. Atkinson continued to hold the President's financial policies in high regard, his opinion of the Democratic Party became increasingly uncomplimentary as the silver interests began more and more to dominate the party after 1892. He looked upon the defeat of the Democrats in the Congressional election of November, 1894, as an encouraging sign. To an English friend he commented, 'I do not consider this revolution as a return to McKinleyism. The fact is the Democratic Party swept the country to their own injury in 1892.... That complete sweep gave the bad element of the Democratic Party the power to exert its malignant influence, and it is an encouraging fact that they had been stamped upon and crushed. Again, the Republican Party is much safer as a party on the silver question and on the fiat money question than the Democratic Party.[1]

At the same time Mr. Atkinson was advising various members of the Administration in respect to banking and currency reform, his ideas were finding frequent expression both in speeches and in public print. He was a frequent contributor to such magazines as *The Forum*, *The Nation*, *Harper's Weekly*, *The North American Review*, and *Bradstreet's* (to mention only a few), and he also had letters and articles printed in an extensive list of newspapers scattered throughout the United States.[2] In addition, the most

---

[1] A letter addressed to Swire Smith, November 10, 1894. A month later he put his feelings on this point into stronger language after Congress had failed to pass any constructive legislation during the current session. 'The incapable mob which calls itself the Democratic Party in Congress having refused to follow its true leaders and having submitted to the dictation of its treacherous and untrustworthy bosses, has been condemned by the people of this country. Still failing to learn this lesson since the election, and apparently about to fail to remedy its own folly in the present session, it yet leaves the Administration in which the public has full confidence, and which will be sustained by men of both political parties, in full power to maintain the credit of the country and to fund the demand notes of any class representing both the forced loans, to any extent that may be needed in order to maintain the confidence of the people in their ultimate redemption. In other words, the public and the Executive sustaining each other will maintain the integrity and honor of the country in spite of the game of politics which members of both parties have attempted to play in dealing with these vital questions. Letter to the editor of the *Evening Post*, December 20, 1894.

[2] Some of the most prominent of these were: the *Boston Advertiser*, the *Boston Herald*, the *Boston Transcript*, the *Boston Globe*, the *New York Evening Post*, the *New York World-Bulletin*, the *New York Times*, the *New York Sun*, the *Chicago Record*, the *Chicago Times-Herald*, the *Chicago Herald*, the *Chattanooga Tradesman*, the *Springfield Republican*, the *Atlanta Union*, the *Galveston News*, the *Washington Post*, the *Sioux City Tribune*, and the

important of his magazine articles appeared later in pamphlet form.

Always a frequent contributor to newspapers and magazines, Mr. Atkinson's work along this line assumed astonishing proportions during the latter part of 1895 when the free-silver campaign was being waged so vigorously. His attention had been called to the effective pamphlets of the opposition printed under the heading of *Coin's Financial School,* and he took steps to see that offsetting material was made available for popular circulation. He co-operated in this matter with the Sound Money Committee of the Reform Club of New York which had organized what was, in his opinion, 'the most complete system of distribution of pamphlets, leaflets, broadsides, plate matter and the like that has ever been witnessed in this country.'

As early as May, 1895, Mr. Atkinson was, in addition to his other work, writing two articles per week for several Southern and Western papers, setting forth the benefits of the gold standard and the evils of free silver. A little over a year later he was writing regularly for some forty Democratic papers, besides preparing a series of articles for *Leslies' Weekly* and *Harper's*.[1]

In his newspaper and magazine articles, Mr. Atkinson did not add anything to the criticisms and proposals already noted, except perhaps to emphasize the selfishness of the silver interests in attempting to force the silver standard upon the United States. He put it, 'I regard these silver mine-owners and their retainers in the House and the Senate, one of whom in the Senate told me "he didn't believe in the damned rot, but he had got to vote for it," as a set of knaves and scoundrels who propose to cheat the people of this country without any regard to the honest advo-

Seattle Post Intelligencer. Other magazines to which he contributed on occasion included: the *Southern Review,* the *Country Gentleman,* the *Bankers' Magazine,* the *Literary Digest, The American,* and *The Independent.*

[1] During the few months previous to the November elections of 1896, Mr. Atkinson was relieved of his duties as president of the Boston Manufacturers' Mutual Fire Insurance Company, and two secretaries were placed at his disposal by the Company in order that he might spend his entire time in preparing anti-silver material.

cates of bimetallism. On that line I propose to pitch in and make it thunder all around.'[1]

It is, of course, impossible to tell how much influence his work had upon the final results of the election. He was one of a large number of writers who helped flood the country with campaign material. That his help was greatly appreciated and eagerly sought is shown by numerous letters from editors and others requesting him to send them material to combat the arguments of the other side.[2] It may be said, however, that his pleasant style and convincing manner of writing made his articles excellent ones for the purposes of propaganda.[3]

Mr. Atkinson's writing did not, of course, escape criticism from his opponents. The editor of a Colorado paper said of him, 'Mr. Atkinson is the champion liar of the world, and Ananias was very discreet in getting born early, as he would have had no reputation compared to Mr. Atkinson if he had waited until now.'

In a letter to the *Chattanooga Tradesman*, Henry Carey Baird admonished his readers, 'Let the South, therefore, turn its back upon and flee from the economic fallacies of Mr. Edward Atkinson, as it would from the plague, the black death, or from leprosy, for these fallacies are microbes that breed a social leprosy.'[4] These and other criticisms did not perturb Mr. Atkinson, as he looked upon them as indications of the fact that his comments

[1] Extract from a letter to Robert Treat Paine, July 2, 1896. He said of Bryan: 'The Popocrat candidate [the term applied to the combination of Democrats and Populists] is a specious, plausible orator without any staying power, wholly incapable of defending his own attack upon the principle of free trade and free contract on which he is now entered by becoming the advocate of a forced circulation of bad money. Had he possessed any original powers of reasoning on this question, he would never have been deceived by the shrewd attorneys of the privileged class of the silver miners on whose behalf he proposes to become Executive in forcing bad money into circulation.' Letter to the editor of *Bradstreet's*, July 15, 1896.

[2] A letter dated March 10, 1896, to the Secretary of the New York Reform League from the editor of the *Belton Journal*, of Belton, Texas, stated, 'If you wish to assist us down here in Texas in our fight against 16 to 1, get some competent person, say Edward Atkinson, of Boston, to review the speech of Honorable J. W. Bailey delivered in the House of Representatives on Wednesday, February 12, 1896.'

[3] In connection with this campaign and in a special effort to reach the masses, Mr. Atkinson developed a technique of writing his articles with words of as few syllables as possible. He prided himself on the fact that many of his writings contained a remarkably high percentage of words of one syllable.

[4] Issue of March 15, 1895.

had attracted attention, or had perhaps touched a vulnerable spot in the silver armament.

Like many others who favored sound money and low tariff, Mr. Atkinson was placed in an awkward position by the attitude which most of the Democrats took in respect to silver, and by the high protective sentiments of the majority of the Republicans. Early in February, 1895, he tried unsuccessfully to get William B. Allison to head '*the sound money, tariff reduction party*, which under the influence of the West is going to sweep the country and wipe this Democratic mob, who have not the common sense to recognize a great leader when they have one, out of existence.'[1]

The Republican nomination in 1896 of McKinley for President could not be expected to please Mr. Atkinson.[2] As a result of this nomination, and in anticipation of Bryan's nomination, he predicted an 'enormous bolt from both parties in support of the business men's candidates in Congressional districts.' This move he hoped would assure control in the House of Representatives, and would prevent any unwelcome action either in respect to the tariff or currency. Following Bryan's nomination and the declaration by the Democrats in their convention at Chicago in July, 1896, for free coinage of silver, Mr. Atkinson urged that the 'true Democrats' call a convention for the primary purpose of controlling the House.[3]

Although he did not attend the subsequent convention that the bolting Gold Democrats held at Indianapolis, Mr. Atkinson

---

[1] Allison's failure to follow his suggestions was disappointing to Mr. Atkinson. He wrote to Wells: 'What a pity Allison has not more sand. If Allison had Cleveland's pluck and would lead off for low tariff with the West behind him and for sound money — he would have a walkover. I wrote him and he says he has nine months to think of it! What a dam'd fool.' Letter dated March 12, 1895.

[2] He said of the Republican candidate, 'McKinley is a respectable mediocrity, without mental capacity or comprehension either of the tariff question or of the money question.' Letter to Professor Goldwin Smith, June 10, 1896.

[3] On July 10, 1896, Mr. Atkinson directed a telegram to W. E. Russell, Democratic Governor of Massachusetts, who was attending the Democratic Convention at Chicago: 'Suggest immediate call for third party convention of True Democrats to organize for control of Congressional districts and balance of power — without separate candidate for President. Platform — Gold standard, take Government out of banking and rest for one term on general tariff question until money question is settled.'

did, at the suggestion of William D. Byman, chairman of the Executive Committee, prepare materials for the proclamation calling the convention. He was enthusiastic about the Gold Democrats, making the prediction to Wells that 'the Party born yesterday at Indianapolis corresponds to the old Free-Soil Party in its origin. It will as surely rule the country in four or eight years as that party did when it had gained its position under the name of Republican, since so misused.'

Recognizing the fact that the new party had no chance of electing a President, Mr. Atkinson was deeply concerned lest Bryan should win. As election day approached, however, he felt fairly confident that the result would be a sweeping victory for the Republicans.[1] In July and August he was not happy over the prospect of having to vote for McKinley. He wrote to a friend, 'I expect to vote for McKinley, but it goes hard with me.'[2] But, as the Republican candidate carried out his campaign on a sound-money platform, Mr. Atkinson partially revised his earlier opinion, and was able to say in September,... 'McKinley has shown to me an unexpected ability in his treatment of the money question, and as that is the paramount issue, it has become a necessity that he should be elected, as I have little doubt he will.' But he added, 'In his treatment of protection, notably wool, he shows the

[1] The following letter, written to his friend Lord Farrer in England on the eve of the election, gives an interesting picture of conditions as they then existed; 'We now count by hours the time which must elapse before the tremendous strain upon us will be removed. As the time for the verdict approaches and the magnitude of the issue has become apparent to everyone engaged in affairs, great nervousness is exhibited. One can hardly imagine what would have happened had not the Lord again "helped the fools, the drunken men and the United States." The rise in wheat and cotton is all that has saved us from a terrible calamity even in anticipation of the election. As it is, there is a steady, slow withdrawal of deposits from savings banks, which might become panicky at any moment, and there is evidently an enormous investment in gold and in foreign exchange, depleting what is called the money market and carrying the rate of interest to a high point. Yet there have been no great failures and no failures except of previously insolvent persons or of men who like one great commission house had gone into speculation. The business community is strong and the two years have been marked rather by the absence of profit than by any very large losses in well-established business. I have no fear of the result and expect a sweeping victory, but as Tom Reed related the other evening of a man who went up to the top of the Washington Monument and looked out, remarking, "Nobody ever did fall from here, but if one did, how much would be left of him?" That is about the way we are feeling.' Letter dated October 30, 1896.

[2] Extract from a letter to Alfred Shepperson, July 29, 1896.

same sophomorical lack of elementary knowledge that has always appeared in his speeches on the subject.'[1]

Mr. Atkinson was of course gratified with the results of the election and looked with considerable optimism to the future. He summarized the election to Lord Farrer:

> We have avoided a great danger.... My confidence in the intelligence of the western farmer is more than fully justified. Now comes financial reconstruction, the tariff, etc. In this matter I believe that the Sound Money Democrats or National Democratic Party, organized at Indianapolis, will hold the balance of power. It was through that influence that McKinley has been elected by the vote of free-traders. That fact is acknowledged. Heretofore both the old political parties have truckled to the silver States: hereafter the National Democratic Party will, like the old Free-Soil Party, hold the balance of power, and although small in number they will in a forceful manner control events.
>
> We shall have no return to McKinleyism. In fact the representatives of every branch of industry in the country, agriculture and manufactures alike, have become aware that the efficiency of our mechanism is so great as to over-stock this market in short order with every product. Hence, the most eager attention to our increasing exports at high wages coupled with low cost of production. When the public mind is turned in that direction the tariff for revenue only must become well assured.[2]

There was but one incident which disturbed Mr. Atkinson's high regard for Mr. Cleveland. This was the Venezuelan boundary controversy which for a time seemed about to bring the United States into war with England. The dispute between England and Venezuela over the boundary between the latter country and British Guiana began in 1841, and had subsequently cropped up from time to time with no progress being made toward settlement. Venezuela had appealed in 1876 to the United States to aid in settling the matter, and Cleveland offered, during his first term, to arrange for a mediation of the question, only to have England decline to submit the controversy. After returning to office for the second time, Cleveland again urged that the matter be settled by submission to an arbitration board, and with

---

[1] Letter to Professor Goldwin Smith, September 18, 1896.
[2] November 23, 1896.

the backing of Congress, approved a message sent to England by Secretary of State Olney which invoked the Monroe Doctrine as a basis for our interest in the affair. The denial on the part of Great Britain that the Monroe Doctrine applied in this case caused the President to send his famous message to Congress on December 17, 1895, which declared in no uncertain terms that the United States would resist any attempts at aggression by England against Venezuela, and he asked that he be allowed to appoint a commission to investigate the situation.

This message came as a distinct shock to the country, for there could be little mistake concerning the attitude of the President. To Mr. Atkinson the message seemed extremely unwise and ill-advised. His efforts had been directed, through the advocacy of low tariffs, toward bringing about closer economic relationships among the various nations of the world, progress toward which would be seriously retarded by such a conflict. He was greatly perturbed by the war spirit expressed by many Americans, and deplored the readiness with which numerous persons hastened 'to twist the Lion's tail.' Even before the President's message, he had prepared an article entitled 'Jingoism, a War Upon Domestic Industry,' in which he brought out the harm done to industry and commerce by the agitation for war. The war spirit, he thought, had its origin 'in the extreme view of protection, of which the seeds were planted by Henry C. Carey, that all imports from other countries of goods which might be made in this country even at higher cost constitutes a war on domestic industry.' A statement in one of the *Coin's Financial School* pamphlets, to the effect that war with England would be both popular and beneficial, completed the association of jingoism with the two movements against which he was working hardest. Finally, the fact that he had numerous friends in England and was distinctly an Anglophile made the prospect of a conflict between the two countries even more abhorrent.[1]

[1] In general Mr. Atkinson agreed with one of his business associates, Arthur T. Lyman, president of the Lowell Manufacturing Company, who wrote to him on December 19,

Mr. Atkinson's immediate reaction to the President's message to Congress reflected these feelings. 'If the purpose of this message is war under any circumstances by perversion of the Monroe Doctrine to this boundary question, it is a crime against humanity and civilization. If it does not mean war on a final joining of this petty question, it is the most stupendous blunder ever committed by a public man of position. If it is a bid for Jingo support in politics, it is a degradation to everyone connected with it. The sober sense of the country will condemn this Jingo spirit whether it emanates from Lodge and Chandler, or their imitators and followers, Cleveland and those who sustain him in this course.'[1]

To the President he wrote directly: 'Your closest friends and most earnest supporters here, Democrats and Mugwumps alike, on whose judgment you have heretofore depended, are shocked by the position which you have taken, more grieved than any others, and will not sustain you, but are doing everything in their power to overcome the danger to which the country has been exposed.'[2]

Mr. Atkinson lost no time in attempting to arouse sentiment both in the United States and England which would relieve the tension which existed between the two countries. He looked upon a suggestion made privately by William E. Russell, former Democratic Governor of Massachusetts, that the Monroe Doctrine itself should be arbitrated, as offering a possible solution to the situation, and made it the basis of a cable he sent to Lord Farrer, dated December 20. This message read: 'Suggest Lord Salisbury proposal to Cleveland to arbitrate and define Monroe Doctrine on behalf of England, and States, with whom it jointly

---

'What can the President mean by this foolish, illogical, reckless, business-destroying, currency upsetting and infernal war message? Who really cares anything about the Venezuelan boundary except the Fenians, the utter protectionists, the newspaper reporters who never heard of the place, the fellow who is said to have a claim or a concession from Venezuela, or the "politicians" of one side or the other who are trying to distract attention from the currency which they dare not talk of? These classes and "war and free silver" make up the people who are talking of acting in mad haste.'

[1] To J. Sterling Morton, Secretary of Agriculture, December 19, 1895.
[2] December 20, 1895.

originated, thus laying down conditions for permanent peace [between] English-speaking peoples.'

This cable was followed by letters to Lord Farrer, Lord Playfair, and George J. Goschen, the last of whom was a member of the British Cabinet, which gave his plans in more detail.

At home Mr. Atkinson worked to get members of the Senate to delay and to defeat any action leading toward the appointment of any arbitration board as suggested by the President, in order that things might quiet down before any rash action was taken. He also communicated with Professor Henry Sedgwick whose wife was a sister of Lord Balfour, outlining his plans to have the matter brought to a peaceful settlement.

Throughout the latter part of December, and all of January, this problem held Mr. Atkinson's attention almost to the exclusion of other subjects. He pushed his idea of having the Monroe Doctrine subjected to arbitration with a view of deciding whether this dispute rightfully came under its operation. This suggestion, in view of the uncertain status and meaning of the Monroe Doctrine, was not without merit, although of course it was not likely that the United States would consent to any interpretation by outside parties.[1]

Mr. Atkinson was anxious for the Administration to recede

---

[1] Early in January Mr. Atkinson made a suggestion which has been both voiced and felt by many other lovers of peace. In a letter addressed to the editor of the *New York Evening Post* on January 8, 1896, he said:

'A question has arisen as to whether Jingoism is a chronic disease affecting any great number of persons or only a superficial eruption or eczema developed by the itching for notoriety of a few persons who occupy but do not fill high positions, irritating but not dangerous. A conclusion could be easily reached upon these two phases of the question by drawing up a petition to the Senate and House of Representatives of the United States somewhat in the following form:

'"It is requested that an act may be passed to the effect that any citizen of the United States who proposes to force this country into a war with Great Britain or with any other country on a dispute about boundaries or any other similar issue, shall be immediately conscripted or entered upon the army roll for service from the beginning to the end of any such war when it shall occur. It is suggested that Senators of the United States shall be assigned to the position of general officers in this addition to the army upon the ground that their military capacity must certainly be equal to their political intelligence.

'"It is next suggested that Representatives in Congress shall be assigned to the command of brigades upon the ground that their capacity to lead military bodies had been proved by their capacity to mislead civil organizations. It is suggested that all other persons such as the heads of police departments and the like shall be ranked in the subordinate

somewhat from the position first assumed by the President. Senator J. R. Hawley had written him: 'Cleveland steps into the diplomatic field like an ox or an elephant, but he is right in the essential point that we object to England's policy of aggrandizement, and especially practicing it on the little fellows in America. He could have said substantially the same thing in the unimpassioned courteous way of diplomacy without creating a ripple.... The war scare was utterly senseless. But what astonishes me is that so many good men have talked as if there never could be a righteous war and never could be another war of any kind. The war to suppress the Rebellion was absolutely and wholly righteous and just and in accordance with the commands of God. War is a terrible thing, but there is one thing worse than a wicked an unnecessary war, and that is a cowardly peace.'[1] To this Mr. Atkinson answered: '... that there can be any reasonable

offices or as privates according to the relative energy which they may have exhibited in the development of the Jingo policy."

'Of course men who in high public position have held that patriotism should not be made subordinate to dollars and cents, and who have expressed such an earnest desire to assert and defend the honor of the country at any cost, would most enthusiastically vote for this enactment and would immediately enroll themselves for active service in the field.

'If the Jingo spirit is deeply seated, the army thus recruited would be ample for the defence of the country; while on the other hand, if it is a merely superficial or skin disease of a slightly contagious kind, that fact would be proved by the lack of enrollment of gentlemen in the higher positions which would leave the Jingo army short of officers even if the number of privates should be sufficient to make two or three regiments out of our seventy million people. But if the number of officers proved to be sufficient then that discrimination might be made use of in the disposal of the forces. The place for most effective service would be upon the disputed territory in South America lying between Guiana and Venezuela. A Lodge might there be found in some vast wilderness of the Orinoco, from which source the centre of direction could be given to the Jingo army. Effective work would be found for young men of previous experience in the police departments of northern cities in the Provost Marshal department of the Jingo army. A place could also be found in the Courts Martial of the Jingo army for the Judges who fear that without an occasional war the young men of the North will be enervated and will become too much imbued with that Christian spirit which we have become so accustomed to consider as one making for peace, order and human welfare. With this Northern Judge advocate of occasional war might be joined the Southern Judge who has lately been actuated by a similar principle and who carries concealed weapons for the purpose of shooting the counsel whose briefs are not acceptable in his Court.

'This proposal for the immediate enrollment of the Jingo army will at once develop the sincerity of purpose of the advocates of aggression and violence by their enlistment. An indirect but great benefit would then ensue by the removal of these persons from the high positions in which they have proved their incapacity to deal with questions of peace, order and industry and to give them the opportunity to exert and prove their military prowess.'

[1] Letter dated December 27, 1895.

cause for war among the English-speaking peoples, I do not believe.... There is one thing worse than a cowardly peace, a cowardly and unnecessary war. Our Mexican War was such a war.'[1]

Meanwhile the strain between England and the United States was relieved as British attention was diverted by the message of the German Emperor to President Kruger of the South African Republic on January 3, which showed that England was more concerned over trouble with Germany than with the United States.[2]

After this incident, events began to move toward a peaceful settlement of the affair. Success was assured when England agreed to arbitrate the matter after certain safeguarding provisions had been made. The matter was finally settled when a treaty was signed at Washington on February 2, 1897, between Venezuela and England which accepted the decision of an arbitration board.[3]

Mr. Atkinson shared the general feeling of relief experienced by all advocates of peace when the war danger began to subside. It was not in his nature, however, to let the affair pass into history without making an effort to promote more friendly relations between the two countries. To this end he proposed that a comprehensive treaty be negotiated which would assure a peaceful settlement of any further disputes, and which would lead eventually to a close commercial union among the English-speaking countries. Chief among the provisions which he proposed, for such a treaty were the following: First, any question of land titles should be referred to a court of three judges, one chosen by each of the contesting parties, and a third by those two. Second, international damages or claims other than those involving land should be subjected to arbitration. Third, private property on the seas, other than contraband of war should be immune from seizure. Fourth, privateering should be abolished. Fifth, unarmed cities should not be bombarded or attacked.

---

[1] December 30, 1895.
[2] Cf. Rhodes, J. F., *op. cit.*, vol. VIII, pp. 450 ff.
[3] *Ibid.*, p. 452.

Sixth, rights of smaller states, especially in the Americas, shall be guarded. Seventh, the Sandwich Islands and insular places should be neutralized and made open to the commerce of the world.[1] Finally, all precautions should be taken to bring other countries into the agreement, and to prevent armed conflict whenever possible.

Most of these ideas were, of course, not new or original with Mr. Atkinson. The provisions did, however, show an appreciation of the types of controversies that lead to conflict between nations and anticipated to a certain extent the arbitration treaty agreed upon by Secretary Olney and Lord Salisbury.[2]

Following his customary procedure, Mr. Atkinson urged the adoption of these principles by sending letters to influential persons on both sides of the Atlantic who were favorable to lasting peace between the two countries. A communication on the subject to President D. C. Gilman of Johns Hopkins University, a member of the President's Commission on the Venezuelan affair, was presented by the latter to the Commission and received favorable comments.

That his ideas were favorably received abroad is well demonstrated by the following communication from Sir John Lubbock, who wrote on March 18, 1896:

> I have duly received yours of the 18th ult., and read it with great interest.
> The feeling on our side seems to have been the same as on yours, namely, that a war between England and the United States was out of the question, and the President's threat filled us with blank amazement.

---

[1] This particular provision was one to which Mr. Atkinson had given a good deal of attention. Soon after Cleveland's return to the Presidency, Mr. Atkinson had suggested to him that the Sandwich or Hawaiian Islands be made the object of an international treaty which would insure their neutrality and would make them open to the commerce of the world. Nothing had come of the suggestion. Early in 1895, Mr. Atkinson again set forth his ideas in a communication which was presented directly to the President by Mr. Farquhar. Mr. Farquhar wrote to Mr. Atkinson February 19: '... in regard to the Sandwich Islands, what you said evidently pleased the President. He fully agreed with our view of the case, but he convinced me that with the present Congress he could accomplish nothing in that direction.' Mr. Atkinson accordingly let the matter rest until the opportunity to incorporate his ideas into the proposed treaty presented itself.

[2] Cf. James, Henry, *Richard Olney and His Public Service*, pp. 143-52, 257 ff.

Our ideas seem to have been very much on parallel lines, for I suggested in the House of Commons, before receiving your letter, that we might accompany the great increase in our Navy by the reconsideration of the Declaration of Paris.

I have talked both to Balfour and Goschen about it, and there would I believe be every disposition here to prohibit privateering, and make private property free from capture and seizure at sea.

We should I think be ready to agree that undefended cities should not be plundered, without surrendering the right of occupation. If this could be arranged it would be a great step forward.

In April, Mr. Atkinson attended the meeting of the National Arbitration Conference which met in Washington. The Conference was the result of a voluntary movement on the part of a distinguished group of American citizens who organized for the purpose of promoting an arbitration treaty between the United States and Great Britain.[1] Mr. Atkinson had the honor of speaking before the Conference and was made a member of the Executive Committee.

As the immediate excitement over the Venezuelan situation began to subside, Mr. Atkinson's interest was again reabsorbed by other questions, and his subsequent action on this matter was confined to working quietly through the Arbitration Conference.

Mr. Atkinson looked forward with considerable optimism to the inception of the McKinley Administration. As has been noted, he felt that the proponents of cheap money had been defeated without any danger to the progress of the tariff reform begun under the Wilson Bill. 'So far as we can learn,' he wrote to friends in England, 'the personnel of the next Congress will be better than that of any recent Congress. The Republicans have

---

[1] Among the more noted members were Carl Schurz, Major-General Nelson A. Miles, Lyman T. Gage, William E. Dodge, William H. Taft, President Charles W. Eliot, and Gardiner G. Hubbard.

[2] Mr. Atkinson was one of the signers of a statement issued by the National Arbitration Committee on May 24, 1897, which read in part: 'The rejection, by our National Senate, of the treaty initiated in accordance with the joint resolution of Congress passed in 1890, and concluded by the representatives of the United States and Great Britain, January 11, 1897, we believe to have been against the highest interests not only of the two nations immediately concerned, but also of the world. Nor can we doubt that the rejection was against the prevailing national conviction. By every available mode of expression, the people, without distinction of party or locality, manifested their desire for the ratification of the treaty. Seldom has a national measure received a popular support so cordial.'

been forced to put up strong men, and while there may be a show of high tariff legislation merely to satisfy appearances, I do not think there will be any reversion to what is known as McKinleyism. The chief support of that system was in this section of the country and the men who gave it will be the last men to seek a return to the uncertain conditions of excessive protection.'

But his confidence in the Republicans was misplaced. Within two days after his inauguration, President McKinley called a special session of Congress for the purpose of passing a new tariff law.

Mr. Atkinson was disturbed at the outlook. In February, he had written to A. B. Farquhar, 'My son has lately been in Washington and he brings back the word that the new [tariff] bill will be a very obnoxious one, all sorts of log-rolling in it, some of the worst types of McKinleyism, and that it will probably go through the House with a rush unless there is an organized resistance developed.' [1]

Mr. Atkinson gave active support to the movement, led by Mr. Farquhar and others, to block the passage of the new higher tariff legislation, but it was a hopeless task, as the Republicans were determined to restore the protective principles which had been threatened by the Wilson Bill.

Obviously, Mr. Atkinson's position as an avowed supporter of low tariffs deprived him of influence among the staunch defenders of the Republicans' tariff policy, while his actions against silver had caused many of his friends among the Democrats to turn against him.

Among the Gold Democrats in Congress, he continued to exert a considerable influence, but their position was much less important than he had anticipated.[2]

---

[1] February 18, 1897.

[2] The attitude of the staunch Republicans toward the Gold Democrats was probably typified by Senator George F. Hoar. Mr. Atkinson wrote to him on March 13, 1896, saying in part, 'The Republicans have been put in power by the Sound Money Democrats, who have sunk all other differences in order to save the honor of the Nation; yet the purpose of the Republican Party seems to be to ignore the Sound Money Democrats on the tariff, a question of minor importance in mere dollars and cents, but next in importance to the money question in the conduct of government in the minds of thinking men; objectors

Mr. Atkinson did not give up without a fight and sent letters and data to various members of the House and the Senate trying to prevent the return of 'McKinleyism.' In May, the outlook was sufficiently encouraging to prompt him to write to Wells:

> You may expect to see the tariff bill held in the Senate for months while the Tariff Reform Senators constitute themselves an independent committee for giving hearings to the opponents of the Bill, and placing the whole substance of their protests before the Senate day by day. I think the Committee will be obliged to withdraw both bills.

But a month later he had decided to drop the question. He wrote on June 2, to Senator Caffery who was leading what amounted to a forlorn hope in the Senate against the Dingley Bill:

> I have your two very gratifying letters of May 31. If my works, such as they are, shall be of service to you I shall be glad.

becoming more and more numerous even among those who have previously supported the so-called protective policy without full consideration. If there is to be a reversion to what is called the McKinley policy of 1890; that is to say, the policy of 'protection with incidental revenue,' on a bill which is being framed today in much the same manner that the McKinley bill was framed, namely, by a combination of the demands of particular interests to the public for purposes of private gain — there will be nothing to prevent the Silver Democrats and the Populists sweeping the country in the next election of the House of Representatives.'

To which the Senator replied: 'It is needless to say that I find nothing in it with which I agree. The Republicans were never put into power by Sound Money Democrats. The country in 1894 declared itself by a most emphatic majority against the Sound Money Democrats and all other Democrats and Populists. They favored the adoption of protection and repudiated the wretched, sectional Wilson Bill. I should think the misery which that bill has caused might teach some of you gentlemen a little modesty. But they seem to thrust up their heads and repeat their old exploded arguments with as much confidence as if they had not been again and again refuted by reason and by experience. We should have carried the country triumphantly against the Silver Democrats and their Populist allies if there had not been a Sound Money Democrat in the world. We carried it on the platform which nominated McKinley at St. Louis, and the country accepted and acted upon the pledges we gave. The suggestion that we should abandon them is a suggestion, to Republicans, of personal dishonor.' Letter dated April 19, 1897.

And Mr. Atkinson's prophecy that the Gold Democrats would be joined by many Republicans in favor of lower tariffs evoked the answer:

'If you think a great party and a President are to abandon the convictions of their lifetime and to break the pledges on which they were placed in power for fear that somebody will desert them, I think you are much mistaken. The Democratic Party, professing to be for free trade and to believe that protection was both unconstitutional and criminal, undertook to put into a free-trade measure protection for Democratic interests and Democratic States, and it went down. If the Republican Party, being a party believing in protection, as all our statesmen of any account have believed in it since the foundation of the Government, undertakes to please Mugwumps and traitors by mingling free-trade notions with its measures, it will go down. It may go down, if it do not. But in that case it will go down with honor, in the other with infamy.' Letter dated May 6, 1897.

As to the present conditions I confess that I hesitate. I am in a position wherein I have no right to let my name appear in an aggressive movement which might seem to the members of the Company with which I am associated, to be unsuitable for one holding my position, whatever view there might be on the merits of the case itself. Therefore I have corresponded mainly with Mr. A. B. Farquhar who thoroughly knows my position and I have given him such information as might enable him to serve you, benefitting, in my belief, my own clients rather than injuring them by serving you in your efforts to prevent the enactment either of the Dingley Bill or of the Aldrich Bill. Yet I cannot go on in that line. Within the last three or four days my knowledge of many conditions has become such that I should myself doubt the expediency of delay on the lines which have been undertaken. Your letters confirm me. The opponents of excessive duties are not united. The conditions in many branches of industry are so bad as to make any settlement perhaps more conducive to a favorable change than any further delay. The spectre of the free silver hangs over every one. I have therefore concluded to make no further effort lest I might do more harm than good and might prejudice the interests of my clients more than I might benefit them. I have therefore written Mr. Farquhar to this effect. I have done my part in the late campaign and that is fully admitted. I can do no more and in this matter wiser heads than mine must decide what course to pursue. I shall try to lay this case aside and I think it possible that I may take a short trip abroad during the ensuing summer.

Mr. Atkinson's three months' trip to Europe during the summer of 1897 turned his attention to other matters during the period when the Dingley Bill was finally becoming a law.

Although he did not lose his interest in the subjects of tariff and monetary reform after 1897, Mr. Atkinson's chief political and social interests were, during the subsequent three or four years, centered upon the issue of imperialism which assumed such importance during McKinley's Administration. This issue was precipitated by the events preliminary to, during, and following the Spanish-American War.

The principal causes of the brief and decisive contest between Spain and the United States can be traced to the unsatisfactory state of conditions in Cuba under Spanish rule which had, for a number of years, irritated a substantial number of American citizens and had been the cause of a more or less continuous revo-

IMPERIALISM

lution in Cuba for several decades. This reminder of European monarchy in the new world was in itself odious to lovers of democracy, a feeling which was carefully cultivated by the Cuban revolutionists, who found ready sympathizers in the United States.[1]

Cleveland and Olney had successfully maintained peace with Spain during 1895 and 1896 in spite of obstacles which at times threatened war.[2] Although conditions in Cuba did not improve, President McKinley's sincere desire for peace kept the situation from reaching a crisis during 1897. But the explosion of the Maine on February 15, 1898, precipitated the long-delayed (and probably inevitable) crisis, with the result that war was declared against Spain some five weeks later.

Mr. Atkinson's reaction to the Venezuelan episode foreshadowed his attitude toward the possibilities of a Spanish-American war. In his correspondence, however, he made no reference to the conditions in Cuba or to the increasing war-spirit in the United States until after the catastrophe to the Maine. In March he wrote to one of his English friends: 'There is naturally great sympathy with what appears to be the effort of the native Cubans to secure their independence. This has been aggravated by the disaster to the Maine which I am inclined to attribute to the gases developed in bituminous coal, coupled with electricity. Time will tell. Yet in spite of this sympathy the blatant promoters of war have no influence and are coming into contempt. So it would be in the case of any prospect of disturbance with any other nation, especially with Great Britain.'[3]

[1] More specific grievances against Spain in respect to her conduct of affairs in Cuba included the following: first, the United States had difficulty in enforcing neutrality with such a long coast line and with so much sympathy displayed by its citizens for the Cuban cause; second, the unsanitary conditions in the chief Cuban cities during the troubled times of revolution menaced the health of nearby mainland cities; a third complaint arose out of the disturbed commercial relations with Cuba which hindered an otherwise profitable trade with the United States; fourth, American investments in plantations, sugar mills and the like were inadequately protected; and, finally, there was a serious doubt in the minds of many Americans whether Spain would ever be able to subdue the revolutionists.

[2] Rhodes, J. F., *The McKinley and Roosevelt Administrations*, pp. 44, 45.

[3] Letter to William Fowler, March 9, 1898. In a later communication to Mr. Fowler, on March 22, he expands his theory concerning the destruction of the Maine:

'I have never wavered in my belief that the disaster to the Maine was from internal

Mr. Atkinson applauded the President's firm stand for peace during the latter part of March and early April. He wrote a letter of encouragement to Mr. McKinley on March 25, saying, in part: 'You have attained the respect and confidence of all citizens of repute in this State without distinction of party. You may rely upon their support in every effort to avoid the hell of war, and if in adverse conditions and through forces which you cannot counter or resist the country is forced into the hell of war, you will have the same support in its conduct that you now have in its avoidance.'

As the prospect of war began to loom more and more as a possibility, Mr. Atkinson took more active steps to combat the war sentiment. He suggested, for example, that the churches of America should unite in sending memorials to Congress protesting against war. He advised certain members of Congress to support the President and to hold back the war-spirit 'by long and earnest debate in Congress until it shall become first an object of derision and finally of contempt.'

Once war had been declared, Mr. Atkinson took the view that it probably would have been impossible for the United States not to have taken this step eventually. For the benefit of his European friends he summarized the situation as it existed in the United States at the end of April ending with the statement: 'Intervention at the risk of war would sooner or later have become an obligation on the people of this country. All that could be done was to put off the bitter alternative of war until it could no longer be avoided. That delay was in the power of the President

cause. The Maine carried large quantities of bituminous coal, of a type which is liable to spontaneous combustion, in its coal bunkers, which are between the ammunition chambers and the outer skin of the ship, separated from the ammunition only by a sheet of steel. There have been two narrow escapes in two other ships from the heating of the coal, in one case setting the wooden boxes of ammunition on fire. In your ships there is a cold chamber between the ammunition and the coal bunkers and why our constructors can have neglected such a precaution is beyond belief. It has fallen to me to investigate the spontaneous combustion of coal more fully than any other person on account of the risk in the factories that I insure. One of the most complete treatises on this subject was obtained by me from England, I think published by the Admiralty, and that document I lent to the Naval Department at their own request. Yet this very dangerous mode of construction has been continued. How long these huge battleships will be considered of any value or service is an open question even among the naval men themselves, as I find.'

and would have been continued for a much longer period had not bad politics and a misapprehension on the part of many of the uncertain members of Congress as to the real feeling of the country, led Congress to force the hand of the President and to put us in the wrong even on what ultimately might have been an absolutely right conclusion.'

Mr. Atkinson paid comparatively little attention to the progress of the war, if one may judge from his correspondence.[1] He was highly critical, however, of the administration of the War Department and urged that its prosecution of the war be made the subject of a careful investigation and inquiry. On his own initiative Mr. Atkinson gathered evidence from returned soldiers and officers which showed the incapacity of the army authorities in the Cuban campaign. This evidence he presented to the committee appointed by the President in the fall of 1898 for the purpose of making an inquiry into the conduct of the war.

As a result of this work, Mr. Atkinson's interest became stimulated in the subject of the general effect of the tropics on the morale and health of white troops stationed in those regions. He was appalled by the reports from official British and French sources which showed that a high percentage of European colonial troops were victims not only of tropical fevers and diseases but of the horrible effects of venereal diseases as well.

Meanwhile, the question of what to do with the Philippines became one of growing concern and the subject of controversy. The United States had entered the war with Spain with the avowed purpose, not of annexing Cuba, but of freeing that country from the obnoxious rule of the Spanish. This policy was faithfully executed. The Philippine Islands, on the other hand, had become an unexpected responsibility as a result of the successful prosecution of the war. To hand them back to Spain was of course un-

[1] His reaction to Dewey's victory at Manila Bay may be of interest. Again writing to an English friend he said: 'If we had not built the new navy, there would have been no Maine to be blown up in the harbor of Havana, and if we had not had the misfortune to have a modern fleet in China when the war was declared, we should not now be bothered with the Philippine question. But on the other hand there is something to stir the imagination in joining with you to ameliorate the condition of semi-barbarous people by using force for the maintenance of commerce.' To Henry Yates Thompson, August 10, 1898.

thinkable in view of the current opinion in the United States of the Spanish colonial policy. To turn them over to some other nation was an unattractive alternative. On the other hand, to give the residents their immediate independence seemed to be ignoring an assumed moral responsibility, and yet to make them a part of the United States meant a departure from a long-established policy of isolation into the realm of imperialism. Tremendous pressure was brought to bear upon the President to take the islands for the United States by the expansionists who were thrilled by the prospects of 'planting the American flag on two continents,' and who looked forward to important trade benefits from the occupancy of this region.

The prospects of American expansion greatly disturbed Mr. Atkinson.[1] In addition to the dangers to which American soldiers would be subjected by the combination of the tropics and army life, he had other serious objections. His solution of the dilemma facing the President was to have the islands neutralized under a joint treaty signed by the great naval powers of the world, which would allow the United States to share the commercial advantages of the islands without the expense of maintaining a colonial

[1] On August 25, he called the attention of the President 'to the profound danger of the policy now called imperialism. It is hoped,' he continued, 'as I believe by all men of repute of whatever party, representing the solid sense of this community, that you will use the same good judgment and discretion in getting out of the Philippine Islands that you have used in conducting the war with Spain. It is held that an extension of the functions of this country over distant colonies is uncalled for, totally foreign to our system of government, not within our duty, and that such a danger is one to be deplored.

'We also trust that the honor of the country will be maintained by not adding the West India Islands to the territory of the United States. We shall have accomplished the declared purpose of the nation, and while we must assume responsibility for good government, there is neither right nor duty upon us in annexing these tropical islands. It is held that the functions of this country are those of peace, order and industry, freedom from violence and that we are not called upon to adopt a colonial system, which cannot be done without complete departure from the very principles of government on which this Nation is founded.

'I may take this opportunity to say that I hope and trust you will give orders for such a complete investigation of the conduct of the War Department as the circumstances seem to require while it is still in your power to do so of your own motion. The testimony which is coming in from the very best sources of information, of incompetence, bad judgment and even worse, in the conduct of the Quartermaster and Commissariat Departments, the abuses to which the returning soldiers have been subjected from which they might have been protected, and other charges will bring about a state of exasperation of which you within the atmosphere of Washington — which I know from previous experience keeps out a vast deal of information — may have little conception.'

policy. As has been already noted, he was strongly opposed to the maintenance of large armies or navies which to him were one of the evils of protectionism in addition to being a drain upon the economic resources of the nation so burdened. His final objection was based upon the theory that 'the Constitution followed the flag' which would entitle the Filipinos to all the rights of American citizens.

By the fall of 1898 the question of imperialism had become one of the important issues of the day. Partisans of both sides presented their arguments to the country *via* the newspapers, speeches, and pamphlets. The question cut party lines as well as economic prejudices. Democrats and Republicans, protectionists and free-traders, found themselves allies on the same side of the question.

Mr. Atkinson entered into the fight with enthusiasm. One of his first efforts was to assist in the organization of the Anti-Imperialist League, the most important of the agencies opposed to expansion on the part of the United States. The League, founded in Boston in November, 1898, soon became national in its scope and included among its officers and supporters some very distinguished persons.[1] This organization sent out literally thousands of copies of pamphlets, broadsides, and newspaper articles on the subject of imperialism.

In addition to being a vice-president of the Anti-Imperialist League, and contributing material for use by that organization, Mr. Atkinson printed and distributed his own series of pamphlets. He made a special effort to reach groups such as clergymen, labor leaders, members of Congress and others who were in positions of influence. The response to his pamphlets was such as would be expected on such a controversial question. By some he was branded a traitor to his country, others praised his efforts as being highly patriotic and made substantial monetary contributions for the continuation of his work. Some of his former associates in the tariff and silver fights turned against him, while on the

---

[1] J. G. Carlisle, Andrew Carnegie, David Starr Jordan, John Sherman, Charles Francis Adams, and Grover Cleveland were among the honorary vice-presidents of the Anti-Imperialist League.

other hand, some of his strongest opponents found common ground with him on this issue.[1]

In April, 1899, Mr. Atkinson conceived the idea of sending some of his pamphlets to some of the officers and soldiers stationed in the Philippines. He outlined his purpose to the Secretary of the Treasury, Lyman J. Gage on April 22: 'In this morning's paper a correspondent of the *Boston Herald* states that the Departments are going to "*expose*" the Anti-Imperialist League and others who have as alleged stirred up discontent among the troops in Manila. I do not think the Executive Committee of the Anti-Imperialist League have yet taken any active measures to inform the troops of the facts and conditions here. The suggestion is, however, a valuable one and I have sent to Washington today to get specific addresses of officers and soldiers to the number of five hundred or six hundred so that I may send them my pamphlets, giving them assurance of sympathy. I shall place the same lists in charge of the Executive Committee of the League to keep up the supply.'

Naturally, no such list of names was forthcoming. In order to test the case, Mr. Atkinson mailed copies of his pamphlets to a small group of officials and prominent persons in Manila.[2] On the orders of the Postmaster-General, these documents were

---

[1] F. C. Moore, who had co-operated with Mr. Atkinson on the tariff wrote on July 14, 1899:
'I am in receipt of a copy of the *Anti-Imperialist*, with arguments against the present war in the Philippines, and feel called upon to say that I am thoroughly and earnestly opposed to your views of the matter. The sending to me of the book, with the suggestion to aid in its distribution, warrants me in expressing an opinion which otherwise I would not have troubled you with.

'I believe emphatically in the Spanish war; in the conquest and assumption of the territory of Cuba, Porto Rico and the Philippines, and if I did not believe in it I would favor it and do all I could to assist the President of the United States and Congress, for I believe it to be the duty of every American citizen to take it for granted that the Government is right, for if each citizen can take it upon himself to oppose the Government and carry out his own views and force them upon the soldiers in the service of the Government, this great republic would be no longer a government but only a mob.'

On the other hand, Henry Carey Baird, disciple of the Henry Carey school of economics, wrote: 'It is seldom that I find myself in accord with you in political questions, but in your opposition to McKinley and his foreign schemes I am heartily with you.'

[2] The copies were addressed to the following: Admiral George Dewey, President Schurman, Professor Worcester, General H. G. Otis, General Lawton, General Miller, and J. F. Bass, correspondent of Harper's Weekly.

seized by the postal authorities in San Francisco and orders were issued that these pamphlets were under no circumstances to be forwarded by mail to the Philippines, although their circulation in the United States was not prohibited.[1]

That the postal officials had the legal authority to take this action seems doubtful, although no test of their power arose out of this particular incident. But, as was pointed out at the time, from the point of view of the Administration, it would have been a better policy to have had the documents seized by the military authorities at Manila. Be that as it may, and whatever may have been the advantage of keeping Mr. Atkinson's pamphlets away from the Philippines, the result of the publicity attendant to the incident caused him to be overwhelmed with requests for copies of his 'seditious' publications.[2]

The months following this unexpected action on the part of the postal authorities were strenuous ones for Mr. Atkinson, who was hard pressed to meet the many demands upon his time and energy. He worked to sustain the public interest on the question of imperialism just as long as possible. On June 23, he wrote to Nordhoff: 'I think the members of the Cabinet have graduated from an asylum for the imbecile and feeble-minded. They have evidently found out their blunder because the Administration papers suddenly ceased their attacks on me all on the same day, and I miss the free advertisement. I am now trying to stir them up again to provoke another attack.' He continued to bait the governmental officials from time to time thereafter but with no success.[3]

[1] 'Washington, May 2. The Postmaster-General has directed the postmaster at San Francisco to take out of the mails for Manila three pamphlets issued by Edward Atkinson, of Boston, vice-president of the Anti-Imperialistic League. This order does not apply to the circulation of the pamphlets by a mail in this country, but bars their dispatch from this country to the Philippines, discontent, and even mutiny, among the soldiers being stated by the department to be the design of these publications. The three pamphlets are specifically described, and in no circumstances are they to be forwarded by mail to the Philippines.' News bulletin in the *Atkinson Collection*.

[2] Altogether about 135,000 copies of Mr. Atkinson's various pamphlets on imperialism were distributed during 1888 and 1889.

[3] In September he called the attention of a friend to another of his pamphlets which he characterized as 'my strongest bid yet for a limited residence in Fort Warren.' Letter to Herbert Welsh, September 6, 1899.

In the fall of 1899, Mr. Atkinson shifted the main part of his work to the Chicago branch of the Anti-Imperialist League which was in thorough sympathy with his aims and desires.[1] He maintained an active interest in the question, however, and overlooked no subsequent opportunities to urge that independence be given to the Philippines.

The Presidential election of 1900 again found Mr. Atkinson in the position of favoring neither candidate. McKinley's capitulation to the policy of imperialism made him unwelcome as a candidate in Mr. Atkinson's eyes, but Bryan's adherence to the silver issue made him even less desirable; and of the two men, Mr. Atkinson, true to the principles of sound money, preferred McKinley. There was some talk of drafting Cleveland as a candidate, a procedure which would of course have been most acceptable to Mr. Atkinson, but Bryan's hold on the Democrats was too secure for this action.

Forced by the nominations of both parties to an unwelcome choice, Mr. Atkinson again suggested the plan advanced four years before, which was to concentrate upon the House of Representatives in an effort to elect members who were safe on the money issue, and yet at the same time against a policy of imperialism.

He took little part in the campaign save to discourage the various branches of the Anti-Imperialist League in their attempts to support Bryan. He commented on the outcome of the campaign: 'The election somewhat disappointed me, and yet I think and feel very sure that we Anti-Imperialists have won. The fracture in the Republican Party is developing rapidly.'[2]

Mr. Atkinson did not, of course, confine his attention after 1892 to political matters alone, but maintained his customary enthusiasm for a large variety of subjects (most of which have already been discussed). By far the most unusual of his non-political activities arose in connection with the part he played in the development of the art of cooking and the science of nutrition.

[1] The New England branch had not approved of the attempt to send his pamphlets to the Philippines with the result that the relations between him and the local branch were not entirely harmonious.
[2] Letter to Nordhoff, December 14, 1900.

SOCIAL REFORM

His initial interest in these subjects had begun in 1866. At that time he was treasurer of a cotton mill which, because of the unsettled business conditions, was operating only four days per week. In an effort to help his workers during this period of hard times, Mr. Atkinson expended considerable effort in instructing them in how to purchase and prepare food economically, with the result that (to use his own words), 'at the end of a year they told me they had been better off on the wages of four days in the week than they had previously been on the wages of a week.'[1]

He explained his later interest in the subjects of cooking and dietetics: 'I then [1866] devised some crude methods of cooking in a water oven, but as time went on, conditions improved. I dropped the subject for many years until one day, after I had taken up my present profession, insurance underwriter, I was going through a new mill at noon when the workmen were eating cold victuals out of their dinner pails. The aspect of this food was such as to compel my attention. I then made up my mind that I would renew my investigation and develop a true system.'[2]

It was in the 'eighties that Mr. Atkinson renewed his investigations of cooking and began experimenting on what finally evolved as the Aladdin Oven. This cooking apparatus, in its most improved form, consisted of a rectangular outer case of wood about one inch thick. This outer shell was insulated by an inner lining made of asbestos. Between this layer of insulating material and the oven proper, which was made of steel, there was a space which allowed a circulation of air around the entire oven. This box-like device stood upon four legs which elevated it sufficiently to allow a kerosene lamp to be placed underneath.[3] A hole in the bottom of the box permitted the heat from the lamp to circulate through the air passages, while the food to be cooked was placed in the oven by a door on the side. An oven thermometer completed the outfit.[4]

[1] Letter to William T. DeForest, January 15, 1896.
[2] Ibid.
[3] A gas burner could be used instead of a kerosene lamp.
[4] The standard size of Aladdin Oven had inside measurements of 18 inches in width, 12 inches in depth, and 14 inches in height, and was fitted with movable shelves. Cf.

In the development of his oven, Mr. Atkinson sought primarily to achieve two results. One was to eliminate the tremendous waste of heat which was characteristic of the iron ranges and cook stoves then in common use, and second, to get a type of cooking device which would permit slow cooking of foods at comparatively low and controlled temperatures.[1]

With the Aladdin Oven, Mr. Atkinson accomplished both of these purposes. By applying the principles of insulation to the apparatus, he was able to prepare astonishing amounts of food at very low costs for fuel.[2] And by cooking slowly at controlled temperatures, he produced meals in his oven which, according to all contemporary accounts, were most acceptable to epicurean appetites. Of particular significance for Mr. Atkinson's purpose was the fact that the cheaper grades of food, especially meat, could be very much improved by this method of cooking.

But Mr. Atkinson's interest in this subject did not stop at this point. He found, upon investigation, that although over fifty per cent of the income of the poorer classes was spent for food, very little had been done toward determining the proper rations for human beings. As he put it a few years after he renewed his investigation of the question: 'If it were a question of feeding horses, cows or pigs, all the necessary information could be found in almost innumerable popular treatises, magazines and agricultural papers. Any one can learn in a day how much and what to give to a trotting horse; how much and what to feed a working horse; how much and what to put before a milch cow or a pair of oxen; but if one... had asked, only a little while since, how to select the right ingredients and proportions of food for the nutri-

Atkinson, Edward, *The Science of Nutrition*, p. 43. Although he got his original idea from what was known as the Norwegian type of fireless cooker, the Aladdin Oven, as Mr. Atkinson evolved it, was essentially his own devising.

[1] A preliminary study of the effect of heat upon food had convinced him that fast cooking at high temperatures destroyed much of the nutriment as well as the flavor of the food prepared in this fashion.

[2] By the use of one of his ovens, Mr. Atkinson estimated that a family of five persons, 'can do everything but fry; they can stew, simmer, bake, and roast; and can readily prepare twenty pounds of food a day, with a consumption of oil not exceeding two cents' worth.' Atkinson, Edward, *The Industrial Progress of the Nation*, p. 341.

tion of men and women,... [he] could only be referred to some abstruse and scientific treatises.'[1]

Mr. Atkinson accordingly determined to make the subject of dietetics the object of an extended scientific investigation. He was able to enlist the financial aid of several wealthy persons (including Andrew Carnegie), who donated some six or seven thousand dollars for the purpose of furthering the study.

To carry out the necessary experiments connected with the development of his project, Mr. Atkinson drew upon the services of a number of well-qualified experts. The first of this group was Professor A. W. Atwater, of Connecticut Agricultural College, who had already made some studies of the nutritive values of foods. The second member was Mrs. Mary Hinman Abel, author of a prize cook book and a founder of the New England Kitchen. The third person who assisted Mr. Atkinson was Mrs. Ellen Richards, of the Massachusetts Institute of Technology, well known as a chemist and, with Mrs. Abel, a co-founder and proprietor of the New England Kitchen.

The results of the experiments of this group plus the findings of numerous experiments carried on by himself, were collected and published (in 1896) in a volume edited by Mr. Atkinson entitled *The Science of Nutrition*.[2] Included within its pages were directions for the construction and operation of the Aladdin Oven, written by Mr. Atkinson; a list of dietaries computed by Mrs. Richards; the results of tests of slow cooking in the Aladdin Oven, made by Mrs. Abel; and tables of the nutritive values of food, prepared by Professor Atwater. The volume also contained a large number of recipes for the preparation of food by the slow cooking process.

Using the information gathered by himself and his associates, Mr. Atkinson estimated that the average, hard-working manual laborer in 1896 need not spend over 24 cents a day for food, if he purchased carefully and prepared his meals upon an Aladdin or

---

[1] Atkinson, Edward, *The Science of Nutrition*, p. 14.
[2] Through the co-operation of Andrew Carnegie, copies of this book were placed in all of the public libraries in the United States.

similar type of oven. The cost per person for individuals doing less strenuous physical labor was of course lower. A man at moderate work could live upon 21½ cents per day; a man doing light work or a woman doing moderate work, 17¾ cents per day, and a woman doing light work, 16½ cents per day.[1]

These dietaries which Mr. Atkinson suggested were not theoretical abstractions, for he showed, by numerous demonstrations with the Aladdin Oven and the types of food included in the low-cost menus, that palatable meals could be prepared by the methods which he proposed. He took delight in getting someone who was inexperienced in the art of cooking to prepare a meal on the Aladdin Cooker in order to demonstrate the simplicity of the operation of his device.

While *The Science of Nutrition* was a definite contribution to the study of dietetics and cooking, Mr. Atkinson was unsuccessful, in spite of reports from a considerable number of enthusiastic users of the device, in his attempt to secure a widespread use of the Aladdin Ovens.[2] He did not attempt to profit from his invention, but made arrangements whereby they could be purchased at cost from a small manufacturing company. Public apathy seemed to be due to several causes; the poorer classes, which Mr. Atkinson especially hoped to reach, were on the whole suspicious of his motives because they thought he was trying to reduce their costs of living in order that their employers might reduce wages proportionately;[3] and in general, it may be said the slowness of the

---

[1] Atkinson, Edward, *The Science of Nutrition*, pp. 19–20. That Mr. Atkinson had in mind no meager or 'starvation' standard of subsistence is shown by the following table. The average amount of food per person per day which he estimated could be purchased on the above allowance was as follows:

Meats ....about	10 oz.	Bread ....about	14 oz.
Suet or fat about	1 oz.	Hominy, oats and corn meal about	6 oz.
Salt pork..about	1 oz.	Beans or peas ....about	2 oz.
Butter....about	1½ oz.	Sugar..................about	3 oz.
Fish ......about	3 oz.	Roots or other vegetables ...about	12½ oz.
		Total	54 oz.

Atkinson, Edward, *op. cit.*, p. 19.

[2] Among its users were: The New England Kitchen, Tuskegee Institute, the Clark Thread Company of Newark, the Elmira State Reformatory, and the Hull House.

[3] Cf. *post*, pp. 271–72.

cooking process, the cost of the oven, and the difficulty encountered by any innovation, combined against the widespread use of the device.[1]

Mr. Atkinson was especially disappointed at his failure to interest the poorer classes in the use of the Aladdin Cooker, for he had a genuine interest in improving the condition of these groups. During the latter years of his life he became convinced that he should have first tried to 'save the rich' with his cooking apparatus, because it seemed so much easier to get the poor to adopt something already in use by the wealthier classes than something designed for their own particular use.

Mr. Atkinson's attempts to secure the adoption of the Aladdin Oven and his participation in the controversy over the annexation of the Philippines were the last questions upon which he worked with the intensity that had marked his earlier activities in respect to tariff and money. The five years after 1900 found him interested in a number of subjects of a political, economic and scientific nature, with no one taking precedence over the others.

In the political field, for example, he continued in his attempts to get the Administration to withdraw from the Philippines. He hoped for a time during the latter part of 1900 that the opponents of imperialism in Congress would be able to hold up the appropriations for the army bill, which would necessitate a withdrawal of American troops from the islands because of lack of funds. He aided the opponents of the Administration's Philippine policy, especially Senators Hoar and Caffery, by furnishing data pertinent to the cost of the occupation of the Philippines and information concerning the hardships suffered there by American soldiers.

Mr. Atkinson also tried to start another investigation of the sinking of the Maine. He was far from satisfied with the conclusions of the American board of inquiry to the effect that the cause of the explosion was external. His efforts in this direction were checked by the unwillingness of the Administration to allow the

---

[1] It is to be noted how much the design of Mr. Atkinson's oven anticipated the modern use of insulation which is such an important feature of the present-day gas and electric ovens.

case to be reopened, and he was unable to secure any public demand for such an investigation, much to his disappointment.

Consistent in his opposition to all things connected with war and its prosecution, Mr. Atkinson condemned the building of battleships and other navy equipment. He objected not so much to the waste involved in their construction as he did to the destruction of shipping during time of war, and he scornfully dubbed them 'commerce destroyers,' not an appellation which would appeal to members of the navy.

To protect property during time of war and to eliminate as far as possible the necessity of constructing warships to protect such commerce, Mr. Atkinson extended his idea of the neutralization of certain islands and countries, to include a neutralization of the entire Atlantic Ocean and certain trade zones elsewhere on the high seas. He tried to enlist the aid of prominent persons in Europe as well as in the United States in this plan, and was pleased to have it presented at a meeting of the International Peace Congress which met in Boston in 1905.

Although the success of the Republicans in the elections of 1900 and 1904 insured the maintenance of the protective tariff, Mr. Atkinson never lost faith in the tariff reform which he felt was inevitable. In 1902 he wrote his friend Arthur Lyman, of the Pacific Mills, recalling his own part in guiding tariff legislation in former years along lines which would not harm manufacturers in New England. He continued: 'I think the same intervention may be of great use at the present time. I think very few have any comprehension of the tidal wave moving in the West. I have been expecting it for months, and I know what is coming. I want to be on the lead to help guide it and to prevent stopping the Pacific or any other mill even for a time, and I am certain that I can use my influence.'[1] And in 1905, he tried to get Senator William B. Allison to assume the leadership of a party which would 'sweep into office' on a tariff reform policy.

Mr. Atkinson paid considerable attention after 1900 to the conditions of the Negroes in the South. He was highly indignant

---

[1] September 22, 1902.

at the failure of more of the Southern States to give the Negroes franchise, and at the deficiencies in providing adequate educational facilities. A great believer in the effectiveness of education, Mr. Atkinson laid the blame for the backwardness of the black man to the lack of free public schools in the South. He took a great interest in the efforts of Booker T. Washington and others to further colored education,[1] and felt on the whole that where the Negroes had had equal opportunities they had advanced much more than had the 'poor white' classes of the South. He attempted in a series of magazine and newspaper articles to call the attention of the Southerners to the errors of their ways, but his success was no more than could be expected from an attempt to solve this complicated problem.

Another question which challenged his attention was the adulteration and 'doping' of patent medicines, cosmetics, and the like. He tried unsuccessfully to secure State legislation in Massachusetts which would force makers of such products to print the formulas upon the labels of the containers, which he felt would do much to correct this evil.

His experiences with the patent medicine vendors and the jingoists made Mr. Atkinson favorable to universal woman's suffrage on the grounds that the feminine influence in politics would tend to eliminate such evils as these.

He also found time and energy to interest himself in some experiments designed to test the value of cornstalks as fuel and possibly as a substitute for wood in making paper. He persuaded Professor Norton to make some experiments upon the tensile strength of cotton fiber which he thought would be of aid to cotton manufacture. He again entered a controversy with his British opponents over the future supply of wheat, maintaining his position that the United States would be able to furnish an increasing supply of wheat at constantly lowered prices.

No picture of Mr. Atkinson's life would be complete without a mention of the enthusiasm which he was able to impart to others

---

[1] Mr. Atkinson knew Booker T. Washington personally and on one occasion entertained the latter at dinner at his home in Brookline.

for various subjects and activities in which he found interest. Ever ready to discover possibilities in both old and new fields, he seemed able to transfer some of his own abundant energy and vitality to those with whom he came in contact. He was especially interested in aiding those who were just beginning a career or who were trying to find themselves. This quality of Mr. Atkinson's character is spoken of by Henry Adams in his *Education of Henry Adams*. After describing his efforts to get a fresh start in Boston upon his return from diplomatic service abroad with his father, he says of himself, 'At the end of three months the only person, among the hundreds he had met, who had offered him a word of encouragement or had shown a sign of acquaintance with his doings, was Edward Atkinson.'[1]

The range of the foregoing subjects illustrates the fact that Mr. Atkinson during the latter years of his life had lost little of the diversity of interests which had characterized his earlier activities. It would not have been astonishing if he had occasionally felt the need of a vacation from his many duties, for in February, 1901, he had celebrated his seventy-fourth birthday. But although he found it necessary at times to conserve his strength, he was in good health and had lost little of his vigor or capacity for hard work. There is no suggestion in his letters during the last few years of his life of any tendency to live in the past. On the contrary, his feeling was well expressed in a statement he made to his friend Nordhoff in December, 1900: 'I think the world is more interesting than it ever was before, and I have greater confidence in progressive human welfare.'[2]

Mr. Atkinson died as most men would like to die, in full possession of his faculties and engaged in the work he loved so well. On December 11, 1905, while on his way to his office in Boston, he was stricken with a heart attack, and he passed away shortly thereafter, being spared any lingering and painful illness. Two

[1] Page 242.
[2] December 14, 1900. A year before he had written to Nordhoff: 'I am about having a new set of front teeth mounted on platinum posts in the roots of the old ones, and I have proposed to shave my white beard and put on a brown wig, so as to get back to about sixty. That would give me fifteen or twenty years more of good work.' June 23, 1899.

statements made by him, just before the end, contain the text which had guided him throughout his life, and the hope with which he faced another existence. His regret at leaving the world he found so interesting was expressed, 'So much to do, so little done.' And in contemplation of the next world he said, 'I hope God has a lot of things for me to do up there, I shouldn't be happy if he didn't.'

At the time of Mr. Atkinson's death French, German, English and American papers united in carrying stories of his life and his many contributions to human welfare and social advancement. Of the many fine tributes to him, the following seem to have caught his spirit and personality with the clearest understanding. The Reverend Doctor William H. Lyon, pastor of Mr. Atkinson's church, said, in part: 'In a time like this, when so much iniquity is coming to light in the world of affairs, when suspicion runs about wildly through high places and low, wondering whom next it will find to have dropped his self-respect in the hot chase after money, it is refreshing to tarry awhile by the memory of one who, both outwardly and within, led the simple life; who tried to teach others the gospel of plain living and high thinking, who found refuge from the utter sorrows that came upon him, not in excitement, natural or artificial, but in the serene atmosphere of large and impersonal truth. A handsome man to look at in the flesh, he lived a life of no less beauty within.'

And Desmond Fitzgerald, one of Mr. Atkinson's closest associates, in describing what seemed to be the outstanding qualities most appreciated by the latter's friends wrote of:

> the great love which he had for humanity and which led him to manifest the true spirit of kindness towards everyone, and under every circumstance, whether in the thick of battle over some public or private measure, or calmly enjoying the passing events of the day.
> It was perhaps in Mr. Atkinson's case a quality as much of the heart as of the head; his nature seemed to contain the source of some perennial spring of kindness for all humanity. To me, and I think to most of his companions at the round table, this was his strongest claim upon the steadfast regard of his friends. Courage, energy and honesty are the common heritage of the great majority of mankind. They are met in greater or less degree on every hand and in every walk in life, but

where shall we turn for that constant charm of kindly feeling which always greeted us when Mr. Atkinson arrived to complete the social circle? I can see him now, as he flashes an intelligent criticism upon some common subject of conversation, or offers a word of praise for a piece of work well done; how naturally his hand seeks his capacious pockets to bring forth some striking example of practice or experiment illustrating the progress of the times, in which his alert mind was ever engaged; the discussion may perhaps wax a trifle warm, but after it comes the sweet reminder of friendly regard like a dash of sunshine breaking through a rift in the clouds.

All of us will recall personal experiences of this magnetic side of our friend's nature. His heart was so big that there was always room for more subjects upon which to exercise the talisman of kindly sympathy. Now it was for a poor orphan, struggling to express the gift of musical talent, but overcome with poverty and discouragement; and now it was for some powerful movement of mankind for the good of the race; to both in turn our friend was ever ready to extend a tender of a sympathetic hand.

We shall all miss those hospitable entertainments upon Heath Hill, when the capacity of the 'Aladdin Cooker' was tested to its utmost. What a charming host! How dearly he enjoyed to be surrounded by as many as could crowd around that ample board, over which he presided with dignified cheer and magical presence.

Silently the chairs close the vacant space left by the passing of the visiting angel, but long in the future will our thoughts reconstruct the familiar form in the old accustomed place, and our hearts beat the quicker as we think upon our loss; our friend may have left us, but his memory will ever remain as a bright glow in the shadows.

And finally, the *Brooklyn Eagle* said editorially of Mr. Atkinson's place in public life:

By the death of Edward Atkinson, Boston loses a venerable citizen, Massachusetts an aggressive reformer, the United States a business magnate of integrity and of wisdom, and the world a statistician and a moralist who deserved the confidence which he inspired, and the attention which he commanded.

The *Eagle* totally differed from Mr. Atkinson in his views touching Expansion, but his objection to that policy was absolutely sincere and his statements against it were the most difficult to meet of any that were advanced from any quarter.

Aside from all that and far more than all that, this wise, learned, earnest, and intellectually tolerant American stood for the best type of thought and action which has honored Massachusetts in the past, and which honors Massachusetts in the present. There was no gathering of great Bostonians that was complete without him. Every such gathering was richer while he lived and for a long time will be poorer because he is dead.

There was no service to any worthy cause that he could render which he withheld. There was no appeal in his judgment or to his knowledge which he did not gratefully answer. There was no kindness and there was no courtesy which he did not more than requite. He was among the chief delights of one of the most delightful cities and states in the world.

CHAPTER VII
ECONOMIST AND PUBLICIST

MR. ATKINSON owed his initial interest in the subject of economics to the writings of Frederick Bastiat, with which he became acquainted as a young man. In addition to being attracted by the French writer's attacks upon protection, many of which formed the basis of his own pronouncements in respect to that subject,[1] Mr. Atkinson found an economic philosophy to which he could thoroughly subscribe in Bastiat's contradiction of the gloomy conclusions of the English Classical School, and in his exposition of the inherent harmony that exists in the economic functioning of society.[2]

The later development of his economic views Mr. Atkinson described as being 'derived mainly from observations taken during a long period of active business; taking to the books either to confirm or change my views if I found that the book men knew more than I did.'[3] And, although he was acquainted with the writings of the economists of his day,[4] there is reason to believe that Mr. Atkinson got his fundamental principles largely from Bastiat, and, to a certain degree, from Adam Smith, and that, with the possible exception of Francis A. Walker, he was little influenced by later writers.

As Mr. Atkinson's later observations were taken chiefly from the United States, in which a rapidly increasing population was

[1] Cf. *ante*, p. 77.

[2] Cf. Bastiat, Frederick, *Harmonies of Political Economy*.

[3] Extract from a letter to Thomas T. Barret, May 18, 1900. Mr. Atkinson attached great importance to the efficacy of observation as a means of developing a true picture of economic conditions. To the graduating class of the University of South Carolina, on June 26, 1899, he said: 'I am inclined to think that it may be an advantage for anyone who has a reasonably good faculty of observation, coupled with the power of reasoning from the facts which are now easily brought within the observation of any student, that his mind should be free from the bias which comes to the special student who crams himself with book knowledge.' Atkinson, Edward, *The Industrial Progress of the Nation*, p. 10.

[4] Included in his library were the works of such economists as J. S. Mill, Alfred Marshall, Walter Bagehot, J. A. Hobson, F. A. Walker, Henry Fawcett, Thorold Rogers, C. F. Dunbar, F. W. Taussig, C. F. Bullock, and J. E. Cairnes.

enjoying a rising standard of living, and in which land was in many cases practically a free good, he found much to substantiate his opinion that Bastiat's reaction to the teachings of Ricardo and Malthus was correct, and that the future of mankind was not to be viewed through the eyes of the 'dismal' scientists.

This tendency to develop an optimistic view in respect to the economic future of man places Mr. Atkinson with a group of American economists of the middle and latter part of the nineteenth century, who were also influenced to a considerable degree by their environment. Differing sharply on some points,[1] such writers as H. C. Carey, Francis Bowen, Amasa Walker, Professor A. T. Perry, Simon N. Patten (to mention only the most important) found common ground in refusing to accept the pessimistic implications of Malthusian and Ricardian economics, and in reflecting the optimism of a new and growing country.

Mr. Atkinson gave expression to his optimistic attitude toward the nature of this worldly existence in the following words: 'To him who has faith in a higher power which is both supreme and wholly beneficent, no matter from what source he may have derived his idea of the Eternal, there can be but one conception of life itself. The premises on which that conception may be based must be, that this world is the best world that could have been made; that the conditions of this life are the best conditions that could have been established for the development of mankind; and that the struggle for existence, hard and severe as it seems to us, must be the necessary school by which man could have been elevated above the beasts of the field. If there could have been a better world or a better method for the development of mankind, man would have the right to ask his Creator why it has not been established.'[2]

---

[1] H. C. Carey and Professor Perry, for example, were opposed on the question of protection, yet they found common ground in a generally optimistic attitude toward the future. Cf. Carey, H. C., *The Harmony of Interests, Agricultural and Commercial* (pamphlet), and *Past, Present and Future*; and Perry, A. L., *Political Economy*, pp. 237-40, 283-88, 461-580.

[2] Atkinson, Edward, *The Industrial Progress of the Nation*, p. 2. In these expressions, Mr. Atkinson shows definitely the influence which Bastiat's writings had upon his philosophy. Cf. Bastiat, Frederick, *op. cit.*, pp. 33-46.

Mr. Atkinson set out to prove that 'this is the best possible of worlds' by a sweeping attack upon the principles of the Classical School. 'I take issue,' he said in addressing the New England Cotton Manufacturers' Association, 'with the English school of economists on three points; on the so-called law of population as propounded by Malthus; on the so-called law of diminishing returns; and on the Ricardian theory of rent in which the properties of the soil are considered as a basis of rent, rather than the capacity of the man who works the soil.'[1]

But in his consideration of land and the forces giving rise to rent, Mr. Atkinson does not make entirely clear whether he disbelieves the actual operation of the law of diminishing returns at a given time or whether he believes that the ingenuity of man will be such that improvements in the technique will adequately take care of any future increases in the population. Concerning the nature of land, he said:

> Raw land, if such an expression may be used, itself possesses no more value than free air or running water. A price may be paid, or a contest may be waged for a time, in order to secure the opportunity to reap and dispose of the harvests which are due to the original fertility; but, with very rare exception, the virgin properties of the soil are soon exhausted, and what is known as 'economic rent' almost wholly disappears; then land ceases to be a mine and becomes a laboratory, only yielding product, and therefore only yielding wages and profits, according to the measure of the labor put into it, and the intelligence with which both capital and labor are directed. At last land may cease to yield either wages or profits in response to labor and capital unless both are combined under the direction of skill and experience.[2]

It will be noted that in the foregoing quotation he admits that soil exhaustion may bring about a tendency toward diminishing returns, but that he does not consider this factor to be significant. He suggests two other circumstances under which the law would operate.

> The present condition of Great Britain, under the system of large entailed estates which have been cultivated for a comparatively short

---

[1] April, 1885. Published as a pamphlet entitled, *Necessary Relations of Capital and Labor*, p. 8.
[2] Atkinson, Edward, *The Industrial Progress of the Nation*, p. 56.

historic period to the present time, mainly by tenant-farmers under leases which prevent free use, gives one example of the failure of land to yield adequate returns for the kind of labor and the method of directing the capital expended upon it. The failure may not happen for lack of abundant product, but because the product is of high cost and not suitable to present conditions. It does not follow that some other method would not yield adequate returns. Again, the present condition of many parts of the continent of Europe under the system of forced subdivision of land, by which the parcels have become too small for application of machinery to them, affords another example of the limited truth of the hypothesis of diminishing returns.

But both in Great Britain and on the Continent examples may be found of such exceptions to this supposed law as to invalidate the rule; while, again, the whole area in which this alleged rule apparently finds limited support constitutes so small a fraction of the surface of the earth as to make any deduction from the results obtained from it a mere exception, or else a result attained under such exceptional conditions as to be of no force whatever in sustaining a universal law supposed to cover general production.

He further states:

A given area of land of high fertility may be divided into parts by a line. On one side the cultivation may be carried on as in the foregoing examples, and the land may be finally exhausted, so far as that kind of cultivation is concerned. On the other side the land of the same quality, treated by different men, or by a succession of men of a different or more intelligent type, or working under better institutions, may yield a larger and larger product through a period of at least a century. This has been proved in the history of this country. A fair example may perhaps be found in the relative conditions of the central part of the State of New York, as compared to some of the more fertile portions of the land of Lower Canada inhabited by the French population. In one case a steadily increasing product may be found in proportion to the capital and labor; in the other, diminishing returns in ratio to population, accompanied by the forced migration of the French *habitants*.

Land of the same original quality, in the same field, divided only by a line, may, therefore, on the one hand, prove the law of diminishing returns, and may be cited as an example of the entire loss of economic rent; while on the other side of the line, under a better mode of treatment, a law of increasing returns and of higher rent may be proved. Of course there may or must be a final limit, and by admitting a final limit it may be held that the hypothesis of Malthus is so far justified; perhaps, however, at so remote a period as not to be entitled to present consideration, if ever.

Mr. Atkinson concludes his observations on this point by stating:

> Land itself may be exhausted when treated as a mine; it may be maintained when worked as a laboratory. Its potential in the increase of fertility and production, when used as a tool or instrument for diverting nitrogen and carbon from the atmosphere and converting these elements into food for man and beast, is as yet an unknown quantity.[1]

In respect to Malthus' belief that population tends to increase with every increase in the means of subsistence, Mr. Atkinson offered the following:

> Our statistics of population do not yet cover a single century with any approach to accuracy, yet a law of diminishing population begins to be perceived even in the prosperous and peaceful countries, in spite of the huge abundance in the means of living and the improvements in distribution, and notwithstanding that the average duration of human life is prolonged in each century beyond that of the previous one. Statistics begin to prove that there is a law governing the growth of population which is not enforced by any artificial method of limiting the existing population to the present means of subsistence. On the basis of this creed, as I have called it, I have ventured to seek for some broad generalization, which may not yet be capable of proof, and which may be still only an hypothesis, but which shall be wholly consistent with the conception of a beneficent power creating and governing the world and ruling all things well. I have ventured, therefore, to say that on the basis of the statistics compiled in recent years, it may soon be proved to be a rule or law of life that the power of mankind to consume the means of subsistence is limited, while on the other hand, the power of mankind to produce and distribute the means of subsistence is practically unlimited.[2]

Incidentally, Mr. Atkinson pays little attention to the factor of distance in determining rent.

> The low cost of railway service in the United States makes the distance between the farm and the factory of little consequence as long as there are no artificial obstructions to commerce. The whole country is one great neighborhood in which each man serves the other; and this is its true strength. The wages for one day's work of an

---

[1] Atkinson, Edward, *op. cit.*, p. 158.
[2] *Ibid.*, p. 159.

average mechanic in the far East will pay for moving a year's subsistence of bread and meat a thousand miles or more from the distant West.[1]

These views concerning land as a factor of production are based upon several rather common errors concerning the principle of diminishing returns, its effect upon the welfare of man and its influence upon the shares of the national product going to land and the other factors of production. Mr. Atkinson was led astray in his denunciation of the principle by confusing its operation with the effects of soil exhaustion, by neglecting to see that it applied to a given stage of the arts and by not distinguishing between value productivity and physical productivity.

His concept of a definite piece of land as a laboratory upon which (at any given stage of the arts) capital and labor may be applied in an almost unlimited quantity, and from which products would come in a flow which increased more than proportionately with every additional application of capital and labor, is without foundation in actual experience, and cannot be said to constitute any valid attack upon the principle of diminishing returns as laid down by Ricardo.

Mr. Atkinson's observations concerning the lowering birth rate in face of an increase in production is much more to the point as an attack on Malthusianism, for while Malthus admitted this possibility if men would exercise 'prudence,' neither he nor Ricardo, nor later, J. S. Mill, believed that population would be limited to any considerable extent by the exercise of foresight. As proof of his statements, however, Mr. Atkinson's observations are far from satisfactory, for he produces no statistical evidence to confirm his views, nor does he inquire into the reasons behind the suggested fall in the birth rate, save to impute divine influence. For these reasons, one is led to suspect that his conclusions, however correct, were founded more upon hope than facts.

It is to be expected that Mr. Atkinson's repudiation of the principle of diminishing returns would make the remainder of the body of economic theory which he espoused somewhat dif-

[1] Atkinson, Edward, *The Industrial Progress of the Nation*, p. 61.

ferent from the principles commonly held by more orthodox thinkers on the subject. Such was the case.

By practically eliminating rent, the problem of the division of the national income is considerably simplified. To quote Mr. Atkinson directly:

> The two forces which are engaged in the production of the substances which constitute food, fuel, means of shelter, or the materials which may be converted into additional capital, are of course, labor and capital. Land itself is but an investment, being useless and valueless unless labor and capital are employed upon it. By the co-operation of these two forces, an annual product is made.[1]

This annual product is divided in the following manner:

> For instance, given the question, 'What is the value of the annual product of the year 1884?' It would consist of the following elements: first, the wear or consumption of fixed capital previously accumulated; the proportion of the quick capital or product of the year 1883 brought over to and consumed in the year 1884, in order to begin work. Let these two elements be called a. To them would be added the actual product of the year. Let this be called b. From this product a certain proportion would be carried over to begin the work of the year 1885. Let this be called c. The formula could then be stated in the following terms: $a + b - c = x$, the annual product which is subject to subdivision and to consumption.
>
> Let profits be called d, sum of all wages, e, persons engaged in gainful occupation for a given rate of wages, f, and the average rate of wages, i. The complete formula would then be as follows:
>
> $$a + b - c = x$$
> $$x - d = e \div f = i$$
>
> If i be the average of all there is, one wage-earner will earn less, another more, according to relative capacity and opportunity, and by competition each with the other; but these earnings, differing each with the other, will be absolutely within the limit of i; while i itself will annually stand for an increasing share of an increasing product, if my premises are sustained.[2]

Mr. Atkinson considered wages as a residual element dependent in magnitude upon productivity of labor. He says:

---

[1] Atkinson, Edward, *The Distribution of Products, or the Metaphysics of Exchange*, p. 24.
[2] *Ibid.*, p. 30. For Mr. Atkinson's reasons for believing that labor will get an 'increasing share of an increasing product,' cf. pp. 253–54.

Wages are held to be a consequence — a result — a remainder over after capital has received such profit as will have induced it to undertake the work; *the rate of wages cannot therefore be considered a true measure of the cost of production.* Wages are a consequent result and their measure or rate is, and must be determined in the long run, by what the product will bring, and not by what the capitalist may either promise or be willing to pay for a given time.[1]

For an individual plant or industry, the prior claims to that of labor on the product are subdivided into the following categories: From the sum of money representing the annual product must be deducted:

> First, a portion or sum sufficient to restore the depreciation of the capital used, in other words, to keep the machinery in effective condition.
> Second, a sum equal to the average rate of profit on capital invested in the very safest securities, and, in addition to that rate, as much more as is necessary to compensate the owner for the greater risk of one branch of work as compared with another.
> Third, the cost of materials. [This presumably could be reduced to labor and capital costs for industry as a whole.]
> Fourth, the sum needed to secure the very best administration.
> Fifth, the proportion of the national, state, and municipal taxes which are collected from the consumers of the goods through the instrumentality of the person, firm, or corporation owning the property; which taxes enter into the money-cost of the product and must be recovered from the sales.
> Lastly, the remainder over constitutes the wages or earnings of the laborer, whatever that remainder may be.[2]

In his discussion of wages, Mr. Atkinson placed great emphasis upon the proposition that wage rates were not a cause or indication of high cost of production. He developed this idea in connection with his advocacy of low tariffs, in order to meet the well-known 'pauper-labor' argument of the protectionists. Mr. At-

---

[1] Atkinson, Edward, *op. cit.*, p. 53. It may be of interest to note the similarity between the wage theory outlined by Mr. Atkinson and that developed by Francis A. Walker. Walker, for example, assumed that from the total national product, rent, interest, and profits are extracted, the remainder going to labor in the form of wages. He also assumes, and in this Mr. Atkinson would thoroughly concur, that any increased product due to an increased efficiency on the part of labor would be paid in its entirety to labor. Cf. Walker, Francis A., *Political Economy*, pp. 252–58.

[2] Atkinson, Edward, *op. cit.*, p. 70.

kinson saw clearly that the large amount of machinery and raw materials per laborer in countries like the United States or England so increased the efficiency of the workers that no pauper, hand laborer of the more backward countries (industrially speaking) could compete in the production of manufactured goods. Mr. Atkinson did not go so far as to propose that the payment of high wages would lower costs. There was no causal connection thus established; rather wages were in most cases the gauge of costs; high wages indicated low cost of production, and low wages, high cost of production.[1] He felt confident that with the increase in capital and the progress in invention in the United States, wage rates would continually advance.

It is easy to appreciate and applaud the emphasis Mr. Atkinson put upon this phase of the money-cost of production, even though it was a principle well recognized by contemporary economists. There is probably no sophistry of the ardent protectionist which is more convincing to the uninformed than the plea to protect the highly paid American worker from the pauper-labor of Europe or the Orient.

Mr. Atkinson's treatment of capital and interest follows somewhat orthodox lines. Interest is paid for the use of capital and not for the use of money. While short-time fluctuations of the interest rate may be affected by banking or monetary conditions, the long-time rate of interest on safe loans is determined by the supply of capital relative to the demand.

In respect to the nature of capital, Mr. Atkinson presents somewhat different concepts. Usually he considers capital as machinery and partly processed materials, referring at one point to, 'the quantity of actual capital which exists at a given time in a reproductive form, that is to say, in corn and potatoes, iron and steel, cotton, wool, lumber, lead, etc.'[2] At another place he speaks,

[1] 'Low rates of wages are not essential to a low cost of production, but on the contrary usually indicate a high cost of production — that is to say, a large measure of human labor and a large sum of wages at low rates. Conversely, high wages may, and commonly do, indicate a low cost of production — that is to say, a small proportion of human labor and a small proportionate sum of wages at high rates in a given quantity of product.' Atkinson, Edward, *The Distribution of Products*, p. 63.

[2] Atkinson, Edward, *What Makes the Rate of Interest* (pamphlet), p. 24.

however, of capital, 'as a force and the capitalists are those who direct this force.'[1] And again, he speaks of the only capital of permanent value as being immaterial, 'the experience of generations and the development of science.'[2]

The supply of capital, according to Mr. Atkinson, comes from two sources; from the wealthy who cannot, or do not, from force of habit, spend their entire incomes on consumer's goods, and from the laboring classes who save a portion of their wages to provide for emergencies or old age.[3] He is not clear, however, in his analysis in respect to the supply of capital, for he says: 'It is the abundance of wheat, cotton, and corn which in part determines the rate of interest. The rate of interest must therefore be determined by their abundance relative to the demand for their use.'[4] Mr. Atkinson seems confused on this point, for considering wheat, cotton, and corn as capital goods, it would seem inaccurate to assume that their abundance or scarcity should have any direct effect upon the rate of interest. Changes in their supply would affect the prices at which they were bought and sold, but it would be the supply of funds available to borrowers, which would have a direct effect upon the rate of interest.

Mr. Atkinson advanced several propositions in respect to the saving and investment of capital:

> First, that the saving of capital at the beginning, however little it may be, is due to prudence, self-denial, economy, and sagacity. Second, the productive use of capital, after it has been saved, calls for intelligence, skill, and mental capacity. Third, the larger the capital the greater the mental capacity required for its application to productive purposes. Fourth, unless capital is directed to productive purposes, whether invested in land, mills, railroads, or works of any kind, it yields neither rent, interest, profit, nor earnings. When productive, it increases production more than it secures as income. Fifth, unless labor did in fact secure a better subsistence in the service of capital, the workmen would refuse to work for the capitalists.[5]

---

[1] Atkinson, Edward, *The Distribution of Products*, p. 147.
[2] Atkinson, Edward, *The Industrial Progress of the Nation*, p. 153.
[3] Mr. Atkinson gives no consideration to the effect of the rate of interest upon the supply of capital. Presumably it would have little effect.
[4] Atkinson, Edward, *What Makes the Rate of Interest*, p. 28.
[5] Atkinson, Edward, *Distribution of Products*, p. 299.

From the foregoing statements, it can be seen that Mr. Atkinson was inclined to separate the functions of the capitalist and that of the directors or entrepreneurs of business. He says further, 'It is necessary to true welfare that the mental capacity and power of direction of the capitalist or his agent shall be recognized as a prime factor in production, especially by those who attribute abundance to the mere application of mechanical or manual labor to work.'[1] Again: 'As the margin of profits has diminished, a higher order of intelligence, a much closer method of business, and a more strict application of science have been called for in all large undertakings. Therefore, while the earnings of workmen have increased, the earnings of those who have been charged with the direction and application of capital have also increased, possibly even in inverse proportion to the lessening ratio of profit on which the remuneration of capital depends, while mere possession of capital has become less and less remunerative to the owner. Thus the work of the director or administrator of capital, whether its owner or agent, has assumed a position of supreme importance.'[2]

It is not surprising that Mr. Atkinson should fail to make any sharper distinction than the foregoing between the functions of the capitalist and the business man as an entrepreneur. The difference between profits and interest had just begun to attract the attention of contemporary economists during the latter part of the 'eighties.[3] Furthermore, in the cotton industry, with which he was most familiar, the companies, although incorporated for the most part, were usually operated under the guidance of boards of directors, the members of which usually had a large financial interest in the business. This condition tended to center

---

[1] Atkinson, Edward, *The Industrial Progress of the Nation*, p. 178.
[2] *Ibid.*, p. 179.
[3] In 1867, F. A. Walker, by the presentation of his rent-of-ability theory of business profits (*Quarterly Journal of Economics*, vol. I, pp. 265–87), precipitated a discussion on the part of the prominent economists of the day which did much to clarify the concept of the function of the business man. Cf. *Quarterly Journal of Economics*, vols. I–III. Although Mr. Atkinson knew Mr. Walker personally, and with some exceptions admired the latter's contributions to the field of economics, he makes no mention of Walker's theory of profits.

the functions of ownership and administration of capital in the same individuals.

Whatever may have been the precise functions of the capitalist in Mr. Atkinson's mind, he was greatly impressed by the importance of the services rendered by those who directed the business activities of the community and by the low cost of those services. 'The mind of man, mental energy, is the prime factor in material production. Land, labor and capital are either inert or ineffectual unless co-ordinated and directed by mental energy — a very rare quality, entitling those who possess it to the largest remuneration because they add vastly more to the sum of all utilities than they take from it even by way of their incomes.'[1] One of his favorite methods of illustrating this point was to cite the case of railroad development under the direction of Cornelius Vanderbilt. He pointed out how the New York Central Railroad reduced the freight rate per thousand miles on a barrel of flour from $3.45 in 1865 to 68 cents in 1885. Then, in respect to the 68 cents, Mr. Atkinson raised the question, 'What profit did he [Vanderbilt] make? Fourteen cents a barrel; no more; sometimes less. Not so much as the value of the empty barrel. What if he did make $200,000,000 or more by the job, he and his father working together 25 or 30 years? Wasn't he a cheap man to employ as a teamster? Vanderbilt made his $200,000,000 by cheapening the cost of carrying the flour, and saving each of us $2.77 on our flour.'[2]

In respect to the relative portions of the national income going to capital on the one hand and labor on the other, Mr. Atkinson subscribed fully to the statement of Bastiat to the effect that 'in proportion to the increase of capital, the absolute share of the total product falling to the capitalist is augmented, and his relative share is diminished while, on the contrary, the labour's share is increased both absolutely and relatively.'[3]

---
[1] Letter to Thomas T. Barret, April 27, 1900.
[2] Atkinson, Edward, *Addresses upon the Labor Question* (pamphlet), pp. 15–16.
[3] Bastiat, Frederick, *Harmonies of Political Economy*, p. 212. Mr. Atkinson made this statement of Bastiat's the motto of an essay entitled *What Makes the Rate of Wages*, which he read before the British Association for the Advancement of Science, August, 1885.

Mr. Atkinson put great emphasis upon the point that 'the more the capitalist increases his wealth and applies it to reproduction, the more the welfare of the laborer is assured. The competition of capital with capital tends constantly to decrease in the ratio of the profit of capital to the total production, and of necessity tends also to a constant increase in the rate of wages of the laborer, thereby more than counter-acting the tendency of the competition of laborer with laborer to diminish wages.'[1]

The subject of value was one to which Mr. Atkinson gave little attention. His principal comment on the subject was to the effect: 'There is no absolute measure of the value of anything. It depends upon where it is and who wants it. Its value as an article at a particular place for conversion into terms of money for purposes of trade is *fixed by* the time and labor saved to him who buys, not by the time and labor expended by him with whom the product originated.'[2] Mr. Atkinson's use of the phrase '*fixed by*' is unfortunate, for while it may be conceded that the potential saving in time and labor (disutility) to be derived from the object in question would set the upper limit of the price which will be paid for the article, it is obvious that the maximum is not always paid for an article.[3]

Mr. Atkinson paid considerable attention to the subject of taxation. His interest, in part, was drawn to this subject as a result of his activities to get the tariff reduced to a revenue basis, and, in part, by an interest in the problems arising in connection with internal revenue policies. In general, he favored taxes based upon the principle of 'ability to pay.' His treatment of the subject, however, was marred by an over-simplified theory of the incidence of taxes, which was that all taxes, with the exception of income taxes, but including land taxes, no matter how levied

---

[1] Atkinson, Edward, *The Industrial Progress of the Nation*, pp. 63–64. The last part of this statement would be challenged by anyone who believes in the validity of the principle of diminishing returns as being applicable only under certain conditions. If, for example, the population were increasing at a faster rate than the supply of capital, it is difficult to see how wage rates could rise. But by denying the validity of diminishing returns, Mr. Atkinson conveniently disposes of this and other troublesome population problems.

[2] Letter to Thomas T. Barret, May 5, 1900.

[3] Cf. Taussig, F. W., *Principles of Economics*, vol. I, pp. 128–37.

originally, were shifted to the consumer.[1] Such a combination of theories left only taxes on the consumption of luxuries and the income tax as desirable sources of governmental revenue.

Few students of the subject would agree with Mr. Atkinson's view that all taxes, even excluding land taxes, are shifted entirely to the consumer. The incidence of taxation is too complicated a subject to be thus dismissed by a sweeping generalization. Mr. Atkinson's aberration from the common view that taxes upon economic rent are rarely shifted may be accounted for when his view concerning the nature of rent is recalled. Because he believed that in most cases the product of land is due entirely to the capital and labor expended thereon, and that little, if any, of the product is due to the superior qualities of one piece of land as compared to another, it is understandable that he should come to the conclusion which he did.[2]

On the whole, it is fair to say that Mr. Atkinson did not possess any thorough or profound knowledge of economic principles. His analysis in respect to many of the important aspects of value and distribution is fragmentary at best, and in some instances shows a complete misunderstanding of the principles involved. His exposition suffers from a lack of precision in the use of terms,

---

[1] Cf. Atkinson, Edward, *The Distribution of Products*, p. 14.

[2] In view of his interest in the subject of taxation, it is not to be expected that Mr. Atkinson would fail to enter the discussion which followed the publication of Henry George's *Progress and Poverty* in 1880. Nor is it unexpected, in light of his economic beliefs, that he would disagree with Henry George at almost every point of the latter's analysis. Mr. George believed that industrial progress had resulted in poverty instead of plenty, and had widened the gap between the rich and the poor. He believed that the reason for the failure of inventions and scientific discovery to improve the conditions of most of mankind lay in the fact that land, which had been appropriated by the wealthy, had become increasingly important as a factor in production, with the result that the owners exacted more and more of the social income as tribute. His solution was to tax economic rent, which would relieve the burdens of taxes from the poor, and eliminate the most important cause of poverty. Mr. Atkinson on the contrary, as has been noted, believed that the industrial progress had bettered the conditions of the poor, and would continue to do so in the future; that rent, as a payment for the uses of land, was becoming of less importance, and to tax land as George proposed would only result in the tax being passed on to the consumers, including the poorer groups.

It is unnecessary to discuss the relative merits of Henry George's proposals or Mr. Atkinson's criticisms of them. The latter's refusal to concur in George's views of the cause of, and the cure for, poverty is consistent with his belief that the greatest future improvement in the condition of the poorer classes would come as a result of the free operation of economic laws and with little change of existing institutions.

which makes it most difficult to follow his line of reasoning in many instances.[1] This fault is due in part at least to the fact that he was not interested in economic theory as such. In spite of the fact that Mr. Atkinson in many instances chose titles for his writings and speeches which would suggest that he wrote extensively in the field of pure theory, such was not the case. Almost without exception his work was directed toward some specific end, and he possessed neither the inclination nor the time to work out any well-ordered system of economic theory.

In justice to Mr. Atkinson it should be said that he looked upon many of his conclusions as being only tentative, and he expressed the hope that his work should serve to induce others to make further inquiry into the subjects which he presented. In fact, his work was at times a deliberate attempt to arouse controversy and discussion on topics. There was no question in his mind, however, about his fundamental objections to the conclusions of Ricardo and Malthus, at least in so far as those conclusions might be applied to the United States, and he felt confident that further studies would support his denial of the validity of the principle of diminishing returns and the implications usually drawn from that principle. To a critic who said that Mr. Atkinson's conclusions would not be accepted 'when his very inadequate comprehension of the theories of Malthus and Ricardo is called to mind,'[2] Mr. Atkinson replied: 'In this statement my critic presents an example of the danger to which the student of books is exposed in becoming a mere interpreter of the hypothesis of writers who may have failed to adopt a true inductive method, or who may not have been capable observers. Possibly Malthus and Ricardo may have applied great ability to false theories, by which a vast deal of mischief has been done,

---

[1] One competent critic said, in part, of Mr. Atkinson's work as an economist: 'How is it that a man so capable of lucid statement should have such exceedingly misty conceptions on the important subjects of profits, services, and products? It is due to the common fault, the besetting sin of the practical man, who openly despises or tacitly ignores theory and definition.... Because in his mind the word "profits" represents indifferently the income of capitalists and the savings of capitalists, he reasons as if everything true of one must be true of the other.' Hawley, F. B., 'Mr. Atkinson's Economics,' *Forum*, May, 1889, p. 298.   [2] Hawley, F. B., *Quarterly Journal of Economics*, vol. II, p. 362.

and it may not be consistent with true economic science to adopt their hypotheses.'[1]

The true science of economics he thought might be developed by breaking away from the English influence upon the subject and adopting an inductive approach. He queried:

> Have the orthodox English economists since Adam Smith ever overcome the insular quality of their work, or sufficiently counted upon the mind of man as a factor in material production? Perhaps these questions would occur only to one who has studied economic problems by the observation of the facts of life rather than in the treatises on which our economic reasoning has heretofore been based. Is it not desirable that more attention should be given to the method of Adam Smith than to the dogmas of Malthus, Ricardo, and Mill? If so, then the facts which are now being gathered by statisticians, especially in this country, may hereafter serve to give a broad extension of the narrow and insular habits of thought which the students of political economy have derived mainly from English writers. Let it not be supposed for an instant that I assume that there can be an American system of political economy as distinguished from an English system. Such a conception would be utterly inconsistent with any true idea of science. Yet, is it not true that habits of thought are unconsciously controlled by the environment of the writer?[2]

He expanded his belief in the future of statistics.

> I venture to believe that although the province of statistical science has been held subordinate to that of political economy or political science, it may yet become of paramount importance to the development of either branch of study. Doubtful as statistics may be, much as they depend on the sincerity of purposes and integrity of him who compiles them, and easy as it is for them to become twisted and confused, even by the unconscious bias of the observer or compiler, they may yet become a necessary foundation for any true inductive method in political economy, and must, therefore, be placed on an even plane, to say the least, in the estimation of the student.[3]

It is not surprising that Mr. Atkinson should attach such importance to the study and use of statistics. He was a pioneer in this particular study and his ability both as a compiler and an interpreter of data was recognized even by those who disagreed at times with his conclusions. Although his methods, viewed in

---
[1] Atkinson, Edward, *The Industrial Progress of the Nation*, p. 155.
[2] *Ibid.*, p. 160.   [3] *Ibid.*, p. 161.

the light of modern statistical procedure, were crude and his conclusions in the field of economics weakened by his lack of a theoretical background, nevertheless his widespread reputation as a statistician was well deserved and his contributions to this field of study of considerable significance.

As was previously indicated, Mr. Atkinson was primarily concerned with the application of economic principles to practical social problems, and it was in this field that he acquired his chief reputation as an economist.[1]

Aside from the tariff and monetary questions, to which attention has already been called,[2] the problems in the field of applied economics which were of most interest to Mr. Atkinson had to do with the relations between the capitalist and the laborer. This subject engrossed him, especially during the 'eighties and early 'nineties, and to its discussion he brought all the optimism which characterized his observations on distribution. In 1884, preliminary to a discussion of *What Makes the Rate of Wages*, he gave the key to his interest when he wrote: 'All men who have studied the phenomena of wages are somewhat appalled by the indications of the contest which seems to be approaching in every civilized state. This struggle takes the aspect in one place of a contest between the landlord and peasant; in another between mill-owner and operative; in another between privileged class and proletariat; in another between rich and poor; and in another between the needy and the well-to-do, whether the latter be rich or only well off.'[3]

This approaching struggle he blamed in part to the false teachings of the followers of Ricardo and Malthus, and in part to restrictive legislation and the burdens of war in European countries. While he felt that in the United States, 'which is no longer subject

---

[1] One observer, speaking of the status of economics in the late 'seventies, said, in part, 'The men best qualified to stand in the front rank of American economists are not the authors of systems or general theories, or textbooks of principles, but writers on special subjects — David Wells, William M. Grosvenor, Albert S. Bolles, Francis A. Walker, Edward Atkinson, William G. Sumner, C. F. Dunbar, and Simon Newcomb.' A quotation taken from Cliffe Leslie by Lewis Haney in *History of Economic Thought*, p. 614.

[2] *Ante*, pp. 57–98, 135–61, 178–222.

[3] Atkinson, Edward, *The Distribution of Products*, pp. 1–2.

to the inherited wrong of slavery, in which birth gives no privilege, and in which all have or may have equal opportunity to attain material welfare, the working men and women who perform that part of the work or production which is either manual or mechanical are steadily securing to their own use and enjoyment an increasing share of an increasing product; while on the other hand, both the material capital which has been saved in a concrete form, and also the element which is yet more necessary to material abundance, the capital which is immaterial, i.e., the mental factor in all productions, are being placed at the service of those who do the primary work at a lessening rate of compensation or profit. Nevertheless, when all Europe is a prey to fears of anarchy, nihilism, socialism, and communism, and when it seems to be as impossible for the standing armies and national debts of the Continent to be sustained as for the armies to be disbanded or the debts repudiated without violent revolution, may it not be well for us to take an inventory of our resources and to review our present methods of distribution, lest we also should perhaps be called upon, again and again, to apply force in sustaining rights of property both in land and capital, which need no force for their defense when fully comprehended and justified by the service to humanity which their possession makes their owners capable of rendering in ever-increasing measure? May not the harmony of interest between labor and capital be disclosed by the statistics of the nation to everyone who can read what underlies the columns and is written between the lines? May it not therefore be well for all to give their attention to what are indefinitely termed the "claims of labor," lest for want of thought, that which is right should be misconstrued and assumed to be wrong by those whose narrow or monotonous conditions of life limit the scope of their thought and may possibly lead them to misdirect their acts.'[1]

[1] Atkinson, Edward, *The Industrial Progress of the Nation*, p. 207. It is perhaps needless to point out that this implicit faith in the harmony of interests between labor and capital is somewhat naïve. No one will deny, of course, a certain identity of interests between capitalists and laborers in so far as they may be considered as partners in the joint enterprise of production. But no one conversant with the facts can overlook the fact that on many questions, such as wage rates, hours of employment, and the like, the immediate interests of the two classes are in definite opposition.

Mr. Atkinson took upon himself the task of clearing away some of the misconceptions which he felt were endangering the fundamental harmony existing between capital and labor. His work proceeded along several well-defined lines. In the first place, he gathered statistical evidence to show that the capitalist, contrary to popular opinion, currently received only a small share of the national income. Second, he sought to prove that Bastiat's proposition, to the effect that labor was destined to get an ever-increasing share, both absolutely and relatively, in the national dividend, had been, and would be true of the United States. Next, he outlined the evils arising from combinations of laborers and from restrictive legislation. And, finally, he advanced his own suggestions as to how the conditions of the laboring classes might be improved.

Mr. Atkinson faced a difficult task in attempting to determine the relative shares of the national income which went to the capitalist (in the form of business profits, rent and interest) on the one hand, and to the laborer (in which class he included all who received salaries or wages) on the other. Chief of the difficulties which he had to meet was the lack of statistical material upon which to base adequate conclusions, particularly the data on incomes and profits which have now been made available to the modern investigator (though, to be sure, not in as complete a form as might be desired).

Mr. Atkinson proceeded in his investigation in the following manner.[1] The census figures for 1880 placed the value of the annual (physical) product of the United States at approximately $8,500,-000,000, exclusive of articles which were consumed directly without being bought or sold. Checking this figure by material from other sources and estimating the value of the goods consumed directly (chiefly on the farms), Mr. Atkinson placed the national dividend at a figure of $10,000,000,000. The next step was to determine the share going to labor. To get this figure, he divided $9,000,000,000 (not $10,000,000,000, although he doesn't explain why the $1,000,000,000 consumed domestically should not be

[1] Cf. Atkinson, Edward, *Distribution of Products*, pp. 31-34.

included in the total income) by the number of persons in gainful occupations, 17,300,000, which gave a figure of about $523 as the average *per capita* gross income. After deducting eight per cent for taxes and ten per cent for the share going to the capitalist, Mr. Atkinson arrived at $433 as the average net income to all workers gainfully employed. Although he does not explain why he chose ten per cent of the total income as the reward to the capitalist, the fact that his result of $433 checked with the earnings in specific industries — according to the census data — made him conclude that this figure was correct.[1]

Mr. Atkinson's conclusion from the foregoing analysis was that the amount going to the capitalists was not over ten per cent of the total national income. As he put it, 'In a normal year under normal conditions, I am of the profound conviction that not exceeding ten per cent of the total product can be set aside as either rent, profit or savings; and that nine-tenths constitutes the share of the laborer, which, by subdivision, becomes expressed in terms of personal wages.'[2]

Mr. Atkinson's findings in respect to the national dividend

---

[1] Mr. Atkinson gave the following summary of the data which he used in the foregoing calculations:

Approximate estimate of the value of annual product of the census year		$10,000,000,000
Domestic farm consumption, estimated		1,000,000,000
Commercial Product		9,000,000,000
Estimated profits of capitalists	$450,000,000	
Estimated savings of other classes	$450,000,000	900,000,000
Wages fund		$8,100,000,000
Number of persons engaged in all gainful occupations in round figures	17,400,000	
Deduct soldiers, marines, and persons engaged in subordinate positions in the Government service	100,000	
Remainder	17,300,000	
Administrative force, i.e., mental rather than manual work		1,100,000
Working force, i.e., wage-earners or small farmers		16,200,000
Average remuneration of the administrative force, per year		$1,000
Average wages or earnings of the working force, per year		$432
Gross amount of national, State, and municipal taxes in census year over		$700,000,000

Or eight per cent of the commercial product.

Atkinson, Edward, *Distribution of Products*, p. 91.

It will be noted that the method implied in this table is different from the one followed in the text, but the result is almost the same, namely, $432 as compared with $433.

[2] Atkinson, Edward, *op. cit.*, p. 27.

for 1880 and its distribution did not pass unchallenged. His book, *The Distribution of Products*, which contained the foregoing analysis, was critically reviewed by Frederick B. Hawley, well-known contemporary economist.[1] In the course of his review, Mr. Hawley made the following criticisms of Mr. Atkinson's conclusions: First, the omission of the one billion dollars' worth of products consumed domestically was unwarranted, as this amount certainly belonged in the total 'wages fund.' Second, he felt that the national dividend, including domestic consumption, was nearer eleven than ten billion dollars. Thus, as he agreed with Mr. Atkinson's estimate of the average net wage of the workers, those differences alone would change the percentage going to the capitalist from ten per cent of the total to approximately twenty-six per cent of the total. To these omissions, however, Mr. Hawley added a third and more serious one. This was the share of the national dividend which must be attributed to personal services, and the services of capital goods and land, none of which is included in Mr. Atkinson's estimate of the national dividend. Allowing for this discrepancy, but taking Mr. Atkinson's estimate of the value of the physical product as correct, Mr. Hawley arrived at the following results:[2]

Material products marketed	$9,000,000,000
Material products unmarketed	1,000,000,000
Services rendered by persons	1,200,000,000
Services rendered by wealth	800,000,000
Total	$12,000,000,000

Deducting the $8,100,000,000 'wages fund' from this figure leaves $3,900,000,000, or 32½ per cent (if 11,000,000,000 is accepted as the value of the physical products, 37½ per cent) of the national income which went to the capitalistic class in the form of business profits, rents and interest, instead of 10 per cent as Mr. Atkinson suggested.

It is impossible to verify the national income figures given by both men, as reliable studies of the national dividend are of com-

[1] *Quarterly Journal of Economics*, vol. II, pp. 362-71.
[2] *Ibid.*, p. 367.

paratively recent origin, and do not extend back to the date under consideration (1880). There can be little doubt, however, of the validity of Mr. Hawley's criticism to the effect that services and goods consumed domestically should be considered as a part of the national dividend. As both agreed on the absolute share going to labor, it is probable that Hawley's estimate of the total dividend, and therefore the proportion going to capital and labor, is more nearly correct than Mr. Atkinson's estimates.

Mr. Atkinson, in his rejoinder to Mr. Hawley,[1] refused to admit the force of the latter's criticism, and denied that services can be included as a part of the national income. He continued: 'If this theory is a true one, to wit, that all wages, profits, and taxes which are liquidated in money must of necessity come within the limit of the salable value of that part of the product which is bought and sold, it follows of necessity that "neither the earnings of those persons who are engaged in personal and professional service, nor the sons who are engaged in personal and professional service, nor the support of horses, railways, and telegraph companies used for other than business purposes, nor the services performed for us by various forms of accumulated wealth" can be added to a sum which already covers the entire value of everything produced.'[2] It was this point, of course, which Hawley refused to admit, as personal services, capital services, and the like were not included in the value of the physical production which Mr. Atkinson took as representing the entire national income.

Mr. Atkinson tacitly admitted in his original exposition that the incomes of capitalists are larger than his figures indicated when he wrote: 'It will be observed that the savings [by which he means incomes in the form of rent, interest, and profits] are something quite different from the measure of that which would constitute the profits [incomes] of individuals; for instance, the manufacturer or merchant may make a very considerable profit out of his work, but he then distributes a very large portion of

[1] Atkinson, Edward, *The Industrial Progress of the Nation*, pp. 137-62.
[2] *Ibid.*, pp. 143-44.

this profit in his family expenses, thereby sustaining a large number of persons who are included among the so-called working classes or wage-earners. The final end or contribution to the capital [capitalists] of the nation is therefore a very much less sum than the apparent profits which accrue either from the rent of real estate or from the income derived by the individual owners of manufacturing, railroads, or other investments, or from business.'[1]

In his rejoinder to Mr. Hawley, he supplemented the foregoing by saying: 'The richest man rarely consumes more than a small part of his income in what may be called unproductive consumption; what he and his family cost the country is the measure of their actual consumption in their own persons; what they spend constitutes the income or share of the annual product of those among whom it is spent. Every capitalist is a distributor as well as a consumer.'[2]

These statements need no further comment except perhaps to indicate that they lead to the untenable conclusion that a man who spends his money for services receives no income, and is no burden to society because he merely distributes income to those who perform those services, whereas the man who spends an equal sum for food, clothes, and the like does receive his income and is a cost to society to the amount of his spending.

On the whole it may be said that Mr. Atkinson's lack of training in economic theory betrayed him into making statements which, with a more thorough understanding of the principles involved, he would have avoided. And, in so far at least as it applied to this analysis by Mr. Atkinson, one is forced into agreement with Mr. Hawley's statement 'that statistical investigation can rarely be fruitful of any valuable results except in the hands of an investigator well grounded in economic theory.'[3]

Mr. Atkinson's attempt to prove the validity of Bastiat's statement concerning the inevitable tendency for labor to get an in-

---

[1] Atkinson, Edward, *The Distribution of Products*, p. 95.
[2] Atkinson, Edward, *The Industrial Progress of the Nation*, p. 145.
[3] *Quarterly Journal of Economics*, vol. II, p. 362.

creasing share of the national dividend [1] is scarcely more convincing. Mr. Atkinson took his data to substantiate this tendency from the accounts of two successful New England cotton factories for the period between 1830 and 1884.[2] During that period the yearly wage rate increased from $164 to $280, the number of employees remaining constant, while the rate of profits, he assumed, remained at ten per cent on the same amount of capital. As the production of cloth had increased tremendously during these years, Mr. Atkinson therefore concluded that labor was receiving a larger proportion of a larger product, and he assumed, after checking his results with a number of other factories, that what was true of the cotton industry was true of industry in general. Without questioning the validity of generalizing from such a limited number of data, it may be said that this conclusion does not necessarily follow from these data. One may admit, for example, that wage rates throughout industry did rise simultaneously with a fall in the interest rate during the fifty years after 1830, without being committed to the proposition that labor received in 1884 a larger percentage of the total product than it did in 1830. To arrive at the proportions of the total product going to capital and labor, it is necessary to know the number of laborers and the total amount of capital, in addition to their rates of return. (This statement would apply with equal force if profits are taken to include both interest and business profits, as Mr. Atkinson uses the term, except that the number of persons receiving profits and the rate would also have to be known.)

As reliable data on the functional distribution of the national income do not cover the period under consideration, it is again impossible to check Mr. Atkinson's conclusions by more recent figures. Careful studies of the period between 1913 and 1925 show, however, that the percentage of the national income going to labor, in the form of wages, salaries, pensions, etc., increased from 53 per cent in 1913 to 57 per cent in 1925.[3] While this twelve-

---

[1] Cf. *ante*, p. 253.
[2] Atkinson, Edward, *Distribution of Products*, pp. 116–26.
[3] Copeland, Maurice, *Recent Economic Changes in the United States*, p. 767. Incidentally,

year period is much too short a time from which to draw any conclusions as to any general trend, these data would seem to indicate that Mr. Atkinson's faith concerning the future of labor was justified. But, if Mr. Atkinson's figures of the relative shares going to the capitalistic classes and to labor in 1880 are taken, to wit, 10 per cent and 90 per cent, then, as between 1880 and 1913, labor found itself in an increasingly worse position, relatively speaking. There is little reason to believe that this was the case, however, a fact which gives further evidence that Mr. Hawley's ratio for 1880, of 37½ per cent to 62½ per cent, was probably a much more nearly correct estimate of the distribution of the national income.

In concluding this particular discussion, it may be assumed that Mr. Atkinson did not go beyond demonstrating that real wages had risen between 1830 and 1884. Proof as to whether laborers are destined to improve their future position relative to the property-owning classes must await further investigation extending over a much longer period of time than has thus far been possible.

Having demonstrated to his own satisfaction that labor was going to assume an increasingly advantageous position in respect to the distribution of the national income, Mr. Atkinson's next step was to outline the conditions under which this result could be achieved. The most important requirement, he felt, was that there should be a minimum number of restrictions placed on the operation of economic laws, which, if left undisturbed, would not only bring out the fundamental harmony existing between capital and labor, but also would insure the greatest efficiency in the production of goods and services.

This belief was posited on a profound faith in the benefits to be derived from the free play of competitive forces. It is in this attitude toward competition that Mr. Atkinson shows most clearly the influence of Adam Smith on his thinking. He joined Smith in giving what almost amounted to a religious sanction to the

the share going to capital as interest increased from 4 per cent to 5 per cent of the total during the same period.

principle of *laissez-faire* when he stated: 'Not only does enlightened self-interest coincide with, or lead toward moral and material welfare, but even unenlightened self-interest, as represented by the mere money-getter, the mere capitalist, or by the man who has himself no knowledge of his own function, yet works of necessity in promoting an increased product and a reduction in cost of all necessaries of life, under which the great mass of the community cannot fail to attain better conditions of welfare.... It was said by the prophet of olden time, that "The Lord maketh the wrath of man to praise him." It might be said by the prophet of the present, that the Lord maketh the selfishness of man to work for the material welfare of his kind.'[1]

It was not that Mr. Atkinson denied the necessity of Government regulation. But he felt that legal enactments of the Government should not go beyond the point necessary to secure the greatest freedom to the forces of competition. Its true purpose should be only 'to promote justice and to give equal opportunity to everyone.' He was fond of the statement, 'that country will prosper most which requires least from its Government, and in which the people, after having chosen officers, straightway proceed to govern themselves according to their common habit.'[2] By this he meant that men, in most of their relations with one another, are able to conduct their affairs without interference by Government.[3]

Thus believing that in the absence of artificial obstacles labor as a class would of necessity achieve an increasing share of the social dividend, Mr. Atkinson became highly impatient at the attempts of laborers to secure shorter working hours, minimum wages, uniform wages, or similar measures, either by legal enact-

---

[1] Atkinson, Edward, *The Industrial Progress of the Nation*, p. 208. Cf. Adam Smith's famous statement concerning the guidance of 'an invisible hand' which leads men, unwittingly, in their pursuit of personal interests to contribute to the gain of society. *Wealth of Nations*, vol. I, p. 400.

[2] Atkinson, Edward, *op. cit.*, p. 79.

[3] In the future he felt that the 'function of the officers of Government will become less important than they now are, and it need not long be necessary for able men to make a great sacrifice in order to take a share in the executive work. Ordinary men will do the ordinary work to be done.' Letter to Daniel G. Thompson, November 24, 1891.

ment or by the organization of labor unions. He denounced the 'subtle restrictions upon individual liberty, affecting all the methods of production and distribution... imposed by secret societies.' He further prophesied: 'The effect of these various restrictions upon personal liberty may be to prevent the abundance of the means of subsistence from becoming as ample as it might be, and may continue to take from the many a part of the fruits of their labor for the benefit of the few. Yet this country has been endowed with such abundant resources that we shall continue to thrive in spite of the blunders of legislatures and the interference of labor associations, whose objects may be as right as their methods of attaining them are wrong.'[1] He urged the laborers to organize themselves as 'Squires of Work,' in opposition to the currently strong Knights of Labor. The purpose of the Squires of Work would be to achieve the benefits of an association, without coercing members into accepting laboring conditions prescribed by the unions. He expressed the conviction that the term 'scab,' like 'Yankee,' should eventually become an appellation to be accepted proudly by the independent workman.[2]

Concerning the future of the labor unions, he said:

> There is no great power either in statute laws, or in the by-laws of the associations; the real power which governs the people of this country is the power of public opinion; and public opinion sooner or later will utterly condemn every association, under whatever name, that undertakes to restrict the individual liberty of adult men. When this principle is recognized, Labor will suffer no defeat, because there will be no contest in which it can be defeated.[3]

In a speech before the Central Labor Lyceum on May 1, 1887, Mr. Atkinson expanded upon the ineffectiveness and dangers of labor legislation. He said:

> In 1842, the men and women who worked in the cotton mills worked 13 or 14 hours a day and they could not begin to make as much

---

[1] Atkinson, Edward, *op. cit.*, p. 245.
[2] 'If there is one thing meaner than a rich man who does not admit that wealth has duties as well as rights, it is a workman who tries to prevent his neighbor from making his own bargains in his own way, and who, when he fails, as he always will fail, next tries to make him contemptible by nicknaming him a "scab."' Atkinson, Edward, *The Margin of Profits*, pp. 49-50.   [3] *Ibid.*, p. 108.

cloth in a day as they do now.... It was just the same in every other kind of work then as it was in the cotton mill, longer hours, harder work, poorer pay; too long, too hard; but it took all that time and all that labor to raise food enough or to make cloth enough, or to get fuel enough to go around; where it took 13 or 14 hours, it now takes but 10 hours.... I think it very likely that your children will be able to get just as good a living, and perhaps a better one than you do by working 8 hours a day; but they won't get it by acts of the Legislature. If you can pass a law to shorten the general hours of work (and it won't be fair unless you make it general), if you bring every kind of work down to 8 hours or less, there will not be houses enough to give you as good rooms as you have now, there won't be clothes enough, and there may not be food enough.[1]

As Mr. Atkinson viewed the problem of social reform, there were but three ways by which the condition of the laboring classes could be improved. One was to enlarge the total production. A second method was to take away from the wealthy or capitalistic class and give to the poor. And the third and most effective way to secure social betterment was to eliminate the waste in the consumption of the income already going to the poorer groups.

Enough has already been said concerning Mr. Atkinson's attitude toward the first of these methods to indicate that he had great faith in an increasing social product. For the 'impatient' social reformer, however, this process, which of necessity must extend over a number of years, was too slow. Therefore, Mr. Atkinson devoted considerable attention to the problems involved in the alternative ways of social reform.

As might be expected, he was utterly opposed to a redistribution of wealth or incomes as a method of improving the conditions of the laboring classes. In the first place, as he estimated that the total amount going to the capitalists was only ten per cent of the total national income, he felt there was little chance for any substantial increase in the incomes of the working people from this source.[2]

---

[1] Atkinson, Edward, *The Margin of Profits*, an address delivered before the Central Labor Lyceum of Boston on Sunday evening, May 1, 1887, p. 24.

[2] Mr. Atkinson put this point: 'If the workmen or laborers or if the classes consisting of laborers, receivers of small salaries, small farmers and the like, who now constitute the great majority of the community, do now actually obtain for their own use and consump-

Mr. Atkinson based his second objection to a redistribution of incomes upon the following line of reasoning. He said:

> Capital is a force, and capitalists are those who direct this force. By the direction which the owners or the administrators of capital give to this force, which requires mental work of the most uncommon kind, the joint product of labor and capital is so much increased that, even though the capitalist secures to his own use a large part of the joint product, what is left to the working-man is more in quantity and in value than he could otherwise have attained by his own unaided efforts. In all commerce, in all manufactures, in all industries, in all work of every kind, the forces of labor and capital must co-operate, and must render mutual service to each other. This law cannot be impaired by either without disaster to both. The capitalist adds more, by his service, to the joint product than he can possibly take away or divert to consumers in any form of rent, profit, or interest.[1]

Mr. Atkinson implies, although he doesn't discuss the subject in any detail, that without profits, the services of the capitalists would not be forthcoming. This being true, he felt that labor could scarcely afford to encroach on profits as a source of income.

Having thus indicated that profits were neither a large nor an expedient source of income available to labor, Mr. Atkinson turned to what he considered to be a practical method of improving the condition of the working class. This was to eliminate the waste of consumption; more specifically, the wastes in the preparation and consumption of food.[2]

Mr. Atkinson estimated that in the 'eighties the cost of food absorbed about one-half of the income of nine-tenths of the population ninety per cent of the gross annual product, then there is little margin for improvement except through an increase of the product itself.' *The Industrial Progress of the Nation*, p. 139.

[1] Atkinson, Edward, *The Industrial Progress of the Nation*, p. 147.

[2] It is interesting to note how the subject of waste attracted Mr. Atkinson's attention throughout his life. As has been noted, in his first pamphlet, *Cheap Cotton by Free Labor*, he called attention to the loss involved in the then common practice of letting cotton seeds rot away in huge piles by the sides of the ginneries. His primary purpose in suggesting the Atlanta Cotton Exposition was to eliminate the waste involved in the poor preparation and packing of cotton. As a fire insurance executive, his principal concern was to eliminate the losses due to preventable causes of fires. His chief objection to war was based upon the wasted man-power involved in the maintenance of standing armies and large navies, as well as the actual destruction of material during conflicts between nations. And during the latter part of his life, he became intrigued by the idea of utilizing the tremendous annual supply of cornstalks by converting it into paper, fuel briquettes, and similar substitutes for wood.

lation. It was his conviction, based upon his study of dietetics, that most of the food bought by rich and poor alike was ill-prepared and subjected to heavy loss of food value in the process of cooking. He queried: 'How much human force is wasted in consequence of bad cooking? How much does dyspepsia or indigestion, caused by bad cooking, impair the working capacity of the people of the United States and diminish their product? How many cooks are there who know what food to buy and how to cook it?'[1]

He further estimated that a saving of only five cents per day for each individual in the average family among the poorer classes would mean the difference between crowded living quarters and comfortable surroundings. And he challenged the 'anarchist, the communist, the socialist, the protectionist, the free-trader, the co-operator, the paper-money man, the knight of labor, the eight-hour man, or the sentimentalists [to] invent or suggest any other method of changing the direction of the industry of the whole community which would on the whole be so effective in improving the conditions of all, as one which would save five cents a day on food and fuel, the money saved to be devoted to providing better dwelling houses in which people may live.'[2]

As a practical demonstration of what could be done in the utilization of food, Mr. Atkinson offered his experiences with the Aladdin Oven, and urged that it be widely used by those interested in lowering food costs and in the better preparation of meals. By the use of his oven, and by following the rules of cooking which he helped to develop, Mr. Atkinson estimated that the average family could not only save at least five cents per person per day, but in addition would enjoy immeasurably better-prepared food.

Laborers and their leaders, on the whole, did not take kindly to Mr. Atkinson's efforts to aid them in this manner. He was suspected of attempting to get them to live cheaper in order that their employers would be enabled to pay lower wages. One labor leader in the course of a debate with Mr. Atkinson said: 'My friend says the men must save, must economize, must eat beef at five cents a pound, instead of twenty. Starve our stomachs to

[1] Atkinson, Edward, *op. cit.*, p. 239.   [2] *Ibid.*, p. 240.

save our food! Better and more nutritious will the food be? Is this recommended because it is better, or because it is cheaper? If because it is better, the working class need not be appealed to; everybody will soon find that out. If because it is cheaper, we answer, nothing is too good for us. We know that the more expensive we are the higher will our wages be, for that is determined by the cost of living; an iron law Ricardo calls it. If all laborers could save in cooking, the employers would profit by the saving, not the workmen.'[1]

Eugene Debs was another who scorned Mr. Atkinson's attempts to aid the laborers by means of improved cooking. As editor, he wrote in the *Locomotive Firemen's Magazine* for June, 1892: 'He may teach men the science of the shinbone diet, and chuckle as he sees his degenerate disciples live on 10 cents a day, and glory in his success in teaching Americans how to live like Huns, but American working-men are resolving not to be further degraded, scientifically or otherwise, and Mr. Atkinson, were he a thousand times more erudite than he is, will find out at last, at no distant day, that his mission is a miserable failure.'[2]

This statement of Debs typifies the attitude which most labor leaders maintained toward Mr. Atkinson and his labor policies. By them he was regarded as an able, and therefore doubly dangerous, representative of the capitalist class.[3]

A general criticism may be leveled against Mr. Atkinson's labor policies on the grounds that he put too much faith in the automatic operation of the laws of competition to secure equitable results for the worker. Experience since the advent of the Industrial Revolution has demonstrated that the economic laws are not self-enforcing, and it is necessary to supplement their action with

---

[1] 'Reply to Edward Atkinson by R. M. Chamberlin,' in Edward Atkinson's book, *The Margin of Profits*, pp. 56–57.

[2] Page 538.

[3] Debs, in the same publication quoted above, said of Mr. Atkinson's opposition to labor organizations: 'Mr. Atkinson proclaims himself the foe of such organizations. He is not so much of a fool as to attempt to destroy labor organizations by an appeal to the courts, but he is nevertheless so hostile to them that he advises men and women to keep away from them, and is probably more relentless in his hostility than any other writer or speaker in the country.' Page 538.

legal enactment, as well as voluntary associations, in order to overcome, somewhat, the frictional elements involved.¹ It is generally recognized, for example, that labor unions tend to equalize the bargaining power between capital and labor, and enable the employees to deal on more even terms with their employers on matters involving conditions of employment, wages, and the like.²

The extent to which the Government should attempt to regulate the hours of labor, working conditions, wage rates, etc., is still a highly controversial question, sixty or more years after Mr. Atkinson first began to write on these subjects. Yet conservative public opinion has largely accepted the position that minimum wages for women, limited hours of employment for both women and children, the protection from injury and poor conditions of employment in all types of work, and the enactment of laws providing for workmen's compensation, may rightfully fall under the jurisdiction of the State.³

On the whole, Mr. Atkinson's attitude toward labor unions and Government regulation of the conditions affecting business represented the opinion of the more enlightened business man of his time. He was not, however, without an appreciation of the responsibility which the business men themselves should assume as owners or directors of large capital or wealth. Speaking before the New England Cotton Manufacturers' Association in April, 1885, he said: 'I know of no class of men upon whom graver responsibility rests than upon you, and those like you, upon whose

[1] Included among the frictional elements which prevent the free operation of the competitive system are ignorance, monopoly, custom, and the general immobility of the factors of production.

[2] Not only do associations of employees remove the disadvantage which exists when one laborer attempts to bargain with an employer, but as it is true that in most industries there is a considerable range within which wage rates may be set by skillfully bargaining, the employees as a group may be able to secure a share of the product which might otherwise go as profits. Especially is this true in the case of a progressive state of industry.

[3] Mr. Atkinson would probably agree with these statements in so far as they applied to the working conditions of women and children. Beyond this, it is doubtful if he would have been willing to extend governmental regulation. Adult male workers, he felt, were able to take care of themselves without any aid from the Government or associations.

judgment, forbearance, and sense of responsibility rests the welfare of the multitude. You are employed by them, and in the service which you render as well as that which you receive may be found your own justification as well as the justification of the capital which you direct.'[1]

In spite of the fact that Mr. Atkinson's opinions were at odds with many of the real or fancied interests of labor, there can be no question that he was thoroughly sincere in his desire to improve the conditions of the working class. The questioning of Mr. Atkinson's motives in respect to the Aladdin Oven, by Debs and others, was absolutely unwarranted, especially in view of Mr. Atkinson's belief in the desirability and inevitability of high wages, and his renouncement of everything Ricardian, including the implications of an iron law of wages. It is true, of course, that he hoped to make labor more content with conditions as they were, but primarily in order that there might be no interference with the progress toward better conditions as they were to be.

It is easy in light of present-day standards to be critical of much of Mr. Atkinson's work in the field of applied economics. But in view of the fact that industrial and social changes were occurring so rapidly and that he was trying to apply a strict *laissez-faire* policy to an economic and social organization which was becoming increasingly complex and unresponsive to the influence of an 'invisible hand,' it is not unexpected that many of his conclusions now seem unwarranted. Moreover, he had good authority for his position in respect to the desirability of a *laissez-faire* policy, for most of the professional economists of his time shared this attitude.

It is evident from the large number of letters of encouragement and appreciation which followed the frequent publication of his

---

[1] Atkinson, Edward, *The Necessary Relations of Labor and Capital* (pamphlet), pp. 23-24. Mr. Atkinson deserves a generous measure of credit for being consistent in his belief in *laissez-faire* as it applied to legal restrictions on international trade. He was unlike many of his contemporaries who believed in being 'let alone' in their relations with labor, but who were anxious to accept governmental assistance in the form of a protective tariff.

pamphlets and articles, and the extensive circulation which his works enjoyed, that Mr. Atkinson's expressions on economic as well as other subjects were followed by a large audience, and that he exercised an important function in arousing interest in contemporary problems.

No small share of his popularity as a writer was due to the pleasing style which he used in treating the subjects about which he wrote. For, while his work at times suffered from a lack of careful editing and revision, due to the pressure of his many activities,[1] he had a facility for expressing himself in an effective manner. One competent critic has observed: 'Looking at Mr. Atkinson's career with the eyes of a literary man, it seems clear to me that no college training could possibly have added to his power of accumulation of knowledge, or his wealth in the expression of it.'[2]

Not the least impressive characteristic of Mr. Atkinson's writing is the fact that he was able to speak with no small measure of authority on a variety of fairly technical subjects. Included, for example, among the titles of articles which he wrote for a single year (1889) were the following: 'An Easy Lesson in Statistics,' 'The Art of Cooking,' 'Consumption Limited, Production Unlimited,' 'How Society Reforms Itself,' 'Instructions for Use of the Aladdin Oven,' 'Lessons from the Boston Fire,' 'Missing Science,' 'The Problem of Poverty,' 'Reforms that do not Reform,' 'Religion and Life,' 'Remedies for Social Ills,' and 'The Future Situs of the Cotton Manufacture of the United States.' To the manufacturer he spoke as a manufacturer, to the banker as a banker, to the cotton-grower as one who knew considerable about cotton culture, to the cook as a cook, and so on through the range of his interests. Yet, while his articles were written for the most part for rather specialized audiences, they can be read with interest even by the uninitiated.

[1] In some of his writing, Mr. Atkinson engaged in numerous digressions from the subject under discussion, which made it difficult to follow the main thread of his argument.
[2] Higginson, Thomas Wentworth, 'Edward Atkinson,' in *Proceedings of the American Academy of Arts and Sciences*, vol. XLII, p. 3.

Mr. Atkinson sought in his writing (and his speeches) to arouse interest in the subjects under discussion, and if possible, to incite criticism which would call attention to the issues involved. He would often deliberately overstate his case in order to attract such attention, often remarking that an article or a speech was of little use unless it 'stirred things up.'

Mr. Atkinson's fame as a writer scarcely exceeded his reputation and popularity as a speaker. His services were in such demand from various groups that he might have taken up oratory as a profession. Tall, of massive build, dignified, yet benign in appearance, he made an impressive figure upon the platform. His manner of delivery was as positive as was his manner of writing, a positiveness which emanated from a supreme confidence in the truth of his utterances.

His speeches and his audiences reflected the diversity of his interests, ranging from a technical dissertation of banking policies before the American Institute of Banking to a philosophic discussion of the relation between economics and religion before the Alumni of Andover Theological Seminary.

It cannot be said that Mr. Atkinson lacked courage to make statements which might not be pleasing to his listeners. His remarks to Southern audiences after the war to the effect that 'no man can be a true Democrat who does not maintain the equal rights of every man, without distinction of race, color, or condition, to speak, act, and vote as he freely chooses,'[1] and his statement to a group of laborers that 'if you attempt to force any man to work for a certain rate of wages, and in a certain way, under certain restrictions enforced by way of the statutes of the State or by the by-laws of a club, you introduce the first step which ends in slavery,'[2] could not have been made by anyone afraid to express what he felt were unpleasant truths.

When Mr. Atkinson's contributions as a speaker and a writer are added to those already credited to him in other fields of activities, it may be said, to use the words of one of his contemporaries,

---

[1] Atkinson, Edward, *Address Given in Atlanta, Georgia*, p. 12.
[2] Atkinson, Edward, *To the Workingmen of Providence, Rhode Island*, p. 29.

that 'when the amount of useful labor performed by the men of this generation comes to be reviewed a century hence, it is doubtful if a more substantial and varied list will be found credited to the memory of anyone in America than that which attaches to the memory of Edward Atkinson.'[1]

[1] Higginson, Thomas Wentworth, *op. cit.*, p. 9.

THE END

APPENDIX B

FREE LABOR COTTON COMPANY[1]

WHEREAS it is believed that the permanent relief of the Freedmen upon the Mississippi River, in whose behalf large donations are now being asked, requires that employment should be given them as soon as possible, in order that they may become self-sustaining,

We the undersigned do hereby constitute ourselves the 'Free Labor Cotton Company' for the purpose of leasing and carrying on plantations upon the Mississippi River or elsewhere upon humane business principles, and we agree to pay the sums set against our respective names for that purpose upon the following terms, conditions, and agreements.

1st. Such sums are to be paid to Edward Atkinson as Trustee for the subscribers hereto, and in case of his demise during the continuance of this Company, such trust shall thereby be transferred to John H. Stephenson, and in case of his demise to such person as may be chosen by the subscribers.

2nd. No liability of any kind is to be incurred by said Trustee or by any other agent or person whatsoever on behalf of this Company.

3rd. It is to be the duty of said Atkinson to receive such sums as are hereto subscribed and to deposit the same with the Assistant Treasurer of the United States, or to lend them upon such security as by him may be deemed sufficient, until called for on account of the business of this Company, and he shall be authorized to pay out the monies thus received upon the draft or receipt of A. H. Kelsey or his successor as hereinafter provided, and to receive from said Kelsey or his successor the avails of the crops raised under his supervision, and to divide such avails among the subscribers hereto pro rata, and upon his, the said Atkinson's performing such duties without defalcation, all responsibility or liability upon his part or that of his successor shall cease and terminate.

4th. It is understood and agreed by and with said A. H. Kelsey that he shall lease certain plantations and carry on the same for the cultivation of cotton or other crops, that he shall draw upon Edward Atkinson, Trustee, for the amount of the subscriptions hereto, or for such portion of the same as he may need from time to time, and use the same in the conduct of such business, and that he shall conduct such business with strict economy in the name of A. H. Kelsey, that he may hire such assistants and employ such labor as to him may seem fit, and that he shall charge his own expenses while engaged upon this business to the same, and that he will attend to all sales of produce and generally to all busi-

---

[1] Copy of the original agreement in the Atkinson Collection.

ness connected with this undertaking as if for his sole account; that he shall render to said Atkinson Trustee full and accurate accounts of all receipts and disbursements on account of said business as often as once in three months; and that in case of his demise the before named Edward Atkinson Trustee or his successor may appoint a successor to take charge of the business hereby undertaken by said Kelsey as Trustee.

5th. Said Kelsey may associate with himself in this undertaking any person as a partner, provided he shall have the consent of said Atkinson Trustee or his successor to such partnership.

6th. Said Kelsey shall pay over or account for to said Atkinson Trustee or his successor all proceeds or avails of any crops which may be raised on plantations leased under this agreement, and at the close of the business with his account shall render an accurate inventory of all produce, stock, tools or other property which may remain on hand belonging to the Company.

7th. This business is undertaken for a single planting season, and a final settlement is to be made as soon as the business of a single season can be closed.

8th. One teacher for each hundred children upon the plantations leased by said Kelsey, may be employed by him at the expense of the business.

9th. No subscription shall be made to this Company for less than Five hundred dollars, and the total amount shall be limited to One hundred and fifteen thousand dollars, unless it shall be found desirable by said Atkinson Trustee or his successor to increase said amount during the season, in which case he may call a meeting of the subscribers, of which meeting he shall give two weeks' notice, to act upon the matter, and to make such arrangements for such increase as to them may seem fit.

10th. If subscriptions to the amount of fifty thousand dollars are made within two weeks from the date of this agreement, then said agreement shall take effect, but not otherwise and any subscription not paid within two weeks after due notice shall be forfeited.

11th. Of the proposed subscription of One hundred and fifteen thousand dollars, the sum of fifteen thousand dollars shall be retained at the disposal of said Atkinson Trustee, to be subscribed by him and said Kelsey and partner if any, one third each at any time prior to April 1, 1864.

12th. The third part of the profits of this undertaking, if any there be, is to be paid to said Kelsey and partner if any, as compensation for the conduct of said business.

13th. A full printed report shall be made and circulated at the cost of the business.

14th. The first assessment shall be five per cent, on receipt of which said Kelsey and partner, if any, will leave for the Mississippi to explore

FREE LABOR COTTON COMPANY

the ground and if they find it expedient they shall notify the said Atkinson to call in the balance of the Capital; if not such   per cent shall be returned to the subscribers, less the expenses which may have been incurred.

15th. John H. Stephenson and   shall be an advisory committee to have access to books and papers at all times, and to see that the business of the Company is conducted in an economical and business-like manner.

Boston, December 22, 1863.

Names below are copies of signatures except when otherwise noted.

1. Edward Atkinson — One thousand dollars
2. John A. Blanchard — $1,000
3. B. A. Gould — $1,000
4. Geo. Wm. Bond — $ 500
5. John B. Stephenson — $1,000
6. Charles Heath — $1,000
7. Daniel N. Spooner — $1,000
8. J. S. Higginson — $ 500
9.   Ditto for H. F. H. — $ 500
10. Chas. U. Cotting — $1,000
11. Chas. W. Scudder — $ 500
12. Chs. W. Pierce — $2,000
13. R. H. Jackson — $ 500
14. Wm. Endicott Jr. — $1,000
15. J. P. Williston — $1,000
16. Henry Lee Jr. — $1,000
17. Tuttle Gaffield — $1,000
18. Edward W. Hooper by R. W. H. — $1,000
19. A. L. Williston by J. P. W. — $ 500
20. George O. Hovey — $1,000
21. J. C. Howe by E. Atkinson — $1,000
22. Chas H. Dalton by E. Atkinson — $ 500
23. Mrs. Geo. R. Russell per letter — $1,000
24. M. Brimmer — $1,000
25. Thos. J. Lee — $ 500
26. E. R. Mudge by E. A. per order — $ 500
27. Wm. D. Philbrick — $1,000
28. Edwd. S. Philbrick by W. D. P. — $1,000
29. Jas. L. Little by E. A. — $ 500
30. Chas S. Norton by E. A. — $ 500
31. Benj. E. Bates — $1,000
32. Joseph C. Tyler — $ 500
33. Jerome W. Tyler by J. C. T. — $ 500
34. Jno. C. Dalton — $ 500

35.	Sml. R. Payson by E. A.	$ 500
36.	Chas. Francis by E. A.	$ 500
37.	I. Amory Davis	$ 500
38.	F. S. Richardson by E. A.	$1,000
39.	J. M. Forbes by E. A.	$1,000
40.	Saml. Williston per letter	$1,000
41.	Stephen Decatur by E. A.	$1,000
42.	[illegible] Dwight	$ 500
43.	Jas. M. Barnard	$1,000
44.	Wm. S. Eaton	$2,000
45.	W. N. Thompson by E. A.	$ 500
46.	J. A. Higginson by E. A.	$ 500
47.	H. P. Rogers per letter	$1,000
48.	Chas. D. Hind by E. A.	$1,000
49.	G. W. Higginson by E. A.	$ 500
50.	S. B. Russel by E. A.	$ 500
51.	W. S. Bowditch by E. A.	$ 500
52.	Geo. S. Winslow by E. A.	$ 500
53.	J. W. Putnam by E. A.	$ 500
54.	W. S. Bullard by E. A.	$1,000
55.	Jas. Jackson by E. A.	$1,000
56.	A. W. Kelsey by E. A.	$1,000
57.	M. S. Scudder by E. A.	$ 500
58.	S. M. Standish by E. A.	$ 500
59.	Daniel Wheeler by E. A.	$ 500
60.	Caleb Wm. Loring by E. A.	$ 500
61.	Eben White	$2,500
62.	J. B. Glover	$ 500
63.	J. S. Wright	$2,500
64.	Nathan Durfee	$1,000
65.	Caldos Pierce	$2,000
66.	Geo. P. Blake	$1,000
67.	J. E. Oliver by E. A. Lynn	$1,000
68.	J. Homans Jr. for G. H. Homans	$2,500
69.	Geo. H. Homans	$2,500
70.	E. B. Welsh, Boston	$1,000

BIBLIOGRAPHY

1. Primary Sources

A. Unpublished primary material.

This material consists, first, of copies of Mr. Atkinson's correspondence for the period between 1850 and 1905; and second, of letters written to him during the same period. Copies of the letters which Mr. Atkinson wrote are preserved in copy-books, some seventy-eight in number, these containing a total of over fifty thousand pages of manuscript material. Of the letters written to Mr. Atkinson, approximately twenty thousand of the more important have been kept. This entire collection is on deposit at the Massachusetts Historical Society.

B. Published primary material.

The following list includes all of the magazine articles, pamphlets and books written by Mr. Atkinson, arranged according to date of publication.

1	1861	*Cheap Cotton by Free Labor*, Boston, 52 pp.
2	1862	'Is Cotton Our King,' *Continental Monthly*, vol. I, pp. 247–56.
3		*Cotton Manufacture*, Boston, 21 pp.
4		'Taxation No Burden,' *Atlantic Monthly*, vol. X, pp. 115–18.
5	1863	'The Cotton Question — Mr. Atkinson's Report,' *The Living Age*, vol. 77, pp. 464–65. [Reprint from the *Boston Daily Advertiser*.]
6		*The Cotton Kingdom*, Boston. A statistical map.
7	1864	*Future Supply of Cotton*, Boston, 23 pp.
8	1865	*Cotton and the Cotton Trade*, Boston, 1 p. [To the President of the United States. Address by Edward Atkinson and others relative to the reconstruction of the Southern States after the war.]
9	1866	*On Cotton*, New York, 55 pp.
10		*Remarks Upon the Proposed Tax on Cotton*, April 20, 1866, 3 pp.
11	1867	*The Cotton Tax. Report of a Committee of the Boston Board of Trade*, Boston, 16 pp.
12		*On the Collection of Revenue*, Boston, 70 pp.
13	1868	*National Debt*. Speech delivered at Worcester, Massachusetts, and published by the Washington Republican Congressional Committee, 8 pp.
14		*Senator Sherman's Fallacies, or Honesty the Best Policy*, Boston, 39 pp.

BIBLIOGRAPHY

15   'Speech of Edward Atkinson of Brookline at Republican Meeting in Salem, October 12, 1868,' *Reform League*, Boston, 1869–70, v. 1. [Discussion of Gen. Butler's views on resumption of specie payments.]

16   1871   *Memorandum in Regard to Equity in the case between the Government and the Union Pacific Railroad*, Boston, 22 pp.

17   *Inefficiency of Economic Legislation*, Cambridge, Massachusetts, 10 pp.

18   *Revenue Reform*, Boston, 31 pp.

19   1872   *Reply to John L. Hayes*, Woonsocket, Rhode Island, 16 pp.

20   'The Visible and Invisible in Protection,' *Atlantic Monthly*, vol. XXIX, no. CLXXII, pp. 212-24.

21   1873   *Argument before the Railroad Commission*, Boston, Wright and Potter, State Printers, 40 pp.

22   *How to Pay for the Hoosac Tunnel*, Boston, 16 pp.

23   1874   *Argument for the Conditional Repeal of the Legal Tender Act*, Boston, 32 pp.

24   'An Easy Lesson in Money and Banking,' *Atlantic Monthly*, vol. XXXIV, pp. 195–206.

25   'Righteousness of Money Making' (periodical unknown), December, pp. 686–93.

26   *The State of the National Finances*, an address at a mass meeting at Cooper Institute, New York, 6 pp.

27   1875   *Argument for the South Boston Flats Railroad*, Boston, 23 pp.

28   'Commercial Development,' *Harper's Monthly*, vol. LI, pp. 260–68.

29   1876   *The Cotton Manufactures of the United States of America*, Boston, 34 pp.

30   *Export of Cotton Goods*, Boston, 31 pp.

31   1877   *Letter to President Grant*, Boston, 8 pp.

32   *Argument for a Change in the Law in Regard to Taxing Foreign Corporations*, Boston, 24 pp.

33   *Cotton*, Boston, 58 pp.

34   1878   'Oil Report,' appendix of *Report of Semi-Annual Meeting of the New England Cotton Manufacturers' Association*, Boston, pp. 54–79.

35   1879   'An American View of American Competition,' *Fortnightly Review*, vol. XXXI, no. CXLVII, pp. 383–96.

36   *Cotton and Cotton Manufactures in the United States*, Boston, 44 pp.

37   *Labor and Capital; Allies not Enemies*, New York, 98 pp.

38   *Memorandum in Regard to Instruction in the Mechanical Arts*, Boston, 11 pp.

39   'Vibration of Mill Buildings,' *American Architect*, vol. VI, pp. 94–95.

BIBLIOGRAPHY 285

40 1880 *Address in Atlanta for the Promotion of an International Cotton Exhibition*, in October, 1880, Boston, 36 pp.
41 *Commercial Progress*, Boston, 11 pp.
42 *Fire Engineer, the Architect, the Underwriter; their Relations*, Boston, 27 pp.
43 *Memorandum in Regard to the South Boston Docks and Flats*, Boston, 29 pp.
44 *Our National Domain*, chart on cotton privately published, Boston.
45 *Progress of the Nation*, a chart, Boston.
46 *Railroads of the United States*, Boston, 36 pp. [Reprinted from *Fortnightly Review*, vol. XXXIV, pp. 83–104.]
47 'Solid South?' *International Review*, vol. X, pp. 197-209.
48 'Unlearned Professions,' *Atlantic Monthly*, vol. XLV, pp. 742-53.
49 *What is a Bank? What Service does a Bank Perform?* Lecture before Finance Club of Harvard University, published by Society for Political Education in New York, 36 pp.
50 1881 'The Atlanta Cotton Exposition' (periodical unknown), pp. 23-30.
51 'Boston as a Centre of Manufacturing Capital,' pp. 95-110 of *The Memorial History of Boston*, vol. IV, Justin Winsor, editor, Boston, Osgood and Company, 1881.
52 'Elementary Instruction in Mechanic Arts,' *Century Magazine*, vol. XXI (old series), pp. 901-10.
53 *Industrial Exhibitions; Their True Function in Connection with Industrial Education*, Boston, 29 pp.
54 'Kentucky Farms,' *Harper's Monthly*, vol. LXIII, pp. 124-28.
55 'The Railroads and the Farmer' (no.1), *The Journal of the American Agricultural Association*, vol. I, pp. 194-222.
56 *Right Methods of Preventing Destructive Fires in Cities, and Securing Indemnity Against Loss by Fire at Cost*, Boston, 28 pp.
57 'What Makes the Rate of Interest?' (periodical unknown), pp. 21-32.
58 1882 *Address at the Opening of the Fair of the New England Manufacturers and Mechanical Arts Institute*, Boston, 32 pp.
59 'Leguminous Plants Suggested for Ensilaging,' *Agricultural Review*, vol. II, pp. 149-50.
60 'Railroad and the Farmer' (no. 2), *Agricultural Review*, vol. II, pp. 20-34.
61 1883 *English Cotton Mills and Methods*, Boston, 14 pp.
62 *Plan for Textile Laboratory and Museum*, Boston, 10 pp.

BIBLIOGRAPHY

63		*The Standard of Adequate Railroad Service*, New York, 56 pp.
64	1884	*The Law of Competition*, a statistical graph, Boston.
65		*Mutual Insurance of Rubber Works*, Boston, 10 pp.
66	1885	*Application of Science to the Production and Consumption of Fuel*, Salem, Massachusetts, 74 pp.
67		*Common Sense in Regard to the Silver Question*, Bankers' Publishing Association, New York, 12 pp.
68		*The Distribution of Products*, New York, G. P. Putnam's Sons. [This volume included nos. 49, above, and 71, 73, below.]
69		'Is Gold Becoming Scarce?' *Bradstreet's*, vol. XII, pp. 357–60.
70		*Necessary Relations of Labor and Capital*, Boston, 35 pp.
71		*Railway, the Farmer, and the Public*, published by the New York Society for Political Education, New York, 69 pp.
72		*Statistics of Consumption*, published in the *Proceedings of the Census Convention in Boston*, pp. 42–62.
73		'What Makes the Rate of Wages?' *Canadian Economics*, Montreal, pp. 277–89.
74	1886	'Capitalist and his Work,' *Bradstreet's*, vol. XIII, p. 230.
75		'Eight Hour Question,' *Bradstreet's*, vol. XIII, pp. 260–62.
76		*Food Question*, published by the Massachusetts Horticultural Society, 24 pp.
77		'The Food Question in America and Europe,' *Century Magazine*, vol. XI, pp. 238–47.
78		'Hours of Labor,' *North American Review*, vol. CXLII, pp. 507–15.
79		*The Labor Question*, Boston, 21 pp.
80		'Land Question,' *Bradstreet's*, vol. XIII, pp. 428–29.
81		'Niagara Falls Water Power Development,' *Bradstreet's*, vol. XIV, p. 277.
82		'Paper Mill Fires,' *Paper World*, pp. 3–12.
83		'Progress from Poverty,' *Bradstreet's*, vol. XIII, pp. 309–11.
84		*Silver Question*, Providence, Rhode Island, 33 pp.
85		'True Insurance, or, Prevention of Loss by Fire,' *Bradstreet's*, vol. XIII, pp. 397–98.
86		'The True Savings Bank,' *Bradstreet's*, vol. XIII, pp. 325–26.
87		'Wage-Earners and the Silver Question,' *Bradstreet's*, vol. XIII, p. 165.
88		'Wages and Prices,' *Bradstreet's*, vol. XIV, pp. 388–89.
89		'Weakness and Strength of Nations,' *Bradstreet's*, vol. XIV, pp. 21–22.
90	1887	*Commercial Union Between United States and Canada*, New York, 13 pp.

91		'Economic Pessimism,' *North American Review*, vol. CXLIV, pp. 540–43.
92		'Economy in Domestic Cooking,' *American Architect*, pp. 238–39.
93		*Factory Mutual Insurance*, 20 pp.
94		'Farm Mortgages,' *Bradstreet's*, vol. XV, p. 744.
95		'Low Prices; High Wages; Small Profits; What Makes Them?' *Century Magazine*, vol. XII, pp. 568–84.
96		'The Margin of Profits,' *Century Magazine*, vol. XI, pp. 923–31.
97		*The Margin of Profits, How It Is Divided*, New York, G. P. Putnam's Sons, 123 pp.
98		*The Relative Growth of Population, Production and Wealth in the United States*, New York, 1 p.
99		'Relative Strength and Weakness of Nations'; 'Strength,' *Century Magazine*, vol. XI, pp. 422–35; 'Weakness,' *Century Magazine*, vol. XI, pp. 613–21.
100		'Report to the President of the United States on the Status of Bi-metallism in Europe,' Fiftieth Congress, First Session, *Executive Document* no. 34, Washington, 280 pp.
101		'What Has Jesus Christ Done for Humanity?' *Christian Register*, p. 803; December 22, 1887.
102		*What is Bi-metallism?* 30 pp.
103	1888	*An Address before the Southern Society*, New York, published in *The Proceedings of the Southern Society*, pp. 31–42.
104		'Cost of Wheat Growing in California,' *Bradstreet's*, vol. XVI, p. 608.
105		'How can Wages be Increased?' *Forum*, vol. V, pp. 477–507.
106		'Mr. Atkinson's Answer to Critics of his Position regarding America's Wheat and World Markets,' *Bradstreet's*, vol. XVI, pp. 142–45.
107		'Must Humanity Starve at Last?' *Forum*, vol. V, pp. 602–12. Reprinted from *The Quarterly Journal of Economics* for April, 1888.
108		'Payment of the Legal Tender Debt,' *Bradstreet's*, vol. XVI, pp. 480–81.
109		'Price of Life,' *Forum*, vol. VI, pp. 350–60.
110		'Progress from Poverty,' *Forum*, vol. VI, pp. 19–33.
111		'The Progress of the Nation,' *Forum*, vol. VI, pp. 125–43.
112		'Single Tax Discussion,' *Bradstreet's*, vol. XVI, pp. 704–05.
113		'Slow Burning Construction,' *Century Magazine*, vol. XV (new series), pp. 565–79.
114		'Some Economic Problems,' *Bradstreet's*, vol. XVI, p. 624.

BIBLIOGRAPHY

115   'Speech of Hon. S. S. Cox before Congress' (including a letter by Mr. Atkinson on the Census), *Congressional Record, Fiftieth Congress, First Session*, pp. 1-2.

116   'Struggle for Subsistence,' *Forum*, vol. VI, pp. 257-65.

117   'The Surplus Revenue,' *The Popular Science Magazine*, vol. XXXIII, pp. 145-49.

118   'Western Farm Mortgages,' *Bradstreet's*, vol. XVI, p. 289.

119   1889   'The Art of Cooking,' *The Popular Science Monthly*, pp. 1-21.

120   *Consumption Limited, Production Unlimited*, 38 pp.

121   'An Easy Lesson in Statistics,' *Forum*, vol. VI, pp. 474-85.

122   'The Future Situs of the Cotton Manufacture of the United States,' *Popular Science Monthly*, vol. XXXVI, pp. 289-319.

123   'How Society Reforms Itself,' *Forum*, vol. VII, pp. 18-29.

124   *Instructions for Use of the Aladdin Oven*, Brookline, 4 pp.

125   'Lessons from the Boston Fire,' *American Architect*, vol. XXVI, pp. 293-95.

126   'Missing Science,' *Lend a Hand*, vol. IV, pp. 407-19.

127   'The Problem of Poverty,' *Forum*, vol. VII, pp. 609-22.

128   'Reforms that do not Reform,' *Forum*, vol. VI, pp. 600-11.

129   *Religion and Life*, published by the American Unitarian Association, Boston, 18 pp.

130   'Remedies for Social Ills,' *Forum*, vol. VII, pp. 156-64.

131   1890   'Agricultural Depression,' *Bradstreet's*, vol. XVIII, p. 198.

132   'Biographical Notice of William P. Atkinson,' in *Report to the American Academy of Sciences and Arts*, pp. 309-10.

133   'Common Sense Applied to the Tariff Question,' *Popular Science Monthly*, vol. XXXVII, Part I, pp. 433-58; Part II, pp. 591-608.

134   'Comparative Taxation,' *Century Magazine*, vol. XVIII (new series), pp. 284-92.

135   'Credit Main Factor in Making Prices,' *Proceedings of the American Bankers' Convention*, on September 4, 1890, pp. 47-68.

136   *Finance and Banking*, Boston, 12 pp. Reprinted from *Shoe and Leather Reporter*.

137   'Free Silver Coinage,' *Bradstreet's*, vol. XVIII, pp. 390-91.

138   *Future Situs of the Principal Iron Production of the World*, published by the *Manufacturers' Record of Baltimore*, Baltimore, Maryland, 51 pp.

139   *The Industrial Progress of the Nation*, New York, G. P. Putnam's Sons, 395 pp. [This volume included nos. 68, 77, 95, 99, 113, 126, 129, 144, above and below.]

140		'Mr. Atkinson's Rejoinder to Henry George,' *Century Magazine*, vol. XVIII, pp. 403–05.
141		'Mr. Atkinson's Views on a New Source of Wheat Production,' *Bradstreet's*, vol. XVIII, pp. 262–63.
142		*The Right Application of Heat to the Conversion of Food Material*, Salem, Massachusetts, Salem Press, 20 pp.
143		'The Single Tax Upon Land,' *Century Magazine*, vol. XVIII, pp. 385–94.
144	1891	'The Development of the South,' *Engineering Magazine*, vol. I, pp. 452–61.
145		*Food and Feeding, Considered as a Factor in Making the Rate of Wages or Earnings*, Boston, 29 pp.
146		'Free Silver Coinage — Why Not?' *Forum*, vol. XI, pp. 350–51.
147		'The Government of the United States in Account with the Taxpayers,' *Forum*, vol. XII, pp. 89–97.
148		'Invention and its Effect on Household Economy,' *Proceedings of Congress*, Washington, 1891, pp. 217–33, of report of addresses at the celebration of the American Patent System.
149		'Lessons of the Park Place Disaster,' vol. II, pp. 137–50 (publication unknown).
150		'Mr. Atkinson's Opinion as to Why Trade is Dull,' *Bradstreet's*, vol. XIX, p. 403.
151		'The Permanent Census Department,' *Engineering Magazine*, vol. II, pp. 297–303.
152		'Question Answered,' *Frank Leslie's Weekly*, vol. LXXVIII, p. 148.
153		'The Real Meaning of the Free Coinage of Silver,' *Forum*, vol. XII, pp. 215–27.
154		'Wheat — Our Financial Sheet Anchor,' *Frank Leslie's Weekly*, vol. LXXVIII, p. 148.
155	1892	'An Address to Bank Clerks,' *Bank Notes*, pp. 4–14.
156		'Australian Registry of Land Titles,' *Century Magazine*, vol. XXI, pp. 586–92.
157		'Farms, Homes and Mortgages,' *Frank Leslie's Weekly*, vol. LXXIV, p. 178.
158		'Incalculable Room for Immigrants,' *Forum*, vol. XIII, pp. 360–70.
159		'Letter to Eugene V. Debs,' *Locomotive Firemen's Magazine*, vol. XII, pp. 536–38.
160		'Overproduction of Cotton,' *Frank Leslie's Weekly*, vol. LXIV, p. 110.
161		'Personal Liberty,' *Popular Science Monthly*, vol. XL, pp. 433–46.

BIBLIOGRAPHY

162   'Protection to Miners of Iron Ore,' *New England Almanack*, 1892, p. 25.

163   'Reciprocity in Trade,' *Reports of the Boston Merchants' Association* of January 2, 1892, pp. 41–54.

164   *Taxation and Work*, New York, G. P. Putnam's Sons, 296 pp.

165   *Thou Shalt Not Steal — a Few Words on the Tariff*, jointly written with Grover Cleveland, William E. Russell, R. Q. Mills, Senator Carlisle, Carl Schurz, and others, Boston, 31 pp.

166   'Veto of Inflation Bill in 1874,' *Journal of Political Economy*, vol. I, pp. 117–19.

167   'The Vicar's Automatic Stoker and Other Appliances in English Cotton Mills,' *Proceedings of the Meeting of the New England Cotton Manufacturers* on October 26, 1892, pp. 59–84.

168   1893 *Automatic Sprinklers*, Boston, 5 pp.

169   'Do We Need State Bank Currency?' *Engineering Magazine*, vol. IV, pp. 497–505.

170   'Edward Atkinson's Tariff Plan,' *Tariff Reform*, vol. VI, no. 3, pp. 1–21.

171   *Every Boy His Own Cook*, Boston, 70 pp.

172   'Free Ore and Free Coal,' *Manufacturers' Record*, vol. XXIV, pp. 329–30.

173   'How Distrust Stops Trade,' *North American Review*, vol. 157, pp. 25–29.

174   *Mill Construction with Self-Sustaining Frame*, Boston, 18 pp.

175   *The Need of Improving our Cotton*, 4 pp.

176   'Suggestions for the Establishment of Food Laboratories in Connection with the Agricultural Experiment Stations, *U.S. Department of Agriculture Bulletin*, no. 17, Washington, 20 pp.

177   'The Transformation of New England,' *Forum*, vol. XV, pp. 115–26.

178   'The Unit of Value in All Trade,' *Engineering Magazine*, vol. V, pp. 555–67.

179   1894 'Cooking of Food,' *U.S. Department of Agriculture, Report* no. 54, Washington, 31 pp.

180   *Evil Effects of Raising Prices by Depreciating Currency, and Forecast of the Future Commercial Union of English-Speaking People*, Boston, 13 pp.

181   *Financial Outlook*, published by the Chamber of Commerce of the State of New York, New York, 23 pp.

182   'The Gold Basis Fixed by Commerce Itself,' *Forum*, vol. XVI, pp. 737–46.

BIBLIOGRAPHY

183		'Our Enormous Annual Loss by Fire,' *Engineering Magazine*, vol. VII, pp. 1–10.
184		'Present Industrial Problems in the Light of History,' *Forum*, vol. XVIII, pp. 42–53.
185		'Productive Industry,' *The United States of America*, vol. II, edited by Nathaniel Southgate Shaler, New York, D. Appleton and Company, pp. 1–64.
186		'Reply to the "Case for Bimetallism,"' *Rhodes Journal of Banking*, vol. XXI, pp. 549–51.
187		*Suggestions on Methods of Investigation in Monetary Science*, Boston, 23 pp.
188		'The True Meaning of Farm Mortgage Statistics,' *Forum*, vol. XVII, pp. 310–25.
189	1895	'The Banking Principle,' *Rhodes Journal of Banking*, vol. XXII, pp. 520–29.
190		'The Battle of Standards and Fall of Prices,' *Forum*, vol. XIX, pp. 143–58.
191		'The Benefit of Hard Times,' *Forum*, vol. XX, pp. 79–90.
192		*Construction of Schoolhouses*, Boston, 15 pp.
193		'Co-operative Competition,' *New World*, vol. IV, pp. 421–28.
194		'The Cost of Our Government,' *Harper's Weekly*, vol. 391, pp. 588–89.
195		'The Cost of Bad Money,' *Harper's Weekly*, vol. 392, pp. 964–65.
196		*Forced Loans*, published by New York Reform Club, 4 pp.
197		'Greater Boston' (periodical unknown), vol. IX, pp. 377–80.
198		*How Every Man Can Become His Own Landlord*, issued by the Real Estate Exchange, Boston, 7 pp.
199		*Improvement of Cotton*, Boston, 36 pp.
200		'Jingoes and Silverites,' *North American Review*, vol. CLXI, pp. 544–60.
201		'Malignant Effects of Free Silver Delusion,' *Engineering Magazine*, vol. IX, pp. 405–12.
202		*Nutrition of the Soil, the Plant, the Beast, and the Man*, Boston, 19 pp.
203		'Pending Reform of Our Monetary System,' *Report of the National Bankers' Convention*, pp. 80–98.
204		'Possibilities of the Peanut' (periodical unknown), pp. 427–29.
205		'Precious Metals; Appreciation or Depreciation,' *Bankers' Magazine*, vol. 50, pp. 905–12.
206		*Remarks of Edward Atkinson on Child Life Insurance*, Boston, 7 pp.

207		'Signs of the Times,' *Engineering Magazine*, vol. IX, pp. 811-22.
208		'Statistician's Views,' *Egg Reporter*, vol. I, pp. 3-5.
209		'Taxation in the United States,' *Engineering Magazine*, vol. X, pp. 194-202.
210		*Use and Abuse of Legal Tender Acts*, Boston, 33 pp.
211		*Why Money is Scarce in the Southwest*, a Broadside, Boston, 1 p.
212	1896	'Cause and Remedy for Business Depression,' *Engineering Magazine*, vol. XI, pp. 611-20.
213		'The Cost of an Anglo-American War,' *Forum*, vol. XXI, pp. 74-88.
214		'The Fallacy of Free Coinage,' *The Independent*, vol. XLVIII, pp. 1285-86.
215		'Increased Production of Gold,' *North American Review*, vol. CLXII, pp. 160-73.
216		'Jingoism, or War Upon Domestic Industry,' *Engineering Magazine*, vol. X, pp. 801-10.
217		'The Money of the Nation; Shall it be Good or Bad?' *Sound Currency*, vol. III, pp. 2-20.
218		'The Philosophy of Money,' *The Monist*, vol. VI, pp. 337-50.
219		*The Science of Nutrition*, Boston, Damrell and Upham, 246 pp.
220		'Treasury Borrowing in Order to Hold a Useless Stock of Silver Bullion,' *Journal of Commerce and Commercial Bulletin*, publishers, 6 pp.
221		'What Free Silver Means,' *The Independent*, vol. XLVIII, pp. 1125-26.
222		'What Makes the Rate of Wages,' *Harper's Weekly*, vol. 402, pp. 827-30.
223	1897	'Argument in Favor of such Discrimination in Framing Tariff as shall Best Promote Industry and Protect American Labor,' *Report of New England Free Trade League*, pp. 16-37.
224		*British Silver and its Cost*, Boston, 20 pp.
225		'Corn Stalks as Food for Animals,' *The Cultivator and Country Gentleman*, vol. 62, p. 993.
226		'The Cost of Producing Silver,' *Sound Currency*, 13 pp.
227		'Farm Ownership and Tenancy in the United States,' *Report of American Statistical Association*, pp. 329-36.
228		*Fibre of Cotton*, Boston, 7 pp.
229		'Home Life; Why Not?' *American Kitchen Magazine*, vol. VI, pp. 145-47.
230		*National Accounts*, published by the New England Free Trade League, 26 pp.

BIBLIOGRAPHY

231   *One Function of the Savings Bank; Its Importance as a Lender's Distribution of Capital*, New York, 34 pp.
232   'Paramount Control of the Commerce World,' *Engineering Magazine*, vol. XII, pp. 561–76.
233   'The Scientific Preparation of Food' (periodical unknown), pp. 277–80.
234   'Shaw Memorial and the Sculptor St. Gaudens,' *Century Magazine*, vol. XXXII, pp. 176–78.
235   1898   'Anglophobia,' *Harper's Weekly*, vol. 42, pp. 1259–90.
236   'The Basis of the Science of Political Economy,' *Proceedings of the American Academy of Arts and Sciences*, vol. XXXIII, pp. 215–21.
237   *The Cost of a National Crime*, Boston, 34 pp.
238   *The Development of the Resources of the Southern States*, 56 pp.
239   'Evolution of High Wages from Low Cost of Labor, *Popular Science Monthly*, vol. 53, pp. 746–57.
240   'Federal Taxation,' *Journal of Commerce and Commercial Bulletin*, May 21, 1898.
241   *Fire-Proof Building*, Boston, 8 pp.
242   *The Hell of War and its Penalties*, Boston, 23 pp.
243   *How to Increase Exports*, 9 pp.
244   *Interdependence of Nations*, 8 pp.
245   *Legal Tender as a Factor in Money*, published by the National Sound Money League, 10 pp.
246   'The Negro Question,' *Dixie*, December, 1898, pp. 42–44a.
247   *Sheep in the Cotton States*, prepared for the Tennessee Industrial League, 30 pp.
248   'The Wheat-Growing Capacity of the United States,' *Appleton's Popular Science Monthly*, vol. LIV, pp. 145–62.
249   1899   *The Anti-Imperialist*, published at intervals by Edward Atkinson, nos. 1–6, June 3, 1899, to October 1, 1900. [These included nos. 237, 242, above.]
250   'Criminal Aggression; by Whom Committed?' *Senate Document* no. 163, Washington, 13 pp.
251   'Reciprocity with Canada,' *The Tradesman Annual*, vol. XX, pp. 133–34.
252   'South and Its Development,' *The Tradesman Annual*, vol. XVII, pp. 80–83.
253   'The Wheat Problem Again,' *Appleton's Popular Science Monthly*, vol. LIV, pp. 759–72.
254   1900   'Distribution of Taxes,' *Popular Science Monthly*, vol. LVIII, no. 1, pp. 54–59.
255   *The Dominion of Iron and Coal*, 13 pp.
256   'Eastern Commerce; What Is It Worth?' *North American Review*, vol. 170, pp. 295–304.

BIBLIOGRAPHY

257   'The Influence of Mechanical Science on the Social Condition of Humanity,' *The Advocate of Peace*, vol. LXII, pp. 176–79.

258   'Lynching versus Industrial Progress,' *The Tradesman Annual*, vol. XXI, pp. 1–2.

259   'Mental Energy,' *Popular Science Monthly*, vol. LVII, pp. 632–37.

260   *Prevention of Loss by Fire*, Boston, 95 pp.

261   'Suppression of War by Science and Commerce,' *The Sagamore*, vol. VI, pp. 3–8.

262   'Public Tests of the Diffusion of Light,' in *Report Upon Diffusion of Light*, by Charles Ladd Norton, Boston, pp. 2–8.

263   'Tonics, Beverages and Compounds,' *The Woman's Journal*, vol. XXXI, p. 397.

264   1901 'Atkinson-Casson Debate; Competitive System a Success,' *Bellamy Review*, vol. I, pp. 301–04.

265   'Atkinson-Casson Debate; Independent View,' *Bellamy Review*, vol. I, pp. 371–72.

266   *British Manufactures and the Policy of Unfettered Commerce; and The Interdependence of Nations*, New York, 44 pp.

267   'The Commercial Aspect of War,' *Advocate of Peace*, vol. LXIII, pp. 42–44.

268   1902 *The Explosion of the Maine*, Boston, 4 pp.

269   *Family Mutual Health Insurance; A Problem*, Boston, 20 pp.

270   *Food and Land Tenure*, Boston, 31 pp.

271   *How to Make and Use an Aladdin Oven*, Boston, 22 pp.

272   *The Outlook for Iron in the Next Ten Years*, Baltimore, 4 pp.

273   *The Protective Tariff*, Testimony before the United States Industrial Commission, Washington, 37 pp.

274   *The Race Problem: Its Possible Solution*, Baltimore, 8 pp.

275   *The Aladdin Oven*, Boston, 14 pp.

276   *Brief Statement to be Made Before the Committee on the Philippines*, Washington, 7 pp.

277   *The Cost of War and Warfare from 1898 to 1902*, Brookline, Massachusetts, 19 pp.

278   *A Department of Insurance Engineering a Public Necessity*, Boston, 8 pp.

279   'Social Bacteria and Economic Microbes, Wholesome and Noxious,' *Popular Science Monthly*, vol. 60, pp. 317–27.

280   1903 *The Cost of Warfare to June 30, 1903*, etc., Boston, published by the New England Anti-Imperialist League, 8 pp.

281   *Fuel; What We Don't Know About It*, published by the New England Water Works Association, Boston, 200 pp.

BIBLIOGRAPHY 295

282   *Occupations in their Relations to the Tariff*, Boston, 15 pp. [Reprinted from the *Quarterly Journal of Economics*, vol. XVII, pp. 280–92.]

283   *Protection and Wages*, published by the American Free Trade League, Boston, 13 pp.

284   *Reciprocity*, published by the American Free Trade League, Boston, 17 pp.

285   *The Retroactive Influence of Duties Upon Imports*, Boston, 24 pp.

286   *Sheep Upon the Upland Cotton Fields*, Charlotte, North Carolina, 31 pp.

287   1904   *The Cost of War and Warfare from 1898 to 1904, Seven Fiscal Years Ending June 30*, Brookline, Massachusetts, 19 pp.

288   *The Cost of War and Warfare from 1898 to 1905 Inclusive, Twelve Hundred Million Dollars*, Brookline, Massachusetts, 27 pp.

289   *Facts and Figures, the Basis of Economic Science*, Boston and New York, Houghton, Mifflin and Company, 202 pp. [This volume includes 290, below.]

290   *A True Policy of Protection*, Boston, 59 pp.

291   1905   *The Cost of War and Warfare, Oversea Expansion and Imperialism, Eight Years to June 30, 1905*, Fifth Computation, Brookline, Massachusetts, 6 pp.

II. Secondary Sources

The following are the books and reports, including magazine articles, from which quotations were taken or to which special reference was made:

Annual Reports of the Boston Board of Trade, 1865–1880.

Annual Reports of the Boston Manufacturers' Mutual Fire Insurance Company, 1878–1905.

Annual Report of the Firemen's Mutual Fire Insurance Company, the Mercantile Mutual Fire Insurance Company, and the Narragansett Mutual Fire Insurance Company, 1931.

Annual Report of the Manufacturers' Mutual Fire Insurance Company, 1931.

Annual Report of the What Cheer and Hope Mutual Fire Insurance Company, 1932.

Barnes, J. G., *John G. Carlisle, Financial Statesman*, New York, Dodd Mead and Company, 1931.

Barrett, Don C., *The Greenbacks and the Resumption of Specie Payments, 1862–1879*, Harvard Press, 1931.

Bastiat, Frederick, *Harmonies of Political Economy*; translated by P. T.

BIBLIOGRAPHY

Sterling, second edition, London, Simpkin, Marshall and Company, 1880.
Brearley, Harry Chase, *Fifty Years of a Civilizing Force*, New York, Frederick A. Stokes Company, 1916.
Brown, Harry Bates, *Cotton*, etc., New York, McGraw-Hill Company, 1927.
Carey, Henry C., *Miscellaneous Works*, Philadelphia, Henry Carey Baird Industrial Publisher, 1872.
Carey, Henry C., *Past, Present and Future*, Henry Carey Baird Industrial Publisher, 1869.
Dewey, Davis Rich, *National Problems*, New York, Harper Brothers, 1907.
Dewey, Davis Rich, *The Financial History of the United States*, New York, Longmans, Green and Company, 1903.
French, Edward V., *Arkwright Mutual Fire Insurance Company*, Boston, privately printed, 1912.
Garner, James Wilford, *Reconstruction in Mississippi*, New York, The Macmillan Company, 1901.
George, Henry, *Progress and Poverty*, New York, D. Appleton and Company, 1880.
Haney, Lewis, *History of Economic Thought*, New York, The Macmillan Company, 1911.
Higginson, Thomas Wentworth, 'Edward Atkinson,' *Proceedings of the American Academy of Arts and Sciences*, vol. XLII.
House Executive Documents, 1865–66, Thirty-Ninth Congress, Second Session, *Special Report* no. 3.
House Executive Documents, 1867–68, Fortieth Congress, Second Session, no. 8.
House Executive Documents, 1867–68, Fortieth Congress, Third Session, no. 2.
Hughes, Sara Forbes, *John Murray Forbes, Letters and Recollections*, Boston, Houghton, Mifflin and Company, 1899.
James, Henry, *Richard Olney and His Public Service*, Boston, Houghton Mifflin Company, 1923.
Massachusetts House Legislative Documents; 1875, nos. 100, 365, 368; 1876, no. 151; 1879, nos. 211, 289; 1880, no. 252.
Massachusetts, Laws and Resolves of; 1875, Chapter 239; 1880, Chapter 252.
McCulloch, Hugh, *Men and Measures of Half a Century*, New York, Charles Scribner's Sons, 1888.
Mendum, Samuel W., 'The Question Clubs and the Tariff,' *North American Review*, vol. CL, no. 3.
Mitchell, Broadus, *The Rise of Cotton Mills in the South*, Baltimore, The Johns Hopkins Press, 1921.
Mitchell, Broadus, *The Industrial Revolution in the South*, Baltimore, The Johns Hopkins Press, 1930.

Noyes, Alexander Dana, *Forty Years of American Finance*, New York, G. P. Putnam's Sons, 1909.
Oviatt, F. C., 'Historical Study of Fire Insurance in the United States,' *Annals of the American Academy of Political and Social Science*, vol. XXVI.
Perry, Arthur Latham, *Political Economy*, twenty-first edition, New York, Charles Scribner's Sons, 1892.
Pierce, E. L., *Memoirs and Letters of Charles Sumner*, Boston, Roberts Brothers, 1893.
Proceedings of a Convention Held in the City of New York, Wednesday, April 29, 1868, for the Purpose of Organizing the National Association of Cotton Manufacturers and Planters, Boston, Prentiss and Deland, Printers, 1868, 105 pp.
Proceedings of the New England Cotton Manufacturers' Association, vols. XXI–XXXI.
Quarterly Journal of Economics, vols. I–III.
Recent Economic Changes in the United States, Report of the Committee on Recent Economic Changes of the President's Conference on Unemployment, Herbert Hoover, Chairman, New York, McGraw-Hill Company, 1929.
Reed, Wallace P., *History of Atlanta, Georgia*, Syracuse, New York, D. Mason and Company, 1889.
'Report of the United States Revenue Commission,' *House Executive Documents*, 1865–66, Thirty-Ninth Congress, First Session, vol. VII, *Executive Document* no. 24.
Richardson, James D., *A Compilation of the Messages and Papers of the Presidents, 1789–1897*, vol. VII, Washington, U.S. Government Printing Office, 1898.
Rhodes, James Ford, *History of the United States from Hayes to McKinley*, vols. I–VIII, New York, The Macmillan Company, 1919.
Rhodes, James Ford, *The McKinley and Roosevelt Administrations, 1897–1909*, New York, The Macmillan Company, 1922.
Senate Executive Documents, Fiftieth Congress, no. 34, Washington.
Smith, Adam, *The Wealth of Nations*, New York, E. P. Dutton and Company, 1910.
Stanwood, Edward, *American Tariff Controversies in the Nineteenth Century*, vols. I–II, New York, Houghton, Mifflin and Company, 1903.
Tarbell, Ida M., *The Tariff in Our Times*, New York, The Macmillan Company, 1915.
Taussig, Frank W., *History of the Present Tariff, 1860–1883*, New York, G. P. Putnam's Sons, 1885.
Taussig, Frank W., *Principles of Economics*, vol. I, New York, The Macmillan Company, 1912.
Taussig, Frank W., *The Silver Situation in the United States*, New York, G. P. Putnam's Sons, 1885.

BIBLIOGRAPHY

Taussig, Frank W., *Tariff History of the United States*, sixth edition, New York, G. P. Putnam's Sons, 1914.

Tomkins, D. A., *Cotton and Cotton Oil*, Charlotte, North Carolina, privately printed, 1901.

United States Statutes at Large, Thirty-Seventh Congress, Third Session, Chapter 73.

United States Statutes at Large, Thirty-Ninth Congress, First Session, Chapter 184.

United States Statutes at Large, Thirty-Ninth Congress, Second Session, Chapter 169.

United States Statutes at Large, Fortieth Congress, Second Session, Chapter 5.

Walker, Francis A., *Political Economy*, third edition, revised, New York, Henry Holt and Company, 1888.

Welles, Gideon, *Diary of Gideon Welles*, vol. II, Boston, Houghton Mifflin Company, 1911.

Woodbury, C. J. H., *Modern Development and Early History of Automatic Sprinklers*, pamphlet, issued by the Boston Manufacturers' Mutual Fire Insurance Company.

INDEX

Abbott, John C., 53, 55
Abel, Mrs. Mary Hinman, 233
Adams, Charles Francis, 90, 91
Adams, Henry, 238
African Cotton, 4, 5
Agriculture, 163–75
Aladdin Cooker or Oven, 52, 231–34, 240, 271, 274
Albert Maple Leaf, 162, 163
Aldrich, Senator, 157, 158
Aldrich Bill, 222
Allen, Zachariah, 100, 104
Allison, William B., 80, 84, 210, 236
American Academy of Fine Arts, 177
American Architect, 113
American Economic Association, 176
American Institute of Banking, 276
American Mutual Fire Insurance Company, 101
American Social Science Association, 73
American Statistical Association, 176, 177
Ames, F. L., 128
Anderscoggin Mills, 34
Anderson, Ellery, 186
Andover Theological Seminary, 276
Andrew, Governor John A., 52
Anti-Imperialist League, 227–30
Arkwright Club, 147
Arkwright Mutual Fire Insurance Company, 101, 105
Arthur, Chester A., 134, 138, 139, 155
Associated Factory Mutual Fire Insurance Companies of New England, 100–09, 119–22, 132, 133
Atkins, Elisha, 39
Atkinson, Amos, 1
Atkinson, Anna Greenleaf, 51
Atkinson, Anna Greenleaf Sawyer, 1
Atkinson, Caroline Penniman, 51
Atkinson, Charles Heath, 51
Atkinson, Edward Williams, 51
Atkinson, John, 1
Atkinson, Mary Heath, 51
Atkinson, Robert Whitman, 51
Atkinson, William, 51
Atwater, Professor A. W., 233
Automatic Sprinklers, 103–06, 114–20, 126

Baird, Henry Carey, 209
Balfour, Arthur James, 215, 219

Baring Brothers, 192
Barker, C. J., 35
Barker Mill, 35, 36
Bastiat, Frederick, 74, 77, 242, 243, 253, 264
Bates Manufacturing Company, 34
Bates, Mr., 34, 35
Bear, William E., 164
Beard, Alanson W., 56
Beecher, Henry Ward, 83
Belmont-Morgan Syndicate, 194, 205, 206
Bi-metallism, 142, 143, 155, 156, 191, 200, 203, 204, 209
Bingham, Judge, 71
Blackstone Mutual Fire Insurance Company, 101
Blaine, Hon. James G., 64, 98
Blair, Senator, 18
Bland, Senator, 160
Bland-Allison Act, 139, 140, 143, 154, 155
Bland Bill, 160, 161, 202
Borden, Colonel T. J., 117
Boston and Albany Railroad, 42, 45, 47
Boston and Maine Railroad, 41
Boston and Northwestern Railroad Association, 44–50
Boston and Providence Railroad, 45
Boston Board of Trade, 40, 41, 42, 47
Boston Boot and Shoe Club, 155, 156
Boston Herald, 228
Boston Manufacturers' Mutual Fire Insurance Company, 36, 49, 99–101, 105–14, 119–23, 131, 133, 135, 166
Boston Post, 125, 126
Bowditch, William I., 53
Bowen, Francis, 243
Bradstreet's, 155, 156, 164, 165, 207
Brawley, Senator, 179
Breckinridge, C. R., 150, 151, 179, 188
Breckinridge, W. C. P., 141, 147, 150, 151
Bright, John, 8, 29, 30
British Economic Association, 177
British Guiana, 212–15
British Society for the Advancement of Science, 162, 163
Broadsides, 63, 87
Brodwell, Friend, 34
Brookline, 1, 50, 52, 54, 55, 178
Brookline Savings Bank, 55, 56
Brookline Whist Club, 53
Brooklyn Eagle, 240, 241

INDEX

Brown, H., 11, 12
Brown, Henry W., and Co., 132
Brown, Durrell and Company, 128
Bryan, William J., 195, 203, 210, 211, 230
Bryant, William Cullen, 90
Bureau of Inspection, 107, 111
Bureau of Statistics, 184, 185
Butler, Benjamin F., 84, 85, 94
Byman, William D., 211

Cabot, J. Elliot, 52
Caffrey, Senator Donelson, 201, 221, 235
Caldwell, Josiah, 40
Carey, H. C., 79, 85, 213, 243
Carey, John, 115
Carlisle, J. G., 151, 153, 179, 180, 184, 193, 196, 198, 200, 205, 206
Carnegie, Andrew, 233
Case Scientific School, 124, 125
Central Labor Lyceum, 268, 269
Chace, Jonathan, 146, 148, 163
Chase, Mr., 13
Chattanooga Tradesman, 209
Cheney, F. W., 187, 188
Chicago Tribune, 83
Civil Service, 161
Civil War, 3–10, 17, 18–26, 31, 63
Clement, Miss, 55
Cleveland, Grover, 138, 141, 143, 147, 148, 149, 156, 159, 161, 178, 180, 190, 192, 196, 204–07, 212–16, 223, 230
Coates, Benjamin, 4, 5
Cohoes Mills, 2
Coin's Financial School, 208, 213
Commission of Plantations, 10
Congressional Globe, 70
Continental Mills, 34, 35
Cooper Institute, 94
Cornstalks, 237
Cotting, Charles U., 56
Cotton, 2–30, 32, 37, 38, 57–69, 72, 86, 163, 166–75, 237
Cotton and Woolen Manufacturers' Mutual Insurance Company, 101
Cotton Exposition in Atlanta, 168–70, 174, 175
Cotton Manufacturing, 2–4, 7, 13, 17, 23, 24, 26, 28, 33–37, 59–65, 81, 166–75, 180, 181, 190
Cotton Mills, 2, 3, 33–36, 67, 150, 151, 166, 167, 170–75, 180, 231, 265
Cotton Price Fluctuations, 25
Cotton Purchase Bill, 19, 20
Cowan, Senator, 19
Cox, J. D., 90
Crisp, Charles L., 160

Crowinshield, Mr., 60
Cuba, 222–25
Currency, 31, 32, 81–86, 93–97, 138–42, 156, 178, 192–95, 199–207, 219

Dabney, Dr. C. W., 132
Dana, Richard H., Jr., 85
Dartmouth College, 177
Davis, Jefferson, 18
Dawes, Henry L., 93, 151, 152, 157, 158, 165
Debs, Eugene, 272, 274
Democrats, 90, 91, 138, 144, 145, 153, 154, 156, 157, 161, 178–80, 184, 188–90, 193, 207, 210–14, 220, 227, 230, 276
Dewey, F. O., Company, 108
Dharmapala, Anagarika, 52
Diffusion of Light, 123
Dingley Bill, 221, 222
Division of the National Income, 248, 249, 260–66, 269, 270
Draper, General W. F., 150, 183
Dunbar, C. F., 54

Eastern Railroad, 41
Economics, 242–75
Economy Club, 53
Educational Commission, 8, 9
Egyptian Cotton, 38
Eliot, Charles, 126
Ellsworth, Captain T. E., 11
Emmons, Professor Frank, 52
Endicott, William, 9, 90
England, 26, 28, 29, 162–66, 212–19
Ensilage, 169, 171
Enterprise Mutual Fire Insurance Company, 101
Examiner Club, 53

'Factory-ribbed' glass, 123
Fairchild, Charles S., 206
Fall River Manufacturers' Mutual Insnrance Company, 101
Faneuil Hall, 41, 125, 126, 158
Farm mortgages, 164–66
Farquhar, A. B., 206, 220
Farrer, Lord, 52, 212, 214, 215
Fessenden, William P., 13, 14, 16, 86
Fire-escapes, 125–27
Fire hose, 111
Fire Inspection, 106–09, 111, 116
Fire Insurance, 99–123, 132, 133
Firemen's Mutual Insurance Company, 101
Fire Prevention, 99, 100, 102–33
'Fireproof' wood, 123
First Parish Church, 55
Fishing rights, 162, 163

# INDEX 301

Fitchburg Railroad, 43, 45, 47
Fitzgerald, Desmond, 239
Forbes, J. M., 11, 14–18, 20, 21, 23, 24, 26, 32, 90
Force Bill, 157
Forum, The, 207
Foster, Charles, 179
Foster, Dwight, 8
Fowler, William, 138
Franklin Company, 34, 35
Freedmen's Bureau, 9
Free Labor Cotton Company, 10
Free trade, 24, 64, 65, 68, 69, 73, 75, 76–81, 84, 92, 93, 136, 144, 148, 149, 153, 154, 161, 183, 184, 186, 187, 189, 191
Free Trade League, 78, 79

Gage, Lyman J., 228
Garfield, James A., 134, 178
Geikie, Archibald, 52
George, Henry, 141
Georgia, 9, 26
Gilman, D. C., 218
Godfrey, Ambrose, 114
Gory, Mr., 60
Goschen, George J., 215, 219
Grant, Ulysses S., 10, 85, 87, 88, 91, 93–97
Great Britain, 26–28, 37, 75–78
Greeley, Horace, 89–91
Green, Mayor, 126, 127
Greenbacks, 31, 32, 82–85, 93–97, 198, 199, 201–03
Greenough, Mr., 71
Grimes, J. W., 16, 80, 84
Grinnel, Frank, Company, 116, 117
Grosvenor, William, 88, 89
Guerillas, 12

Hadley, A. T., 54
Hale, Rev. E. E., 9
Hamilton, General, 26
Hamlin, Charles, 205
Harper's Weekly, 207, 208
Harrison, Major A. Stewart, 115
Harrison, Benjamin, 193
Harter, Michael D., 160, 179
Hartford and Erie Railroad, 41, 43
Harvard College, 2, 177
Hawkes, R. R., 148, 149
Hawley, Frederick B., 262–64, 266
Hawley, J. R., 216
Hayes, Rutherford B., 98
Head, Charles D., 53
Heath, Mary Caroline, 5, 51
Heath Hill, 51
Herschell, Lord, 52

Hoar, George F., 235
Home Market Club, 147, 152
Honorary degrees, 176, 177
Hoosac Tunnel, 41–45
Hope Mutual Fire Insurance Company, 101
Houston, Governor, 8
Hovey, George O., 2
Howe, J. C., and Company, 2
Howe, Timothy O., 16
Hunt, Mr., 12

Imperialism, 222, 226–30, 235
Income tax, 188, 189
Indian Orchard Mill, 33, 36
Indirect illumination, 123
Industrial Mutual Insurance Company, 101
Inflation Bill, 94
Insurance Engineering Experiment Station, 122–24
Interest, 250–54, 260–66
International Cotton Exposition, 169, 170, 174, 175
International Peace Congress, 236
International Statistical Society, 177
Interstate Commerce Act, 137, 138

Jingoism, 213, 214, 237
Johns Hopkins University, 218
Johnson, Andrew, 30, 72, 83, 85, 86
Jordan, C. N., 205
Jordan Marsh Company, 126
Journal of the American Agricultural Association, 137
Journal of Commerce and Commercial Bulletin, 201

Kelsey, Captain A. H., 12
Kelsey, A. Warren, 12, 13, 26, 27, 29
Kerckoff, C., 38
Keystone Mutual Fire Insurance Company, 101

Labor, 248–50, 254, 258–74
Labor Unions, 267–69, 273
Labouisse, J. W., 71
Laissez-faire economics, 73, 267
Landlord's Liability Insurance Company, 130
Lanterns, 108, 109
Laughlin, J. Laurence, 54
Laurence, Amos A., 55
Law of diminishing returns, 244–46
Lee, Colonel Henry, 52, 53
Lee, General Robert E., 18, 22
Leslie's Weekly, 208
Lincoln, Abraham, 3, 13, 14, 16, 18–20

INDEX

Little Rock and Fort Smith Railroad, 39
Locomotive Firemen's Magazine, 272
London *Times*, 164
Lowell, Judge John, 52
Lowell Railroad, 43
Lubbock, Sir John, 218, 219
Lubrication oils, 109, 110
Lyman, Arthur, 236
Lyman, Colonel, Theodore, 52
Lyon, Dr. William L., 239

McCulloch, Hugh, 16, 19–24, 26, 27, 32, 69, 78, 80–83, 86, 93, 139, 140
McCune, Dr., 179
McKinley, William, 152, 182, 194, 195, 207, 210–12, 219–26, 230
McKinley Bill, 151–54, 161, 185
McPherson, J. R., 151, 153, 179, 189, 190
Maine (The Battleship), 223, 235, 236
Malthus, T. R., 243, 244, 246, 247, 256, 258
Manning, Daniel, 144
Manton Mutual Fire Insurance Company, 101
Manufacturers' Mutual Fire Insurance Company of Providence, Rhode Island, 101, 105
Maritime Provinces, 162, 163
Masconomet Mills, 36
Massachusetts Central Railroad, 43, 45
Massachusetts Institute of Technology, 109, 122, 123, 125, 176, 233
Massachusetts Legislature, 46–50, 55
Massachusetts Public Buildings, 122
Materielen, 142
Mechanics' Mutual Fire Insurance Company, 101
Mellen, Mr., 21
Memorial Hall, Harvard, 125, 126
Mercantile Mutual Fire Insurance Company, 101
Merchants' Mutual Fire Insurance Company, 101
Mill construction, 112–14
Mill, John Stuart, 247
Mill Owners' Mutual Fire Insurance Company, 101
Mills, Roger Q., 150–52
Mills Bill, 150
Minot, William, 53
Mississippi Valley, 10–12
Mitchell, Broadus, 173, 174
Money, 134, 155–60, 179, 192–95, 199–207, 219, 222
Monroe Doctrine, 213–15
Morrill, Justin S., 18, 60, 81, 97

Morrison, William, 136, 144–47
Morse, Leopold, 147
Mugwumps, 138, 189, 214
Mutual fire insurance companies, 99–109, 119, 122, 132, 133

Nation, The, 29, 56, 207
National Arbitration Conference, 219
National Association of Cotton Manufacturers, 108, 117
National Reform League, 88
National Republican, The, 7
Negroes, 3–13, 22, 30, 84, 86, 236, 237
New England Cotton Manufacturers' Association, 166, 167, 169, 244, 273, 274
New England Freedmen's Society, 8, 16
New England Kitchen, 233
New England Loyal Publications Society, 87
New York and New England Railroad, 43–45, 47
New York Central Railroad, 253
New York Evening Post, 11, 66
New York Herald, 167
New York Reform League, 186, 188
New York Tribune, 91
Nordhoff, Charles, 52, 62, 66, 71, 78, 134, 141, 146, 147, 149, 178, 204, 205, 229, 238
North American Review, The, 207
Northampton Company, 12
Norton, Professor Charles L., 123, 124, 237
Nourse, B. F., 22, 38

Ogden Mills, 2
Olney, Richard, 195, 196, 200, 213, 218, 223
Ordway, Professor John, 109, 110

Pacific Mills, 150, 182, 236
Page, Walter Hines, 52
Paper Mill Mutual Insurance Company, 101
Parmelee, Henry S., 116
Parmelee Sprinklers, 117
Parsons, Thomas, 53
Patent medicines, 237
Patten, Simon N., 243
Peel, Sir Robert, 136, 143, 147
Perforated-pipe sprinklers, 115, 116, 119
Perry, Professor A. L., 54, 78, 243
Perry, O. H., 68, 148
Phi Beta Kappa, 177
Philadelphia Manufacturers' Mutual Fire Insurance Company, 101
Philbrick, Edward, 4, 11, 53
Philippines, 225–29, 235
Philpot, Mr., 148
Pierce and Bacon, 21

INDEX 303

Pierce, E. L., 8
Pierce Hall, 55
Pierce, T. W., 21
Playfair, Lord, 215
Poor, Henry V., 53
Potter, Thomas, 52
Price, Bonami, 52
Protection, 64, 65, 68, 71–81, 91–93, 138, 144, 146, 149, 150–53, 181–86, 191, 210, 212, 236, 242
Protection Mutual Fire Insurance Company, 101
Public Schools of Boston, 129

Question Clubs, 149, 150

Railroads, 7, 39–50, 137
Railroad and the Farmer, 137
Railroad rates, 137
Railroad transportation costs, 163–66
Randall, Samuel J., 144, 146
Raum, Mr., 179
Read and Chadwick, 2
Reform Club of Boston, 177
Reform Club of New York, 177, 185, 208
Reform Republican Convention, 63, 88–90
Rent, 246, 247
Republicans, 63, 67, 86, 89, 91, 138, 149, 152, 157, 161, 179, 195, 207, 210, 211, 219, 220, 227, 230, 236
Resumption Act, 82, 95
Revenue Commission, 57–59, 62, 70, 77
Rhode Island Mutual Fire Insurance Company, 101
Ricardo, 243, 244, 247, 256, 258, 272, 274
Rice, Alexander H., 30
Richards, Mrs. Ellen, 233
Richards, Professor Robert E., 52
Richardson, William A., 93
Rideout, Miss C. M., 55
Ripley, W. Z., 52
Rise of Cotton Mills in the South, 173
Risely, Mr., 21
Roof hydrants, 131, 132
Rubber Manufacturers' Mutual Insurance Company, 101
Russell, William E., 214

Saint-Gaudens, Augustus, 176
Salisbury, Lord, 214, 218
Saltonstall, Henry, 39, 40, 145, 182, 185
Sands, Mahlon, 90
Science of Nutrition, 230–34, 270–72
Sedgwick, Professor Henry, 215
Seligman, E. R. A., 53, 54
Seward, William H., 14, 72

Shaw, Colonel Robert G., 176
Shaw Monument, 176
Shawmut and Old Colony Railroad, 44
Sherman, Senator John, 16, 97, 157, 158, 160
Sherman Silver Purchase Act, 141, 143, 154, 155, 160, 192, 195, 197–99, 202
Silos, 169
Silver, 135, 138–43, 154–63, 178, 191–210, 220, 222
Skinner, Francis, and Company, 34
Slavery, 3, 4, 6–9
Slocum, General Henry W., 12
'Slow-burning construction,' 112–14, 121, 124
Smith, Adam, 242, 257, 266
Smith, R. D., 53
Smith, Sir Swire, 52
Soetbeer, A. D., 142
Sound Money, 82–85, 94–97, 138–42, 161, 179, 191, 192, 195, 201–12, 230
South Carolina, 8
South Carolina, University of, 176
Southern Farmers' Alliance, 179
South, New, 138, 166–76
South, Rehabilitation of, 38, 39, 87
Spain, 222–26
Spanish-American War, 222–26
Specie redemption, 81–87, 93–97, 139–42
Springer Bill, 206
Springfield Republican, 9
Stanton, Edwin McM., 14
Stanwood, Edward, 53, 174, 175
State Mutual Fire Insurance Company, 101
Statistics, 257, 258
Stewart, A. J., and Company, 28
Stock fire insurance companies, 99, 100, 102, 109, 119, 122
Sumner, Charles, 8, 17, 80, 83, 84, 86, 90
Sumner, William G., 148

Tariff, 57, 58, 63–92, 134–54, 160–62, 178–91, 210–12, 219–22, 236
Tariff Act of 1890, 150, 151, 153
Tariff Commission, 135
Tariff Reform, 185
Taussig, F. W., 54, 142
Taxation, 15, 21, 30, 31, 57–88, 154, 183, 185–88, 193, 202, 254, 255
Taxpayers, Union, 87–89
Tennessee, 6
Texas, 6–8, 22, 26
Thayer, Samuel, 127, 128
Third National Bank of Boston, 200
Thompson, Henry Yates, 52
Thursday Evening Club, 52, 177

INDEX

Tin-plate, 151
Trumbull, Senator Lyman, 90
Twentieth Century Club, 177

Union Club, Round Table at, 53
United States Commission for the relief of the National Freedmen, 9
United States Department of Agriculture, 38

Vance, Z. B., 151
Vanderbilt, Cornelius, 253
Venezuela, 212–19
Vicksburg, 10–12

Wadsworth, General, 11
Wages, 249–54, 258–66, 273
Walker, Amasa, 243
Walker, Francis A., 52, 71, 176, 242
Walker, Robert J., 140
Ward, George L., 64, 65
Ware, Emma, 17
Washington, Booker T., 52, 237
Water supply, 131

Wedgewood, Geoffrey, 52
Welles, Gideon, 13
Wells, David A., 52, 57, 58, 62, 63, 66, 68–73, 78, 79, 81, 84, 89–92, 134–36, 141, 146, 147, 153, 159, 178, 184, 185, 221
Wenzie, J. A., 42
What Cheer Mutual Fire Insurance Company, 101
Wheat, 164–66, 192, 237
White, Horace, 54, 80, 83, 90, 153, 156, 187
Whiting, William B., 107, 111, 131
Williams, Maurice, 26, 29
Williams, Moses, 52, 53, 55, 195, 196
Williston, J. P., 11
Wilson Bill, 187–90, 220
Wilson, Henry, 19, 67, 79
Wilson, William L., 151, 160, 180, 187
Winchell, Reverend, 12
Woman's suffrage, 237
Wood, S., 53
Woodbury, C. J. H., 114, 116, 118
Wool and Woolens Act, 71, 72
Worcester Manufacturers' Mutual Insurance Company, 101

The Right Wing Individualist Tradition In America

An Arno Press/New York Times Collection

Bailie, William. **Josiah Warren:** The First American Anarchist. 1906.

Barber, Thomas H. **Where We Are At.** 1950.

Barnes, Harry Elmer. **Pearl Harbor After a Quarter of a Century.** Left and Right: A Journal of Libertarian Thought, Vol. IV. 1968.

Barnes, Harry Elmer. **In Quest of Truth and Justice:** De-Bunking the War Guilt Myth. 1928.

Barnes, Harry Elmer. **Selected Revisionist Pamphlets,** n.d. 1972.

Bromfield, Louis. **A New Pattern for a Tired World.** 1954.

Burgess, John W. **Recent Changes in American Constitutional Theory.** 1923.

Carroll, Charles Holt. **Organization of Debt into Currency:** and Other Papers. 1964.

Fleming, Harold M. **Ten Thousand Commandments:** A Story of the Antitrust Laws. 1951.

Flynn, John T. **As We Go Marching.** 1944.

Harris, George. **Inequality and Progress.** 1897.

Individualist Anarchist Pamphlets, 1867-1904. 1972.

Knight, Bruce Winton. **How to Run a War.** 1936. New Preface by Bruce Winton Knight.

Lane, Rose Wilder. **The Discovery of Freedom:** Man's Struggle Against Authority. 1943. New Foreword by Robert LeFevre. New Introduction by Roger Lea MacBride.

Left and Right: Selected Essays, 1954-1965. 1972.

The Libertarian Forum. 1969-1971. Murray N. Rothbard and Karl Hess, editors.

McGurrin, James. **Bourke Cockran:** A Free Lance in American Politics. 1948.

[La Monte, Robert Rives and H. L. Mencken.] **Men Versus The Man:** A Correspondence between Robert Rives La Monte, Socialist and H. L. Mencken, Individualist. 1910.

Montgomery, Zach[ariah], compiler. **The School Question:** From a Parental and Non-Sectarian Stand-Point. 1889.

Nock, Albert Jay. **Our Enemy, The State.** 1935.

Olds, Marshall. **Analysis of the Interchurch World Movement Report on the Steel Strike.** 1922.

Oppenheimer, Franz. **The State:** Its History and Development Viewed Sociologically. 1926.

Paterson, Isabel. **The God of the Machine.** 1943.

Phillips, C. A., T. F. McManus and R. W. Nelson. **Banking and the Business Cycle:** A Study of the Great Depression in the United States. 1937.

Schoeck, Helmut and James W. Wiggins, editors. **Scientism and Values.** 1960.

Scoville, John W. **Labor Monopolies or Freedom.** 1946.

Scoville, John and Noel Sargent, compilers. **Fact and Fancy in the T.N.E.C. Monographs.** 1942.

Snyder, Carl. **Capitalism The Creator:** The Economic Foundations of Modern Industrial Society. 1940.

Society Without Government: 1969-1970. 1972.
 Tannehill, Morris and Linda and Jarret B. Wollstein.

Spooner, Lysander. **Let's Abolish Government,** 1852-1886. 1972.

Sprading, Charles T., editor. **Liberty and the Great Libertarians.** 1913.

Sumner, William Graham. **What Social Classes Owe to Each Other.** 1883.

Tolles, Frederick B. **George Logan of Philadelphia.** 1953.

Tucker, Benj[amin] R. **Instead of a Book:** By a Man Too Busy to Write One. 1893.

Vreeland, Hamilton, Jr. **Twilight of Individual Liberty.** 1944.

What Is Money? 1884-1963. 1972. Rothbard, Murray N. and I[saiah] W. Sylvester.

Williamson, Harold Francis. **Edward Atkinson:** The Biography of an American Liberal, 1827-1905. 1934.

Winston, Ambrose Paré. **Judicial Economics:** The Doctrine of Monopoly as Set Forth by Judges of the U.S. Federal Courts in Suits under the Anti-Trust Laws. 1957.